Enterprise SOA:
Designing IT for Business Innovation

Other resources from O'Reilly

Related titles

Enterprise Services Architecture

Open Source for the Enterprise

Essential Business Process Modeling

UML 2.0 in a Nutshell

UML 2.0 Pocket Reference

oreilly.com

oreilly.com is more than a complete catalog of O'Reilly books. You'll also find links to news, events, articles, weblogs, sample chapters, and code examples.

oreillynet.com is the essential portal for developers interested in open and emerging technologies, including new platforms, programming languages, and operating systems.

Conferences

O'Reilly brings diverse innovators together to nurture the ideas that spark revolutionary industries. We specialize in documenting the latest tools and systems, translating the innovator's knowledge into useful skills for those in the trenches. Visit *conferences.oreilly.com* for our upcoming events.

Safari Bookshelf (*safari.oreilly.com*) is the premier online reference library for programmers and IT professionals. Conduct searches across more than 1,000 books. Subscribers can zero in on answers to time-critical questions in a matter of seconds. Read the books on your Bookshelf from cover to cover or simply flip to the page you need. Try it today for free.

Enterprise SOA:
Designing IT for Business Innovation

Dan Woods 9/14/06

Dan Woods and Thomas Mattern

O'REILLY®

Beijing • Cambridge • Farnham • Köln • Paris • Sebastopol • Taipei • Tokyo

Enterprise SOA: Designing IT for Business Innovation
by Dan Woods and Thomas Mattern

Published by O'Reilly Media, Inc. 1005 Gravenstein Highway North, Sebastopol, CA 95472

O'Reilly books may be purchased for educational, business, or sales promotional use. Online editions are also available for most titles (*safari.oreilly.com*). For more information, contact our corporate/institutional sales department: (800) 998-9938 or *corporate@oreilly.com*.

Editor: Mary O'Brien	**Indexer:** Julie Hawks
Developmental Editor: Deb Cameron	**Cover Designer:** Mike Kohnke
Production Editors: Reba Libby and Adam Witwer	**Interior Designer:** Marcia Friedman
Copyeditor: Audrey Doyle	**Illustrators:** Robert Romano and Jessamyn Read

Printing History:

April 2006: First Edition.

 This book uses RepKover™, a durable and flexible lay-flat binding.

ISBN: 0-596-10238-0
[M]

CONTENTS

A HUMBLING CHALLENGE NOW FACES ALL OF US IN INFORMATION TECHNOLOGY (IT). IN THE PAST, OUR imaginations ran far ahead of what we could do with the state of the art. We could easily think of processes and applications that would be useful but that we could never build. Those who succeeded in making IT support a business did so because they understood the domain of the possible and did their best within those boundaries.

With the arrival of the Enterprise Services Architecture (ESA), which is the acronym for an Enterprise Service-Oriented Architecture (SOA), IT now faces a dramatic expansion of the world of the possible. All of the things that used to be hard—designing and automating differentiating processes, adapting and optimizing existing processes, expanding the reach of applications to more users, integrating with partners—will become much easier.

Using services as building blocks is the first step toward ESA. Turning those services into a platform and ecosystem is the second step. This book will show the progress that SAP® is making toward creating a true business process platform supported by services.

The third step will happen in companies that put ESA to work. As a full inventory of services becomes available and companies are able to combine them, using modeling to compose user interfaces (UIs), processes, and information, IT will transform from an operational concern to a strategic weapon. The humbling challenge is that we will be limited more by our imaginations and our ability to grow and manage change than by the constraints of what is possible.

IT will play a new role. Instead of managing the complexity and innovation of the technology, IT staff will manage the complexity and promote innovation of business processes. The chief information officer will transform into the chief process innovation officer. For this transformation to take place, technology will change, and so will the organization.

The goal of this book is to explain ESA so clearly and completely that companies take the idea off the shelf of promising ideas and start putting it into their project plans.

ESA is the next major architectural paradigm, following the rise of client/server, and then Internet-based applications that came before. But unlike the previous paradigm shifts, where the focus was primarily on how the technology was changing, ESA is as much, or even more, about how to organize a business.

With both the business and the technology sides thinking in terms of enterprise services, a thicket of communications problems disappears. Businesses can model their processes in terms of high-level process components assembled into scenarios. Then they can easily flesh out such models into detailed processes powered by enterprise services that provide gateways to business objects. Thick, hard-to-understand requirements documents become outdated. The models become the requirements.

The silos in organizations and applications will recede in importance. Processes, not applications, will now be at the center of everyone's thinking. Innovation can rise again as a habit because by using ESA, businesses can implement new ideas affordably and in a timely fashion.

The build versus buy tradeoff also disappears, replaced with buy and extend. Unlike many proponents of more technically focused, service-oriented architectures (SOAs), SAP is not just delivering the tools to build services; it is delivering an entire inventory of ready-made services described in a searchable repository that makes them accessible for modeling. Once businesses buy ESA-based solutions, a process of building and adapting the service-based solutions can begin. Companies can easily shape solutions built on enterprise services to meet many more business requirements than solutions built using architectures of previous generations.

The key question we hear most often does not concern whether ESA will work. SAP has a reputation for solving the whole problem, and solving it well. SAP bases all of its applications on ESA. It builds all of its technology to deliver ESA. The future of SAP rests on the success of ESA. Yes, ESA will work.

The question we hear most often in our visits to customers and analysts concerns how ESA will work. That's what we've written this book to explain.

Of course, the best examples of how ESA will work come from our customers, who are unleashing the power of service-based IT into their industries. Companies such as SupplyOn are using ESA to make their auto-industry hub more useful and configurable. Companies such as Day & Zimmermann are using ESA to expand service offerings. This book is full of many such examples.

The days of the "my way or the highway" dictatorial software company are long gone. Large companies such as SAP cannot give orders anymore. But the resources and past successes have conferred on SAP the privilege of setting the context.

ESA is our context for creating business value with IT. ESA explains how SAP, Independent Software Vendors (ISVs), systems integrators (SIs), and hardware vendors work together with customers to make IT work better for business. We are eager to make this concept work for you at your company.

Ori Inbar, Senior Vice President, Solution Marketing SAP NetWeaver, April 2006

ORGANIZING AND EXPLAINING ALL OF THE WISDOM ABOUT ENTERPRISE SERVICES ARCHITECTURE clearly and directly was a major challenge that required several innovations. To help this book to serve the needs of a broad audience from business analysts to enterprise architects, we have employed a question-and-answer format for the chapters to help readers find the portions of the book that are right for them. To partition ESA into more digestible portions, we have boiled everything down into six concepts, each with its own section in the book:

- Part One, *The Context for ESA*, covers new ways of thinking about IT and explains how you must plan for ESA.

- Part Two, *Conceiving a Vision for ESA*, delves deeper into the technical aspects of ESA.

- Part Three, *Consuming Services*, explains simple ways to use services to create value.

- Part Four, *Composing Services*, covers the way that composite applications are constructed from services.

- Part Five, *Creating Services*, explains how services are created and managed.

- Part Six, *Controlling Services*, discusses new forms of governance based on services, as well as life cycle management, operations, security, and standards.

Inside each section are the following chapters:

Part One, *The Context for ESA*

Chapter 1, *ESA in the World of Information Technology*, provides an explanation of the forces that led to the creation of ESA and how it fits into the world of enterprise computing.

Chapter 2, *The Business Case for ESA*, is a summary of the business value of ESA.

Chapter 3, *Evolving Toward ESA*, explains the complexities of managing the technology and organizational changes that are part of ESA.

Part Two, *Conceiving a Vision for ESA*

Chapter 4, *ESA Fundamentals: Learning to Think ESA*, is a survey of ESA-related concepts.

Chapter 5, *The Structure of ESA*, takes you on a top-to-bottom tour through the technology architecture of ESA.

Chapter 6, *The Enterprise Services Community*, explains how SAP is creating a customer and partner ecosystem.

Chapter 7, *Creating a Roadmap with the ESA Adoption Program*, provides a survey of the process created to help manage ESA adoption.

Part Three, *Consuming Services*

Chapter 8, *The Enterprise Services Repository and the Enterprise Services Inventory*, explains the repository and inventory of enterprise services.

Chapter 9, *Project Mendocino: A Product Based on Consuming Enterprise Services*, explains the joint SAP/Microsoft effort to use Microsoft Office to access SAP enterprise applications.

Chapter 10, *ESA at Work: Examples from the Field*, comprises a survey of examples of how ESA has been used in various industries and processes.

Part Four, *Composing Services*

Chapter 11, *SAP xApps Composite Applications for Analytics*, analyzes how analytic functionality works and why it is so important to enhancing the value of composite applications.

Chapter 12, *The Architecture and Development Tools of Composite Applications*, provides a survey of the architecture and development tools used for creating composite applications.

Chapter 13, *Supporting Composite Applications*, explains all of the support that SAP NetWeaver provides to enhance the functionality of composite applications.

Part Five, *Creating Services*

Chapter 14, *Web Services Basics*, explains the fundamental web services concepts and architecture.

Chapter 15, *Creating Enterprise Services in ABAP*, explains how to create enterprise services in ABAP.

Chapter 16, *Creating and Consuming Services in Java*, explains how to create enterprise services in Java.

Part Six, *Controlling Services*

Chapter 17, *ESA and IT Governance*, analyzes how ESA will affect IT governance.

Chapter 18, *ESA Life Cycle Management and Operations*, analyzes how ESA will affect life cycle management and operations and how SAP will provide support.

Chapter 19, *ESA Security*, analyzes ESA security issues and discusses how SAP will provide support.

Chapter 20, *Standards and ESA*, explains the vital role that standards play in ESA.

Despite all of our sincere efforts, the best that this book can be is a snapshot of where ESA is in 2006 and where it is going. We hope this snapshot explains the context for IT that we are trying to create so that you and your organization can best use ESA to transform your business and succeed in every way you can.

Safari® Enabled

 When you see a Safari® Enabled icon on the cover of your favorite technology book, that means the book is available online through the O'Reilly Network Safari Bookshelf.

Safari offers a solution that's better than e-books. It's a virtual library that lets you easily search thousands of top tech books, cut and paste code samples, download chapters, and find quick answers when you need the most accurate, current information. Try it for free at *http://safari.oreilly.com*.

How can I comment on this book?

To comment on this book, look in the ESA area on the SAP Developer Network (SDN; *http://sap.sdn.com*) for the discussion area dedicated to this book, or send email to the authors at *ESABookFeedback@sap.com*. For questions for the publisher, send email to *bookquestions@oreilly.com* or contact:

O'Reilly Media, Inc.
1005 Gravenstein Highway North
Sebastopol, CA 95472
(800) 998-9938 (in the United States or Canada)
(707) 829-0515 (international or local)
(707) 829-0104 (fax)

This book's web page can be found at *http://www.oreilly.com/catalog/enterprisesa/*.

Acknowledgments

A book such as this one, which covers so many technical topics, must be a community effort. Actually, we produced this book with the effort of several communities. We interviewed more than 200 people inside and outside of SAP to create this book's content. Starting with engineers, product managers, developers, and solution marketers inside

SAP, we then extended our research to customers, partners, and analysts. Perhaps the most inventive use of community came in December 2005, when we published early versions of certain chapters for feedback on SDN. This book at its best represents the wisdom about ESA harvested from all of these people.

And of course, many people deserve our thanks.

First, this book would not exist if Shai Agassi, Peter Graf, Ori Inbar, and Peter Zencke did not believe in the project and provide their enthusiastic support. Thomas Balgheim, Pascal Brosset, Archim Heiman, Franz Hero, Peter Kabuth, Klaus Kreplin, Jürgen Kreuziger, Carsten Linz, Nimish Mehta, Doug Merritt, Dennis Moore, George Paolini, Stefan Schaffer, Rolf Schumann, Emiel van Schaik, Vishal Sikka, Jim Hagemann Snabe, Klaus Weber, and Jason Wolf gave generously of their time and made valuable resources on their teams available to us.

Several people made especially large contributions to the book, and we would like to offer our sincere gratitude. Scott Feldman, Claus Fruehwein, and Isabell Jaeger helped us obtain the customer case studies. Scott Jones and the SDN team set up the SDN public review. The writing team at Evolved Media Network, including Greg Lindsay, Noah Robischon, John Verity, and Deb Cameron, produced enormous amounts of clear copy.

We are also indebted to the SDN community members who provided feedback that significantly improved the book and enhanced our understanding of how to write about ESA: Richard Andrulis, Asher Benbenisty, Theo Bolta, Shashank Date, Jean-Jacques Dubray, Robert Eijpe, Mark Frear, Lucio Frega, Wenning Gao, Andy Heldt, Vladimir Hert, Christian Hissler, Andreas Huppert, Sujesh Kc, Shehryar Khan, Michal Krawczyk, Cedric Laridon, Raghavendra Pothula, Srinivas Reddy, Luis Rincones, Ivan Schreter, John Showers, Kamaljeet Singh, Srikanth Soundappan, Holger Stumm, Ramesh Suraparaju, Paul Taylor, Tarun Telang, Alexey Telitsin, and Raj Vuppala.

Many SAP customers generously provided their experience with ESA in the form of examples, which helped bring the book from the theoretical to the real world. We are thankful to each and every one of them: Eric Brabänder (IDS Scheer AG), Thomas Büsch (LHI Leasing GmbH), Jason C. Childers (Whirlpool Corporation), Manish Choksi (Asian Paints), Carlos Cruz (Agile Solutions), Kevin deKock (CSA Group), Michael P. Friess (Day & Zimmermann), Timm Funke (syskoplan AG), Andy Heldt (Kimberly Clark), Michel Hellmann (Arcelor), Alexander Hildebrand (Wacker Chemie AG), Brian J. Moore (Raytheon), Guiseppe Pagnotta and Mauro Tedesco (Elsag Domino), Claus Qvistgaard (Arla Foods), Andreas Schachtner (TRW OSS Engineering Europe), Holger Schloermann and Lutz Schwiedernoch (Nordzucker AG), Christian Stoecklmayer (SupplyOn AG), Masaki Takahiko (Mitsui & Co., Ltd.), Frédéric Tribel (Solvay), Richard Vinches (Manchette Publicité), Frank Wegner (CSC Ploenzke AG), and Alexander Wüest (Zuger Kantonalbank).

Two analysts, Randy Heffner (Forrester Research) and David Smith (Gartner), also provided valuable insight for which we are grateful.

We authors needed support through this difficult project, and three people helped us beyond measure. We owe special thanks to Matthias Haendly for believing in this project and playing a major role in making it happen. He is a paratrooper and a gentleman. Tobias Weiblen, our intern on the project, was a godsend who made project management a joy rather than a difficulty. Only great things are ahead for Tobias. Uli Golle, our intern for the final stages of the project, came up to speed quickly and was of enormous help—we thank him heartily.

Finally, we would like to thank the experts—the enterprise architects, developers, solutions managers, product managers, solutions marketers, field staff, NetWeaver advisors, and those from industry development. Their thoughts make up the message we crafted in this book. Without them, we would have had nothing to say. They are: Werner Aigner, Thomas Anton, Sheejo Arvind, Michael Augsburger, Koby Avital, Oliver Bahner, Fritz Bauspiess, Michael Bechauf, Joerg Beringer, Frands Bennetsen, Karol Bliznak, Jochen Boeder, Carsten Boennen, Martin Botschek, Carsten Brandt, Rainer Brendle, Claus Bruckner, David Brutman, Ruediger Buck-Emden, Roman Bukary, David Burdett, Eugene Cherny, Kevin Cox, Matthew Czwikla, Gerd Danner, Massimo D'Attoma, Till Dengel, Thomas Ellenberg, Marty Etzel, Timm Falter, Wolfgang Fassnacht, Mark Finnern, Claudius Fischer, Georg Fischer, Kevin Fliess, Andreas Frank, Franz-Josef Fritz, Sindhu Gangadharan, Holger Gockel, Sidney Goodman, Alexandra Gorman, Thomas Grassl, Claus Gruenewald, Sunil Gupta, Stefan Hack, Thomas Hassing, Christian Hastedt-Marquwardt, Ariel Hazi, Christopher Hearn, Lothar Henkes, Franklin Herbas, Stephan Herbert, Martin Hermes, Patrick Hildenbrand, Ramin Hummel, Jennifer Huntington, Martin Huvar, Hanif Ismail, Achim Ittner, Lutz Jaeger, Susanne Janssen, Michael Joergensen, Stefan Kaetker, Robert Kapanen, Karl Kessler, Margret Klein-Magar, Panagiotis Kokkalis, Nir Kol, Stefan Kraus, Jewgeni Kravets, Juergen Kremer, Hardy Kuhn, Andre Labahn, Jennifer Lankheim, Peter Latocha, Sven Leukert, Bernd Lober, Salvatore Lombardo, Kaj van de Loo, Phong Ly, Holger Mack, Marina Marscheider, Peter McNulty, Paul Medaille, Nimish Mehta, Holger Meinert, Helge Meyer, Atsushi Minakuchi, Frank Mittag, Gordon Muehl, Christoph Nake, Harald Nehring, Arnold Niedermaier, Gerard O'Neil, Gilad Parann-Nissany, Bill Pataky, Bao Huong Phan, Gunther Piller, Rainer Pochlatko, Thomas Pohl, Georg Rau, Michael Redford, Christine Regitz, Claus von Riegen, Ralf Rieger, Susanne Rothaug, Gunther Rothermel, Ingo Rothley, Dieter Scheerer, Eric Schemer, Michael Schenk, Stephan Schindewolf, Christian Schloegel, Andreas Schmidt, Horst Schnoerer, Ulirich Scholl, Christine Schroeder, Martin Schroter, Lothar Schubert, Manfred Seidel, Jeff Sharpe, Stefan Sigg, Sue Spaulding, Sebastian Speck, Lisa Strizzi, Bernhard Teltscher, Peter Tillert, Johannes Tulusan, Udo Urbanek, Tzvetomir Vassilev, Thorsten Vieth, Christian Violi, Andreas Vogel, Thomas Volmering, Udo Waibel, Marcus Wefers, Andreas Weiskam, Aaron Williams, Joerg Wolf, Brian Wood, Richard Yim, Renato Zadro, Gerlinde Zibulski, and Martin Zurmuehl.

We hope we have not left anyone out, but if we have, we thank you as well.

Dan Woods and Thomas Mattern, April 2006

PART ONE

The Context for ESA

CHAPTER ONE

ESA in the World of Information Technology

ENTERPRISE **S**ERVICES **A**RCHITECTURE **(ESA)** IS **SAP'S** BLUEPRINT FOR HOW ENTERPRISE SOFTWARE should be constructed to provide maximum business value. The challenge facing most companies is not whether to adopt service-oriented architecture (SOA), but when and how to do so. There is always a lag between technological vision and business feasibility. It also takes time to fully realize the potential of existing technologies, a process that does not stop the moment the new thing arrives. But when the value of a new approach such as ESA starts to make a difference and produces a competitive advantage, the motivation to change skyrockets. The time to change becomes now and the hunger for learning grows. The goal of this book is to satisfy the hunger for information for those who suspect that ESA may be a gateway to transforming Information Technology (IT) into a strategic weapon.

The current state of the art is a long way from ESA. Most enterprise software programs now use Internet-inspired technologies, such as portals, web-based user interfaces (UIs), application servers, and XML-based messaging services, but they still cling to client/server and even mainframe architectures. This will change dramatically over the next five years. IT will become connected by networks, awash in data, faster, more adaptive, more in sync with business. Companies that understand how to unlock the business value of this new architecture before their competitors do will have a huge advantage.

The skeptics among us cannot help but ask, "Has something really changed?" Buzzwords—*web services, service-oriented architecture*, and *enterprise service bus* are the current rage—come and go, but the network, the Internet, is here to stay. However, the classic mainframe and client/server architectures make only minimal use of it. In dribs and drabs, enterprise applications have taken advantage of network-enabled functions, but the core architecture in many ways remains untouched. ESA represents a refactoring of the core architecture of enterprise applications to make sense of a flock of new possibilities and to bring them in formation to the level of business, application, and technology architectures.

IT will change not simply because new things are possible, but because most markets are presenting companies with a whole new set of requirements that traditional IT is having a hard time meeting. Most companies live in a world in which business models change every year, or even more frequently. An implementation cycle of a year or more on an IT project can no longer be tolerated. New processes must be designed and built in three months, six months, or nine months. The systems of record that provide the context for most business activity have been built out. Now the challenge is to quickly build a new layer of flexible processes based on those systems of record in a way that preserves flexibility so that future adjustments are affordable.

This book will explain—in more detail than ever before—what ESA is, and how SAP is bringing the concept to life in all of its products as a platform supported by an ecosystem. The first book written on this subject, *Enterprise Services Architecture* (Woods and Mattern, O'Reilly), described in general terms the context for ESA, the business case for it, and outlined the shape of an ESA platform. Because SAP has made so much progress in fleshing out the details of ESA, many questions can now be answered in great detail. For example, this book will answer the following questions:

- How will UIs be modeled and constructed in ESA?

- What new components will need to be created to support creating composite applications?

- What is the role of business intelligence and analytical functionality in a service-oriented world?

- How will process orchestration knit together new processes from the parts of all of the enterprise applications participating in composite applications?

- How will the application logic of enterprise applications have to change to best support ESA?

- How will a unified process, information, and UI model be constructed out of a collection of distributed services?

- What new level of container will replace the collection of functionality now kept inside an enterprise application?

- What projects will allow companies to build the right skills needed to adopt ESA?

- What is the ecosystem of customers, Independent Software Vendors (ISVs), and systems integrators (SIs)?

- How will SAP NetWeaver evolve to enhance and broaden the support of ESA?

- Which products does SAP offer in 2006 to help customers moving from a classic mainframe/client/server architecture toward an open Enterprise Services Architecture?

If these questions seem rather technical, well, they *are*. That such detailed questions about technology can be answered indicates how much ESA has matured. But our attention to technology questions will never distract us from the role that technology plays in supporting business.

Who is this book for?

ESA should be of primary concern to anyone charged with making IT support a business. The intended audience of this book includes:

Enterprise architects
> Those involved in looking at the whole company from an architecture perspective.

Business analysts
> Those who look at different business processes to assess the best way to run them.

Senior executives
> Those who rely on IT to support their business and need to know what is expected of their IT departments, enterprise architects, and business analysts.

Developers and engineers
> Those who will have new roles in this new world and will need to learn the new skills they will require.

This list is a broad umbrella that encompasses a range of responsibilities from reducing total cost of ownership (TCO) to decreasing development time to choosing new platforms and development methodologies. This wide perspective matches almost exactly the domain of ESA shown in Figure 1-1.

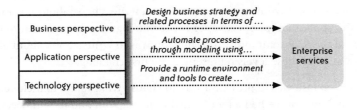

FIGURE 1-1. Three perspectives on ESA

What distinguishes ESA from all other approaches to SOA is that ESA explains how the business, application, and technology should be organized to produce maximum value. The business strategy and process design, the application architectures, and the way technology supports applications are synchronized in relation to enterprise services. Figure 1-1 is an accurate oversimplification, but as our explanation proceeds, it will become clear that a unified approach to designing services is the first step. From that first step flows the ability to create a unified process model, a unified information model, and a unified approach to building UIs. All of these things combined comprise the engine of value that makes new innovations possible based on existing systems of record.

Synchronizing business strategy and technological applications through enterprise services has two enormous advantages. First, the business architecture is defined by exactly those processes that are supported by enterprise services. Second, this synchronization brings business executives, analysts, and technologists onto the same playing field as application experts and engineers. Each group has clearly defined responsibilities. Business analysts define and modify processes and UIs using modeling and simplified tools based on services. Technologists build services and tools based on services for use by business analysts. Each group manages its own domain of complexity and can talk about enterprise services from its own perspective. The conversation is structured. Business analysts request services and UIs when they are missing and then modify them from there. Technologists provide these services. The communication disconnect that plagues business and IT is conquered by a form of information hiding in which each side has its own domain, and communication is structured. Improved communication may be the most profoundly valuable contribution ESA can make.

Why so many questions?

If the questions and ideas mentioned so far sound interesting, then you are ready for the rest of this book and you are ready for the format.

When we sat down to write this book, we were quickly awed by the breadth of topics under the ESA umbrella. ESA starts with a perspective on how business should view IT through modeled processes and information entities and then explains how applications should be constructed and technology should support these applications along with a range of related issues. It would easily be possible to write a book about just the business perspective, the application perspective, or the technology perspective. But to really provide a service to the SAP community, our mission was to write a book about all three. Covering ESA at all of these levels represented the first challenge.

The second related task was to provide a way to choose what topics to include. To cover these perspectives meant we had a lot of territory to map out and then navigate. Within each perspective there is a wide variety of material. The question we struggled with was how to guide readers to the material that was most useful to them.

Most technology books do this by constructing a narrative or a story that explains things from one perspective. The problem with that approach is that whichever perspective we chose to use to organize the narrative would leave the other two groups searching for what they needed to know.

Our solution was to imitate one of the forms of content that was made popular on the Internet, the Frequently Asked Questions or FAQ document. ESA is so large and affects so many different people in different ways. There are hundreds of stories inside the world of ESA. So, we gave up on the idea of telling one story or making one perspective dominant. Instead, we present questions and answers, lots of them, so readers can quickly find the information they seek. We chose to write each chapter as a series of answers to questions so that the table of contents was a long list of questions. We assembled these questions into chapters aimed at a particular audience so that related questions handled at a similar level of business or technical detail were grouped together.

While we try to keep a natural sequence between the answers to the questions, with one question leading to another, this structure abandons any form of story and instead leaves it to readers to find what they need to know. Our intent was to write a book that would be more useful to more people than any other approach. Only experience will tell, and we would love to hear from you. Now we will begin with the most fundamental question of all.

What forces created ESA?

Modern businesses need functionality that is both distributed and centralized. Existing systems of record, such as Enterprise Resources Planning (ERP), Customer Relationship Management (CRM), Supply Chain Management (SCM), and so on, serve the needs of key segments of the organization. But at the same time, a need for many new processes has arisen that requires a flow that moves from one system of record to another, with the context for the process kept outside of any of the existing systems. The traditional way of building enterprise software is not well-suited to these new requirements and does not take full advantage of the new world of pervasive networks, reusable services, and distributed data. Treating an application as a self-contained world no longer meets the needs of business.

In the past, enterprise applications contained the end-to-end processes that were being automated. One program running on one computer automated a workflow process that began and ended inside that application. A single database was the central mechanism of integration. All elements of the stack were contained within one program, as shown in Figure 1-2.

Figure 1-2 actually shows a prettier picture than what exists in many mainframe applications. Even after workflow mechanisms were in use and points of integration were designated, process and integration logic ended up strewn all over the stack and was mixed in

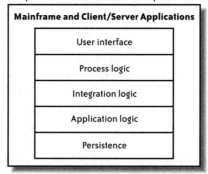

Mainframe and client/server applications had complete control of the stack from top to bottom.

Mainframe and Client/Server Applications
User interface
Process logic
Integration logic
Application logic
Persistence

Developers were able to control a vertical slice when coding from UI to persistence. A single, consistent database was the point of integration.

FIGURE 1-2. *Mainframe and client/server architecture*

with application and UI logic. This structure, however, captures the spirit of mainframe applications, which at their best were organized into the following layers:

- The UI layer

- The process logic layer (which controls the automation of the steps)

- The integration logic layer (which controls the way the programs interact)

- The application logic layer (which controls what the program is actually *doing*)

- The persistence layer that serves as the database (where all the information is stored)

From a development perspective, the mainframe and client/server tools gave developers control over a vertical slice of this stack, from the UI to the persistence layer. If functionality in other slices was to be reused, the developer would have a conversation with the developers of the other slices to figure out how to use their functionality. Everything came together and had to be carefully reconciled in the database, which was the central point of integration. One of the major points of ESA is to transform such conversations about reuse from an ad hoc event into a formal design based on the needs of business processes.

It is possible to access the functionality in a mainframe/client/server stack through application programming interfaces (APIs). But there was no template for this; each time an API was developed, it came with its own assumptions about how it worked and how it should be used.

The mainframe/client/server applications did anticipate the need for customization through metadata, different variables controlling an application's behavior, and templates for UIs. Customization, however, is a one-time reuse, and as we will see, services are created to be reused in a context unknown at design time. The mainframe/client/server stack worked well when used by competent hands, and huge leaps forward in automation and productivity were made based on this architecture. But because the stack was contained within one application, with the UI, process, application, integration, and information layers tightly coupled at design time, it was impossible to break open a mainframe application and restructure it to solve new problems.

Application proliferation: systems of record are built out

In the late 1980s and 1990s, ERP systems showed the power of the mainframe/client/server stack. Despite growing pains, the widespread success of ERP—with SAP leading the charge—led to the creation of other applications, as seen in Figure 1-3.

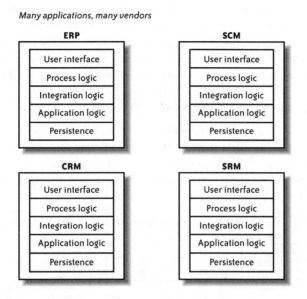

Many applications, many vendors

ERP
| User interface |
| Process logic |
| Integration logic |
| Application logic |
| Persistence |

SCM
| User interface |
| Process logic |
| Integration logic |
| Application logic |
| Persistence |

CRM
| User interface |
| Process logic |
| Integration logic |
| Application logic |
| Persistence |

SRM
| User interface |
| Process logic |
| Integration logic |
| Application logic |
| Persistence |

F I G U R E 1 - 3 . Many applications, many vendors

While ERP was focused primarily on only the financial and management aspects of a company—before it expanded throughout the 1990s to sales, distribution, and other key functions—new applications such as CRM, SCM, and supplier relationship management (SRM), among others expanded the range of automation.

This led to a proliferation of applications for most companies under the label of "best of breed." The idea was to get the best application for each purpose. This allowed the VP of sales to have the best CRM application, the VP of manufacturing the best SCM application, and so on. The main benefit of this proliferation was the creation of a comprehensive collection of systems of record that automated common business processes from end to end.

But solutions from different vendors created a problem because they took away the central point of integration in the mainframe/client/server world: the single database. Data was scattered all over the system landscape, or even worse, was duplicated in multiple systems. For example, the same customer data ended up in the CRM system and in the ERP system, sometimes with variations. Perhaps worse, it was difficult to get applications from different vendors to communicate properly, making it more difficult to maintain data consistency.

Communication and integration among applications became even more important when companies realized that essential processes may flow through several enterprise applications. The process that starts with taking an order and ends with the receipt of money, the so-called "order to cash" process, involved many enterprise applications. A financial transaction in the ERP system would move to the SCM system for a factory order, which then went to the CRM system for service questions, and then back to ERP for the final confirmation of the order. Other processes, such as procure to pay and sell from stock, had a similar cross-application structure and required better interaction among all the systems. The best-of-breed model left no one company in charge of making everything work, and whenever a company bought a new solution, it came with "some integration required." Getting it to work at all actually required expensive, hard-wired integration projects.

Bridging the gap among systems of record

The next challenge facing companies using enterprise applications was integration. How could all of the best-of-breed applications be made to work together to serve the needs of the cross-application processes that were becoming the key to increased efficiency and innovation? As shown in Figure 1-4, the key question concerned how to bridge the gap among systems of record.

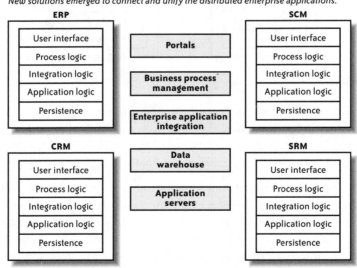

FIGURE 1-4. Attempts at bridging the gap

Many different technologies emerged to bridge the gap, so a cross-application, integrated view of enterprise applications was created, based on the new possibilities of the Internet as a pervasive network and emerging technology standards such as HTTP, HTML, Java, and XML:

- Portals emerged as web-based UI technology that enabled one UI to connect to functionality from the different applications.

- Data warehouses collected data from all of the different databases within the applications in one place.

- Enterprise Application Integration (EAI) technology created engines that allowed one application to send an XML message—a standard for data formatting—to another application. The receiving application could send a response back, and all sorts of fancy alerting, monitoring, and triggering could happen in central systems for routing and transforming messages.

- Business Process Management applications for process modeling and management were frequently coupled with EAI technologies to create a new way to define and execute processes in the center.

- Many of these integration tools were powered by application servers, a new sort of structure for applications based on standards such as Java 2 Enterprise Edition (J2EE) that were created for the world of the Internet.

These new technologies started to bridge the gap among isolated enterprise applications and enabled some cross-application coordination and development. The results were encouraging. Portals could bring together UI elements from different applications, as well as gathering information from different sources and displaying them in one place. Data warehouses created one view of distributed information, albeit with a delay caused by batch-oriented extraction processes. EAI technologies connected applications, but these connections were complex and threatened a new layer of unstandardized spaghetti. Parts of the gap were bridged with these approaches and the requirements for cross-application processes were met to some extent. These capabilities fell far short of a unified approach to UI, process, and information integration, however. They also ushered in a new set of problems—integration of the integration technologies.

Portals might need to talk to the data warehouse, which may need to send and receive data through the EAI system, which could be working with a Business Process Management system. The same sort of integration problems that these technologies were designed to resolve among enterprise applications arose among the integration technologies, which also generally came from a variety of vendors. It was "best of breed" all over again, except this time, it concerned integration tools, not applications.

Consolidation: mySAP™ Business Suite and SAP NetWeaver

The cost of integrating enterprise applications and integrating integration technologies quickly mounted, leading customers to ask, "Is this really our problem to solve?" SAP thought not, and solved this problem in two ways. First, SAP assembled its own solutions for ERP, CRM, SCM, SRM, and so forth into a unified collection called the mySAP Business Suite. Second, SAP integrated all of the integration technologies into a unified whole, called SAP NetWeaver. Furthermore, SAP started to develop all of its mySAP Business

Suite applications using SAP NetWeaver: in other words, integrated applications built on integrated technologies as a platform.

This created the situation shown in Figure 1-5 in which an integrated set of tools could help manage processes across a set of enterprise applications designed to work together.

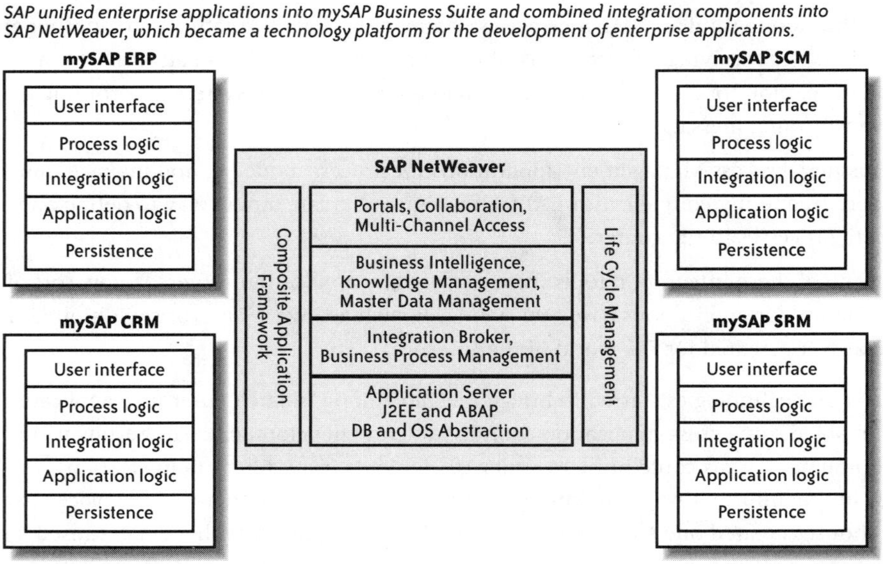

SAP unified enterprise applications into mySAP Business Suite and combined integration components into SAP NetWeaver, which became a technology platform for the development of enterprise applications.

FIGURE 1-5. SAP NetWeaver and mySAP Business Suite

This approach solved a large portion of the problem of connecting enterprise applications and integration technologies to each other.

SAP NetWeaver is a single, integrated set of technologies used to unify a huge collection of integration and development functionality, including the portal, the data warehouse, EAI, application servers, Business Process Management, and a variety of other systems for supporting mobile devices, for constructing UIs, and for distributing data and managing master data.

SAP NetWeaver allows you to write programs not only in ABAP—the language that has been used for more than 20 years to write applications in SAP—but also in Java. This helps solve the problem of integrating the integration tools, but still the problem of getting all of these applications to talk to each other remains.

Bringing all of the applications together in the mySAP Business Suite helped solve the second half of the cross-application integration problem in a variety of ways. Because the integration points between the enterprise applications started to become well-known, SAP could support them as part of the product, not as a special integration task. SAP was able to add business packages to configure enterprise applications to work together. This left the challenge of integrating legacy applications and products from other vendors into the mix—and finally solving the "best-of-breed" dilemma.

The challenge still remained, however, to be able to recombine systems of record to solve new problems. The connections made possible by SAP NetWeaver allowed some processes to flow from one enterprise application to another, and solved a host of other problems as well. Much of the power of enterprise applications was still locked in the monolithic structure. Businesses needed to change faster than the connections between applications could be constructed.

The web services era

A new phase in the evolution of enterprise application architecture started with the emergence of web services based on XML. Web services comprise a family of interrelated standards that work together to provide a simple way to allow program functionality in different languages and on different platforms to interoperate.

Web services are based on sending XML back and forth in a way somewhat similar to EAI systems. But they use a simpler protocol—typically based on HTTP—and inside it they can embed XML using protocols such as SOAP so that one web service can send another web service a message very easily. This interaction provides interoperability across applications and technologies from different vendors. Because every vendor supports the basic web services standards, messages can be passed from one service to another, regardless of the architecture of the underlying application.

Web services (described in detail in Chapter 14) emerged as a standard and became popular very quickly. Almost every vendor adopted and implemented basic web services standards immediately and, for once, a standard was quickly agreed on by the entire software industry.

The arrival of web services offered an exciting way to solve the problem of how applications from different vendors could communicate based on a common standard, as shown in Figure 1-6.

One implementation detail here is that SOAP is just one of the communications protocols that could be used with web services. It is possible for other protocols to be used as well, but in practice, most web services use SOAP through HTTP to ensure interoperability. Also, each web service is described in something called a Web Services Description Language (WSDL) file. This file could be stored in a repository that was defined by the Universal Description, Discovery, and Integration (UDDI) standard, which allows the storage, search, and retrieval of WSDL files.

Web services provided a jolt of excitement to IT because they promised a solution to the challenge of connecting many enterprise applications in a standard way. They also offered a solution to breaking apart layers of the application trapped inside the monolith. Any enterprise application could use web services to present its functionality for reuse. Any platform, such as Microsoft Windows, could use web services from another platform, such as Unix, because they were based on HTTP and other standards that were supported on all platforms. Web services could be implemented in any programming language. When programmers wanted to use something that was encapsulated in a web service, they didn't

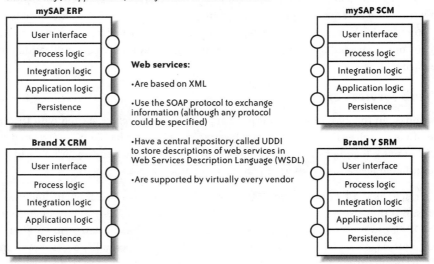

Web services offered the possibility of exposing services based on existing enterprise applications, creating a standard way for applications from any vendor to talk to each other.

Web services:

•Are based on XML

•Use the SOAP protocol to exchange information (although any protocol could be specified)

•Have a central repository called UDDI to store descriptions of web services in Web Services Description Language (WSDL)

•Are supported by virtually every vendor

FIGURE 1-6. Web services

have to learn a proprietary API. And UDDI promised a way for everybody to learn what web services were out there.

The biggest new idea to emerge from the concept of web services was called *service-oriented architecture* (SOA). The idea of SOA had its roots in many other ideas and approaches that had been circulating in the computer science world for a while. CORBA, DCOM, and EDI are similar in approach and intent to SOA. The notion is simple: think of components as *reusable* parts and *reusable* services. It is a powerful notion, one that discards the underpinnings of the mainframe and client/server architectures. SOA was a collection of data and functionality that is reusable across different programs. In many ways, SOA is an external, cross-application form of object-oriented programming. SOA created reusable collections of data and functionality, which are similar to objects.

So with SOA, instead of a monolithic, big-black-box, mainframe type of application, you could build a series of services that you could recombine each time you needed to solve a new problem. You would not have to constantly start from scratch. The functionality in the layers inside the monolith were now set free. No longer tightly coupled to each other, the functionalities could be put to new uses. With this new approach came new terminology. Systems of record now also became known as *service providers*. Applications that used services from systems of record became known as *service consumers*.

The Web services and SOA spawned a lot of work on standards and how to standardize and build applications. XML was a very important way of expressing those standards. Standards started to emerge for making web services more secure to create standards for global data types for reliable messaging. The UDDI standard was created to help people find services. Development of industry standards was also accelerated. This raised the question of what sort of application would be built on top of service providers, as shown in Figure 1-7.

Because web services were quickly and widely accepted, interest in the idea of service-oriented architecture was reignited. The question then became: what would be built on top to tie all of these together?

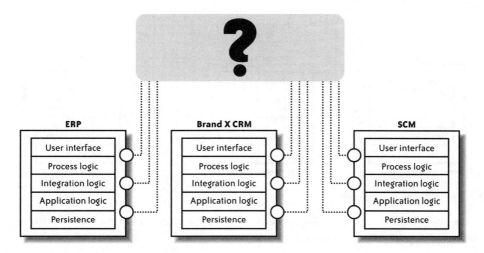

FIGURE 1-7. Service-oriented architecture

SOA became the blueprint for new forms of applications that bridged the gap and automated new processes based on services from systems of record. These applications clearly were going to be different from the mainframe/client/server applications. Everything would not be contained within one application. Processes could start in one application and be handed off to another, coordinated by the center. Communication inside the composite applications was going to be far more standardized, based on a unified approach to UIs, processes, and managing information. Data would be distributed across many different repositories. These new applications were called composite applications, as shown in Figure 1-8.

For companies such as SAP, which is focused on providing business value, SOA was a great idea, but primarily a technical one. Composite applications are the way that SOA would be brought to life and put to work. To create new functionality, you could use web services from existing systems of record to provide the base for a new composite application that might have to add just a few new services to perform a task. This made profound business sense because many years and much money had been put into creating these applications, and they worked well, solving the problems they were intended to solve. (Remember, you also can think of legacy applications as applications that work well to solve stable problems.) But new problems were emerging that needed to be solved, and innovation was becoming more important, not just as a way to secure a leadership position in the market, but also as a way to survive. Composite applications promised a way to

Composite applications, applications based on services provided by other applications, were designed to bridge the gap between applications and provide flexible, repurposable automation.

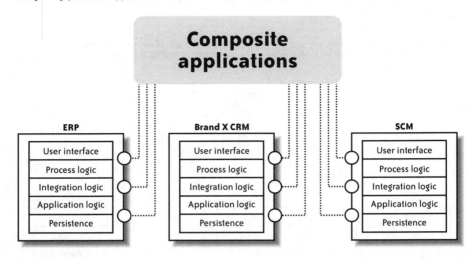

FIGURE 1-8. Composite applications

use services from a variety of different enterprise applications that were exposed through web services and then to create a new sort of application.

And because composite applications were reusing parts of other applications, you could separate the process logic for a process such as order to cash from the underlying systems that were implementing it. That made it easier to change and optimize the orchestrated process and helped reduce IT as a bottleneck.

Moreover, UIs could be separated from the application logic, which allows composite applications to have UIs tailored for different process automation roles. For example, one person might need to see the process from end to end, and another person might need to see one step of the process. The UI could simply show what each role needed. All of this ended up creating a new sort of architecture for a composite application, as shown in Figure 1-9.

This simple vision for composite applications is particularly popular for companies selling professional services, as well as selling tools to build web services. The underlying assumption is that the arrival of web services and the tools to build them mean that IT departments should immediately begin building their own services and using them to create composite applications under the SOA umbrella. After the bill for creating and maintaining custom web services increases, this approach will again lead to the question, "Is this really the IT department's problem to solve?"

SAP's answer is no, and a simple automotive analogy explains why. A Porsche Boxster has 70 percent of the same components as a Porsche 911. The remaining sections of the Boxster are simply new parts added to the 911, producing an entirely new car altogether. This

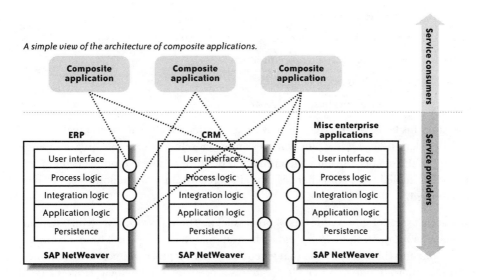

A simple view of the architecture of composite applications.

FIGURE 1-9. Composite application architecture

is possible because a huge inventory of reusable parts exists, and they were constructed specifically to be reused; just the idea of having reusable parts is not enough.

The idea of composite applications is not enough either. A reusable inventory of web services will allow the creation of new applications from existing components. But for this to work, you don't just need the idea of reusable parts; you need reusable parts that were constructed in a way that promotes reuse.

What is ESA?

Now we are at the doorway of ESA. The simple view of composite applications and SOA leaves many questions unanswered about how the reusable parts will be constructed, who will build them, what tools will be used, and what will make them work together. Here are just a few questions that must be answered to derive the full business value from composite applications:

- How should the portions of the stack be distributed across this architecture?
- How should the portions of the stack talk to each other?
- What is the right structure for each portion of the stack?
- When should multiple structures for a portion of the stack be supported?
- How should the UIs be constructed?
- How should the process orchestration take place?
- How should development methods change?
- Where is the persistence?
- How is distributed data managed?

- How can complexity be managed?

- How can the process of adapting applications be simplified?

- How can developers be made more productive?

- What is the right division of labor?

- Who should solve all of these problems?

The rest of this book is dedicated to answering questions such as these in great detail. To get started, let's look at a few different areas more closely. For example, in a composite application, the data is distributed over many repositories. How can one version of the truth be assembled? How can changes that affect records in many repositories be synchronized?

There are all sorts of different forms of process logic. There is workflow, which happens within an application; there is process orchestration, which happens within a composite application; and there is the logic that is required when a process is handed from one enterprise application to another—let's call this process integration logic. How is all of that logic going to be dealt with? How are the different portions of the stack for process logic, integration logic, application logic, and so on, going to be distributed across the structure? Will all the logic be in the center? Will the enterprise applications have to become smarter? (For the rest of this book, we are going to use the term *process orchestration* to refer to all of these sorts of process logic.)

How should applications be developed? Are new development methods needed? How can things be simplified? Who is going to do the work of creating the services that are built on top of the enterprise applications? Is there any standard for those?

How will industry standards be incorporated and made useful? How will all interested parties in the architecture communicate and participate in the ongoing design process?

It is quite clear that there are plenty of questions to ask. One, however, is perhaps the most fundamental: who should answer the questions? Each IT department?

SAP, living up to its traditional dedication to solving the whole problem, is not satisfied to just leave these questions to IT departments to solve on their own. One of the most important aspects of ESA is the blueprint it provides for building composite applications based on the principles of SOA with all questions answered and details filled in. As part of its commitment to ESA, SAP is not only filling in the architectural details, but also creating the collection of reusable parts (the Enterprise Services Inventory), a repository for searching through the parts and using them to create programs (the Enterprise Services Repository), and an ecosystem that includes input from partners, customers, and standards bodies in a systematic way (the Enterprise Services Community, or ES-Community).

To simplify the explanation of ESA we have created a basic stack, as shown in Figure 1-10, that serves as a unified model for UIs, processes, and information, with a clear separation of duties for each layer.

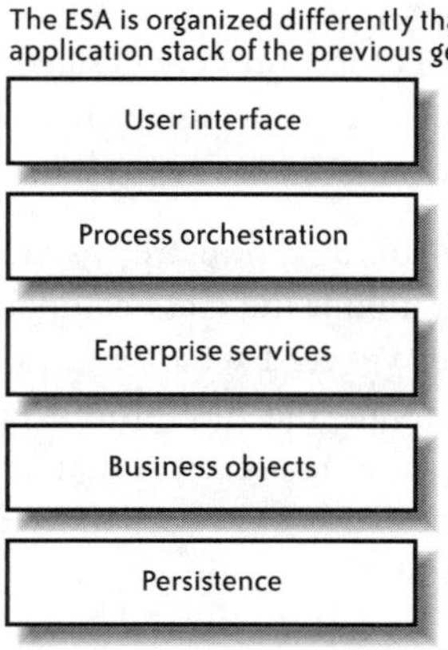

The ESA is organized differently than the application stack of the previous generation.

User interface

Process orchestration

Enterprise services

Business objects

Persistence

FIGURE 1-10. The ESA stack

Later sections of this book will examine each area of this stack in detail. But to prepare for further learning, here is a quick, top-to-bottom explanation of each layer of the stack that shows how it answers many of the questions previously raised.

User interface

UIs in ESA have much more structure than in previous generations of enterprise applications. Most of the time UIs are created through modeling, or by using patterns as building blocks, or both. For example, the UI patterns of work center and control center will be a standard part of ESA applications. Work centers are UI elements designed to take a user through the steps needed to complete a process. Control centers show the status and are the central point of access for all of the work centers that a user may be involved in. Common approaches to managing lists of tasks have also been created. The goal is to reuse configurable components and adjustable patterns to reduce the complexity of building and using UIs for enterprise applications.

Process orchestration

Process orchestration is the notion that process logic will be separated from all other kinds of logic. Process orchestration will happen at many different levels. Composite applications will use process orchestration as the coordinator and integrator of a set of process steps available through enterprise services provided by enterprise applications. Service providers such as existing enterprise applications will use workflows for processes within their boundaries and will use layers of process integration logic to accept incoming or send outgoing processes to and from other systems. Individual services may use process orchestration to create composite services. The goal in ESA is to make process orchestration easier to build and modify so that applications can be changed quickly, cheaply, and by a wider group of people than is now possible.

There are two main flavors of process orchestration. Frontend process orchestration is conversational. It is focused on collaboration and interaction with users. A technology called *guided procedures* can walk a user through a set of steps that may involve many different enterprise applications. Guided procedures are designed to enable you to easily maintain a context for a process by allowing documents to be attached. They are also flexible and allow you to change the process flow for one instance of a process on the fly.

Backend orchestration is about long-running, primarily asynchronous processes. An example of backend process orchestration is the cross-component Business Process Management functionality in the SAP NetWeaver Exchange Infrastructure (SAP NetWeaver XI), which has a high-performance, robust business process engine for using enterprise services to automate complex, long-running processes that are triggered by events, send and receive alerts, and coordinate the activity of many transactions asynchronously.

Enterprise services

Enterprise services come in many forms. Usually the term *enterprise services* refers to services that are being exposed by the enterprise applications or by other service providers to participate in the support of business processes. Reusable utility functionality offered by SAP NetWeaver can also be presented as enterprise services. So can services that specialize in managing a process or engine for special-purpose calculations of taxes.

Although enterprise services are based on web services standards, they are different from plain web services in that enterprise services are created to participate in reusable processes, not necessarily in just the functionality that has been exposed at any level of granularity. Enterprise services live in the Enterprise Services Repository that stores data that describes the services' interfaces, how the services would be used in model-driven development tools, and how the services fit into models that describe business processes.

SAP has both external and internal processes for controlling the growth and design of the Enterprise Services Inventory, the name for the sum total of all enterprise services.

Business objects

Business objects are the collections of related data and functionality inside a service provider. Business objects also can be units of modeling, a description from a modeling perspective of related functionality. In the purest form of ESA, enterprise services are extensions of business objects. In other words, enterprise services expose the functionality of business objects to the outside world. Business objects also show up inside composite applications, where they consume services and can be the building blocks for services provided to other programs. One of the major challenges of ESA is that enterprise services must be constructed on enterprise applications and other service providers that were not originally designed for ESA. These applications don't have the equivalent of business objects inside them that make it easy to build services. The challenge of building enterprise services on enterprise applications based on the mainframe/client/server stack is that the functionality in the application is not separated into reusable chunks. In attempting to create a reusable enterprise service, one must take care not to have any unwanted side effects.

Distributed persistence

In ESA, the core assumption of the single database that was so central to the mainframe/client/server architecture is no longer valid. The ESA stack assumes not only a distributed repository, but also certain levels of redundancy. Part of this is handled through aggregation and distribution mechanisms such as SAP NetWeaver Master Data Management (SAP NetWeaver MDM) and SAP NetWeaver Business Intelligence (SAP NetWeaver BI) that create a logically normalized information model on a physically distributed collection of repositories. But the whole solution requires more. Composite applications must have their own robust persistence mechanisms when they store new information that extends systems of record. Distributed database transaction mechanisms that allow many repositories to be updated in a consistent manner are also defined by ESA.

How will ESA change how applications are designed and built?

Perhaps the most important aspect of the ESA stack to keep firmly in mind is that it does not live in just one application. The ESA stack exists in every part of a network of service consumers and in service providers that are participating to automate a process. Figure 1-11 shows the transition to this architecture from the mainframe stack.

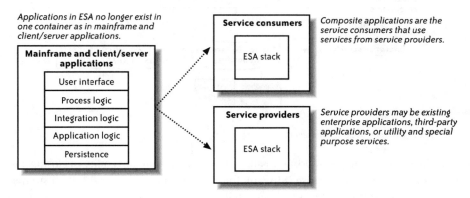

FIGURE 1-11. Application structure in ESA

Service consumers use the ESA stack to do their jobs, as do service providers. Each type of application may use more or less of each layer in the stack.

The layers of the ESA stack are also constructed differently than in the mainframe era, in which development was performed primarily with languages such as Java, ABAP, and C/C++. All of these languages are still used in ESA, but their focus is to build components that fit into a composition environment in which modeling is the primary method of building applications. Chapter 12 covers how composite applications are structured and how model-driven development tools are used to build them.

Figure 1-12 illustrates how development tasks are separated between developers and programmers who focus on the more technically challenging task of creating enterprise services, and business analysts and process experts who use modeling and orchestration techniques to assemble new applications from existing parts. The UI can be rendered in many more forms quite easily because of the model-driven development techniques.

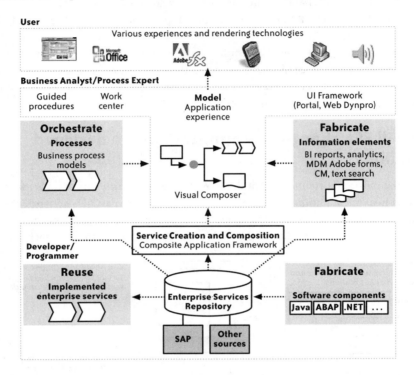

FIGURE 1-12. ESA composition environment

Finally, the structure that ESA brings to applications creates the possibility of closing a gap that has long existed in enterprise software. In order to communicate with its customers, SAP has created a system of business maps that describe the scenarios and groups of processes that exist in a particular industry. These maps are of great value in explaining how a product such as mySAP ERP will support a business. The maps show the main areas of the business and break them down into scenario groups, then into individual scenarios and further into processes that enterprise applications automate. You can then divide those processes into process steps that are associated with specific tasks in UIs. SAP has long promoted this sort of high-level modeling as a way to bring clarity to the design of businesses and business processes. The ARIS modeling tool from IDS Scheer has been SAP's recommended approach for business modeling. The ARIS tool, which will become part of the suite of tools surrounding the Enterprise Services Repository, creates the sort of process component models that are shown in Figure 1-13.

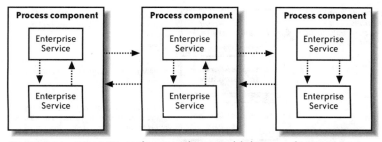

Process components are groups of processes that are modeled in terms of Enterprise Services.

FIGURE 1-13. *Process component modeling*

Process component modeling defines the process components, the interaction among the process components (called integration scenario modeling), and the interaction between two process components (called process interaction modeling). Inside the process components the processes are modeled using enterprise services and business objects. The value of this modeling is that it closes the gap between business modeling, which takes place in terms of process components and modeling how those process components will be implemented. In the current forms of business modeling, there is a leap from the scenarios to the processes, and this leap does not connect the two as clearly as process component modeling does. This sort of modeling is yet another way that ESA brings the business and IT onto the same playing field.

What supporting infrastructure does ESA require?

This new world of service consumers, service providers, and model-driven development and composition requires a host of supporting elements, each of which plays a crucial role, as shown in Figure 1-14.

Model-driven, pattern-based development tools

Applications in ESA are based on a division of duties among the various layers of the ESA stack. This structure serves to contain the complexity within each layer and to simplify the interaction between them. Further simplification is provided through the use of patterns and model-driven development tools. Modeling is used at many different levels in ESA. UI and application modeling using tools such as SAP NetWeaver Visual Composer helps you to create UIs rapidly. In certain cases, SAP NetWeaver Visual Composer can simplify the task enough so that business analysts can configure applications or even build them themselves. Modeling tools are also available for high-level business processes (ARIS models from IDS Scheer), for backend business processes (SAP NetWeaver XI), and for configuring business processes (SAP Solution Manager). Various abstraction layers such as Web Dynpro provide more detailed representation of an abstract UI that modeling tools can use. Modeling simplifies development and application change and helps to support many platforms with less work.

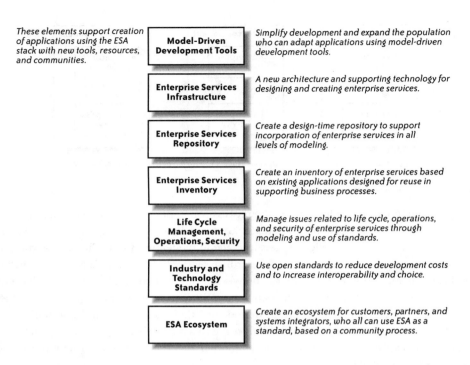

These elements support creation of applications using the ESA stack with new tools, resources, and communities.

Model-Driven Development Tools — Simplify development and expand the population who can adapt applications using model-driven development tools.

Enterprise Services Infrastructure — A new architecture and supporting technology for designing and creating enterprise services.

Enterprise Services Repository — Create a design-time repository to support incorporation of enterprise services in all levels of modeling.

Enterprise Services Inventory — Create an inventory of enterprise services based on existing applications designed for reuse in supporting business processes.

Life Cycle Management, Operations, Security — Manage issues related to life cycle, operations, and security of enterprise services through modeling and use of standards.

Industry and Technology Standards — Use open standards to reduce development costs and to increase interoperability and choice.

ESA Ecosystem — Create an ecosystem for customers, partners, and systems integrators, who all can use ESA as a standard, based on a community process.

FIGURE 1-14. Supporting elements of the ESA stack

Patterns amplify the power of modeling by bringing together large assemblies of components into higher-level structures that repeat themselves. Patterns can be applied to UIs, processes, or the entire structure of applications. Developers who use them have a huge head start compared to having to start from scratch.

The use of model-driven development and patterns is key to delivering the increased productivity and the ability to quickly and easily change existing processes that are crucial to the success of ESA.

Enterprise Services Infrastructure

The Enterprise Services Infrastructure is a coordinated set of technology, infrastructure, and tools for designing and building enterprise services and ensuring that they operate in an optimized fashion. ESA spells out what service work will be done in the application calling the enterprise service, what will be done in any intermediate layer, such as a service broker, and what will be done in the application providing the service. The Enterprise Services Infrastructure enables developers to create services according to this architecture, to take advantage of web services standards, to help implement patterns, to use global data types, to support security and transactions, and to optimize invocation of services and message traffic between them. The Enterprise Services Infrastructure provides many of the functions that are associated with the idea of the enterprise service bus.

Enterprise Services Repository

In order for enterprise services to be reusable, it must be possible to find enterprise services, determine what they do, and then bring them into development tools. The Enterprise Services Repository is a directory of enterprise services that does all of these things. An easy way to understand the Enterprise Services Repository is to think of what an automotive engineer would need if he were creating a Boxster from reusable parts. First, he would need a directory of all reusable parts. The Enterprise Services Repository is a searchable archive. Once he found a part, he would want to know what it did and how it was intended to be used. The Enterprise Services Repository stores a variety of types of modeling data. It stores how any enterprise service is linked to higher-level business processes that may be part of business scenarios and process component models that describe how an enterprise application or an industry process works. The description for the service interface that is used to invoke the service, the WSDL file, is also stored, and development tools use it to invoke the service or use it in modeling. The Enterprise Services Repository also stores how an enterprise service is related to business objects that implement it. A variety of other documentation and metadata about the service are also stored. Finally, the automotive engineer would like to know if any of the parts were built and available. The Enterprise Services Repository also stores how the service may be accessed at runtime.

Enterprise Services Inventory

The Enterprise Services Inventory comprises the services that SAP is creating, based on the mySAP Business Suite and SAP NetWeaver, to support the creation of composite applications. Enterprise services are described in the Enterprise Services Inventory in such a way that business analysts can easily understand them. In 2005, the first batch of enterprise services were described in the Enterprise Services Preview on the SAP Developer Network (SDN; *http://sdn.sap.com*). WSDL files and process descriptions were provided for hundreds of enterprise services based on mySAP ERP and some industry-specific solutions. In the first quarter of 2006, the first implementations of services in the Enterprise Services Inventory started to arrive, along with xApps and other composite applications that use those services; since then, implementations have proceeded in quarterly installments. The composite applications include Project Mendocino for Microsoft Office integration of SAP applications, and composite applications for analytics, self-service, and other key processes that extend and improve the functionality of the mySAP Business Suite. In the future, SAP partners and customers will add to the Enterprise Services Inventory by implementing services created through the ES-Community.

Life cycle management, operations, and security

ESA changes what software vendors provide to customers and what is available for reuse. In the mainframe era, applications and parts of applications had life cycles. They were delivered, installed, configured, maintained, and retired. SAP has used modeling in the SAP Solution Manager to simplify the process of configuring applications. Now the world of life cycle management will become a lot more challenging. Instead of a modest number of applications and parts of applications, thousands of services will be delivered to customers. Each will have its own life cycle. Managing this world will require new, model-driven configuration tools and support models. Operations and security practices will also have to change to accommodate the new world of services. (All of this is discussed in Chapters 18 and 19.)

Industry and technology standards

ESA could not exist without the hundreds of standards that have been developed to make application development and interoperability much easier than they have been in the past. ESA creates an environment in which the value of standards can be harvested in terms of both technology and business semantics. At all levels of the stack, ESA uses technology standards such as J2EE, WS-Reliable Messaging, WS-Policy, and so on, to improve interoperability and reduce implementation costs. ESA takes all of these technology standards and provides the context and plumbing for them to work together in a way that maximizes the value each can create. In isolation, technology standards provide a certain level of value, but when combined, a synergy is created. In the same way, enterprise services also bring semantic industry standards to life. Standards such as RosettaNet and CIDX describe standard document formats and provide guidance for how these formats should be used to support various business processes. A set of enterprise services that uses these standards can be put to work quickly to automate business processes among companies so that new partner relationships can be implemented in days rather than months.

ESA ecosystem

The ESA ecosystem consists of all of SAP's capabilities, plus those of its partners, brought to bear in a coordinated way to solve problems for customers. SAP is promoting ESA adoption by software vendors in important vertical markets. Companies such as Intel, Cisco, Microsoft, and others have agreed to support ESA in their products and are certifying a wide variety of products to work in an ESA-compliant manner. The ES-Community will allow partners and customers to work with SAP to design enterprise services to solve emerging technology and industry problems. This ecosystem will make it easier for SAP, partners, and customers to gain more value from ESA.

Is ESA compatible with event-driven architecture?

Event-driven architecture (EDA) is another architectural paradigm that is often mentioned in conjunction with SOA. While EDA is fundamentally different from SOAs such as ESA, the two styles are not contradictory, and in fact, they work together well. ESA is a request/response architecture. Service consumers make requests of services and wait for responses. The idea of EDA is "fire and forget." Systems are constructed to respond to events that occur in software or in the real world. Once an event has occurred, a cascading process begins in reaction to the event. Perhaps alerts are sent to people, tasks are assigned, or automated responses are executed. EDA meets ESA in terms of this process of reacting to events. For example, if an event requires a task to be performed, users can use a composite application based on ESA to execute that task. In processing the task, more events can be raised, initiating more chains of events. SAP has long recognized the importance of events in modeling and automating business processes. More than 2,000 core events exist on business objects in the mySAP Business Suite. SAP has created a new infrastructure for turning these core events into business events that can be the foundation of a new generation of event-driven solutions. See Chapter 5 for an expanded discussion of SAP's plans for EDA.

What is the promise of ESA?

Looking back to the answer we provided to the question "What is ESA?" reveals that the answer so far has primarily explained the ESA technology architecture. The next question in this chapter refers to ESA at the application level, and the following chapter is devoted to exploring all of the questions related to understanding the business value of ESA.

The technology architecture came first because that is how most enterprise architects start their understanding of a new trend or idea. First they understand the mechanisms, then they understand what they can do with those mechanisms, and then they determine whether the trend has any relevance to their company's IT situation.

Based on all of the mechanics of ESA that we have explained thus far, we can summarize the likely benefits of systems created using ESA:

- Greater flexibility
- Expanded reuse of existing functionality
- Improved communication between IT and business
- Faster time to market through improved developer productivity based on model-driven development, removing IT bottlenecks
- Easier adaptation through modeling and role-based tools
- Clearly defined roles from the business analysts to the developers
- Better encapsulation to allow heterogeneity or outsourcing
- Lower TCO
- A foundation for an ecosystem
- A foundation for harvesting value from standards

For many SOA vendors, these benefits are promised without the sort of complete, top-to-bottom explanation that we are providing in this book.

But even though SAP's vision is complete, nobody expects the fulfillment of that vision to be rapid or effortless. If Hasso Plattner could wave a magic wand and all of a sudden bring every enterprise service needed by SAP and all its customers into existence, what would be the result? How would this work? What would be the benefit for SAP and its customers?

Another way of thinking of this is to ask the question, "What will the world of enterprise software and IT be like in a completely enabled Enterprise Services Architecture?" Here's one vision.

The first major difference in the world of a complete Enterprise Services Architecture is in the nature of software requirements and documentation. Instead of having lengthy requirements documents that describe systems, a series of models would be used that would always be accurate because the applications would be generated from them. At the highest level would be models of the business showing the relationships among process components. Next, each process component would be modeled in terms of the enterprise services that would automate the business processes. The enterprise services themselves would be modeled from business objects. All of this modeling would be used to create service providers. Composite applications would be generated the same way from UI models, process models, and modeling to create business objects in the composites through service composition. Thanks to Plattner's magic wand, all of the services to enable all of this automation would exist in the repository.

Unfortunately, there is no magic wand, and instead, SAP and its customers and partners must gradually build the inventory of enterprise services, the repository to hold their descriptions, and the modeling and development tools to construct service providers and composite applications. The next question addresses how that is likely to play out.

How will the transition to ESA occur?

ESA is too large a change to happen in a big bang. Over the next few years, each release of the mySAP Business Suite will become increasingly service-enabled, model-driven, pattern-enhanced, and easier to configure and change. At a macro level, the change that ESA will bring will have the following shape:

- The starting point is the world of SAP R/3 and the mySAP Business Suite as they existed before ESA. Processes are automated inside the applications and are configured with metadata. Almost 100,000 UIs exist in a wide variety of forms. SAP NetWeaver is used for integration and to support processes that move from one enterprise application to another, such as order to cash. ESA-style development is possible using SAP NetWeaver, but the supporting set of tools and the inventory of tools are limited.

- The midpoint comprises the current versions of the mySAP Business Suite, SAP NetWeaver, and those that will be released in 2007 and 2008. These versions come with the Enterprise Services Repository populated with an increasing number of services built on the mySAP Business Suite and described in the context of a high-level process component model. SAP NetWeaver Visual Composer, SAP Composite Application Framework (SAP CAF), and a variety of other model-driven tools that use patterns will be available for the development of composite applications. An increasing number of xApps will be delivered by partners, and special-purpose composite applications such as Project Mendocino or SAP xApp Analytics will be delivered to address urgent problems.

- The destination will be the world of the business process platform. In this world, a fully populated Enterprise Services Repository will be available for use with SAP's model-driven development tools. The power of patterns will reduce the number of UIs that SAP delivers with the mySAP Business Suite from 100,000 to 10,000 or less. These UIs will be easily customizable so that each customer can optimize his processes and productivity. Partners will tailor basic UIs for an increasing number of verticals. The mySAP Business Suite will be delivered as a set of service providers and composite applications.

While the transition described here is oversimplified, it does get to the essence of the change that is taking place. The engine of value creation will be composite applications based on ESA. Application design will change from a process focused on solving one problem to a task centered on assembling—or creating, if needed—enterprise services. In essence, the design process will no longer be about how one application supports a process; instead, it will be about how a set of services can be constructed to support many different end-to-end processes implemented by composite applications. (The Enterprise Services Design Guide, available on SDN, is a comprehensive look at this sort of service enablement.)

But the shift to this new way of thinking about processes and applications will be incremental, as the three phases just described suggest, as will the implementation of the new applications. To improve our understanding of how ESA will affect enterprise applications, we will explore in more detail the general areas in which ESA will improve applications, and then move on to how ESA will affect the current installed base of SAP applications, how the next releases will change, and how applications will be structured in the long term. Figure 1-15 shows when various ESA-related products will be generally available.

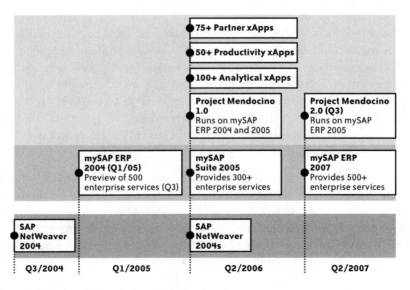

FIGURE 1-15. General availability of selected ESA-related products

ESA's areas of focus for applications

As the "What is ESA?" answer explained, ESA affects all levels of the application stack. So, what will be the value? If ESA can improve many things, what will SAP decide to improve first? Figure 1-16 shows the areas on which SAP is focusing.

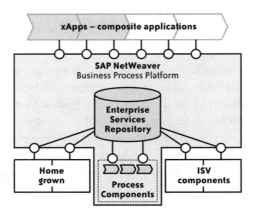

FIGURE 1-16. ESA overview

Here is how ESA will change the application landscape in the long term: SAP will continue to build on xApps, composite applications that SAP and ISVs sell as packaged products, and will create even more composite applications to improve user productivity and extend the reach of mySAP Business Suite solutions. (Project Mendocino is an example of this strategy.) Many of these applications will be intended to promote self-service so that employees and managers will be able to perform by themselves the tasks that power users currently perform. Role-based interfaces that walk users through processes step by step will be one of the key ways that productivity is increased. Providing enhanced analytics capabilities will be another major focus that will be satisfied through composite applications that either stand alone or become embedded in mySAP Business Suite solutions. The analytics applications will not only bring together important information about an issue or task but will also allow action to be taken. Many of these new composite applications will be built with modeling tools such as SAP NetWeaver Visual Composer and other modeling environments that allow business analysts to participate in the construction and configuration of composite applications.

Composite-application building will be supported by an increasing inventory of enterprise services that the Enterprise Services Repository will describe. The first step in this service enablement was the ESA Preview system on SDN, released in mid-2005. Starting in the first quarter of 2006, the first implementations of services in the Enterprise Services Inventory based on the mySAP Business Suite were released, providing a new gateway for composite application development. The composite applications for the purposes mentioned earlier will use these services, but they will also be available for use by SAP customers and partners, who will be able to use the SAP NetWeaver Developer Studio, the SAP CAF, SAP NetWeaver Visual Composer, and other development techniques to put these services to work or to configure and adapt composite applications created by SAP. As each release of mySAP Business Suite solutions and SAP NetWeaver arrives, the Enterprise Services Inventory will grow and enterprise services will become easier to create. Modeling tools for service composition to create enterprise services will arrive and business objects will start to show up in the mySAP Business Suite solutions that will allow the automatic relation of services that support UI and application patterns.

Configuration and administrative functions for applications will be supported with tools for life cycle management. SAP Solution Manager relates high-level business processes to processes automated by applications using a cascading set of models.

While the big picture is helpful to know, most companies that use SAP software are interested in how ESA can help them today. The answer depends on where you are starting.

ESA today: SAP R/3

Many companies that are running SAP R/3 4.6c think they must upgrade to mySAP ERP 2004 or mySAP ERP 2005 to implement ESA. While more is possible with later versions, SAP customers have made excellent progress on their ESA strategies on SAP R/3 4.6c using the tools and functionality provided by SAP NetWeaver. Figure 1-17 clarifies how enterprise services relate to R/3.

For SAP customers running SAP R/3, ESA provides a framework for extending functionality based on services. Using SAP NetWeaver components such as the Portal, Exchange Infrastructure, and Web Services Infrastructure, SAP R/3 functionality can be exposed as services and used to construct simple composite applications that consume services or support integration with other applications based on services.

Business perspective	Services are used to extend reach of SAP R/3 to provide role-based views for internal and external customers and to support B2B integration.
Application perspective	Basic consumption of services used to build skills and create simple composite applications.
Technology perspective	SAP R/3 RFCs and BAPIs are service-enabled through custom development based on SAP NetWeaver in ABAP Workbench accelerated by the Web Service Infrastructure.

FIGURE 1-17. ESA today: enterprise services and SAP R/3

You can use SAP R/3 4.6c to create composite applications by using the SAP NetWeaver Developer Studio to create web services based in BAPIs and Remote Function Calls (RFCs) in ABAP or in Java. Creation of such web services can be accelerated through the Web Service Infrastructure, which automatically generates proxy code for accessing RFCs, BAPIs, Enterprise JavaBeans™ (EJBs), IDOCs, and other interfaces. The SAP NetWeaver Portal or other programs can use these web services. SAP NetWeaver XI can be used to model processes based on web services and other services described in the SAP NetWeaver XI Integration Repository.

With SAP R/3 4.6c, ESA is much more a do-it-yourself activity resembling the offerings of tools vendors; if you use these techniques, you can create flexible and powerful composite applications.

ESA in mySAP ERP 2004 and mySAP ERP 2005

In mySAP ERP 2004 and mySAP ERP 2005, SAP provides a complete environment for gaining the benefits of ESA. Figure 1-18 explains the relationship of ESA to mySAP ERP 2004 and 2005.

For SAP customers running mySAP ERP 2004, mySAP ERP 2005, the support for ESA is expanded by providing ready-made services described in a repository that supports model-driven development. The scope of requirements that can be met and custom processes that can be supported using the mySAP Business Suite is dramatically enlarged.

Business perspective	Composite applications make IT more flexible and responsive. Standard applications can be tailored to automate more business processes. Innovation cycles accelerate. An ESA ecosystem coordinates SAP, partners, and customers.
Application perspective	Composite applications extend and amplify the power of mySAP Business Suite in all directions while allowing rapid innovation and flexibility. Business analysts start to play a greater role in developing applications.
Technology perspective	Enterprise Services Inventory and Repository provide the foundation for a new generation of model-driven development tools that accelerate development and provide for unprecedented flexibility.

FIGURE 1-18. ESA today: mySAP ERP

Composite applications for the purposes mentioned earlier, such as Project Mendocino and self-service, will be provided. The Enterprise Services Repository and Enterprise Services Inventory will be populated. Advanced tools for creating composite applications such as SAP NetWeaver Visual Composer and SAP CAF will become available.

With all of this support, companies can start to use these services and development techniques to solve new problems right away. Applying composite applications to the most pressing problems facing a company, as well as to areas in which innovation is important, can increase the quality of IT support for the business and reduce time to market for new ideas.

Based on SAP's support for ESA, companies can start the process of cultural change. They can learn to think of their IT infrastructure in ESA terms and build their skills so that increasing value can be created.

ESA in the future

In future releases of SAP products, the composite application architecture will expand its scope. More and more extensions of mySAP Business Suite solutions will be delivered as composite applications. Parts of the mySAP Business Suite functionality may also become composite applications. Models will become more visible at all levels of development. The complexity of adapting SAP products will be reduced. Many more role-based and industry-specific applications will be supported at an affordable cost. In this world, the differentiator will be the quality of the business vision for automating processes. Companies that gain the vision and skills required to take advantage of ESA will have an important advantage over those that do not. Figure 1-19 describes the future of ESA.

In the Business Process Platform, the mySAP Business Suite applications are reorganized around business objects with methods based on patterns. Services can be created automatically based on these patterns, and UI and process templates create standard structures. Automation is extended through event-driven processes that assemble UIs on-the-fly based on patterns to address exceptions.

Business perspective	The gap between IT and business is closed. CIOs become focused on process innovation, and IT is transformed from a cost-center to a strategic weapon.
Application perspective	Event-driven automation covers more business processes than ever, as management by exception becomes the default paradigm. Modeling escapes the world of development and becomes a tool of business design at the highest levels.
Technology perspective	The Enterprise Services Inventory and Repository provide the foundation for a new generation of model-driven development tools that accelerate development and provide for unprecedented flexibility.

FIGURE 1-19. ESA in the future

How can ESA be addressed at a tactical level?

ESA is a topic with such a wide range and such depth in terms of its effect on IT that it can be difficult to understand where to start. You can find part of the answer by using offerings such as the ESA Adoption Program, explained later in this book, that provides approaches for understanding how ESA can help a business and for creating a long-term roadmap.

But on a tactical level—the level of today's project list—ESA can be pursued every day. To help understand how ESA can relate to almost every project, it can be useful to think of the five Cs of ESA. These levels are important, because you cannot just push a button and make ESA a part of your business. You must integrate it in steps.

Figure 1-20 shows the five tactical levels. The first is *conceiving,* which involves making sure you know what you want ESA to do. The next is *consuming,* the task of putting services to work in simple ways to attack projects that are easy to complete. The skills built into consuming services can support the next level, *composing,* in which more innovative and complex applications based on services are created. The task of composing applications generally starts with existing services, but if the job cannot be done with services already in the repository, then the next tactical level is required. *Creating* services is perhaps the most technically challenging level, in which you design and create new services by using a variety of development tools. Finally, *controlling* concerns tactics focused on policies for IT governance related to the security and operational issues surrounding services.

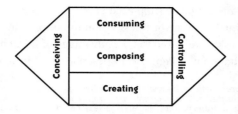

FIGURE 1-20. *The tactical levels of ESA*

Each part of this book will focus on a different tactical level. The goal is that each tactical step will create more flexibility and build more skills. The process of creating a roadmap for ESA (described in Chapter 7) shows how to synchronize all of the tactical work so that infrastructure improvements, software upgrades, system consolidations, and so forth, focus the power of ESA on bringing flexibility and rapid evolution to the parts of a business that will have a strategic impact.

The challenge in discussing ESA is that it can bring up many issues at once, and discussions sometimes wander and become confusing because too many topics are in play. One tool for achieving clarity is a map we created for our use in this book. This map combines the five tactical levels with the three architectural perspectives to create the map shown in Figure 1-21. You can use this sort of map to identify quickly the areas that any discussion is touching on so that you can address issues one at a time and with a clear context.

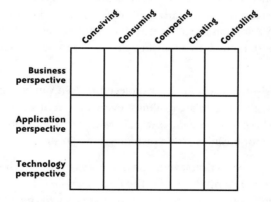

FIGURE 1-21. *The ESA map: perspectives and tactics*

For example, if a businessperson comes up with an idea for a composite application that automates a process across many different lines of business, how can you carry on a discussion about what must be done? One way would be to go through each box in Figure 1-21 and bring up the issues and questions related to each box. Normally, not all boxes apply. At the end of such a process, you will have a to-do list that you can easily allocate to those in charge of each perspective.

Why does ESA matter?

ESA matters most because for the first time in IT history, we have a blueprint for all levels of the enterprise architecture. We have a blueprint not just for an application, but also for a platform for flexible automation of business processes.

ESA matters because it provides the ability to align the business architecture, the application architecture, and the technology architecture using a framework that allows all aspects to understand each other. ESA brings the three basic levels together using enterprise services as a common building block.

ESA matters because it standardizes business semantics by providing services that can be used to implement standards and make them useful, or to model and implement relationships among companies.

ESA matters because it makes flexible composite applications possible. When the complexity of applications is encapsulated in reusable enterprise services that are orchestrated through modeling, new ideas can come to life more quickly, a culture of innovation can be created, and the experience gained each day in interacting with customers can be put to work more rapidly to improve the business.

ESA matters because it bridges the gap between buy versus build. Instead of buying an application and having to live with whatever can be configured or customized at a high cost, ESA provides products as composite applications based on models that can be changed in part where it makes sense for a business. The paradigm becomes buy, build, and compose where you need to.

ESA matters because it delivers a different IT, one that is not a bottleneck and a barrier, but a lever and a springboard. We will expand on these topics in Chapters 2 and 3.

What are the core values of ESA?

At this point in technology development, the idea of SOA is far better developed than the actual technology in the field of SOA. Many solutions that are implemented in the real world of IT cannot take full advantage of all of the elements discussed in this book because the right tools, technologies, and infrastructures are not yet available. This does not make the applications any less valuable; it just means that they perhaps were harder to build or that they make certain compromises that won't be required in the future. Many of the examples we will discuss in this book fall into this category. When we discuss them, we will point out how the application lives up to the core values of ESA, even if the technology falls short of the ideal. But what are the core values of ESA?

The core values of ESA represent the themes that run through ESA that are present in almost every application and technology we will examine:

- *Managing complexity*, usually through enterprise services but also in other ways, is perhaps the most frequently recurring theme of ESA.

- *Simplifying development*, frequently through modeling and patterns, is another important theme.

- *Promoting reuse* happens through mechanisms such as the Enterprise Services Repository.

- *Improving productivity* occurs through expanded automation and role- and pattern-based UIs.

- *Increasing flexibility* is based on model-driven development of applications and reusable services.

- *Promoting differentiation* occurs because existing systems can be recombined in new ways to adapt quickly to changing conditions and to enable innovation.

Where can we go for more answers?

The first book on ESA (O'Reilly's *Enterprise Services Architecture* by Woods and Mattern, mentioned earlier) is a good place to get an overview of what ESA is all about. The latest book, called *mySAP ERP for Dummies: ESA Edition* (Vogel and Kimbell), also covers a lot of basic ESA topics, as does *SAP NetWeaver for Dummies* (Woods and Word) (both published by For Dummies). SDN (*http://sdn.sap.com*) is one of the best locations for information about SAP and ESA. The Enterprise Services Inventory preview is there; it shows what kinds of services SAP will be introducing. SAP.com also offers a variety of other high-level information as well as a service marketplace.

ASUG, long a valuable resource for those in the SAP ecosystem, is starting a special interest group for ESA that will include thought leaders such as Paul Kurchina. You can find details on this special interest group at *http://www.asug.com*.

ESA in action: Mitsui

Mitsui is an excellent example of a company that is putting ESA to work to integrate its operation based on a strategic look at key business processes. Mitsui is one of Japan's largest general trading companies, with more than 700 consolidated subsidiaries, 177 offices worldwide, and a global workforce of more than 38,000 employees. The company focuses on the trading of metals, machinery, chemicals, energy, and consumer goods, and the scope of its operations contains everything from domestic sales in Japan to import/export to offshore trading. Mitsui's strategic goal, set in 2000, is to become "the world's strongest general trading company." But rapid globalization—along with the challenges of market expansion, fierce competition, and the rising volume of data that comes with it—forced Mitsui to make important changes in its corporate structure.

To this end, the company embarked on a massive business reform and integration effort designed to streamline companywide business processes and consolidate the more than 400 individual systems comprising the supporting IT infrastructure. Mitsui's overarching goal was to replace the individual and diffuse efforts of its subsidiaries with a more integrated and centralized model aimed at optimizing, standardizing, and visualizing the operational processes the Mitsui Group had in common.

Begun in earnest in 2001, the first stages of the company's "business reform project" required four years and 670 project members working around the clock, to identify and redesign core business processes. The project team set four overarching goals for their effort:

- Redesign of the operational processes from the viewpoint of overall optimization
- Support of the redesigned operational processes through use of the latest systems
- Reform of the organization into a shared service center
- Creation of a mechanism for sharing knowledge

With those goals in mind, the team set four corresponding midterm objectives:

- Creation of sales opportunity windows
- Prompt provision of management information
- Small corporate divisions made by professionals
- Thorough digitization

Both the policies and the objectives were at the top of the development team's mind when it finally came time to implement what became known as the MICAN (short for the slogan "Mitsui I can!") Process and the MICAN System, which were composed of three types of reform. Organizational reform was enabled by the Shared Service Center model adopted by the project team. Process reform was introduced using the Process System Integrity (PSI) model based on the Sarbanes-Oxley Act. And the underlying IT reform was realized by the adoption of ESA and was based on SAP NetWeaver—specifically, its SAP Business Information Warehouse (SAP BW) and SAP EP components, with SAP R/3 as the base ERP application.

Mitsui built the MICAN System using SAP NetWeaver as the platform, with SAP R/3 and SAP BW comprising a layer of functionality immediately below. After mapping Mitsui's diverse IT landscape to the streamlined business processes identified in the MICAN Process, approximately 400 commonly used pieces of IT functionality were redesigned as reusable web services, of which 100 to 150 appeared in nearly every cross-company process. A rudimentary Enterprise Services Repository was created, as each enterprise service was assigned an ID number and was registered in a database to aid in the easy visualization of operational processes.

Business processes that were once unique to individual Mitsui subsidiaries have since been integrated and centralized, vastly improving the speed and integrity of data as it flows across the combined enterprise. To make these redesigned processes visible to Mitsui's managers, the project team implemented SAP EP to create a portal that would unify them within a single UI. The finished portal serves approximately 9,000 users via a single-sign-on secured site, with role-based profiles providing the appropriate level of functionality and data to any given user.

Looking toward the future, Mitsui intends to keep the MICAN Process and the MICAN System at the heart of its continuous efforts to streamline its efforts in Japan while rolling the system out to its overseas subsidiaries and affiliates over the next few years.

CHAPTER TWO

The Business Case for ESA

THE FUNDAMENTAL CHALLENGE FACING BUSINESSES TODAY IS TO DETERMINE WHETHER **IT** IS THE solution to problems, or is the underlying problem itself.

Where do you start? For the purposes of this book, we will begin with the problem of *speed*. The pace of business is quickening, no matter how large or small your company is or in what industry you compete.

For example, product life cycles are shrinking, as shown in Figure 2-1. Years of mature profitability have contracted into months, forcing product makers to move even faster to recognize new market opportunities, to tweak and compensate for changes in demand while the next new thing is still in the womb, and to begin planning the next revisions, spin-offs, or successors the moment next quarter's hit (you hope) is born.

All of this, in turn, accelerates the business from the very top in the CEO's office to the very bottom in the toll-free customer service trenches. If launching a new product is a function of executing a business process—that in turn is broken down into hundreds, if not thousands, of process steps—then a dramatic reduction in time to market or time to volume is possible only if the coordination of those steps becomes proportionately faster. And it is becoming faster. Historically, businesses have predicted time to transparency—i.e.,

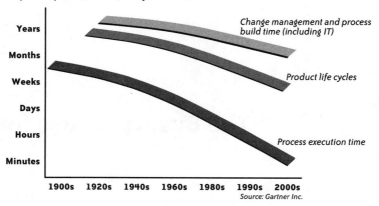

Future growth depends on a customer's ability to change at multiple levels: process, product, culture, and systems.

Change management and process build time (including IT)

Product life cycles

Process execution time

Source: Gartner Inc.

FIGURE 2-1. The prerequisite for future growth

the time between posting a transaction and propagating the data across the enterprise, up the supply chain, and onto the balance sheet—in weeks and months. Today Wal-Mart can predict its quarterly results two months before the end of a quarter. Today you can press a key and produce a P&L statement from a sale within minutes, seconds, or even subseconds.

This transformation is taking place at the bottom of the organization, where thousands of events—a new sale, a customer service record, or a new batch of market research—generate information that is created, sorted, analyzed, and processed by established IT systems. The first generation of enterprise applications—such as Enterprise Resources Planning (ERP), Customer Relationship Management (CRM), Supply Chain Management (SCM), and others of their kind—were created to automate relatively generic, generally stable business processes relevant to single corners of the business. They comprised a hard-wired value chain that willingly exchanged flexibility and extensibility for an optimized operating environment. At the time, the tradeoff was well worth it.

But client/server systems haven't kept up with the accelerating pace of change, nor were they designed to. Neither were they designed to be opened, tinkered with, reconnected to each other, and otherwise recycled and recomposed to serve the actual, real-world business processes of the companies where they are installed.

This is why a corporation's ability to keep up with the pace of change is slipping. Accelerating product and service launches and reducing the speed of execution to near-real time requires changes to business processes that can't be performed unless the corporate structure and culture change, and unless IT supports those changes. Unfortunately, the current enterprise application architecture cannot support such change. Systems of record were built to automate common processes across all businesses and in specific verticals, not for adaptability. Meeting requirements to automate new processes frequently happens too slowly to matter or is too expensive to contemplate.

If the first problem is speed, the second challenge facing every business today is *flexibility*. How quickly and efficiently can you restructure your business to realize gains in speed and seek out new opportunities or answer competitive threats? Cultural preparation is one thing, but for IT to support this shift, the relationship between enterprise software and business processes must first be turned inside out. The internal logic of the applications must be engineered to reflect the external logic of the business process itself, which could be required to change in an instant if a new product is a blockbuster, is a bomb, is rendered obsolete by a sudden acquisition, and so on.

The pace of business is accelerating, but the current generation of IT has become calcified. All too often, *IT is rightfully blamed as the bottleneck; its inflexibility is slowing its owners by standing still.* But let's not get ahead of ourselves. Let's first tick off a few additional challenges facing businesses today:

Companies need to maximize their market by addressing every possible channel, fulfilling all customers' needs. This leads to an array of choices that can sometimes border on the absurd, however, as companies try to satisfy even the most niche customer. It isn't enough for Apple to introduce and perfect the most outrageously successful consumer electronics product of the last five years, the iPod; the company offers a custom engraving option, too. And it isn't enough to have an online-only or retail-only sales channel, either; consumers feel entitled to purchase products whenever, wherever, and however they want, forcing the creation of new touch points and greater complexity. The same principle applies to service industries as well; the ever-finer parsing of customer demographics and desires results in the greater stratification of products and offerings, which in turn leads to shortened product life cycles and proliferating brand extensions in order to discover, capture, or cling to market share. Efficiency is what enables all of this—the Internet, progress in logistics, distribution channels, and analytics—and more products are sold as a result. However, capitalizing on this requires new processes for the more efficient capture, mining, and utilization of consumer data, combined with faster, lighter-weight supply chains and manufacturing operations geared more toward flexible manufacturing than massive, high-volume runs. This is exactly the sort of real-world business process that cuts across enterprise application silos, giving rise to the frying-pan-or-fire choice outlined earlier: either succumb to inertia or suffer painful, expensive, and time-consuming change.

The dilemma of when, how, and how much to outsource and offshore. Given the permanent cost pressures facing manufacturers in almost every industry, outsourcing has become a given for many who have already bundled off increasingly large and mission-critical portions of their manufacturing operations and supply chains to East Asia and beyond. While outsourcing and offshoring themselves are nothing new, the acceleration of the business landscape and the lure of greater efficiency have effectively led to the outsourcing of critical, nearly core activities. It isn't enough for Nike to send an order to one of its suppliers in China, sit back, and wait for delivery in six months. Today, the shoemaker is able to see the available manufacturing capacity of partners in that country at a single glance. Thanks to a key business process innovation in its supply chain,

Nike monitors its outsourcing activities across China as if it were looking inside a single warehouse and production environment. The company is unwilling to offload a critical activity without some measure of control. The challenge for every company going forward is determining what it can outsource or offshore, and in turn, what level of visibility and control is needed for maximum efficiency.

Global markets, global competition, and global regulation. The flipside of offshoring is market globalization. Your customers, as well as your supply chain, are just as likely to live in Mumbai, Singapore, or Seoul as they are in Frankfurt, San Francisco, or Stockholm. Competing for customers on the global stage demands its own supply chain solutions, as well as a new approach to sales and marketing that may require international acquisitions. (This creates another set of problems in terms of integrating your new division's business processes and IT with your existing infrastructure.) Global markets also create new demands on data integrity—sorting currencies and sales orders on the one hand, and conforming to regulatory standards such as the Sarbanes-Oxley Act on the other.

These are somewhat specific tactical and strategic issues facing businesses today, but underlying each are a pair of metachallenges with roots in IT. Before you can meet any of the preceding challenges, you must be able to answer a pair of more fundamental questions:

How much data is needed, how critical is it, and how should you use it? Accelerating the speed of business is a challenge that ultimately boils down to data. New products, new markets, and new channels generate more of it; successful execution in all of these areas depends upon collecting that data, analyzing it effectively, and then passing it into the right hands in the right place at the right time. What is an effective business process if it's not a framework for describing what the right hands, the right place, and the right time are?

The first-generation enterprise applications effectively funneled data to a handful of power users—the CIO and CFO, their respective inner circles, and so on. Today's IT architecture reflects the hard-wired value chain and centralized command and control commonly in place when the architecture was built. As noted earlier, however, the organization of business processes has sped away while IT frequently did not keep pace.

As the decision-making process becomes increasingly decentralized, the data associated with business processes is no longer the domain of a handful of power users, but is spread to knowledge workers across the enterprise. As more employees at varying levels are encouraged to become monitors and decision makers, they need data, analyzed and parsed to the appropriate level, to make these decisions as quickly and with enough context as possible. Institutional speed is the sum of the speed of these individual choices, and perhaps the ultimate challenge facing businesses today is to redesign organizational structures (and the underlying IT) to empower people along business process lines, rather than cultural, political, and ad hoc organizational lines. (Chapter 3 discusses the cultural challenges and changes related to ESA adoption.)

This means that today's corporations face the monumental challenge of redesigning the flow of data through the value chain. Events must complement transactions as the operational focus—an IT architecture should be able to automate the handling of data and embed analytics throughout the value chain in order to foster management by exception—the moment data is passed to the right hands in the right place at the right time. We will discuss how to choose the right hands in more detail shortly, in the section later in this chapter titled "What principles should be driving my IT decisions?"

Just how many enterprise applications, data types, and business processes does anyone need? You can always count on intense competition for at least one thing: market consolidation through mergers and acquisitions. The need (or at least the desire) to add new revenue streams, to add new international divisions, or even to just round out product portfolios sooner or later leads to industry consolidation (and that's just the nature of the software business itself). With acquisitions come a set of integration challenges that go beyond corporate culture. What should you do with the best-of-breed systems your company has just adopted, which you now have to merge, somehow, with both your day-to-day operations *and* your attempts to make sense of your already heterogeneous IT environment? (The result of past acquisitions, perhaps?)

Just as you must extract the logic of business processes from the internal logic of enterprise applications and allow it to drive the use (and reuse) of those applications going forward, you must also extract the data and functionality from those applications in the form of enterprise services to speed up, simplify, and reduce the total cost of ownership (TCO) of heterogeneous environments. The ESA transformation is about using existing systems of record to build a composite application infrastructure that enables cost-effective change. The old model was monolithic infrastructure with integration; the new model is service-oriented architecture (SOA) with composition.

Once they have embraced the new model, businesses can begin to recombine that data and functionality in ways that address all of the challenges outlined earlier. That, in the smallest nutshell, is the promise of ESA; it will free data and functionality from siloed processes, and it will redistribute both in units of enterprise services designed to serve the process logic of the business, not the internal logic of the software. The question then becomes, how will it do this?

What attributes must ESA embody?

You may be saying to yourself, "Well, all of that sounds thoroughly daunting, and no one would disagree that IT, like all segments of the business, could always do better. But how do we address these challenges?"

For most of the rest of this book, we will thoroughly explore the nitty-gritty details of ESA from the application and technology perspectives. In this chapter, we will examine ESA from a business perspective, and from that vantage point, any IT architecture that hopes to improve upon the existing IT architecture (such as it is) must have the following attributes:

Flexibility

Here it is again. Ripping out a generation's worth of monolithic enterprise applications only to replace it with another one isn't going to reduce anyone's TCO or simplify any CIO's life. More than anything else, the next architecture must find a way to free data and functionality from siloed applications, package them properly, and put them at the service of processes. The way forward, at least at a granular level, is already clear—the concept of *web services*, which SAP, Microsoft (.NET and Indigo), IBM, and a raft of smaller software companies have embraced. Web services carve interoperability from enterprise applications that you can call remotely from anywhere using fairly simple exchange protocols such as SOAP. Web services defined without a process context are usually too granular to be useful on their own, but when designed as enterprise services with specific processes and process steps in mind, they accomplish the necessary task of transforming powerful, albeit static applications into dynamically available functions flexible enough to be used and reused repeatedly.

In practice, this means that all of the function calls that comprise, for example, the order to cash business process—the ones involved in time to transparency, which we mentioned earlier—are extracted from their respective silos and are loosely coupled in an end-to-end process that mirrors the real-world business logic. The addition of *business semantics*—e.g., standards, compliance, interfaces, and documentation for data exchange between two business processes—transforms a web service into an enterprise service, a marriage of technical and business standards that didn't exist in previous architectures, as illustrated in Figure 2-2.

FIGURE 2-2. Business semantics needed in addition to SOA

The combination of business semantics and an SOA, which can loosely couple and decouple technical functionality as needed, results in ESA, which is the framework needed for the positive evolution of IT. Instead of enterprise applications shaping business processes from the inside out, knowledge workers at every level can contribute to and help shape IT around real-world scenarios and business processes from the outside in. That also requires ESA or any other architecture to possess…

Simplicity, or at least enough simplicity to be understood outside of the IT domain

If the current IT architecture has one flaw that's more fatal than the others, it is the tremendous amount of complexity involved in integrating combinations of enterprise applications into a coherent operating environment to automate emerging process needs. This difficulty drives TCO and the number of developers on the payroll higher, and it drives managers crazy. This shortcoming also drives the popular perception of IT as the obstacle on the way to innovation. To transform IT into an enabler of growth—and this is at the heart of ESA's promise—a simple system is needed that moves control of the architecture out of the hands of IT and shares it with empowered employees on the front lines of the business, the ones who need IT to support their attempts at process innovation.

Traditional development techniques, even using languages such as Java and ABAP, have improved greatly over the years. However, applications derived from enterprise services can be developed faster and are easier to modify because the complexity is carved up elegantly across systems of loosely coupled services; it is not buried deep in a monolithic structure.

To that end, the next architecture must be model driven. It must enable knowledge workers to create new scenarios or business processes that can be manipulated with graphical tools linked to the enterprise services below. To oversimplify a bit, businesses need a user-friendly approach to their IT investments. And that's what ESA's model-driven approach offers. This has an enormous impact in terms of control and distribution:

Control

For the first time, the primary user of IT isn't an application consultant or an in-house developer, or even the CIO, all of whom will design, consciously or subconsciously, an application according to their interface preferences and (incorrect) assumptions of what line users need. That is why so many of the first generation of enterprise applications reflected the structure of the database, not the model of the business in the user's mind. Instead, a new kind of architect—a manager who is intimately familiar with the day-to-day workings and needs of her operational business unit—will use modeling tools to design new scenarios as needed. And she will be able to adjust these scenarios virtually, on the fly, in response to changing business conditions instead of having to rebuild them in 18 months at a cost of millions of dollars. We will discuss the business analyst role in detail shortly, but it's important to note here that business analysts will not constitute a new mandarin class within the enterprise; they won't be replacing one institutional bottleneck with another. They will organizationally embody another key attribute of next-generation architecture, that of…

Distribution

By liberating enterprise services from monolithic applications, and by allowing assembly of these services by business analysts and beyond, ESA creates the possibility of increasing automation at every level of the business, scaled up or scaled down, depending on the person's place within the enterprise. This is the *role-based* approach to IT, a vision in which business analysts create semitailored roles (for a customer service representative, perhaps, or a factory shop-floor manager) which are basically portal interfaces to a predefined set of data and functionality that helps that role carry out the tasks needed to support a specific process. (As we will see in our discussion of the user interface (UI) throughout this book, a new pattern called the work center provides a reusable, role-based structure.) In this way, business analysts can decentralize the power of enterprise computing, enlarge the population involved in adaptation and innovation, and increase efficiency across the business by empowering employees with just enough functionality.

And that's just within the company. Perhaps the greatest potential within the enterprise services concept is the idea that selected data and services can connect on both a technical and a semantic level outside the boundaries of the firm to partners, suppliers, and customers, each of which can pass and receive data to drive decision making at either end.

Each of these attributes underscores the overarching need to unlock the power and value already residing in the previous generation of enterprise applications. But once you have that power, where do you start?

What principles should be driving my IT decisions?

Geoffrey Moore is a theorist and consultant who developed a very powerful operating model for how companies should assign scarce time, money, and resources in the pursuit of innovation and profit. And considering that you're reading a book about ESA—a sign that indicates you're thinking long and hard about how to assign your company's critical and scarce IT resources for at least the next two to ten years—Moore's model, illustrated in Figure 2-3, might prove of some interest. It's what SAP itself uses to make the business case for ESA. Here it is:

> Any corporate activity that increases shareholder value is core. Anything that doesn't is context.

That's the handy rule of thumb, at least. It sounds simple, maybe even simplistic, but let's pause to think it through for a moment. As Moore notes in his book *Living on the Fault Line* (Collins), "a business process is core when its outcome directly affects the competitive advantage of the company in its targeted markets. Here is the ground upon which companies must differentiate to win power, and the goal of core work is to create and sustain that differentiation."

From that line of reasoning, Moore reaches two conclusions: "For core activities, the goal is to differentiate as much as possible.... And the winning approach to *context* tasks is not to differentiate, but rather to execute them as effectively and efficiently in as standardized a manner as possible." That does not mean that efficient execution of context processes is not a benefit; it's just not the differentiating benefit that will dramatically increase the company's value.

What does all of this mean in practice? Well, here's what it doesn't mean. *Core* doesn't necessarily refer to activities that may be critical to your business, such as customer service

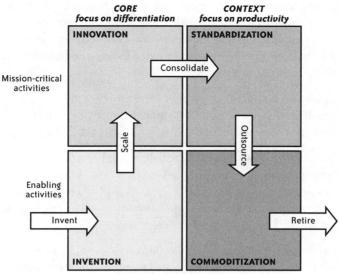

CORE
focus on differentiation

CONTEXT
focus on productivity

INNOVATION

STANDARDIZATION

Consolidate

Mission-critical
activities

Scale

Outsource

Enabling
activities

Invent

Retire

INVENTION

COMMODITIZATION

Adapted from Geoffery Moore's *Living on the Fault Line*

FIGURE 2-3. Business process life cycle

in some industries. Your actual customers might believe it's critical, but if that were true, you wouldn't have seriously flirted with outsourcing the entire operation to Bangalore. If customer service does not differentiate you from your competitors, it's context. (Unless, of course, you're an outsourced customer service specialist.) Back-office operations are context. Outsourced manufacturing is context you've already implicitly recognized as such. If it is core, why don't you have it in-house?

Moore's concept of core isn't about "core competencies." Ever since that term was introduced 15 years ago, it's been diluted to mean anything a company is traditionally good at or is known for. Digital Equipment Corp.'s core competency was in building minicomputers, and that didn't help much in the end. In recent years, Hewlett-Packard, which inherited Digital's legacy, has had a hard time distinguishing between its own core/context activities. The company spun off its scientific measurement arm as a separate company, Agilent, in effort to focus on computing. Today, HP's core is arguably imaging, but what to do, then, with the company's PC and consulting businesses? You can see the dilemmas.

This is not to say that contextual activities are ultimately of secondary importance. A critical defect introduced into a product by one of your Malaysian contract manufacturers, or a bad batch of components purchased by a Chinese subsubsubcontractor, can have an immediate, powerful, and disastrous effect on your business and your ability to deliver increased shareholder value. But Moore's point is that excellence in contextual activities won't differentiate your business and will guarantee neither a competitive advantage nor a nod from the shareholders. He refers to these as *hygiene*. "Hygiene refers to all the things the marketplace expects you to do well," he writes, "but gives you no credit for doing *exceptionally well*." Remember, however, that context processes recombined in ways that differentiate can support new core processes. This framework is powerful but subtle.

Few corporations recognize this. By Moore's estimate, a typical Fortune 500 company has a core-to-context ratio of 20:80, meaning that four times as many resources are allocated to what are either best practices that the competition can copy or purchase, or essentially commodities which, from a purely competitive standpoint (the right one, in Moore's view), is a total waste of resources.

One company's context is another company's core, however. Manufacturing may be context to you—which is why you outsource it—but obviously it's core to that contract manufacturer which must differentiate itself to win your business.

This is how and why SAP came into existence, in fact. It began life by creating the first generation of enterprise applications designed to standardize business activity on systems of record and automate common processes such as payroll and human resources that large corporations preferred not to code from scratch on their own. Its original core was the rest of the world's context.

The current IT architecture of business applications was an originally successful attempt to grapple with the core/context dilemma…up to a point. By standardizing and optimizing discrete sets of functionality—ERP, CRM, SCM, and so on—in single applications, corporate could deploy the pieces as needed and stabilize their own relatively inefficient contextual processes around what SAP and other vendors had focused on and nearly perfected as core. It worked for a while. TCO fell. The first few generations of ERP made good on its guarantee to endow a competitive advantage, albeit a temporary one, to those who were wise enough to install it.

However, two things happened. First, the current generation of IT essentially became commoditized—everyone had ERP, so now what? The investments were made, the ROI was hopefully acceptable, and now everyone had a massive investment on their hands that was gradually becoming increasingly expensive, complex, and hazardous to modify in the pursuit of innovation. Second, the business models of ERP owners changed over time (some suddenly, but most gradually) and what was once considered core became context—which Moore predicted, but enterprise software vendors did not.

What happens when core eventually becomes context?

The reality is that what's core today will not always be core tomorrow. Remember, we're not talking about core competencies here. In this setting, core—a business process, a product, some secret IT advantage, whatever—is anything that differentiates you from your competitors. Over time, core naturally becomes context. An innovation slowly degrades into a best practice, and then into a commodity. What do you do with a core-turned-context process? Moore's answer was simple: outsource it. Find someone who considers that process their core, and if there isn't anyone, then spin out the people responsible for maintaining that process. Let it become their core; put them in charge of innovating it, but whatever you do, get it out of the business if possible.

That might be a little extreme, but Moore has the right idea. When core becomes context, it's critical to divert resources away from that activity as soon as possible in order to give oxygen to a nascent innovation that could become core itself. The IT mechanism for doing so is *consolidation*, the selective culling and repurposing of software and hardware formerly dedicated to core processes that become redundant as they become context and as those resources become needed elsewhere.

At least that's how it should work in theory. In reality, the static nature of today's monolithic architectures impedes consolidation in much the same way it impedes innovation. Faced with a heterogeneous collection of servers and applications that support a core-turned-context process, there is no easy way to abstract the data and functionality from the hardware and software in order to retire unnecessary components or even to identify what those components are.

Along similar lines, there is no prescribed way within the current architecture to cost-effectively recycle and reuse prior investments in context-enabling applications (i.e., ERP and the like) so that they might support core processes about to become context. Within the current architecture, enterprise applications are like barrels in a river about to flow over a waterfall. Once they've gone over—falling from core to context—there is no resource-effective way for those investments to support the core processes that might come floating down the river in the future. The IT components are differentiated from each other, but the process isn't differentiated from competitors anymore. And the business isn't deriving any value from an expensive IT effort that increases spending on context every quarter.

Innovations begin life as nascent processes just beginning to create differentiation, and then become core when they receive the resources to scale into enterprise-wide enablers. Then, as the relentless pace of competition and technology adoption catches up to the innovation, a mission-critical core process shifts to the right. It may still be mission critical, but it is no longer a monetizable difference versus a competitor's process. It's become a best practice. As it shifts to the bottom right, it becomes a process fit for outsourcing to someone who will invest the resources needed to maintain and optimize it as best he can until it finally shifts out of the grid completely and is retired.

For a real-world example of this process life cycle in action, consider Lufthansa. In 1999, the first self-service check-in kiosks began appearing in Frankfurt Airport with a human attendant standing nearby, ready to explain how the system worked. The invention was helping differentiate Lufthansa from its competitors, but it was hardly critical. Two years later, in the wake of long security lines created by 9/11, consumers realized that if they used the kiosk, they could replace a 90-minute wait in the check-in line for a two-minute task at the kiosk. It was a core innovation for Lufthansa by then, one that airports around the world have since scaled up and installed.

However, Lufthansa's competitors—and its own partners—caught up. Every major airline began installing kiosks. Suddenly, it became a mission-critical application. The airline's customers would revolt if the kiosks disappeared, but the airline was no longer differentiating. It had shifted to the right. Lufthansa responded by consolidating. Instead of paying to support its own kiosks, it collaborated with its allies in the Star Alliance to create kiosks that any member airline could reuse. The total cost and the resources involved shrank. Finally, the kiosks became so ubiquitous that the airlines outsourced them completely to third parties, who began placing them in hotels and other public spaces. Today, a Lufthansa kiosk is at SAP's headquarters in Walldorf, Germany. The time elapsed from innovation to commoditization: five years.

How does ESA enable consolidation and reuse?

Through the same set of attributes, actually. Because the enterprise services residing within ESA are loosely coupled, and the composition is not hardcoded, but rather, is assembled through process orchestration and modeling—they're just combinations and recombinations of underlying services, remember?—*consolidation* is simpler. Instead of having to migrate data and applications to a new, streamlined set of best practices running on a different platform, the process in question is already running on that platform; at this point, it's just a relatively simple matter of reconfiguring the underlying scenarios, business processes, and process steps.

Now—as someone once said, this is where the magic happens—those same enterprise services are able to unlock and recycle the functionality that used to go over the cliff. The investment in context now has a greater chance of supporting core activities. Because the process definition has been abstracted from the enterprise applications, it's possible to recombine the resulting enterprise services into new process steps and the like that can support business processes which are *core*. To understand what we mean, see Figure 2-4.

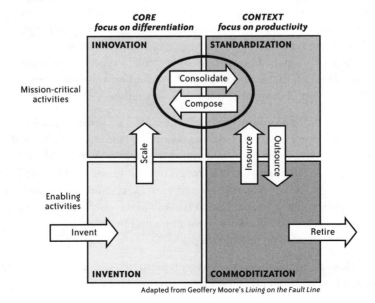

FIGURE 2-4. Consolidate and compose business processes on one platform

These recombinations are grouped together under the banner of *composition*. In the ESA universe, the IT department has a pair of new jobs: one team, the consolidators, is busy consolidating master data, data warehouses, and interfaces and rebuilding them as cost-efficient, contextual processes; a second team, the composers, is busy recomposing entirely new, potentially differentiating scenarios to support the latest and greatest innovation born inside the company's walls. Setting ESA apart from every IT architecture that has come before is the fact that both teams are building upon the same architecture and the same application platform erected from web services. (We'll spend more time talking about these and the other related teams in a new IT paradigm, the repository keepers and the disruptive innovators, in Chapter 3.) The pain points that previously afflicted IT—the high costs and complexity of integration, the expensive but pointless investment in inertia, and so on—begin to disappear.

Turning back to Geoffrey Moore for a moment, consider this: the key to his argument in favor of outsourcing anything and everything that isn't core rests on the premise that resources saved from outsourcing—or at the very least, consolidation—must be reallocated to core activities. As this applies to the business case for ESA, it means that *consolidation can fund innovation, which is made more efficient through composition,* as illustrated in Figure 2-5.

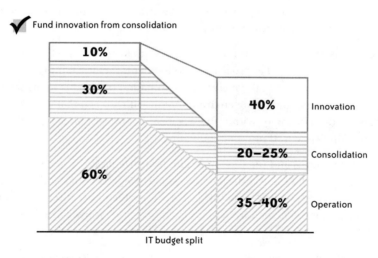

FIGURE 2-5. *Innovation funded by consolidation*

That's just the first step. Consolidation/composition is just the tactical benefit of ESA, one that we will explain next.

What kind of innovation should companies pursue, and how will ESA help them?

It all goes back to speed again and to the beginning of this chapter, actually. Earlier, we mentioned how the time to transparency that encompassed everything from taking a customer's order to passing it up the supply chain to generating a P&L statement had plunged into the subseconds. That was the result of relentless innovation in process execution, a literal race to see who could extract a competitive advantage from the speed of their operations.

However, the final distance between the winner, the runner-up, and the pack wasn't great enough. Light-speed process execution is a best practice well on its way to becoming a commodity. What's next?

The first thought was product innovation; cell phone makers would race to push more models out the door instead of just racing to sell them efficiently. But that didn't happen. For one thing, it wasn't applicable across all industries (it's hard to innovate on something like cement), and in industries with very high rates of product turnover, such as cell phones and consumer electronics, the components are already so commoditized.

So, the last curve left on the graph that appears in Figure 2-1 at the beginning of this chapter is time to change. Can you accelerate and perfect the creation of business process innovations themselves? Call it *process innovation*. Master practitioners of that art already exist in the world. Dell is the consummate process innovator. Dell doesn't invest much differentiation in its actual products, which are assembled almost entirely from off-the-shelf parts. Dell's core is its vaunted supply chain and its ruthless commitment to perfecting that supply chain—a textbook example of process innovation.

The strategic value of ESA lies in its inherent abilities to foster this kind of innovation. The switch from a modeling-based approach to development, the distribution of analytical tools across the enterprise, and the increasing automation of systems to manage by exception combine to create a computing environment in which it is remarkably easy to detect and model patterns of behavior within the business. If a process already mapped to these patterns exists, fine-tune it. If not, then build one.

Examine the big patterns and the tiny ones, and prioritize based on where you can increase revenue and eliminate costs. If a process fails 15 percent of the time and results in a cost of $150 with each failure—and this is a process which runs three million times a year—then the savings to be had from optimizing that process justify the use of ESA already.

Again, that's just thinking tactically. In the long run, ESA's ability to enhance process innovation will have a far-reaching effect on the structure and organization of the business itself. Led by the business analysts, ESA-enabled companies will replace organizational charts with employees organized around processes, and the boundaries between your company and your ecosystem of partners, suppliers, and so on, will eventually become porous, replaced by the automated exchange of data among intelligent systems. The CIO's role will evolve into something more like that of a "CPIO," a chief process innovation officer.

But we're getting ahead of ourselves again. Let's take a step back.

What are ESA's practical implementation issues?

The first step, which Microsoft, IBM, and many others have already taken, is to begin transforming monolithic applications into web services. SAP has gone a step further, seeking instead to create less granular, more sophisticated enterprise services designed to support the business processes and scenarios present in any given company. To that end, SAP has created a preview system with more than 500 defined and published enterprise services. (For a more complete description of SAP's enterprise services, see Chapter 8.)

It then falls to you to think long and hard about the makeup of your current IT landscape. We're back to core/context again. Which scenarios, applications, servers, and so on support core processes, and which ones support context? Which of those supporting services can you buy from vendors? Which are commoditized productivity tools, and which are truly differentiating the company—the processes that can't be bought? All of the services underlying these will be added to the Enterprise Services Repository, a dictionary of services created in the context of business maps, scenarios, processes, and process steps and illustrated in Figure 2-6. Only after you've begun abstracting the functionality from the hard-wired applications are you able to see how a once-ingenious integration solution could just as easily be replaced with an out-of-the-box scenario from SAP or one of a hundred Independent Software Vendors (ISVs). The following checklist offers one step-by-step approach:

- ✓ Understand your differentiators.
- ✓ Identify business process opportunities.
- ✓ Prioritize opportunity versus cost
- ✓ Create a dictionary of services, events, roles, and processes.
- ✓ Reuse services in the platform.
- ✓ Build or buy missing services.

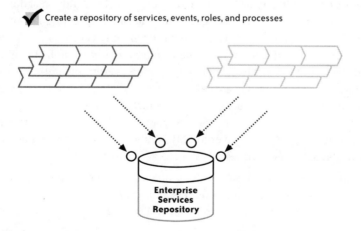

FIGURE 2-6. Creating a repository of services, events, roles, and processes

Once you've done that, map your business processes and start planning how to consolidate context-supporting processes. Do not reflexively invest in development of custom services. Instead, see whether they exist already, buy them, extend them with less effort, and add them to the repository. Stop thinking only in terms of "buy versus build" and start thinking like an architect—like a real one, we mean. If your IT landscape were an actual landscape, what would it look like? What services provide the basic utilities—plumbing, power, and the like—and how does your existing array of applications and data objects comprise the buildings? You might think of it this way: the enterprise applications, like most utilities, are buried; the buildings are assembled from enterprise services stored in the repository, and at a certain height, a composition platform hovers upon which composite applications can be built in the future, pushing your buildings to ever-greater heights.

First, though, you'll need to consolidate activity in certain buildings, renovate them, and demolish the empty ones that are devoid of value.

They're empty because the business tasks that used to be performed within them have moved away and are now the tenants of another building. Think of the all-but-abandoned systems that fell into your hands after the last round of acquisitions. Most of the functionality and data have been migrated elsewhere, but so far, it's been easier to keep those systems standing than to knock them down—to pay for inertia, in other words, instead of grappling with the complexity surrounding their demolition. But now, it's time to do just that. It's time for your first round of ESA-enabled consolidation:

Map your context systems. Again, which parts can you replace with parts off someone else's shelf? Which are already up and running elsewhere in the company? What do you need to keep, and which ones can go? Once you identify those systems, as in Figure 2-7, it's time to consolidate the data associated with those systems and then to retire the hardware.

Consolidate master data. Already we're seeing the power of abstraction in action. Use ESA to create a master data hub that isn't locked into any single application or physical piece of hardware. Why? Because the IT architecture will only become more heterogeneous over time (there are acquisitions to be made and more servers to be bought), and the entire purpose of ESA is to abstract data, processes, everything, onto the platform, beyond the integration headaches that stem from residing in one place all of the time. So, consolidate your data, cleanse and synchronize it, syndicate it back into the environments, and once you're able to manage your data through SAP NetWeaver Master Data Management (SAP NetWeaver MDM), you've essentially transcended your physical systems. Figure 2-8 illustrates this step.

Consolidate your hardware. Stop thinking about one server for each system. Use virtualization to move data out of redundant servers and retire them. Think of it as urban renewal, illustrated in the sparser landscape in Figure 2-9.

Start sharing data and services across the enterprise. Leverage resources across multiple systems; scale functionality as needed to support process innovation, as shown in Figure 2-10.

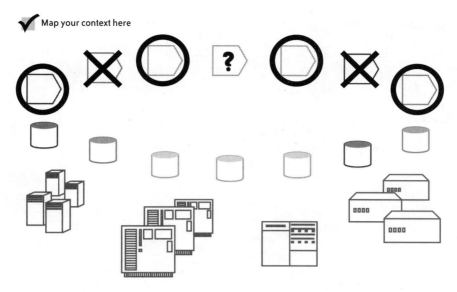

Map your context here

FIGURE 2-7. Mapping context systems

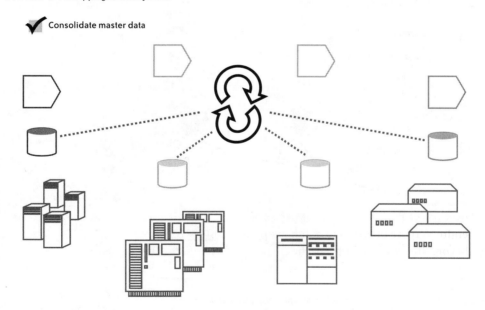

Consolidate master data

FIGURE 2-8. Consolidating master data

Do you see where we're headed with this? Following one of the earliest steps, the creation of the Enterprise Services Repository, you can clearly see which scenarios are core and which are context. Identify which slices' custom-built functionality are context and therefore replaceable; take steps to abstract and cleanly separate essential data from inefficient hardware and processes; and then consolidate all of that down into a virtual platform which can be scaled up again as needed to support the deployment of new services.

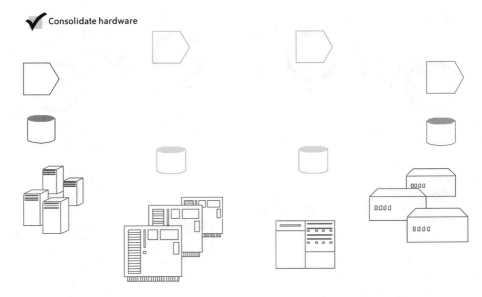

FIGURE 2-9. *Consolidating hardware*

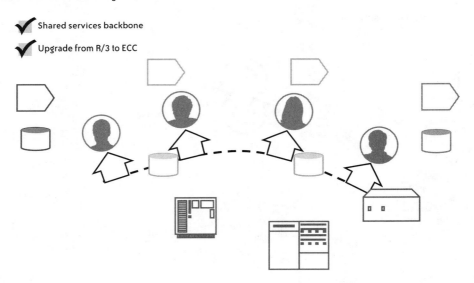

FIGURE 2-10. *A shared services backbone, which enables faster upgrades*

ESA becomes the mechanism for converting core/context theory—which sounds so right on paper but was so hard to realize before now—into action. If that strikes you as a bit of an abstract moral victory, then just concentrate on the reduced TCO.

What's the long-term adoption path of ESA? How quickly will I see ROI, and what form will it take?

Figure 2-11 shows SAP's current roadmap for ESA adoption graphed against the evolution of IT infrastructures once consolidation/composition begins and against the evolution of business process as the model-driven approach to IT begins to transform how scenarios are designed and how businesses are structured. As you can see, achieving the full potential of process innovation is still as long as two years away. And that's what you should expect.

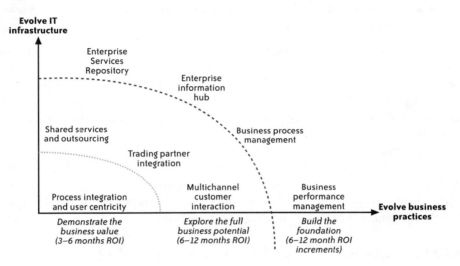

FIGURE 2-11. ESA roadmap

ESA isn't a silver bullet; it's not "best of breed" repackaged under a different name with a new set of marketing materials. It's a complete architecture composed of a business process platform, standards, services, and infrastructure that become easier to use with each passing quarter. Those on SAP R/3 can create applications using services that provide value through ESA principles. This is easier in mySAP ERP 2004 and mySAP ERP 2005, and will be easier still later on. SAP and a large ecosystem of ISVs are committed to making ESA a reality.

"Process innovation" comes in all shapes and sizes, and before business analysts begin building and rebuilding scenarios the way most of us would juggle an Excel spreadsheet, there are small but important gains to be realized.

You may recall that earlier, we made the case that ESA would be a boon for employees in the trenches forced to conform their natural way of working—essentially ad hoc business processes—to the interface limitations of the software. The enterprise applications told them how to work instead of the other way around.

As you can see in Figure 2-11, "Process integration and user centricity" is the very first step. That's already happening in a joint project between SAP and Microsoft, named

Project Mendocino (see Chapter 9). Project Mendocino is an attempt to bridge the gap between daily ad hoc methods of doing business—returning emails, composing documents, passing along those spreadsheets—and the structured information residing in the backbone of the business. Microsoft estimates that more than $2 billion a year in wasted productivity is spent by frontline employees trying to bridge the gap by hand-copying data from SAP applications to Excel and back again, with the possibility of costly transcription errors present at every step. (And that assumes they're even allowed to touch the enterprise application or data warehouse in question, as opposed to handing a presumably contextual task to a dedicated power user whose time is better spent working on core-related process innovation. And so on….)

Project Mendocino attempts to remedy this by recognizing that Microsoft's suite of desktop applications (Office, Outlook, etc.) is the de facto business interface for most office-bound workers. Instead of creating a new, easy-to-use interface for SAP applications, SAP realized that the interface existed, and its job was to use enterprise services to move functionality out of enterprise applications and into all-too-familiar desktop tools. Within Project Mendocino, alerts and other events generated by enterprise services materialize as emails in Outlook. Business analytical tools are embedded in Excel. Reports and other documents that commonly suffer from inconsistent data and version control are automatically synced with data objects hovering in the background. And employees can realize a degree of self-service, filling out forms and correcting data, as needed, within the data object itself, instead of passing along a request to a power user.

What is ESA's long-range impact on corporations?

We won't walk you through all of the organizational and cultural issues involved in making ESA a reality within the enterprise (that's what the rest of the book is for, especially Chapter 3), but we will wrap up this chapter by using the figure of the business analyst to explore ESA's long-range impact on corporations.

The business analyst isn't, in fact, a power user by another name, nor is she an IT administrator or a financial analyst. Tomorrow's business analyst is today's operations person—the line managers in every business unit with a thorough understanding of both the financial performance of their unit and the day-to-day business processes driving that performance.

By handing over the keys to the company's enterprise services in the form of the business process modeling tools resting atop ESA, two major shifts in the organizational structure are about to occur:

- The dismantling of IT as a roadblock to change, and a transformation of IT into a strategic weapon, has begun.

- Henceforth, processes will increasingly dominate corporate organization charts and hierarchies as the company reorganizes itself to reflect real-world concerns. In this role, ESA and the business analyst are enablers of cultural change—because they're able to render formerly obscure and ad hoc business logic visible and transparent, they're able to drive organizational change and break down false barriers between IT and business.

Taking them in order, let's first pause to consider the current model for custom application design in which the nascent business analyst is responsible only for creating the process model that a succession of consultants and developers attempt to map onto the application they are struggling to build with varying degrees of success. They're often starting from blank slates, laboriously writing code from scratch because recomposing code from existing applications is just as costly as and maybe even more difficult than just typing away.

This picture changes dramatically once ESA is in place. In this vision, the business analyst has the modeling tools and the authority to create and adapt UIs using a business-oriented process model and services to support them, and adding insight collected by embedded analytical tools. Then he begins building new scenarios by selecting services from the Enterprise Services Repository, configuring role-based interfaces for employees, and drawing inspiration from user expectations with which he is personally familiar. Only near the end of the process, when IT developers tweak the dynamically generated code created by the modeling tool, does the scenario pass out of the analyst's hands. (For a more detailed description of this process, consult Chapter 17.) The virtues of this model are obvious:

- Application design is decentralized, passing out of the hands of specialists and into those of managers and knowledge workers on the front lines, reducing delays and communication disconnects.

- Modeling tools and a decentralized development process dramatically expand the pool of "developers" to include appropriate business analysts and knowledge workers across the enterprise. And IT's resources are freed to consolidate noncore systems while supporting the organic development efforts of the business analysts. Instead of struggling with standalone applications or fragile integration efforts, IT transforms into an enabler of change—one that supports process innovation occurring on the edge of the enterprise. The chief information officer swaps her title for a new one, chief process innovation officer, because the job is ultimately less about IT than it is about enabling technologies.

This dovetails neatly with the second point from earlier: ESA and its human faces must become the drivers for a larger cultural and institutional shift away from business-as-usual organization charts and more toward a process-oriented structure. Everyone within the organization must be ready, able, and willing to recognize when and how a business process is ripe for optimization, or how a new one might open up a brand-new market opportunity, or steal a competitor's best customers.

ESA can spark a corporate refocusing on process innovation, but the danger exists that ESA will be seen internally as just another doomed initiative by IT, and not what effectively amounts to a corporate cultural revolution. It's impossible to develop pattern-based modeling if employees refuse to understand those patterns and then act upon them. Without widespread sign-on, ESA will fail.

We'll conclude this chapter with that thought. ESA is more than just a path forward for an IT architecture that has otherwise been rendered painfully obsolete. It's a catalyst for the cultural and business process change necessary to create a lasting competitive advantage in a business landscape becoming more complex and more brutal every day.

ESA in action: Nordzucker AG

An excellent example of innovation using ESA is Nordzucker AG. Nordzucker is Europe's second largest producer and distributor of sugar, manufacturing more than 1.9 million tons each year. Headquartered in Germany, with 3,300 employees and revenue of 1.2 billion euros in the 2004/2005 fiscal year, Nordzucker's roots lie with the sugar beet farmers who form the base of its supply chain and who are typically shareholders in the company. With operations scattered across Poland, Hungary, Slovakia, and elsewhere in Eastern Europe, Nordzucker faced significant challenges in exchanging information with and delivering reports to the farmers within its network.

These challenges would be magnified in 2006 when the European Union would relax its rules on sugar importation, opening the market to nonEuropean producers and potentially triggering an across-the-board price drop. With these concerns in mind, Nordzucker set out to strategically overhaul its IT systems in an effort to streamline internal operations and extend as much information and functionality as possible to the farmers themselves. To that end, Nordzucker adopted SAP NetWeaver as its platform to integrate core applications using enterprise services as the blueprint, and to create the "Farmer's Portal" currently used by more than 2,000 of its producers in the fields.

Figure 2-12 shows the traditional IT landscape at Nordzucker in which farmers once waited for weekly status reports to arrive in the mail. Today, however, they log into a web portal containing real-time reports on the quantity and quality of their crop processed at Nordzucker plants that day, quotas for their next deliveries, Nordzucker's internal production forecasts and recommendations, and even their rights and shareholdings in the company. All of this information is available within the portal's interface and as a history of downloadable documents in spreadsheet form. Figure 2-13 shows Nordzucker's new system architecture.

Within 30 minutes of a crop's arrival at Nordzucker's production plants, fresh data begins appearing in the portal window, eliminating the need for the weekly reports that consumed three to four hours per day in paperwork handling by Nordzucker employees. The company has even managed to create a portal interface for PDAs that can collect information from Nordzucker's beet lifters and loaders, such as the quantity of beet lifted, position of lifters, and loading data.

The portal also contains functionality enabling farmers to order seeds, animal feed (i.e., beet pulp), and fertilizer (i.e., carbolic lime) through the same interface, with Nordzucker's systems automatically processing orders for its own products—the animal feed and fertilizer—or else passing seed orders directly to its suppliers. In this way, Nordzucker

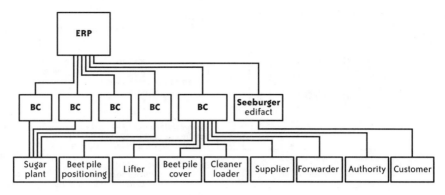

FIGURE 2-12. Nordzucker's IT landscape: yesterday

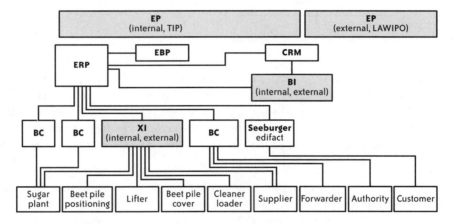

FIGURE 2-13. Nordzucker's IT landscape: today

is able to present the best options to its entire network through a single interface, and then negotiate for discounts and deliveries with its now-consolidated list of suppliers.

Underlying all of this is an IT environment built on a foundation of SAP products. Core functionality embodied in Nordzucker's custom-developed sugar beet management (SBM) system is based on SAP R/3, and is supplemented by implementations of mySAP Supplier Relationship Management (mySAP SRM) and mySAP Customer Relationship Management (mySAP CRM). The portal itself was created using the SAP NetWeaver Portal component, while SAP NetWeaver Business Intelligence (SAP NetWeaver BI) powers its reporting capabilities and interface elements created using the SAP NetWeaver Application Server (SAP NetWeaver AS) pass user input back to the appropriate applications. Meanwhile, SAP NetWeaver Exchange Infrastructure (SAP NetWeaver XI) passes data to the portal from Nordzucker's shippers. Figure 2-14 illustrates the system integration effort at Nordzucker.

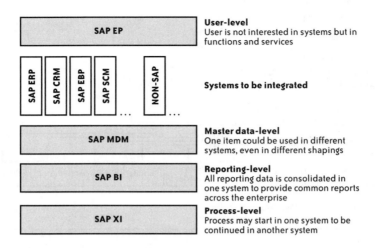

FIGURE 2-14. Levels of systems integration at Nordzucker

To provide the reporting capabilities for the Farmer's Portal, Nordzucker's IT team used SAP NetWeaver to make ABAP service calls to the SBM system. The process is nearly reversed when it comes to ordering seeds and other supplies; the farmers' orders are passed back to the SBM system, which automatically orders and pays for seeds and other supplies and then subtracts the cost from the farmers' accounts with Nordzucker. The orders are then automatically passed to the seed suppliers via XML messages received by the suppliers' own SAP R/3 and similar applications.

Shortly after completing the current version of the Farmer's Portal, Nordzucker reused its collection of enterprise services to create an internal counterpart for its own employees, the transaction and information portal, called TIP. More than 200 employees at the company's Brunswick, Germany, headquarters are now able to log in to a single-sign-on portal individualized for their own needs. Access to formerly disparate and now integrated sources of data has already reduced necessary employee training and improved productivity. And thanks to the flexible, easily recomposed nature of enterprise services, Nordzucker intends to add more features and functionality over time, just as it has to the Farmer's Portal.

CHAPTER THREE

Evolving Toward ESA

•

YOU MIGHT WONDER, "WHAT ARE WE GETTING OURSELVES INTO WITH ESA? THIS ISN'T JUST ABOUT the technology, is it?" ESA isn't "just" about anything. ESA is about changing all dimensions of IT so that every dollar spent, every week of work, every project completed, moves a company toward a new world in which IT is transformed from a no to a yes. Too often today, the answers that IT must provide amount to a no to ideas for innovation. Can we change a process, integrate a partner, offer a new service, outsource a key function? If a project is too expensive or takes too long, the answer, in effect, is no.

However, most organizations would not be ready if IT were suddenly transformed to say yes because the flexibility of ESA expanded the world of the possible. It is similar to the situation that radio frequency identification (RFID) and other real-world awareness technologies present. If most companies instantly turned on RFID and began monitoring real-time information, a flood of data would fill up their databases and disk drives, but those organizations would be able to understand the value of the information in only a few domains at a time. Once the organizations understood the information, they would have to change their processes and systems to take advantage of it. How fast would this happen? Not fast. What would be the impact on the organization? Probably huge. What would a company look like afterward? Probably a lot more responsive, with a new set of processes oriented to sensing and predicting events and then rapidly responding.

ESA poses a similar problem. If IT became a yes, if anything were possible, what would it make sense to do? Of course, the answer would differ from firm to firm, but if the cost of adapting systems to meet new requirements and tailoring general-purpose processes to meet the specific needs of a firm were easy and cheap, it is not a stretch to imagine that the results would most likely be positive and the organization would be transformed.

But neither RFID nor ESA will happen in the blink of an eye. Both take time, and while the work to implement them takes place from the technology and application perspectives, companies that are seeking to maximize the benefit from these ideas will be asking questions about how the business perspective must change. If IT were more of a strategic tool, what sort of evolution of culture, of governance, of organizational structure will be necessary to win in the marketplace? How can ESA help achieve these objectives?

Chapter 2 made the business case for ESA—that it finally provides the platform and methodology for consolidating and reusing your existing IT investment to fund and drive business process innovation. Seen another way, it is also the summation of everything we have learned from more than 30 years of building and fine-tuning our current IT architecture. ESA is not just a vision for the next 30 years; it is already a reality today. Companies that learn to take advantage of that reality faster than their competitors do will find themselves not just with an old-fashioned advantage in total cost of ownership (TCO), but rather, with a strategic advantage in flexibility and clock speed.

Anyone eyeing ESA as just the latest and greatest set of software integration tools is being dangerously shortsighted, however; it's more accurate to describe ESA as a *business process innovator*, or even more accurately put, as a *business process platform*. Once adoption begins—especially if there's enterprise-wide commitment from the start—IT itself is integrated into your business strategy, and then corporate organizational units are integrated and redistributed along the lines of the actual business processes that drive the enterprise processes now embodied in your IT. Ultimately, the business itself is integrated into a larger, tightly knit ecosystem with your suppliers, partners, and customers, to the point where the boundaries between each are fluid and fuzzy as data flows unimpeded back and forth.

No, it's not just about technology or applications. It's about managing a comprehensive change management process, one that will affect virtually every aspect of your company. Only the foolhardy or young would attempt this without some well-organized worrying, but managing such processes successfully and actually changing the nature of a company create competitive advantage. Fortunately, change management is not a complete mystery. It may not be easy, but it presents some wisdom that we can draw on.

The first thing we must do is divide the challenge of ESA into its component parts. The three perspectives of ESA—business, application, and technology—along with the five tactical levels—conceiving, consuming, composing, creating, and controlling—provide a way to organize our thinking into bite-size issues that can be addressed and understood. Trying to think about almost any ESA-related issue without a proper framework can lead to inefficient communication, or worse, bewildering confusion.

We cover the tactical levels of the application and technology perspectives in most of the chapters of this book. This chapter deals with the issues surrounding the tactical levels of the business perspective. How will a company change as it addresses the five Cs? What surrounding issues of culture, organizational structure, and change management must a company address? In addition to discussing these issues directly, we will also look to the example of SupplyOn, the automobile industry productivity hub that is creating standardized processes and services to connect OEMs and suppliers for direct procurement.

So, what are the concerns from the business perspective at a tactical level?

Conceiving

In *Enterprise Services Architecture* (Woods and Mattern, O'Reilly), the first book written on this subject, we described the process of The Big Think. This informal process of understanding the nature of your systems and determining where to apply ESA has been thoroughly formalized and surrounded by service offerings. The process of creating an ESA roadmap helps create a coherent plan that incorporates moves in the infrastructure and application dimensions into a change management program prioritized to maximize impact on business strategy and minimize risk. Skills in modeling of the business and modeling for development of processes and user interfaces (UIs) are usually acquired early on. The ability to use traditional development tools for ABAP and Java plays its proper role in service creation.

However, the organization must change its attitude and structure. Projects do not result in just another automated process, but rather, another set of services that will help automate other processes in the future. This is an investment. Learning which services are available in the Enterprise Services Repository is another sort of investment, one made easier by the search and modeling tools. Learning the skills to compose new applications is yet another investment. As we will see, the organization must change to manage these investments and skills properly.

The culture of no must also be overcome. When the answer to new ideas has been no for too long, people don't waste their time proposing ideas anymore. But even after a small program of service enablement, the answer will be yes more often. Companies must then find a way to turn on and manage brainstorming so that innovation becomes part of the culture.

Consuming

A company must choose its first steps carefully to build credibility that it is serious about transformation. The idea of consuming services is oriented toward simple service enablement put to use in simple ways. From the business perspective, the goal will be to determine where the low-hanging fruit are located in which a small investment can provide a large amount of business value to a wide audience. Once people understand the mechanisms of ESA, they are quick to suggest new services that would be useful. Once a few services are in place, those with business knowledge understand how to combine them to bring information to the right people to increase efficiency and improve the quality of decisions and the timeliness of actions. Consuming services is about solving problems that are probably already well-understood using ESA to make the solutions affordable.

Composing

After experiments in consuming services have proven that ESA can create a new sort of IT, the investments increase. Composing applications is the true engine of ESA. The arrival of composite applications in which new processes are automated by using process orchestration and UI patterns to create solutions that can easily be adapted and improved marks the beginning of an organizational transformation. First, the organization building the composites must be transformed. The repository of services becomes a key resource that must be managed. Business analysts must be trained and empowered to build and adapt UIs and to configure processes. Traditional boundaries between business and IT will become obsolete. The business structure at a high level will be able to be modeled in a way that will cascade from business scenarios such as order to cash, to process components, to processes, process steps, enterprise services, and business objects. The fat, impenetrable requirements document will become outdated, replaced by modeling and UIs constructed as a starting point by the people who intend to use them. With the power to change comes the responsibility to test. IT will expand its traditional processes of testing and quality control to include applications built by newly empowered business analysts.

Creating

The focus of the most technically skilled people in the IT organization will change. On the one hand, they will deliver their skills by creating services. The business side will create applications based on existing services and define the shape of new services. The applications may go into production without the new services and then be improved later when they are created. The business side and the IT department will have to learn to think in terms of services. The interaction between the two will increasingly be focused on deciding which services to build, and in which order. The IT department will also use the same tools as the business analysts to create starter applications that can be further adapted by business analysts. And as always, the IT department will seek out new, potentially disruptive forms of innovation using whatever technology does the job.

Controlling

The arrival of enterprise services will create a new tool for corporate governance that in fact makes governance easier. Departments can be forced to use centrally provided services on the one hand, but could also be empowered to develop their own services for other purposes. The relationships between departments increasingly will be described in terms of who is providing what service and who is consuming it. Service-level agreements between IT and business units and among the business units themselves could be defined in terms of what kinds of services would be provided. The choice between centralized and federated governance will be able to be made with unprecedented granularity, on a service-by-service basis.

In all of these dimensions, a company will transform itself in terms of its culture and its self-image. Those who succeed in this transformation will understand their new identity and manage the process of adopting it with conscious forethought.

Just how much and what kind of change will ESA involve?

One of the promises of ESA is that you won't have to blow up your IT infrastructure and start over. Once they understand ESA, many IT professionals wonder how wide the scope of change will be. They ask, "Will we have to blow up our infrastructure, org chart, and even supply chain, and start over? How is that a benefit?"

No one will have to blow up anyone or anything in the pursuit of ESA, and so far, no one has managed to blow themselves up, either. According to Forrester Research, for example, 75 percent of all large companies (defined as 20,000 employees or more) had begun implementing service-oriented architecture (SOA) components, and their biggest reason by far for doing so was internal integration.* The first phase of adoption is largely used to repair and connect the mistakes and unplanned disconnects within the current architecture. Evolving toward ESA is a continuous process marked by steady improvement as the new architecture gradually replaces the old. It does so organically, not via dynamite.

But if you're serious about adopting ESA, you need to think long and hard about where ESA will take your organization before you worry about how, when, and how much it will cost to get there, "there" being a new relationship between business and IT, as shown in Figure 3-1, that supports process innovation and creates lasting competitive advantage.

That's the purpose of this chapter. You've read the business case for ESA and found it compelling enough to keep reading. Much of the rest of this book is devoted to the technology and application aspects of implementation and evolution—Chapter 7, for instance, contains tactical advice for creating an ESA roadmap. Because ESA isn't IT as usual, realizing its full potential—and, in turn, its potential to transform your business—will require more than your usual IT department. Likewise, unlocking the functionality buried in siloed enterprise applications has limited value if your corporate organization and culture are unwilling to align themselves in tandem with the new, more efficient, process-oriented focus that ESA makes possible.

---

* "Large Enterprises Pursue Strategic SOA," Forrester Research, Inc., April 5, 2005.

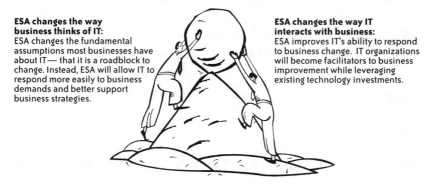

ESA will enable firms to quickly, easily, and cost-effectively optimize existing business processes and innovate both their processes and business models to improve "time to opportunity" and ultimately drive growth.

ESA changes the way business thinks of IT:
ESA changes the fundamental assumptions most businesses have about IT— that it is a roadblock to change. Instead, ESA will allow IT to respond more easily to business demands and better support business strategies.

ESA changes the way IT interacts with business:
ESA improves IT's ability to respond to business change. IT organizations will become facilitators to business improvement while leveraging existing technology investments.

FIGURE 3-1. ESA fully aligning IT and business

Figure 3-2 shows the dimensions along which a company must manage change. The culture, organization, processes, and systems must move forward in synchronized fashion. The goal is to move from process efficiency to the more advanced levels of process flexibility and process innovation that pave the way to business innovation. To drive this transformation, who within the organization will be asking the questions? How will they know which questions to ask? How will the sudden shift from a legacy of saying no to one of saying yes transform the organization? Will simply handing managers the keys to a gleaming business process machine transform them into the "business analysts" discussed in Chapter 2, or, much more likely, will they need to rethink organizational structures, develop new skills, and have ongoing discussions with external partners, et al., about the ramifications of ESA for their business? You should assume, as this chapter does, that evolving toward ESA requires a pair of parallel processes—a technological and a cultural evolution—that require an equal amount of forethought and preparation. Don't make the mistake of underestimating the cultural challenges and looming revolution when mapping a path to ESA, and don't take anyone's word for what the roadmap should be. Each company's cultural transformation will be highly idiosyncratic. The most an outsider can do is talk about its general shape. Each company must bring the specifics to life on its own.

What is IT's role within ESA?

The relationship between the business staff and IT too often is based on obsolete assumptions. That's a good thing because up until now, at times it has not been the best relationship. The relationship between IT and line managers, such as it is now, often boils down to a requirements document: the business side decides what it needs built, and IT is expected to build it. Management doesn't have to peer under the hood, and IT is neither qualified nor expected to ask whether the business side is asking the right questions or has settled on the best solution. This cultural disconnect may lead to a solution that does too much or too little.

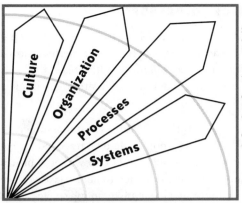

ESA-enabled benefits

System: Improvement of IT's real-time ability to deliver timely, efficient, relevant solutions to business requests

Process: Ability to focus on process improvement through flexibility and innovation

Organization: Ability to develop a common language between IT and business, and to create organizational flexibility to meet market demands

Culture: Ability to develop a process- and opportunity-oriented culture

In order to maximize the benefits of ESA, a company must consider the interdependency of its systems, processes, organization, and culture, and ensure—likely through a comprehensive change management program—that all dimensions receive the right support and incentives to drive company-wide change.

FIGURE 3-2. To achieve ESA benefits, systemic change management is required

Obviously, in a nightmare scenario—or in the world of Dilbert—this is a suboptimal, codependent relationship. Neither side is motivated to understand the limits, capabilities, or opportunities of the other side, nor has the expertise and knowledge to do so anyway. As Figure 3-3 shows, this cultural barrier looms large. The conversations between the two are usually limited to the solution at hand—a new application, an integration task, etc.—rather than the underlying business issues. Answers are built or discussed, but the true questions facing business remain murky. There is a depressing chicken-and-egg aspect to this dilemma. Does this disconnect inhibit IT's flexibility and adaptiveness to ever-accelerating rates of business change, or is it a product of a monolithic architecture in which business logic is buried under layers of application programming interfaces (APIs) and even more arcane interfaces? And does it really matter? It should be obvious to everyone that you can't solve the flexibility issue by adopting ESA without solving a far more fundamental issue: *both sides need to understand business processes before they can adopt ESA.* And that's an organizational and a cultural issue, not a technological issue.

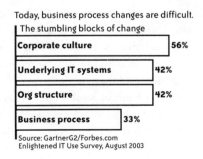

Today, business process changes are difficult.
The stumbling blocks of change

Corporate culture	56%
Underlying IT systems	42%
Org structure	42%
Business process	33%

Source: GartnerG2/Forbes.com
Enlightened IT Use Survey, August 2003

FIGURE 3-3. The obstacles of business process change

What do you mean by "business process?"

By business process, we mean the progression of steps necessary to complete a given task in the pursuit of making more money. These aren't necessarily the steps written down in some manual or encoded in your Enterprise Resources Planning (ERP) installation. These are the steps involved in "how business works," the ballet of data creation, manipulation, and distribution across the enterprise.

An inherent flaw in the current generation of enterprise software is that it assumed that the reigning business processes at the time of their creation could be hardcoded for eternity in a monolithic application designed to be the Platonic ideal of how a set of processes should be performed. "Best of breed" applications were designed to be the last word in their given fields, even though they weren't; they did a great job handling stable tasks, but due to the ever-accelerating pace of competition, business conditions began changing so quickly that processes no longer supported new requirements for processes that crossed application boundaries. Likewise, the underlying software failed to keep up with the dynamic, on-the-fly business processes emerging to meet these challenges, leading to a point where IT and business processes forked. The functionality is now trapped in increasingly obsolete applications while the users have moved on, unconsciously creating ad hoc process steps and relationships to plug the cracks in the monoliths.

As discussed in Chapter 2, ESA's strongest argument in the business case is its unprecedented ability to free that trapped functionality and abstract it to a new service-enabled platform that's flexible enough to keep pace with change.

Before IT can make that happen, *the business side must develop the ability and requisite skill set to think about business logic explicitly in terms of process models and services*. The IT side must be willing and able to listen and to play a new role as process innovator. Figure 3-4 summarizes the new organizational relationship. Enterprise services are a key element to this transition because they represent complete units of functionality designed to automate a business process. Executives and managers must develop the ability to visualize, using enterprise services, the previously occluded steps that bind business logic together. To automate something as simple as "order to cash" might mean you must isolate and highlight a dozen steps that draw upon a half dozen enterprise applications. In a fully realized Enterprise Services Architecture, the business analyst and IT will sit down together and use enterprise services as a common language to map business processes as they currently are, and chart a course for how they could and should be recombined and composed at lower cost and with greater efficiency, and then implemented by IT. The traditional role of the CIO is imagined as being split in two in order to better reflect the role of the business side in IT decision making. As shown in Figure 3-5, the chief process innovation officer (CPIO) evolves to become the C-level link between the two cultures. (We discuss the CPIO in detail later in this chapter.)

As we noted earlier, in our first book, *Enterprise Services Architecture* (O'Reilly), we referred to the first step toward ESA adoption—i.e., conception—as The Big Think. During The Big Think, a steering committee composed of business executives and IT architects sits down

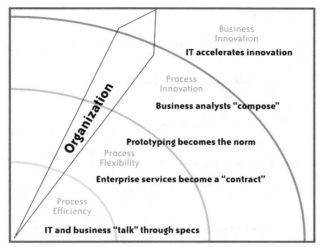

Business strategy and IT strategy need to be aligned, but their goals and tools remain fundamentally different.

FIGURE 3-4. Culture change: from org chart to processes and opportunities

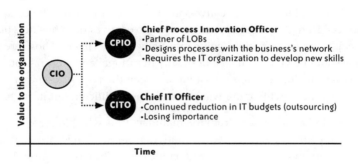

FIGURE 3-5. The new role of the CIO

to trace a map of the company's IT universe as it exists. What are the most important business processes? How many of those processes do existing applications automate? Of those applications, which ones contain data objects and services that might be useful elsewhere? …and so on, drilling down into the enterprise. Until both parties are able to sit at the same table, speak the same language, and identify the business logic embodied in those processes, however, you're not even ready to take the first step. Figure 3-6 summarizes the path to readiness.

That's a good point, but how do you bring the two sides together in the first place?

Putting them in the same room to talk about something other than the latest requirements document is a good start. Bell Canada asks 1,700 business and IT staffers to attend annual "summer camps" of classes designed to bring each side up to speed on the other's most

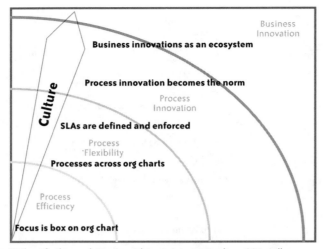

Business
Innovation

Business innovations as an ecosystem

Process innovation becomes the norm

Process
Innovation

SLAs are defined and enforced

Process
Flexibility

Processes across org charts

Process
Efficiency

Culture

Focus is box on org chart

Without further evolution toward a process-centric culture, SOAs will
remain an IT affair and fail to deliver business benefits.

FIGURE 3-6. Culture change: from org chart to processes and opportunities

pressing challenges and foster a real conversation between the two.* The company has
also begun to seed its higher-level IT positions with executives from business backgrounds
in order to keep those conversations going internally on the IT side. Those are two small
steps, but they should give you an idea of the organizational and cultural commitments
necessary to open the lines of communication between the two. Asking them to collaborate on next-generation architecture will be a little more difficult, but it can be done.

ESA adopters might borrow a page from the manufacturers who pioneered the concept of
"concurrent engineering," in which representatives from every relevant department
within the organization imagine entire product life cycles from conception through
design, manufacture, introduction, and even disposal. At every step, designers and engineers can argue for cost-saving modifications or alternate techniques to achieve the same
goals. Through close collaboration, both sides learn what is possible, what is feasible, and
what the larger business goals are. When applied to IT (a concept Forrester Research has
dubbed "concurrent business engineering"), the two sides collaborate on what the shape
of the business itself should be and how they should implement it within IT.† They brain-
storm, prototype, iterate, and test together, instead of haggling over a requirements document and leaving IT to implement everything itself. The continuing dialog accelerates the
speed of development and consensus on the final product, transforming what was formerly a one-sided conversation (i.e., the business side talking down to IT) into a virtuous

* "Digital Business Architecture: Harnessing IT for Business Flexibility," Forrester Research, Inc.,
  November 7, 2005.

† "Concurrent Business Engineering," Forrester Research, Inc., June 20, 2005.

circle of feedback, strengthening the relationship between the two and continually improving the process after each go-round.

Fittingly, this is also an example of how ESA promises to transform business processes across the entire enterprise. If your IT department and line managers can break bread together on this project, then just about anything is possible.

What is IT's role if all of this comes to pass? What does my company look like then?

All right, let's fast-forward for a moment and assume you have a fully realized Enterprise Services Architecture in place. The Enterprise Services Repository has been built and populated, composite applications have been assembled and reassembled from the functionality of your old enterprise software, and your CIO has redubbed herself "chief process innovation officer" because her job ceased to be about wrangling IT resources and morphed into the oversight of gradual, continual tweaking of seamlessly integrated business process steps. Perhaps a chief IT officer is focused on that sort of work. Oh, and your employees in the trenches no longer pass around spreadsheets via email or tortuously retype data from one application to another (introducing the occasional critical error along the way). They're busy responding to the red alerts dispatched by various parts of an event-driven process automation humming along smoothly in the background, such as tactical analytical tools that filter discrete sets of data until some threshold is met, which automatically trigger the alert. This is your business on ESA. So, what's changed?

- The conventional org chart has ceased to matter. Once business processes took center stage in discussions of how the company should operate and be organized, traditional corporate departments began to melt away and re-form along functional lines. Politics and inertia impeded this evolution a bit, of course, but ultimately the corporate structure evolved to mirror the underlying IT. Just as ESA freed functionality from application silos, it also freed employees from their personal silos so that they could participate in the sort of concurrent engineering outlined earlier and made possible by ESA.

- The IT department as you knew it has ceased to exist. Responsibility for simple adaptation of applications has passed into the hands of business analysts, who are using modeling tools and a fully developed business semantics language to manipulate composites and their underlying objects as needed in the course of business. IT's role is now split almost evenly between consolidating noncore systems in search of cost reductions and recomposing services for use by business analysts. (We discuss business analysts and the new role for IT in detail shortly.) The organization may have explicitly reorganized into departments of consolidators and composers.

- These developments have helped foster a culture of innovation in which rank-and-file employees feel more empowered than ever before. Freed from repetitive drudgery and awarded a broad view of the business processes in which each one participates, they've been conditioned to believe that their suggestions can make a difference in the development of a new product or in the optimization of a process. And because IT exists to implement their suggestions quickly, they're encouraged by the instant gratification to be always on the lookout for further optimizations. In other words, ESA has decentralized decision making by handing the tools to the line managers, and it has effectively increased the metabolism of the company by rewarding productivity that wasn't possible before.

- These processes have expanded far beyond the nominal boundaries of the enterprise to incorporate suppliers, retailers, partners, and customers. The business semantics ESA provides offered a lingua franca with which to speak to third parties about aligning supply chains and contract manufacturing, point-of-sale data and market research, and sales channels that are being discovered, ramped up, or phased out all the time. Each company creates its own service-based ecosystem and learns to participate in the ecosystems of others.

The transformation is incremental and punctuated, but across all dimensions, it takes the same shape, moving from efficiency to flexibility and resulting in a new potential for innovation in processes and business models.

What stages will we go through on the way there? What skills will we have to develop?

ESA adoption won't happen all at once. It is still in its early stages at most firms. You've just witnessed a glimpse of a maturity near the end, or at least near the end of how far we can see into the future. But hopefully you have some appreciation of just how different the enterprise will look and function in such a fluid, highly iterative environment.

It's still hard to say whether there will be distinct stages of development as ESA matures. This book won't tell you when to remodel your org chart or when your first batch of business analysts will be ready to take over certain tasks from IT. And as you'll read shortly, one of the more intriguing aspects of ESA is that implementation need not proceed at a uniform, glacial place. You can begin deploying ESA principles and technologies at any time, at almost any scale, depending on your needs.

Are you a CEO wondering whether it's time to rally around the SOA and ESA flags? Then declare an enterprise-level commitment and get to work. Are you a project manager eager to solve a problem in your area of expertise and prove that the ROI is real? You can do that too. According to Forrester Research, you already are doing it. While large corporations are leading the way with increased IT spending and enterprise-level commitments, small firms trying to reduce their IT expenditures have turned to project-level ESA as their method of choice.

Nonetheless, you must master several critical skill sets while evolving toward ESA. As its name implies, ESA calls for a rethinking of IT *architecture*—cracking open enterprise applications, carving out functionality, and piping it along to new enterprise services calls for a radically different architecture than IT departments are used to having. For that reason, companies will need to look very carefully at new roles, responsibilities, and organizations for *IT itself.* Once ESA matures, IT development will become almost entirely *model driven and pattern based*, from the development tools to the WYSIWYG modeling software employed by business analysts—the future offspring of a synthesis of business and IT. Their endless combination and recombination, and their potentially endless tweaking of business processes, demand an entirely new model for governance, as does their ability to be deployed unevenly, which leads to the most pressing question of all: *where does one start, anyway?*

What kind of architecture skills does ESA call for?

We won't delve too deeply into this question, as it will receive its own chapter (Chapter 7), but the fundamental challenges are worth noting here. The ESA universe of process-focused enterprise services, data objects, reusable components, and a platform composed of loosely coupled layers couldn't be more different from the current architecture of monolithic enterprise software and point-to-point, application-to-application integration.

Up until now, in its most pathological form, IT has developed a skill set and organizational framework that revolve around the construction of isolated applications to make up for the shortcomings of other older, isolated applications. It's a skill set that demanded a deep contextual understanding of legacy and enterprise applications, and it required small armies of in-house developers, third-party consultants from "best of breed" vendors or COBOL-coding specialists, and a mindset in which it was always, *always* better to build and keep building—even if what you were building was ultimately redundant—than to attempt to unwind the spaghetti of interdependent applications and hardware that had accumulated over time.

Now, contrast that with the skills needed for ESA, which begin with the disaggregation of the monoliths into the nuggets of enterprise services. ESA calls for carving out functionality, freeing it from context, wrapping and orchestrating services into fluid composites, and always, *always* seeking ways to separate the process logic from the integration logic and application logic and to reuse each as necessary. Whereas the previous generation of IT architects dealt only with all that was solid, ESA's architects are determined to make as much functionality as possible melt into air.

Before that can happen, IT must acquaint itself with an entirely new toolkit of application servers, portals, integration suites, Business Process Management tools, integration servers, and middleware before making any serious attempts to implement ESA on an enterprise-wide basis. A new backbone, or what Gartner called the "backplane," is proved acceptable only for small-scale, vanilla SOA implementations. "For performance, scalability or reliability reasons, other protocols than SOAP must be supported as well," Gartner warns. "Proper integration technology must be used to connect into legacy, non–web services-enabled applications. Dynamic discovery of services, routing of service invocations and mediation, or transformation of service interfaces are at times needed to enable flexible deployments in a distributed environment. Load-balancing, failover management, and other features are required to meet 'quality of service' requirements. Security and management must be enforced by means of externalized 'policies,' and a service registry must be implemented to enable services life cycle management. Tools to design and implement service interfaces and associated client 'proxies' must also be provided." Gartner predicts that by 2009, implementation of a sound SOA backplane will remain the single most important technical obstacle in SOA projects.* Clearly, the time to begin retooling IT resources to build this backbone and to begin preparing for enterprise-wide deployment of ESA is now. And SAP is working on all fronts to help.

How does a cultural transformation happen in the real world? What can SupplyOn tell us about how to manage the change inherent in ESA?

SupplyOn, based in Munich, is a flexible Internet platform for the automobile industry that connects OEMs and Tier-1s engaged in direct procurement to parts suppliers. The OEMs who use SupplyOn include BMW, Bosch, Continental, and Siemens VDO Automotive. SupplyOn has more than 9,000 parts suppliers and 25,000 registered users.

The process of direct procurement, as opposed to catalog procurement, is one in which the OEMs solicit bids from suppliers to make specific types of parts. In each deal, the design for the part must be communicated clearly to the supplier, a deal is struck, manufacturing begins, and parts are delivered. The supply chain in the automobile industry uses a variety of different models for relationships between suppliers and OEMs, such as KANBAN, Delivery Control Monitor, and Vendor Managed Inventory (VMI). All of the communication between the OEM and the parts supplier, from the collaboration on the design to the flow of information needed to manage the scheduling and manufacturing of parts, takes place through SupplyOn.

The advantages to both OEMs and parts suppliers are enormous. OEMs are able to pay one integration cost, that of adapting their systems to use SupplyOn, which then creates thousands of relationships which can be used repeatedly. Both OEMs and parts suppliers participate in customer councils that establish strategic requirements and expert groups that define the detailed processes. SupplyOn then implements these designs. Figure 3-7 shows SupplyOn's architecture.

Each SupplyOn solution supports, standardizes, and automates a different aspect of the OEM-supplier relationship. The collaboration rooms and the business directory are used as relationships are being set up. The sourcing manager provides a framework for the request and offer process, the document manager for document exchange. Web EDI and inventory collaboration direct the flow of information during automated supply chain processes

---

* Gartner Presentation, "Applied SOA: Best Practices from the Best Practitioners," by Massimo Pezzini, October 2005.

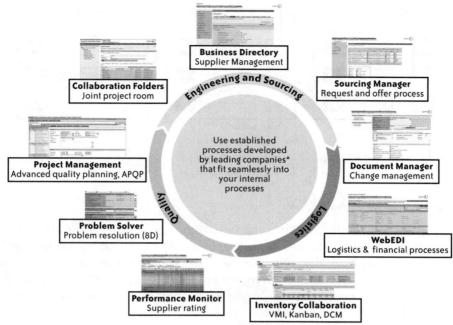

Business Directory
Supplier Management

Collaboration Folders
Joint project room

Engineering and Sourcing

Sourcing Manager
Request and offer process

Project Management
Advanced quality planning, APQP

Use established
processes developed
by leading companies*
that fit seamlessly into
your internal
processes

Document Manager
Change management

Quality

Logistics

Problem Solver
Problem resolution (8D)

WebEDI
Logistics & financial processes

Performance Monitor
Supplier rating

Inventory Collaboration
VMI, Kanban, DCM

* Over 400 man years have flowed into the conceptualization, development and operation of these processes

FIGURE 3-7. SupplyOn's architecture

such as VMI. Problem resolution and performance monitoring of suppliers are also provided.

The way that SupplyOn has replaced thousands of direct, company-to-company connections with a standardized set of relationships automated through a central hub, the way that this implementation process is managed, and the way that services will be introduced to enhance the flexibility of the platform contain several lessons for companies on the path to ESA.

First, the way that SupplyOn changes the relationships, shown in Figure 3-8, is a perfect illustration of the benefits of loose coupling.

Thousands of ad hoc, point-to-point connections are replaced by a much smaller number of standardized relationships that fit into a system of best practices designed by participants. This sort of simplicity through design, heavily informed by users with their process needs in mind, mimics the design process for enterprise services and composite applications. One key element of SupplyOn is a model of all of the business relationships that is stored in a master data repository. This model keeps track of who is delivering which parts, which supply chain processes have to be used, and exactly where they should be delivered, along with several other details.

Second, the process of bringing OEMs and suppliers on board has been standardized. When a new OEM arrives at SupplyOn, the first order of business is to integrate the

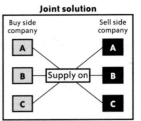

Conventional communication	Company-specific solution	Joint solution

Conventional communication

Buy side company — Sell side company

A — email — A
B — Fax — B
C — Mail — C

The use of different communication media leads to high administrative costs on both sides.

Breaks in media often causes mistakes.

Company-specific solution

Buy side company — Sell side company

A — A
B — B
C — C

Complex IT projects.

High demand of resources and high costs.

Extensive supplier connection.

High operating expense for suppliers.

Joint solution

Buy side company — Sell side company

A — A
B — Supply on — B
C — C

Highly efficient, standardized business processes thanks to a joint solution.

Fast implementation.

Seamless integrated communication with numerous business partners over a single platform.

FIGURE 3-8. SupplyOn reducing complexity

OEM's system with SupplyOn's. Then SupplyOn takes responsibility for reaching out to that OEM's supplier network, convincing them to join SupplyOn, signing contracts, and then performing any integration or training needed to allow the suppliers to use the solutions. To ease the change management required on all sides, SupplyOn offers services for rollout management, process implementation and training, customer support (24/7 in five languages), in addition to technical services for hosting, portal integration, connectivity, and security assurance. *SupplyOn has, in essence, productized the change management process.* While implementers in most companies may not have as clear a target as SupplyOn has, it is clear that similar problems will appear as ESA is applied to different applications and areas of a company, and that developing a standard approach and attempting to build skills and learn from experience is clearly the right approach. SupplyOn implements this approach through close collaboration with the purchasing officers at the OEMs, who work with SupplyOn to craft an adoption plan that takes into account the number of global locations, their readiness to migrate to a new process, the priority of each location, expected barriers to adoption, and so forth. As an organization, SupplyOn has a huge stake in getting change management right because it benefits from increased use of its solutions. This sort of incentive can be a powerful agent of change.

Third, SupplyOn plans to expand its offerings through services at all levels. It also will offer each of its solutions as a suite of services so that an OEM or a supplier has the option of using the services to incorporate SupplyOn solutions into existing portals instead of using the SupplyOn UIs. SupplyOn will be able to use these services to create special-purpose products to meet the needs of various customer groups. On the back end, XML and EDI messages that are used to automate supply chain processes will be supplemented and, in some cases, replaced by enterprise services.

SupplyOn has a focused mission to standardize and automate certain relationships that its users fund. IT departments are essentially in the same position with respect to their companies and could benefit from imitating at a company level some of the architectural and change management ideas that SupplyOn has so successfully implemented.

How will IT change in an ESA world?

As noted earlier, and as illustrated by the SupplyOn example, IT will have its hands full in the early stages, building a fully functional backplane, populating the Enterprise Services Repository, and composing the first few generations of services before modeling tools become sophisticated and pervasive enough to disperse development beyond IT and across the enterprise. (We'll discuss that last point shortly.) But once ESA matures, what will IT's role be?

Recalling the core/context model from Chapter 2, IT's twin responsibilities in an ESA world are to consolidate nondifferentiating "context" systems and to use the savings to reinvest in new, differentiating, and potentially disruptive "core" capabilities that drive process innovation. In an ESA world, debates such as the eternal build versus buy cease to matter. IT is always building core and buying context, and it is implementing both within an architecture that essentially doesn't distinguish between the two.

In this environment, specialization and organization around applications or development languages are obsolete. A new IT department may look more like the vision shown in Figure 3-9 and outlined in the following list:

- The *repository keepers* oversee the care and feeding of the architecture and the Enterprise Services Repository. They define standards and guidelines, manage the service definition process, implement the backplane, keep the service repository clean and coherent, and above all, support the development of new services by the composition and innovation groups (discussed shortly).

- The *consolidators* think about context all day, every day. Once core systems have crossed the threshold from differentiating and mission-critical into nondifferentiating and best practice territory (on the way to becoming commodities), it's the consolidation group's responsibility to abstract data and services from prior investments for ultimate reuse. It's also their duty to replace systems that have outlived their ROI with commodity products or services in an eternal quest for reduced TCO. The consolidators are the ones slashing the costs that make it possible for the next two groups to receive the resources they deserve.

- The *composers* are in charge of mapping real-world business processes awaiting implementation to the underlying services produced by the environment and consolidation groups. They're the ones supporting modeling tool–equipped business analysts with their own sets of model-driven development tools. Within the context of IT, they represent a bridge between the technical skill sets of the other groups and the pure business logic of the analysts. Since the composition team's job is ultimately one of translation, its own skills revolve around its fluency in both languages.

- The heavy lifting is left to the *disruptive innovators*, IT's skunk works operating on the edge of what is currently possible, building new services and applications which cannot be modeled, but which are inherently differentiating and thus are the very essence of "core."

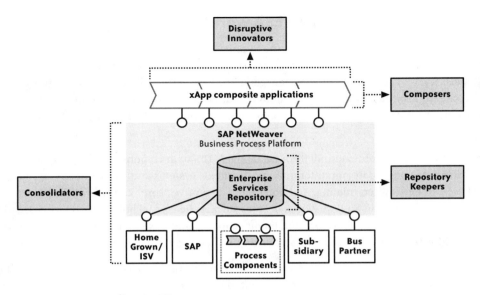

FIGURE 3-9. Transitioning the role of IT

This reshuffling reflects what an ESA-ready IT staff might look like. Getting there will require retooling of skills and a shift in mindset away from static systems and toward the continual massaging of a landscape in flux. New development, testing, Q&A, and internal change management processes will need to be developed and refined to deploy, monitor, and administer the new service-oriented environment. The process will require a comprehensive reeducation program spanning architectures to the most granular operations. And fundamental architecture skills will be demanded of every team member as they labor to bring the ESA transformation to pass.

This transformation could fail at any point if sufficient care and resources aren't set aside within IT to ensure its success. Among the areas requiring most attention are the following:

Communication

Every executive and staff member from the CIO on down who is tasked with leading the charge toward ESA must communicate the urgency of the mission by whatever means necessary using whatever media is at hand. They must impress upon IT that the current architecture and ways of working will be increasingly less viable over time, and that radical change is necessary. This calls for a clear, consistent, and persistent message to the staff. They must understand that this is not "business as usual," or merely some org chart reshuffling. IT must win over those individuals who resist; they must form a general and popular consensus. And the key to all of this is steady doses of information about the why, how, when, and who of the evolution toward ESA.

Training

The world of ESA will demand that IT acquire a new set of skills that have little to do with programming language proficiency. The shift toward a more model-driven architecture, for example, will demand a more conceptual approach to development that's a departure from today's hand-coded methods. Acquiring that expertise isn't as simple as hiring a dozen information architects off the street. In some cases, such as this one, the skills are in such short supply that retraining is inevitable. Before your IT department is able to execute on the ESA vision, it will be necessary to school them in it first.

Performance management

The prospect of a department-wide overhaul will no doubt frighten some staffers and encourage others to resist the change passively. Impressing upon these people the importance of change and retraining staff will still fail if you don't give them proper incentives to support and embrace your efforts. This may mean rethinking your rewards systems—perhaps you should salute programmers for effectively working together with business staff to automate processes, instead of churning out clever code. Creating short-term wins that encourage your staff and prove the ROI to executives on the business side is also essential in keeping up morale and continuing institutional support.

Role modeling

The last and perhaps least understood aspect of this process is role modeling. Not to be confused with other types of modeling discussed in this book, role modeling refers to quickly winning over respected individuals already within your organization and using them to champion change. Previous efforts at engineering organizationwide change, such as General Electric's vaunted "Six Sigma" methodology, included honorifics for leading practitioners—e.g., Six Sigma's "Black Belts," which helped inspire other employees to follow suit. In the context of ESA, your role models may very well turn out to be your first generation of "business analysts," those individuals respected by both the business and the IT sides of the organization, and thus able to command their promise to effect change.

What will the shift to a model-driven world mean for IT, and where will these business analysts come from?

What sets ESA apart from vanilla SOAs is its inclusion of a semantic business language expressed through enterprise services—and, more important, how these are mapped to real business processes—in the form of models. Modeling is the organizing principle of ESA; model-driven development tools will create composite applications that business analysts can build and rebuild, and these business analysts will lead the cultural shift away from siloed corporate hierarchies and toward a corporate organization aligned along business processes. When we say ESA will transform your culture, we're really talking about the change in perception stemming from the dominance of the modeling metaphor focused on processes.

Modeling tools such as SAP Visual Composer are already used to hide complexity and simplify developers' choices when composing new UIs. Other tools also are available for high-level business processes (ARIS models from IDS Scheer), for frontend, conversational, user-centric business processes (guided procedures), for backend business processes (SAP NetWeaver Exchange Infrastructure's Cross Component Business Process Management), and for configuring business processes (SAP Solution Manager). Various abstraction layers such as Web Dynpro provide more detailed representations of an abstract UI that can be used by modeling tools. As we explain in more detail in Chapter 4, modeling makes development simpler, makes it easier to change applications, and helps support many platforms with less work.

A new breed of business analysts, discussed in the previous chapter and elsewhere throughout the book, will handle modeling at the business process level. These business analysts represent the final, complementary fusion of the business and IT sides of a given corporation. Recruited from the business side of the operation, these analysts will be the detail-oriented staff already focused on real-world business processes and the workflow patterns they shape. They will have been sufficiently steeped in the language and in the essence of IT that real conversations are possible about the limits, possibilities, and opportunities presented by the underlying enterprise services. However, they will be shielded from the level of granularity familiar to IT's composition group, which will work with the analysts to assemble services into composite applications of appropriate flexibility and complexity.

This vision presents only one problem at the moment: business analysts are in short supply. And when people with the needed skills are in an organization, they are sometimes reluctant to take the lead. Figure 3-10 shows one possible progression of empowerment, but there will be many. A new class of business executive will need to be trained in IT, integrated into the organization, and granted broad powers over the day-to-day operations of critical business units. While they may be critical to the ESA vision, analysts' institutional and cultural impacts on their respective companies are still a wide-open question. Will they be culled from the ranks of existing managers and be retrained? Or will they be recruited from future generations of MBA graduates? Will they work alongside traditional general managers, or is "business analyst" a retrained general manger by another name? You won't find the answers here because there aren't any. Each company that adopts ESA will have to answer these questions on its own, choosing a model, so to speak, that's most appropriate for it.

These questions will cascade down the architecture as functionality and decision-making powers previously centralized in IT are reduced to services available anywhere within the enterprise. To give just one brief example, consider a model borrowed from Chapter 11. Analytical tools are key to ESA, which, if nothing else, will generate new torrents of data and automated messaging requiring filters and routing mechanisms, a task which today's massive, centralized data warehouses were never designed to perform.

Do you see the organizational and technical challenges mounting? In order to capitalize on the flexibility and model-driven nature of ESA, a new class of users will need to be trained to harness it. In order for those users to make sense of the models they receive, they'll need more tools which have yet to be built, which means IT will need to learn how

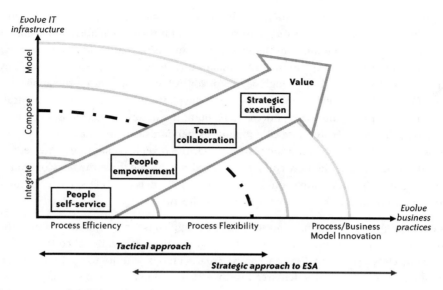

FIGURE 3-10. ESA's path to people productivity

to build them, and after that, the analysts will need to be trained to use them…. The educational and organizational challenges should not be underestimated.

One way of confronting the complexity involved without feeling overwhelmed by it is to consider ESA as a set of both tactical and strategic initiatives. Early in the adoption process, a focus on integration and process efficiency leads to the empowerment of individuals. But as IT begins to flex its new composition-based muscles and business processes begin to migrate across and outside the enterprise, the skills acquired from doing both begin to yield results at the team level, leading to strategic change as new groups, processes, and so on, are incorporated into previously static, stable processes. In other words, users will acquire skills and sophistication as they go along, which will propel the next cycle of innovation.

How will governance function within ESA?

Historically, governance issues have boiled down to a battle between control and reduced costs via synergy on the one side and flexibility and needs for specialized support on the other. Highly centralized governance policies have been successful in enforcing standards, preventing redundancies, and thus driving down costs, but have also paid a price in responsiveness. The more concentrated governance becomes, the more project managers and line executives (or any other precursor to business analysts) are straitjacketed by inflexible policies. Every IT organization faces this tradeoff: suffer in response times now, or face the consequences of a sprawling, out-of-control environment later. Which one will it be?

ESA promises to ease the pain either way, because of its standards and services-based approach, where the repository and platform stand in for the central authority while modeling and recomposition grant considerable latitude to business analysts and other tactical users. In Chapter 17, we explain how ESA makes this "federated" approach possible by abstraction—power users have a high degree of control over their composite applications, while the central authority retains ownership of the platform. Even in custom application development requiring new components to be built, the nature of the repository calls for an orderly process to certify those components as standards compliant and govern their eventual reuse elsewhere within the platform. (Or the reverse could occur. The central committee could decide the new component is redundant and force the development team to reuse a similar, existing component instead.) There is much less danger of the spaghetti code conundrum that bedevils current architectures.

This decoupling—of tactical use and strategic oversight—also frees operational units from a single approach to deploying IT. Just as ESA loosens the organizational constraints imposed by classic siloed applications, it also creates an opportunity to apply governance on an ad hoc basis. By clearly demarcating governance "domains" that stipulate which operational units are subject to which guidelines, the historical friction between business reality and a generic governance scheme is mitigated. In other words, your sales and marketing department is free to deploy new composite applications at a pace and under the guidelines that it sees fit for its own operations without worrying about or even pausing to consider how this might affect the rest of the business. Just as application logic is decoupled from business logic with ESA, so is governance decoupled from the institutional structure.

Of course, this creates its own organizational challenges. In addition to the traditional governance committee overseeing service and platform integrity, the company and the CIO must now address the issues of how much authority to cede to business analysts and their superiors, the size and boundaries of governance domains, and who is entitled within each domain to influence, consult upon, and ultimately make the final decision on governance. A tradeoff still must be made, this time between flexibility and organizational complexity.

How and where should I begin evolving toward ESA?

The short answer is wherever there's a need and however that need can be served best. Because enterprise services are abstracted from the underlying systems of record, and because governance need not progress in a uniform manner, it's possible to begin deploying ESA anywhere within the enterprise at nearly any degree of complexity. Small implementations at the project level aimed at internal integration or creating a new interface for functionality abstracted from a wrapped enterprise application can coexist with enterprise-level efforts toward building the broader ESA platform. In fact, they already do.

Forrester Research surveyed more than 100 IT decision makers in late 2004 and discovered that many were already pursuing SOA adoption on multiple levels; internal integration was the most common use, but usually it was as part of a mixture that included external integration, multichannel applications, and strategic business transformation.*

Early efforts to improve process efficiency incorporate internal integration and first attempts at wrapping application and orchestrating interfaces. As the architecture evolves, external integration in the name of process flexibility extends the scope of services beyond the enterprise to partners and customers, before achieving the more mature states of process innovation and business innovation, in which modeling is used to effect strategic change.

It's not necessarily a linear progression, however. Forrester also found that several participants in its survey were pursuing external integrations before internal ones. But there is a real risk that racing ahead at the project level to pluck the low-hanging fruit of integration will create compatibility conflicts later, once the platform has caught up. It may very well be that the proper path forward is the combination of a long-term, strategic plan for adoption centered on the Enterprise Services Repository, along with numerous short-term, ROI-focused projects designed to reap the benefits of ESA at each step of its evolution.

How will modeling translate between enterprises with different architectures? Will a standards body evolve to resolve potential conflicts?

It's no secret that ESA is SAP's strategy foundation for the future of enterprise software—a market in which SAP's customers expect the company to provide the lingua franca. But it's also true that no one else has come forward with a language or a set of de facto standards for translating a vanilla SOA—a creation of IT, and only IT—into a tool that business users understand.

Erecting an SOA that's technically capable of integrating every one of your systems without involving your managers or your partners is like calling one of your suppliers in China from your cell phone without knowing how to speak Chinese. Cellular networks, undersea cables, and the protocols for transmitting your voice halfway around the world are minor miracles, but what good do they do you if you can't understand the voice on the other end?

SAP developed enterprise services to be the lingua franca spoken by any enterprise that has adopted an SOA. While SAP is leading the charge by virtue of its expertise in this arena, its goal isn't to jealously protect ESA as a proprietary set of standards, but rather to open the definition of services and the platform—the evolution of this language—to the broader community of developers and Independent Software Vendors (ISVs). We explore these issues in detail in Chapter 20.

---

* "Large Enterprises Pursue Strategic SOA," Forrester Research, Inc., April 5, 2005.

This is a new position for SAP. Historically, the company has used its industrial-strength applications and market leadership to define from the top down the roles and opportunities available for its partners. However, that was before flexibility, integration, and reuse took center stage. To date, SAP has spoken to more than 1,000 ISVs about inclusion in the ongoing conversation about ESA, and it has struck partnerships with industry leaders such as Intel, Cisco, EMC, and Adobe for hardware and software support of the architecture. SAP has formalized these relationships in what it dubbed the "Enterprise Services Community" (ES-Community), essentially a steering committee for the future development of ESA. SAP, its partners, and their mutual customers (that would be you) will form the three legs of the stool supporting the ESA ecosystem.

Similar in form to the Eclipse Foundation that formed around IBM's Eclipse platform, the ES-Community is envisioned as a standards organization designed to guarantee interoperability, protect participants' intellectual property, and address issues, such as security, which are relevant to every ESA adopter. Over time, SAP hopes the ES-Community's common inventory and repository of services will become the reference guide and marketplace for every available enterprise service. For a more detailed discussion of this issue, turn to Chapter 6.

With that said, SAP isn't the only one pushing for enterprise services adoption, and in the end, its flagship services may not be the ones most relevant to your industry, or even to your own ecosystem of partnerships. Dominant process innovators such as Dell and (especially) Wal-Mart—which unilaterally dictates the terms of electronic data interchange (EDI) with its suppliers and which brooks no dissent—are setting both the pace and the adoption path for their partners. We cannot emphasize this enough: ESA is about business logic as much as it is about the underlying process logic. It is quite possible—we would hazard to say quite likely—that standards, such as they are, will be driven by the users themselves.

If you aren't already dictating those standards to your partners, chances are they will soon be dictating them to you.

What do the analysts think, and what trouble do they foresee?

If we had to boil it down to one sentence, it would be this quote, drawn from a report by Gartner: "There is no alternative to [SOA] and web services as a basis for future software. The issues revolve around the rate of adoption and the purposes for which it is applied."* In other words, it's not a question of whether an SOA will supplant today's architecture, but rather, how long it will take to complete this evolution.

Technology analysts at Gartner Group—one of the most respected research firms in the field—are generally optimistic about SOA's potential, and have at times made a case for

---

* Simon Hayward, "Positions 2005: Service-Oriented Architecture Adds Flexibility to Business Processes," Gartner Inc., February 2005.

the transformative power of enterprise services that is very similar to what we present in this book. However, the same analysts have also pointed to any number of pitfalls lying in wait for companies just beginning the transformation. Here are a few of their more pressing concerns:

Many of these technologies and their development tools are adolescent, yet overhyped. Companies that decide to begin tackling SOA while in the thrall of industry hype will indubitably become dissatisfied and disillusioned by the real pace of adoption and the many challenges ahead. According to Gartner, "Many projects are running with the intent to deliver SOA. The reality of the effort makes users face the lack of tools, standards and consistency in SOA initiatives. It is harder than expected for most. Many changes in user and vendor organizations and technologies are required before SOA reaches its plateau.... Enterprises are still wrestling with what [web] services do, and their transformational impact will have to wait for more-mature standards and [clearer] examples.... Enterprise expectations for orchestrated, multicompany interactions have reached the peak of their unreasonable hype."*

Service-oriented development is an alien process for today's developers. Don't underestimate how radical the shift is from building traditional application development to SOA. According to Gartner, "The technology issues associated [with] SOA are much more challenging than vendors would like users to think.... Service implementations must be developed and executed on platforms providing the necessary quality of services. Other service implementations must be carved out of pre-SOA applications by using integration tools like adapters and programmatic integration servers. Service consumer applications must be deployed atop platforms capable of supporting multiple devices and presentation styles. Web services protocols must be complemented by more reliable, higher-performance or more secure protocols to support the most demanding requirements. Setting up the infrastructure for SOA entails making [myriad] technical choices in terms of software infrastructure: application servers, portals, integration suites, [Business Process Management] tools, TP monitors, integration servers, various kinds of communication middleware and XML appliances can all play a role in large-scale SOA initiatives. To make proper choices, users must understand the complex world of middleware. Despite the growing popularity of this technology, the risk of making wrong decisions still looms large [for] SOA newcomers."†

Composite applications, which by their nature draw from multiple applications, are proving difficult to build with the nascent services that exist today. According to Gartner, "In many cases, SOA initiatives begin with small projects usually within the scope of a single application such as call center integration or customer self-service portal. These 'test the water' projects usually implement a couple of dozen services to support a few consumer applications.... Projects of this kind usually proceed informally without the support of a

---

* Andrews, Kenney, et al., "Hype Cycle for Web Services, 2005," Gartner Inc., July 20, 2005.

† Gartner Presentation, "Applied SOA: Best Practices from the Best Practitioners," by Massimo Pezzini, October 2005.

hard-core methodology. Mature SOA initiatives expand into a wider scope (multi-application domains or business unitwide)…designing from the outset a scalable SOA-enabling infrastructure is paramount."*

SOA adoption does not provide a quick ROI, but requires strategic investments, including investment in governance and a cultural change to align IT and business. According to Gartner, "In trying to work out an ROI for SOA, users need to take into account three different classes of required investments: 1) Organizational. SOA implies putting in place new, specific processes (for example, to define and validate services, to enforce reuse, to allocate costs) in which many different IT and business players have a role. 2) Architectural. SOA requires development discipline and methodologies that must be defined and enforced; the technical infrastructure of the SOA backplane must be designed; specific technologies must be selected. 3) Infrastructural. Specific software infrastructure products need to be acquired, installed, managed, and so on. Despite the lowering cost of SOA-enabling technology, more widespread know-how and availability of SOA services from systems integrators (SIs), the incremental cost of SOA [versus] a traditional architecture is still significant and—in most cases—cannot be justified for fast-ROI, opportunistic projects."†

What kind of company will we be after ESA?

You will be the kind of company where the traditional barriers between business and IT have fallen. IT, as we know it now, will be practiced on a daily basis by "business analysts" who understand both sides of the equation and who use model-driven tools to refine your business processes continually.

You will be the kind of company where the day-to-day business process that comprises the very essence of your company will be encoded into your IT. Annotated executable models will become the requirements documents.

You will be the kind of company where IT has stopped saying no to most projects because of the complexity and cost. Instead of building applications and then walking away to start new ones, IT will tend to an infrastructure that supports business analysts and other users throughout the enterprise. IT will be dispersed, and it will be summoned within the enterprise as needed.

The boundaries of the enterprise will expand as business processes are automated and extended beyond your own IT systems and into those of your partners around the globe. Your company will continually sense and respond to data received from anywhere within the network, which means business processes will continually be tested and refined.

You will be the kind of company that evolves a little bit every day.

---

* Gartner Presentation, "Applied SOA: Best Practices from the Best Practitioners," by Massimo Pezzini, October 2005.

† Ibid.

PART TWO

Conceiving a Vision for ESA

CHAPTER FOUR

ESA Fundamentals: Learning to Think ESA

THE PRECEDING CHAPTERS PROVIDED AN OVERVIEW OF ESA, ALONG WITH A SURVEY OF ESA'S BUSINESS value and information on how a company can evolve toward ESA. While these chapters effectively set the context for a deeper discussion of ESA, more work remains. ESA is essentially a new way of thinking about how enterprise applications are constructed and how they are used to support a business. At almost every level, ESA reshapes traditional thinking, introduces new concepts, and sets forth a new paradigm for building IT to support the needs of modern businesses. This chapter will introduce and explain the ideas that are fundamental to the transformation of IT that ESA will achieve.

What is architecture and why is it important?

In essence, architecture is a contract that organizes the work of hundreds of thousands—or even millions—of people. It describes the structures used in the course of that work, which in the case of software refers to data and other abstract mechanisms that will have a certain responsibility and that will be connected in a standardized way.

Architecture makes these standard abstract mechanisms or components useful by clearly defining the relationships between them. Complex, unwieldy systems can be reduced to their essence—i.e., to these relationships—and it becomes possible to see which pieces of the system are the most important. It works both ways: if you are attempting to create a piece of software that fits into an existing architecture, you'll need to understand what that piece needs to do, how it will connect to other pieces, and what its relationship to the rest of the architecture will be.

Architecture also defines the life cycle of the components. Who builds them? How are they built? How are they used? How can they be improved, and, eventually, how will they be retired? In other words, how will an architecture come to life, and how long will it live? The answers lie in the details of an architecture's design at specification time, design time, and implementation time, all of which we will explain later in the book.

For now, the key thing to remember is that the architecture circumscribes the capabilities—and the limitations—of any component within it, which is why great care must be spent in crafting the architecture before creating any components. If done properly, everyone who participates in building a system atop the architecture will know—because of the relationships clearly defined by the contract—what they should be doing and how they should be doing it as they create each component.

The goal of any software architecture is to enable the construction of systems to execute some type of task in efficient and flexible ways. For the purposes of this book, the architecture we're focused on is the Enterprise Services Architecture, and the goal of ESA in particular is to enable businesses to use software in a manner that is both more flexible and less costly than any previous generation of software architecture.

What is enterprise architecture and how will ESA change it?

An enterprise architecture is two things, only one of which has to do with IT. The first step to creating an enterprise architecture is to understand how the business should best be organized. An enterprise architecture begins with business goals, which are met through the design of a complex of interrelated business processes. The second step specifies how IT will support that organization and the underlying processes.

Historically, enterprise architects have been limited in their ability to design with processes and IT solutions to support them by the flexibility of enterprise applications such as Enterprise Resources Planning (ERP), Customer Relationship Management (CRM), Supply Chain Management (SCM), and the like. Enterprise applications started as large, complex collections of processes that were configurable up to a point. So an ERP application contained a basic process for running purchase orders or invoices, a CRM application had a basic process for handling a customer inquiry, and an SCM application had various processes embedded within it for interacting with suppliers, monitoring the factory floor, or managing inventory, to name a few.

It is easy to forget that before the advent of ERP and the rest of the enterprise applications that emerged, most business processes lacked standardization. The first generation of enterprise applications created a standard form for the automation of the common processes that appeared in most businesses. The architecture of enterprise applications allowed for configurability, but that was not the main point. When the requirements that these enterprise applications met remained stable, the applications did their job brilliantly.

The challenge for enterprise architects—the managers tasked with defining and refining an enterprise architecture—came when new business requirements and new business processes were needed. They were forced to tailor their organization's appetite for new processes as closely as possible to the business logic embedded in existing applications. It quickly became clear, however, that many processes might start in CRM, move to ERP, and then finish in SCM, and the challenge for these architects and for IT departments became understanding, defining, and adapting these processes to work within these constraints. In many other cases, businesses became frustrated at their inability to adapt the processes embedded in standardized applications to meet their emerging needs.

Enterprise architecture soon became the dark art of splitting the differences between the functionality provided in enterprise applications and the actual needs of your business and then solving urgent problems via expensive and time-consuming custom applications and integration efforts.

ESA was created to satisfy the needs of modern businesses that are interested in process innovation, which means being able to automate new processes as well as improve and optimize stable processes to take advantage of new challenges. Dell, for example, is famously successful, not because of any innovative products (it builds all of its products using off-the-shelf parts), but because of the execution and continual refinement of its supply chain and manufacturing processes.

The demand for flexibility to automate new processes and to improve existing ones changes the landscape dramatically. The standard processes of enterprise applications explode into smaller bundles of enterprise services built to execute proportionally smaller tasks. So now, for example, one service might accept a purchase order and another one might validate that order according to a defined set of rules. A metaservice might control the handoff of data from one service to another as it's passed along a string of orchestrated processes designed to reflect how the real-world business process actually works.

ESA preserves the gains of the previous generation of enterprise applications while introducing flexibility. All of the standard processes that made ERP, CRM, and other enterprise applications so vital to efficient operations will stay in place. Instead of being powered by monolithic architectures, however, they will be powered by services. The existence of services is the engine of flexibility. It's not important where these services originate—whether in ERP, CRM, or SCM—because it's now possible to orchestrate them independently. The Enterprise Services Repository incorporates, a central tank of services that SAP has created for customers, and it will include services that companies create on their own. All of these services will be stored for use and reuse, subject to the rules and standards implicit in ESA.

What does this mean? It means that instead of having to think of business processes within the constraints imposed by the limits of today's enterprise applications, you and your enterprise architects can begin mapping the functionality of a service or collection of services to the actual needs of your business. The barriers to adapting services to your needs are much lower, thanks to their finer granularity. Instead of splitting the difference between the functionality available and your actual need, you can focus on adapting these highly granular services to match your processes perfectly. And because the processes aren't welded together with hard code, but rather are knitted together with modeling tools and process orchestration mechanisms, you should have a much easier time adjusting and readjusting the alignment of these services over time to meet your needs.

In this new world, the CIO is transformed into a chief process innovation officer, someone who focuses less on tools and ensuring that the IT environment does not break and more on perfecting processes and realigning IT resources to support them. The chief IT officer will focus on creating the systems to support these processes and squeezing out costs and inefficiency.

One simple way to think of ESA is as a technical enabler required for process innovation. In the previous generation of enterprise architecture, processes were automated but not flexible. Enterprise services promise to make them automated and flexible at an affordable cost.

What motivated the creation of ESA?

SAP cofounder Hasso Plattner conceived ESA as a solution to the increasingly unwieldy number of enterprise applications appearing in corporate IT environments. As we discussed earlier in this chapter, all the functionality necessary for a given process could no longer be contained within a single application.

Plattner originally conceived of ESA to support *cross-applications* that could cross the boundaries of the enterprise applications beneath them and combine pieces of functionality into a new application running above them. These became SAP's family of packaged composite applications which were branded as "xApps". The creation of xApps overcame several of the implicit assumptions underlying enterprise applications and the previous architecture that no longer applied in the modern business world.

First and most important was the idea of the database as the single point of integration. This was the dominant model during the era of client-server approaches in the late '80s and early '90s. When entering a purchase order into ERP, for example, that order is added to a database that everyone in the system can access. Anyone wishing to revisit that order later can easily retrieve it from the database. But when an xApp begins crossing the boundaries between applications, borrowing data and functionality from each, the customer data may exist in different places—in CRM, SCM, and ERP—and it may not be synchronized across the three, leading to the potential for inconsistency, something that the single-database world was designed to prevent. ESA has many different mechanisms for handling this problem, as we will discuss later in this chapter and later in this book.

Another transformed assumption that ESA had to address was the idea that processes were automated within the boundary of an enterprise application. xApps by definition need to define processes without regard to the existing boundaries between enterprise applications.

The final assumption was the role that standard software would play to meet new business requirements. If emerging requirements were to be met, enterprise software would no longer comprise standard processes encased in enterprise applications. The moving parts would have to be exposed. That need led to the creation of enterprise services. Instead of delivering functionality in the unit of an individual application performing a single task that can't be reused, businesses could free pieces of functionality from their enterprise applications, repackage them as services, and design these services (the job of the architecture) to be flexible and reusable. So, instead of creating a new application every time the business situation changed, you could simply tweak the combination of services within a given application. Now build versus buy has become buy, build, and compose. That's the vision behind ESA; Figure 4-1 provides a visual definition.

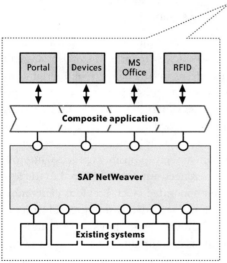

Enterprise Services Architecture is the blueprint of a service-oriented architecture that combines the reliability and functionality provided by SAP's extensive enterprise applications with the flexibility of services based on open standards.

Therefore:
- ESA is a blueprint, not a product
- SAP helps their customers to find their road toward ESA
- IT landscapes/IT products following ESA principles are more flexible and faster to change
- ESA enables co-innovation with partners and customers

FIGURE 4-1. Defining ESA

What are the architectural challenges of ESA?

The architectural challenges of ESA stem from the violation of the implicit assumptions referenced earlier; the ideas of the database as a point of integration and the application as a process boundary no longer apply.

The first challenge is *flexibility*. Once services are created and processes are automated, optimization and innovation depend on a company's ability to not only implement processes, but also be able to change and improve them based on experience. This is a huge challenge, considering the average optimization cycle of today's custom application projects, which may range anywhere from 9 to 18 months—a timeframe that is no longer acceptable. Companies need to implement a new IT system within weeks and months in order for it to have an impact. The tradeoff for flexibility has traditionally been *cost*—it's easier to make changes to a system when development costs are no object. But that implies the system was never very flexible in the first place. Inherent flexibility implies a corresponding reduction in cost to make changes because flexibility has to be affordable in order to be meaningful.

The second challenge facing ESA is *data consistency*—how to unify and synchronize all of the information and process flow in an automated process where data is stored in lots of different databases and lots of applications are supplying services.

The third challenge is *heterogeneity*. The modern enterprise can't assume that all of its software and systems will always come from a single vendor. A heterogeneous computing environment is a given in today's world. In fact, it is inevitable. Even if management consciously set out to choose a single vendor, mergers and acquisitions make it inevitable that systems from a different vendor will arrive with some acquisition down the road. And even if the company is an island, homegrown applications or specialized tools from a niche vendor will ultimately introduce complexity at some point.

The fourth challenge is the *user interface (UI)*. Now that companies have the ability with ESA to combine and recombine enterprise services in any manner they wish, designing the most efficient and the most appropriate interfaces for the delivery of the right functionality to the right person becomes extremely important. As processes are developed, roles must be developed in tandem for the employees charged with collecting information, evaluating that information, and making a decision based on that analysis. But what data, presented in what form and at what level of aggregation, is appropriate for each person in that chain? Torrents of data may be flowing from any given business process, but to be efficient, each role that plays a part in that process needs that data reduced to the level at which people in that role can best perform their appointed tasks. Previous generations of enterprise applications had been built as reflections of the database's internal structure rather than as reflections of the roles people play in the application's process. In practice, this meant that performing a simple, real-world task required using 4, 5, 10, or even 15 UIs reflecting different aspects of the database structure instead of accessing a single screen specifically created so that that person could perform his task. The UI challenge is one of bringing together and making affordable the creation of many role-based interfaces for the convenience of human users.

All of these challenges point to a tremendous impact and change in IT development. The need for inexpensive flexibility, along with the demand for customized interfaces throughout the organization, implies that development must become cheaper and faster in a hurry. That will require the demystification of IT. Development must become simple enough so that not only will highly trained programmers and information architects build and deploy services, but managers outside of IT will as well. SAP has envisioned the role of the *business analyst*, a manager versed in IT but lacking traditional development skills, though she has a much deeper understanding of the actual business processes being automated than the developers in IT do. While IT focuses on exposing services and maintaining the architecture, business analysts will receive the tools to create the necessary applications and interfaces to extend process automation even further.

At this point, the gap between IT and the business will be bridged. IT will supply the business side with those tools, and the resulting conversation—about how to create those interfaces and automate those processes—will replace the lengthy, inefficient negotiations in which the business side explains what it needs to IT, which tries to figure it out and then returns with a requirement spec. And so the traditional dance would have gone on, except that within ESA, the use of services and modeling tools creates a very unconventional development environment.

How does ESA meet those challenges?

The key is the enterprise services themselves. They are the modular, reusable, flexible building blocks of ESA, which are already capable of meeting all of the challenges outlined earlier, provided they're assembled within an environment that is stocked with the appropriate development tools and honors the contract of the architecture.

Enterprise services are essentially pieces of processes. The pieces can be of any size and degree of functionality. One might be a utility function so small as to calculate only the time of day, and another might be large and complex enough to start the execution of a highly automated manufacturing process. But regardless of how large or how small they are, every enterprise service is designed to be a building block of a larger process, meaning they embody a host of attributes that enable them to meet the architectural challenges outlined earlier—the foremost of which is *reusability*. Precisely because they are building blocks, they were always designed to be recombined repeatedly, unlike previous generations of applications.

Because they were designed to participate in process orchestration, they were designed to be *model driven*. Instead of hardcoding services into applications, a new generation of modeling tools will assemble them. In order for a service to participate, it must be able to describe itself to the modeling environment so that its functionality can be adapted and added to the process and connected to other services. This is accomplished using a layer of metadata embedded in the service, metadata that includes descriptions of how to use it, which business processes should be connected to that service, which underlying objects may be implemented using the service, and so on. Metadata can be used to configure the behavior of the service itself and to orchestrate its position within a process chain of services. This solves one of the thornier issues in integrating older applications—the absence of information about their internal workings, which usually leads to unintended side effects during integration efforts. But within ESA, the service metadata is sorted in the Enterprise Services Repository and is summoned by modeling tools at design time to describe the services being used.

ESA also provides a complete *life cycle* approach for designing services, designing the resulting applications, modeling processes, executing the models, and then actually executing the finished code. The architecture specifies and supports all of these things from the moment they are conceived until they are retired. Services built under ESA auspices are guaranteed to work within ESA systems; the ad hoc nature of previous generations' integration efforts isn't an issue here. There are even utility services designed to help knit larger functional services into business processes. (We describe the various types of enterprise services later in this chapter.)

Enterprise services solve the challenges of routing the appropriate data and information to the appropriate interfaces via the use of *analytics* and *roles*. Instead of asking users to hunt through the system for the information they need to make decisions, SAP's analytical tools collect data from every relevant source in the system and synthesize it down to a level appropriate for any given user's needs. Analytic tools solve one of the most serious side effects of increasingly automated processes. Instead of spinning out yet another UI for every process, analytics provide the ability to route the output of each process automatically to a role-specific UI created for each class of user—for example, CEOs, financial analysts, customer service representatives, factory floor managers, and so on. The analytical tools compile and recompile the processes' raw data output repeatedly, assembling it in a form that can then be used as a basis for taking action depending on the user's role within the organization.

The UIs themselves are composed of services, and they can be modeled and attached to automated processes on a flexible, as-needed basis. The result is a *composite application*, which possesses a degree of flexibility unknown in previous generations of applications because it is essentially a mesh of relatively granular, loosely coupled enterprise services rather than monolithic containers of complex functionality. Those applications—ERP, CRM, and the like—will also have services built from them and on top of them so that they can participate within an ESA framework.

The same attributes will solve the problem of heterogeneity by breaking down the integration challenges from absorbing standalone enterprise applications to incorporating much smaller, self-described services designed to operate in an ESA environment in the first place. Businesses won't just purchase enterprise services from SAP; they'll build their own, buy them from third parties, and adapt services from SAP and third parties to meet their needs.

Does ESA make all my existing systems worthless?

Far from reducing the value of existing systems, ESA is likely to extend the lifespan of your existing applications by gradually exposing their core functionality as an increasing number of services. While past generations of software struggled with version control and obsolescence—when even simple upgrades could pose threats to an installed base—ESA is implicitly designed to repurpose these systems.

Service enabling the monolithic functionality of older applications actually increases their value and extends their lifespan by allowing the applications to participate in new processes and composite applications without having to worry about compromising the systems. This flexibility is also extremely useful while still transitioning to ESA, since any system can yield services that are invisible to users and are safe for the underlying systems. Companies are able to choose when, where, and how to adopt ESA principles without tearing anything out and starting over.

What are systems of record?

Systems of record is the term used to describe the role that enterprise applications play in maintaining the state of the enterprise. ERP, CRM, SCM, and all the other enterprise applications keep important information concerning the company's finances, inventory, personnel, business partners, projects, and other issues. When we refer to systems of record, we are emphasizing how enterprise applications are an authoritative database. When enterprise applications were invented, the role of systems of record was perhaps their most important function. As time passed, however, the foundation provided by a consistent and authoritative database laid the foundation for expanded process automation of the sort that ESA expands further still.

What are transactional systems?

Transactional systems or *transactional applications* are names for enterprise applications that emphasize the way these applications record information about transactions and are updated through discrete transactions. Sometimes transactions refer to business transactions, such as taking an order, generating an invoice, and accepting payment. Transactions also include important events such as hiring an employee and recording the terms of a contract in a system. When we speak about enterprise applications as transactional systems, we are emphasizing their role in keeping track of business activity represented as changes to databases in a consistent manner.

What are web services?

Web services are a standard way of creating a self-describing service based on XML that uses the Internet to communicate. What is a *service*? A service is a program that talks to other programs. The self-describing part of web services is the Web Services Description Language (WSDL). Every web service has a WSDL file that describes its interface. This WSDL file, which is expressed in XML, can be used to generate a program automatically to invoke a web service and get information from it. While communicating with a service can be automated, more study is required to understand the information that must be provided to a web service to get the desired result and to use the information properly. The Universal Description, Discovery, and Integration (UDDI) protocol is a standard for creating a searchable directory of WSDL files so that web services can be located and the WSDL files obtained. You can use UDDI when you are designing or running a program. Web services frequently use the SOAP standard for transferring data back and forth, although it is possible to communicate in other ways as well. *OASIS* and the *W3C*, two technology standards bodies, are primarily responsible for the architecture and standardization of web services. The Web Services Interoperability (*WS-I*) Organization has been developing a series of profiles to further define the standards involved for interoperability. New standards for managing web services and improving reliability and security are under development. You can find a detailed description of web services in Chapter 14.

Enterprise services use web services standards to communicate. So, in an important way, enterprise services are web services. But enterprise services are not just web services. Enterprise services have many additional elements, as described throughout this book. Enterprise services are built with semantic standards as well. They are created to help automate processes, and to perform utility functions related to such automation. Descriptions of enterprise services are stored in the Enterprise Services Repository, which contains not only WSDL files but also models that show how an enterprise service is related to business processes and business objects.

What is the difference between a web service and an enterprise service?

A web service is just a standardized interface to a service's functionality. It contains instructions written in WSDL describing how that service is going to be called. And that's all.

An enterprise service is a web service designed as a reusable component in process automation. It exists within the larger context of ESA, and it contains metadata about its functionality and about how it connects to other services. Web services contain much of the same functionality as enterprise services—usually at a more granular level than is useful for process orchestration—but the soul of an enterprise service is that it's there to help you, and it contains enough functionality to make a meaningful difference in processes. Enterprise services are large enough that combining and recombining them is a fairly easy task. In practice, as demonstrated in Figure 4-2, an enterprise service, when called, will execute any number of instructions across any number of underlying applications. A web service will call only the application to which it is related. Therefore, in Figure 4-2, clicking "delete order" in a menu might simply delete the order from an ERP system if one were to use a web service to do so.

The question then becomes, does this act help the larger business process of cancelling an order? The larger scope of that process includes many actions beyond deleting a record in the ERP system. There might also be a CRM system handling the sales aspect, an SCM system containing its own order objects, and so on. Therefore, the business process of cancelling an order contains many steps: revising the supply chain plan, flagging the material in stock, notifying the customer that his order has indeed been cancelled, and so on.

Whereas a web service simply deletes the record, an enterprise service is able to orchestrate the larger process of cancelling an order by sending individual messages to each of its systems, and most likely many more.

Enterprise services typically fall into one of four main categories:

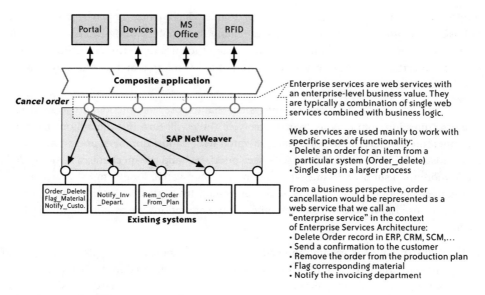

Enterprise services are web services with an enterprise-level business value. They are typically a combination of single web services combined with business logic.

Web services are used mainly to work with specific pieces of functionality:
• Delete an order for an item from a particular system (Order_delete)
• Single step in a larger process

From a business perspective, order cancellation would be represented as a web service that we call an "enterprise service" in the context of Enterprise Services Architecture:
• Delete Order record in ERP, CRM, SCM,...
• Send a confirmation to the customer
• Remove the order from the production plan
• Flag corresponding material
• Notify the invoicing department

FIGURE 4-2. Web services versus enterprise services

Process services

Trigger a process and manage its consistent execution.

Component services

Keep track of the context—the relationships, data, and external information—related to an important business function. Commonly, this context takes the form of a set of rules applied to the operation of other services. When one service inputs data to a purchase order, for example, a second component service determines—based on the identity of the supplier and corresponding contractual relations—how the purchase order should be handled.

Entity or engine services

Provide access to a business object or a discrete piece of functionality, such as a pricing engine, and manage all of the necessary events and activities triggered by the service.

Utility services

Perform a common function for other services. A service providing the required values for a specific field—the "value help service"—is a classic example of a utility service.

Setting all of these apart from garden-variety web services is the fact that enterprise services have been created within a business context, process their own semantic meaning, and are built to be reusable, configurable components that aid in the flexible automation of a greater process.

What is service-oriented architecture?

Service-oriented architecture (SOA) is a term that many different people use in many different ways. Most of the time, SOA refers to architecture for software systems in which services are the fundamental building blocks; that is what we mean by SOA in this book. This is a good, broad definition, but there are many shades of meaning when you start digging into the details of what someone means when they use the term. Sometimes people mean architectures based on web services, and others think that architectures such as CORBA and DCOM are examples of SOA.

Simply put, however, SOA refers to any system that exposes its functionality as services. The next question, naturally, is "what's a service?" We will turn to a metaphor to explain that one: think of services as a mechanical watch with hands, numbers, and an internal mechanism. The hands and numbers are the "interface," and the mechanism is the "code." To do more than simply tell time—to function as a stopwatch, for example—a watch would need additional components, such as mechanisms to start and stop the time, to display the elapsed time, and to reset the timer. Those operations are essentially simple services.

To be useful, the service orientation needs to exist everywhere across applications and systems. The emphasis here should be on the word *across*. As opposed to the old model of developing applications using proprietary languages, customized interfaces, and hardwired packages of functionality, in a service-based world, composite applications are created using a potentially infinite combination of services drawn from these existing applications. It's critical that the service orientation be able to draw upon any application and any database in the system, or else the usefulness of the architecture is crippled from the very beginning.

SOA has led to the creation of many related terms, some that were created because of SOA and others that were given new life. The term *loosely coupled*, for example, refers to a property of systems in which the complexity of the system is partitioned inside a small number of building blocks that are connected in clearly defined ways. Loose coupling means that the building blocks do not depend on each other in complex ways and can easily be rearranged to meet new challenges. The idea of the *service grid* has also gained a lot of currency. A service grid is an infrastructure of many different services all designed to work together. Many terms such as these are being created every year as new ideas emerge.

What is the difference between ESA and other approaches to SOA?

The biggest difference between ESA and other approaches to SOA is that from the ESA perspective, web services are only the beginning of a solution to the larger problems that any enterprise faces when it sits down to draft a roadmap of its business processes and the systems needed to support them.

Web services are very flexible standards, and many vendors already provide the necessary tools for building them and, in some case, modeling applications using web services as inputs. However, the question of where these web services will come from to automate processes is usually left unanswered by the vendors offering SOAs. The general idea is that companies are expected to build their own, and that the SOA vendors will provide help in selecting which ones they need to fit into a modeling environment.

While this approach may work, it doesn't solve the larger business issues, nor does it require the vendor to do much. By contrast, ESA provides a full repository of enterprise services already built and ready to automate processes for its customers.

SAP has gone a step further, creating a full suite of modeling tools at the UI and the process orchestration levels, a framework for the creation of composite applications that is actually embedded in those tools. Not only is SAP committed to building its composite applications composed of services (its xApps line), but also it has created a roadmap for the transformation of its entire product line into collections of enterprise services. ESA adds an "ecosystem" for including its customers and partners in decisions that affect the ongoing evolution of ESA. ESA is therefore more than an SOA; it supports business processes framed in terms of business semantics.

What are composite applications?

Composite applications, illustrated in Figure 4-3, are applications built using services as building blocks. The word *composite* has two shades of meaning that make it easier to understand. As a noun, composite means something that is composed of many different things. For an application to be a composite, it means that it is assembled from many existing parts. This is in sharp contrast to applications that are built through so-called green-field development in which the entire application is created from scratch. The idea of composite applications is that development is accelerated because existing services are used as a starting point and development of new functionality is kept to a minimum. Composite applications are about reuse. Another shade of meaning enters when we think of the verb *composing*. Composite applications are composed rather than developed. Composing means assembling all the required services and orchestrating them so that they work together to perform a new task. Composing frequently takes place through use of modeling rather than coding in traditional languages. Development of composite applications is accelerated in another way. Modeling and the use of services mean that the logic connecting the services is not nearly as complex as traditional applications and is clearly separated into layers. This makes adapting a composite to meet new purposes much easier and faster. So, what are composite applications about? Reuse, speed of development, and flexibility.

Figures 4-4 and 4-5 depict an example of one such composition. They illustrate the composite applications now at work inside a manufacturer that decided to turn its supply chain and manufacturing processes inside out. Instead of thinking of new products, building them, selling them, and shipping them, this manufacturer decided to start with its suppliers first, asking them, "What can you sell me cheaply today?" The manufacturer runs the answers through its APO to compile a list of everything it can build with that day's grab bag of cheap components and then sends that list to all of its distributors, creating an auction in which the distributors bid to distribute and sell whatever the manufacturer

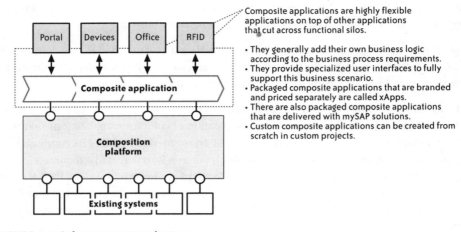

Composite applications are highly flexible applications on top of other applications that cut across functional silos.

- They generally add their own business logic according to the business process requirements.
- They provide specialized user interfaces to fully support this business scenario.
- Packaged composite applications that are branded and priced separately are called xApps.
- There are also packaged composite applications that are delivered with mySAP solutions.
- Custom composite applications can be created from scratch in custom projects.

FIGURE 4-3. Defining composite applications

built that day. When an order arrives through the auction system, the manufacturer goes back to its suppliers, orders the components it needs, manufactures the goods, and then checks to see what it no longer has the potential supplies to make, pulling those orders off the auction block.

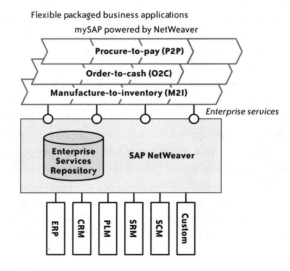

FIGURE 4-4. A packaged business process

The company runs this reverse-auction process using a composite solution assembled with pieces of functionality from its APO, CRM, and supplier relationship management (SRM) applications, including common business processes such as procure to pay, order to cash, and manufacture to inventory. The manufacturer just needed to wire them differently. Normally, however, it might take a company 12 months to figure out what it needs to change in its systems and another 18 months to change it.

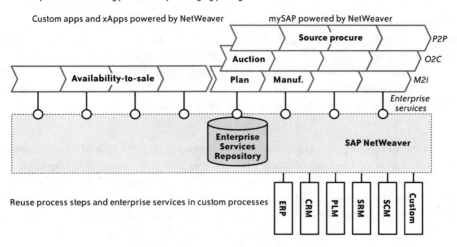

Compose differentiating processes by leveraging packaged solutions

Custom apps and xApps powered by NetWeaver   mySAP powered by NetWeaver

FIGURE 4-5. A custom business process created by leveraging packaged solutions

What are service consumers?

Service consumer is a general term for applications that use services. Services are so versatile that they can fit into many situations. A cell phone can invoke a service. A special-purpose hardware device such as a radio frequency identification (RFID) reader can invoke a service. Services can be invoked by another service. Composite applications are the most common service consumers.

What are service providers?

Frequently when we think of services, we imagine freestanding entities that just exist somehow. However, services are computer programs, and like all computer programs, they must be loaded onto a computer and executed to work. The simplest definition of a *service provider* is any computer program that offers its functionality to other computer programs as a service. For this book, when we say *service*, we usually mean web service, so service providers are programs that offer web services. As a practical matter, though, what kinds of programs are service providers?

The most common kind of service providers are existing enterprise applications that are making their functionality available as services. Most of the first wave of services will be created in this manner. This means that enterprise applications such as ERP and so forth will operate in their traditional manner and will provide their functionality as they always have. They also will provide services that will be used by service consumers, mostly composite applications. Eventually, extensions to ERP may be made as composite applications, and then perhaps someday all of ERP may be architected as a service provider with composite applications on top.

What are xApps?

Even before SAP announced ESA in January 2003, SAP and its partners were using SAP NetWeaver to build composite applications known as xApps. Initially, xApp was an abbreviation for *cross-application*, or an application that implemented processes that spanned across systems of record. Over time, the x in xApps became dominant, and now this term is pronounced *ex-apps*. The unique feature of xApps is that they are created to be sold as products. In this regard, they are examples of what was formerly known as *packaged composite applications*.

SAP created several xApps, including SAP xApp Resource and Portfolio Management (SAP xRPM) for managing large portfolios of projects, and SAP xApp Product Definition (SAP xPD) for managing the product definition process. Partners created xApps such as SAP xApp Integrated Exploration and Production (SAP xIEP) for managing oil and gas exploration. Each xApp was created with early versions of the SAP Composite Application Framework (SAP CAF) supplemented by functionality from SAP NetWeaver. This first generation of xApps did not have the benefit of the infrastructure, such as the Enterprise Services Repository and other parts of SAP NetWeaver built especially to support ESA.

What role does the mySAP Business Suite play in ESA?

The mySAP Business Suite will be the powerhouse of ESA as it becomes service enabled. Each mySAP Business Suite solution will be an important service provider, offering hundreds or thousands of enterprise services for use by service consumers. The mySAP Business Suite will also be the first beneficiary of ESA because each solution will be extended using composite applications for analytics, self-service, and solving special problems for industries.

What role does SAP NetWeaver play in ESA?

SAP NetWeaver is the technology foundation for ESA, for the mySAP Business Suite, and for everything else that SAP creates. SAP NetWeaver, shown in Figure 4-6, is a comprehensive platform designed to make the development, composition, and maintenance of enterprise software as easy as possible. SAP NetWeaver contains an application server that can run code written in ABAP or Java. All of the modern enabling technology for XML messaging, Business Process Management, data warehouses, OLAP, for reporting, searching, collaboration, building and managing UIs, and extending applications to mobile devices exists inside of SAP NetWeaver. SAP NetWeaver has a collection of development tools such as SAP NetWeaver Visual Composer to enable rapid development through modeling, and ABAP Workbench and SAP NetWeaver Developer Studio to implement services. SAP NetWeaver has been extended with such things as the Enterprise Services Repository that stores descriptions of enterprise services and how they work along with many infrastructure layers devoted to the creation and support of services.

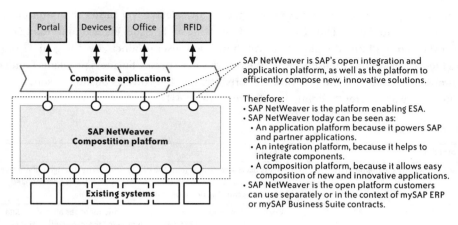

SAP NetWeaver is SAP's open integration and application platform, as well as the platform to efficiently compose new, innovative solutions.

Therefore:
• SAP NetWeaver is the platform enabling ESA.
• SAP NetWeaver today can be seen as:
  • An application platform because it powers SAP and partner applications.
  • An integration platform, because it helps to integrate components.
  • A composition platform, because it allows easy composition of new and innovative applications.
• SAP NetWeaver is the open platform customers can use separately or in the context of mySAP ERP or mySAP Business Suite contracts.

FIGURE 4-6. Defining SAP NetWeaver

As ESA evolves, SAP NetWeaver's role is changing from an integration platform to a platform where the composition of new applications and the recomposition of existing objects and enterprise services will take place. Still later, as ESA reaches maturity, SAP NetWeaver is envisioned as being absorbed into the architecture itself, evolving into the business process platform that supports and offers enterprise architects access to the enterprise services and business objects operating above it (see Figure 4-7).

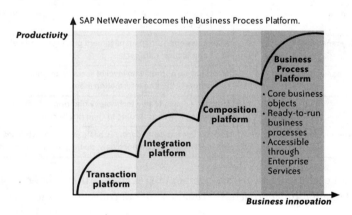

FIGURE 4-7. SAP NetWeaver's evolution to the Business Process Platform

What are IT practices and IT scenarios?

IT practices and *IT scenarios* are SAP's way of expressing the value that SAP NetWeaver provides and the mechanisms used to provide it. When facing any sort of IT project, whether it is ESA-related or not, IT practices and scenarios can provide another tool for analysis, such as the five Cs of ESA, that can help teams of people communicate more clearly about what they need to do.

IT practices are focused on the business impact of SAP NetWeaver rather than on isolated technology components. The idea is that when facing an IT issue, instead of thinking of the portal, a unit of functionality, you will think about user productivity, the goal. IT practices identify how you can use SAP NetWeaver to solve specific business problems familiar to almost any IT organization. IT practices are intended to evolve as business issues change. They are currently defined as shown in Table 4-1.

TABLE 4-1. IT practices

IT practice	Description
User productivity enablement	Helps users and groups improve their productivity through enhanced collaboration, optimized knowledge management, and personalized access to critical applications and data
Data unification	Consolidates, rationalizes, synchronizes, and manages all master data (e.g., customers, suppliers, catalog items, etc.) for improved business processes
Business information management	Increases the visibility, reach, and usefulness of structured and unstructured data
Business event management	Ensures that business events from multiple systems are distributed to the appropriate decision makers within the context of relevant business processes
End-to-end process integration	Makes disparate applications and systems work together consistently to perform business processes
Custom development	Rapidly creates new enterprise-scale applications to drive your company's unique advantages
Unified life cycle management	Automates application management processes and optimizes all facets of an application's life cycle
Application governance	Maintains an appropriate level of security and quality for your intellectual property (IP) and information assets
Consolidation	Deploys a consolidated technology platform with the ability to allocate computing power according to changing business needs
ESA design and deployment	Consolidates and standardizes basic processes while leveraging existing investments to compose new, distinctive business processes

Associated with each IT practice are a number of IT scenarios that support a process-oriented implementation approach. IT scenarios are not collections of technology, such as a portal or a data warehouse; rather, they represent the way that SAP NetWeaver will be used to address an issue related to the IT practice. IT scenarios break down the IT practices, allowing an incremental approach to implementing SAP NetWeaver functionality that maintains a tight business focus. Figure 4-8 shows the different IT scenarios associated with each IT practice.

Each IT practice has multiple IT scenarios—or approaches—that organizations can use to solve a business problem. For example, the business information management practice lists the following IT scenarios:

- Enterprise reporting, querying, and analysis
- Business planning and analytical services

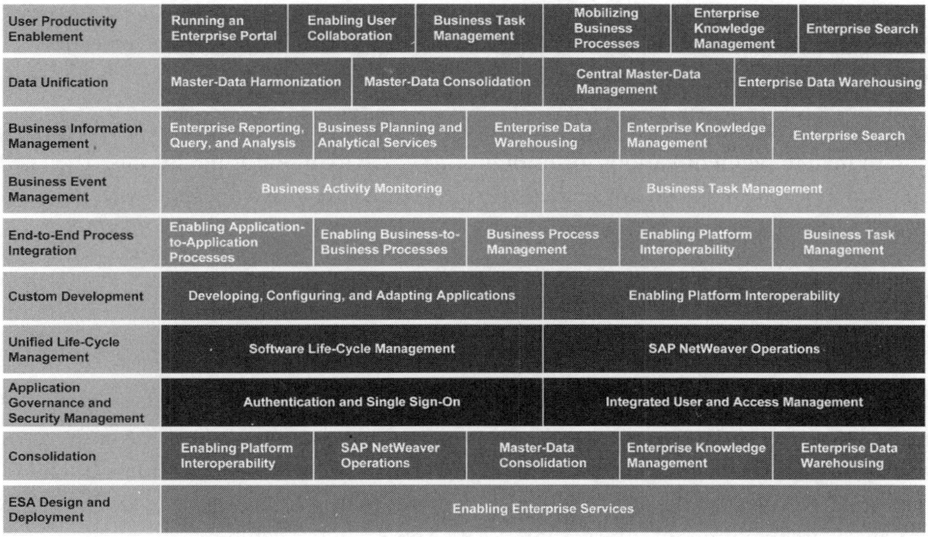

User Productivity Enablement	Running an Enterprise Portal	Enabling User Collaboration	Business Task Management	Mobilizing Business Processes	Enterprise Knowledge Management	Enterprise Search
Data Unification	Master-Data Harmonization		Master-Data Consolidation	Central Master-Data Management		Enterprise Data Warehousing
Business Information Management	Enterprise Reporting, Query, and Analysis	Business Planning and Analytical Services	Enterprise Data Warehousing	Enterprise Knowledge Management		Enterprise Search
Business Event Management	Business Activity Monitoring			Business Task Management		
End-to-End Process Integration	Enabling Application-to-Application Processes	Enabling Business-to-Business Processes	Business Process Management	Enabling Platform Interoperability		Business Task Management
Custom Development	Developing, Configuring, and Adapting Applications			Enabling Platform Interoperability		
Unified Life-Cycle Management	Software Life-Cycle Management			SAP NetWeaver Operations		
Application Governance and Security Management	Authentication and Single Sign-On			Integrated User and Access Management		
Consolidation	Enabling Platform Interoperability	SAP NetWeaver Operations	Master-Data Consolidation	Enterprise Knowledge Management		Enterprise Data Warehousing
ESA Design and Deployment	Enabling Enterprise Services					

FIGURE 4-8. SAP NetWeaver technology solution map

- Enterprise data warehousing
- Enterprise knowledge management
- Enterprise searching

For each IT scenario, second- and third-level maps list various IT activities that need to be performed along with systematic tasks for accomplishing each IT activity.

IT practices and IT scenarios bridge the world between IT's business challenges and technology implementation.

What is event-driven architecture?

Services are request/response mechanisms. A service consumer makes a request and a service provides a response. Essentially, a service consumer calls the service operation of a service, and the information flows through the service interface. Then the service implementation processes the request and provides the information to the service interface that responds.

However, what happens when there is no requestor, and instead something happens that triggers a chain of activity—for example, a sensor shows that the temperature of a tank in a chemical plant is too high or a business object monitoring the inventory level of a product shows that it has dropped too low? Each of these things is an event. *Event-driven architecture* (EDA) is the architectural paradigm used to describe systems that are built to react to various events that may occur. In general, once an event is raised somehow, the program that is notified that the event has occurred attempts to respond appropriately. If the tank temperature is too high for a well-known reason, one of several planned responses may be initiated. If the program cannot figure out what to do, an alert may be raised so that some human being can look at the issue and attempt to take corrective action.

Because of the way in which EDAs constantly wait and observe, companies frequently use them to help implement various forms of business activity monitoring. Because they generally attempt to provide an automated response, EDAs are also associated with the management-by-exception paradigms.

Why are analytics so important to ESA?

Using the flexibility of ESA to embed analytics inside enterprise applications provides the opportunity to close the loop between analysis and action.

Enterprise services provide access to functionality and information across the entire universe of enterprise applications. Services provided by SAP NetWeaver Business Intelligence (SAP NetWeaver BI) and capabilities such as the BI Accelerator, provide the ability to analyze large volumes of information. SAP xApp Analytics combines the ability to analyze what is happening in a process and then take the right actions.

In the past, users were required to leave enterprise applications when they needed to perform some analysis function. In other words, a context switch was required from the enterprise application to an analytical environment. Once insights were gained, another context switch back to the enterprise application was required to move the process forward in the right manner.

Now, hundreds of SAP analytic xApps are being embedded in enterprise applications. This means that management of the business process, analytics, and the means to take action to resolve problems or work with others is part of one seamless environment.

Analytic applications are being created using SAP NetWeaver Visual Composer, a model-driven development environment that simplifies development and allows business analysts to create and adapt analytic applications.

In all of these ways, the development of analytic capabilities acts as a catalyst to crystallize the creation of value based on ESA.

How does ESA provide for easier adaptation and a better requirements fit?

Historically, filling in the gaps between a company's IT needs and the out-of-the-box functionality of any given enterprise application required any number of steps. *Configuration* of the application using metadata might address some needs, and tighter *integration* with pre-existing applications and their processes would address others. If those were not enough, IT was expected to create *extensions*—new components welded onto the application—or even *customized* code written by the company's developers.

As depicted in Figure 4-9, these efforts gradually narrowed the gaps between the customer's requirements for the application and its actual functionality, but at a growing cost of complexity, and its corresponding costs of developer time and resources.

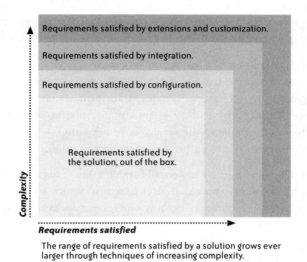

The range of requirements satisfied by a solution grows ever larger through techniques of increasing complexity.

FIGURE 4-9. How requirements are satisfied

Enterprise services fill more of these gaps by creating the reusable building blocks that companies can combine easily to meet new requirements. As mentioned earlier in this chapter, the phrase *loosely coupled* describes enterprise services' characteristic of interacting in well-defined ways without needing to know each other's inner workings. This means that the service's functionality can change without affecting the services that use it, as long as the behavior described in its interface remains the same—that is, as long as it continues providing the functionality it promised.

The opposite of loosely coupled is *tightly coupled*, which means that the internal workings of a system are exposed and that to work with it, you must understand the minute details of its inner workings, resulting in a very high level of complexity. Changing a single piece leads to unpredictable results, which leads to businesses becoming more afraid of potential side effects than excited about improving processes.

But that isn't a problem for enterprise services, which represent much smaller portions of functionality—small enough so that opening the hood and tinkering is a more productive and less intimidating endeavor with a greatly reduced risk of disrupting existing processes. The net result is that it's much easier to adapt an enterprise services environment to meet a much larger set of requirements than it is to adapt a conventional application. When you add the new tools that make development easier and that widen the potential pool of developers, it's easy to see how a much larger set of processes can be automated as needed.

What is the basic structure of an enterprise service?

An enterprise service is composed of two things: the *service interface* and the *service implementation*. The interface is a structure defined by a WSDL file and code that sends and receives messages to and from applications and other services that wish to consume the service, and the implementation contains the functionality and performs the actual work.

The interface itself is composed of *service operations*, or the specific ways a service is invoked. Each service operation has an interface and implementation that understand information received by the service, perform any transformation that takes place, manage any persistent state that is changed, and prepare any information sent back to the caller. Also present is a piece of metadata—the service documentation—that explains the functionality and other inner workings of the service implementation.

It's important to understand that each piece of functionality contained within the service requires a service operation to expose that piece for consumption by a service call from an application. For extremely simple services, only one service operation may be present. But most have at least several operations. Enterprise services are always a gateway to functionality that is provided by an existing system called a *service provider*, which may exist in the form of an exposed enterprise application or which might be built from scratch. Figure 4-10 shows the relationship between service operations, services, and service providers.

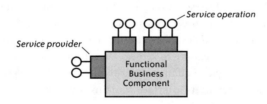

FIGURE 4-10. Services and service operations

It's important to understand here that not all enterprise applications are able to expose the same amount of functionality with the same level of ease via service operations. Enterprise services resting atop business objects—an organized container of functionality and data designed specifically to operate well within an ESA framework—are able to offer a greater variety of service operations more easily than a service consuming functionality from an enterprise application that was never designed to provide discrete services.

What are global data types?

Enterprise services offer revolutionary possibilities for reuse of services, but this revolution comes with challenges and responsibilities. One of the most challenging issues is making sure that the data the services are moving around and managing is the same, and that task is the mission of *global data types*. The easiest way to understand the value of global data types is to think of how you must conduct business without them.

Let's imagine a service that offers the ability to look up the credit score of a consumer based on the consumer's name, address, and Social Security number. If the service required a name that has three fields—one each for last name, first name, and middle initial—but a service consumer that was calling that service had only one field for name that had the entire name in it, some work would have to be done. Either the service consumer would have to parse the name into three fields, or the service would have to change to accept only one name. In practice, the code required to do this sort of translation could be lengthy and error prone.

Global data types are designed to avoid all of this by setting forth one standard way for common types of information to be represented. If everyone uses global data types, then all this nasty translation coding can be avoided. SAP's approach to global data types is to use standards for data set forth by international standards organizations as a starting point, and extending them as needed.

Why is XML messaging so important to ESA?

XML is the language in which the double-sided conversation of services is actually conducted. The message itself can take several forms. The caller of the service might send an XML message and wait until a response is provided—a *synchronous call*—or he might send a message representing a service call that waits while the rest of the application continues—what's known as an *asynchronous call*. XML messages are analogous within ESA to individual neurons firing in the brain; they are the tiny unit of information comprising larger events.

XML is also a key open standard. It provides great flexibility for changing data representations without having an impact on existing components. XML has become the de facto standard for data interchange, enabling integration among partners, protecting the company's investments in its IT infrastructure, and lowering the cost of flexibility.

What is the difference between a frontend and a backend application?

Frontend applications are geared toward user interaction, and backend applications focus on the high-volume automation of complicated processes. Each kind has its own set of features and limitations. Frontend applications are conversational in nature, and they tend to be equipped with collaborative tools and highly customized interfaces. Backend applications are created to handle a number of service calls several orders of magnitude larger than frontend ones experience. Later chapters in this book will discuss tools built for each environment, such as *guided procedures*—an interface designed to walk end users step by step through a business process—or the SAP NetWeaver Exchange Infrastructure (SAP NetWeaver XI) component capable of automating processes that run for days, weeks, or months without human input.

The distinction between frontend and backend applications is ultimately fuzzy, however, as it's not uncommon for a frontend application to call a service provided by a backend-oriented application. The difference ultimately lies in the tools designed for each.

What is service composition?

Just as it's possible within ESA to compose applications from services (thus creating composite applications), it's also possible to compose new services from existing ones. These differ from composite applications in that they are still services that are designed to be consumed by other applications, and thus they contain all of their functionality within themselves instead of consuming them from other services, as composite applications do.

Service composition is especially useful for creating specialized services that might be simpler and better suited to a task than composite applications.

What is the role of business objects in ESA?

Business objects are collections of data and functionality that represent an important business entity. Common business objects are entities, such as business partner, customer, and invoice. Since the beginning of enterprise applications, software designers have used the idea of business objects inside software to represent important parts of the real world. Business objects are not enterprise services, but like them, business objects represent a discrete piece of functionality. And like enterprise services, business objects were created to be reusable, which makes it much easier to build services atop them than to do the same with older, monolithic applications never intended for the purpose. Service providers based on business objects intended to support the creation of enterprise services will automate the creation of certain types of enterprise services. (We discuss business objects further in Chapter 5.)

Conceptually speaking, business objects might contain just about anything. They might exist within composite applications as a piece of dedicated functionality; they might do that and use services to expand the scope of their functionality; or they could be a new piece of functionality that just doesn't exist in any service provider.

How does persistence change in ESA?

The problem with *persistence*—a word describing the storage and synchronization of data in databases—is that the old architecture of enterprise applications assumed there would always be only a single database beneath the application. There would never be a risk of redundancy or duplication, as anyone seeking to change the data would always use that database, which could be kept consistent through rock-solid database transaction mechanisms.

In an ESA world, however, with data from CRM, SCM, third-party applications, partner systems, and beyond, data is scattered all over the system map. Redundancy, duplication, and inconsistency are real problems, and in order for ESA to succeed, it must provide a framework to deal with them.

In the case of ESA, SAP NetWeaver provides the technical capabilities to align and unify, clean, and harmonize data across the system landscape—and to provide a virtual view of that data as though all of it originates from the same database. (SAP NetWeaver Application Server handled persistence-related tasks for a single database in the past.)

From a technology perspective, the information management framework uses capabilities such as Master Data Management (MDM), data warehousing, and business intelligence, as well as knowledge management, to meet the challenge of managing overlapping information in a collection of distributed repositories.

Why does modeling matter? Isn't it just another form of coding?

Modeling is as old as computer programming itself. The first time a programmer added a parameter or two to his code, he created a model. While using modeling to configure and design software is nothing new, it is important to understand how modeling manifests itself at multiple levels, in a variety of forms within ESA, and not just as code. ESA shifts the burden of application development off the backs of IT and onto the shoulders of the emerging business analysts discussed earlier. To enable that shift, business analysts will need models that not only envision code, but also trace the flow of data through business processes, visualize the business objects in which transformations take place, and then finally use modeling tools to produce the code that makes all of this possible. Let's walk through each type of model.

At the highest, most abstract level is process component modeling, where complex business processes are unpacked into functional components that represent business objects and services, such as a purchase order connected to another similarly large financial component. These models don't specify the process automation itself, just the components needed for carrying out that automation. This kind of modeling is how the structure of a business is captured.

After that, business analysts zoom into each process component to orchestrate the process flow and the individual business objects and services comprising that flow, creating a model that's even more detailed. But it's still not a complete picture of the underlying automation, which is what's specified in the code inside those business objects.

In each instance, the models operate at differing degrees of abstraction from the actual code. A *low-level specification model* is essentially another form of coding in which changes to the model or the code are automatically reflected in each other because the specificity in each is roughly equivalent.

A *high-level specification model* manipulates components larger than simple code—the business processes within a process component, for example. These models exchange the flexibility of a low-specification model for the simplicity of fewer objects.

Other kinds of models include *pattern-based models*—which provide large assemblies of model components as a jumping-off point for additional configuration and which can be low- or high-level specifications—and *requirements models*, which are the most powerful of all. In requirements models, instead of a user expressing how she wants something done, the model takes an expression of the user's goals and simply creates the solutions.

To imagine the differences in scope between each kind of model, picture a chef in a kitchen instead of a business analyst hunched over a screen. In a low-level specification model, the chef works alone, using a recipe as his simple model. In a high-level specification model, the chef commands his assistants to produce dishes with a few alterations: make this one spicy, that one sweet, and grill the meat medium rare. A pattern-based, high-level specification model would have the chef ordering his staff to produce a five-course meal in which they substitute a dish or two—salmon for veal, perhaps. And whether they knew it or not, the patrons in the dining room would embody a requirements model at the moment they placed their orders. They know what they want, and now they will wait for their meals to appear from the kitchen.

Modeling is used throughout ESA to create the simplicity and flexibility required for widespread use by nontechnical users and to increase the productivity of technologists. It will be impossible for most businesses to realize the full potential of ESA without the ability to have business analysts lacking specialized knowledge in IT rapidly configure business processes. Several of the challenges mentioned earlier in this chapter—such as the looming proliferation of UIs—will be addressed by spreading the work of building these interfaces across hundreds or even thousands of suddenly empowered enterprise architects wielding simple modeling tools. Such tools already exist in the form of SAP NetWeaver Visual Composer, which was first designed as a high-level specification modeling environment.

Modeling tools use composition languages that represent the relationships among business objects, services, and the applications providing functionality, all of which are then translated into executable code. Modeling tools present to their users a visual representation of the composition language that is even simpler than the composition language itself. While displaying the data of an entity service embedded in a UI table may have a lot of plumbing buried under the service, a visual development environment simplifies that complexity down to the act of joining one object to another with a certain type of connector. The composition language used to represent that connection is much more complex, and the executable version has still greater complexity, but all of this is hidden from the business analyst who may be configuring a piece of software.

Will modeling replace coding?

The goal of modeling is to replace most coding, but modeling will never be able to replace all coding. In every environment that modeling is applied to, new needs will arise that will require more complexity than can be expressed in the modeling environment. Enterprise services and modeling will keep coding to a minimum, and when coding of new enterprise services is done, those services will become usable by others in the future.

How are patterns used in ESA and what value do they provide?

Business analysts will almost never have to start with a blank page. Either they will be configuring an existing application developed using modeling tools, or they will simply be borrowing the accumulated best practices of design embodied in collections of ready-made applications and components known as *patterns*.

Patterns borrow an idea that has always been implicit in programming. Every application ever designed for a desktop operating system follows thousands of patterns—the most noticeable of which are the common windows and menus of the interface—and applies them to the modeling of process orchestrations. Instead of remodeling an interface or process in every instance, why not create a persistent pattern that retains the common attributes?

In a pattern-based modeling environment, development becomes less about writing code and modeling applications from scratch (freestyle modeling) and more about executing best practices embodied in patterns. The patterns themselves become high-level building blocks that spare developers the detailed work of connecting components and instead free them to explore the optimal combinations.

The same holds true at the more granular level of modeling business objects. Objects built according to a pattern—all sharing the same search, save, and read methods, for example—can have those methods translated into services containing their own patterns and can then be used by interfaces or processes or even applications operating according to their own patterns. If done right, cascading automation follows in their wake since it becomes possible to automate service enablement on a massive scale, thanks to their shared patterns.

Patterns also occur during the act of development. Because they embody best practices, and because SAP is embedding pattern recognition in its modeling tools, business analysts and developers are experimenting with the practice of guided development in which the tools automate and enforce best practices for design, development, and testing. Guided development might best be described as the development equivalent of paint-by-numbers: the developer's only responsibility is to fill in the gaps in functionality.

What is process orchestration?

Process orchestration is the act of assembling the enterprise services representing components of a process into a composite application that completes the process. The goal of ESA is to create services with enough size and scope that they can be used inside a simple orchestration mechanism (modeling tools) to configure and orchestrate the process.

If the services are too small and too granular, the advantages of orchestration are lost—you might as well write code from scratch. Model-driven process orchestration is designed to be easier and simpler, an exercise in configuration rather than in gluing components together with customized code. It's not always simpler, however, as some services and business objects may actually have more functionality and complexity than are needed by the process you're trying to orchestrate.

What is process integration?

Process integration is what's needed when process orchestration runs into difficulties because one or more services need help receiving and handing off data to other components. This help can be found in a process integration layer within ESA that essentially attaches translators to the service so that arriving and departing data is accepted and processed smoothly.

How will ESA change the way applications are packaged and delivered?

As ESA continues taking shape, it appears that the basic structure of the future will be the business object, which can best be thought of as containers of functionality where data will be managed and processed. In this vision of the future, business objects that are highly related to each other will exist and will pass messages back and forth without mediation by enterprise services. These business objects will then be grouped together into larger containers, on top of which will rest enterprise services that allow for external access to the business objects beneath. The result is that enterprise applications will no longer be UIs to monolithic functionality and instead will become UIs resting on top of process components composed of related sets of business objects exposed for external use as enterprise services.

What are the special needs of composite applications?

Composite applications face problems previous generations of applications did not have to grapple with.

One problem is *distributed persistence*, which refers to data scattered across a potentially far-flung network of business objects and other structures connected by enterprise services and unaware of each other. It becomes necessary to create mechanisms capable of resolving that distributed persistence, two of which SAP NetWeaver provides: MDM and the SAP NetWeaver BI data warehousing ability. Analytic services are expected to compile and process data from this distributed source and route the results in the right form to the right UI at the right time.

Another problem is flexibility. To handcode composites from scratch is too costly to be effective. Composites need to be intrinsically flexible enough to change easily and quickly without a large investment of time and resources. This is where modeling comes in.

It's also expected that modern composite applications will include or integrate collaborative tools such as email, instant messaging, and lightweight project management tools. Equally important are search and knowledge management capabilities for unstructured documents and information. So are UIs for mobile devices; composite applications simply have higher user expectations than their predecessors. (For more information on composite applications, their architecture, and how SAP supports them, see Chapter 12.)

What is the relationship between ESA, standards, and commoditization?

ESA could not exist without standards. Enterprise services are built upon and depend upon common standards such as web services for general functionality, XML for messaging, and Java and other programming languages for creating the services themselves. ESA creates an environment in which all of these standards coexist and interoperate, and it is inevitable that this interoperability will become standardized (take, for example, standards such as RosettaNet for process orchestration in the high-tech industries), leading to the evolution of the service grid.

Within the grid, automation using enterprise services ceases to be a differentiating factor. What matters will be how you choose to organize your processes and how you choose to structure your business. ESA will have simply become the platform on which all of this happens.

Is buy versus build a false tradeoff in ESA?

In the past, there has been a debate about the tradeoffs between committing the resources to building custom applications versus buying standard (and thus nondifferentiating) applications from vendors. Taking into account all of the short- and long-term implications, what is the total cost of each? And how does this dichotomy apply in the far more granular world of services?

In the world of ESA, organizations will do both—they'll buy some services and build others—but what will really differentiate them from their competitors is the deployment of processes based on those services. Because of that, companies should plan to buy as many necessary services as possible, then use them to automate and improve new and existing processes unique to them. Buy, build, and compose becomes the model. Because of the nature of services, changing them and extending them is a simple matter. Instead of building services from scratch, customers will often adapt and extend services in ways that differentiate them and meet unique business needs. Over time, there will be a core of standardized services, new ones appearing on the market, and custom services created by customers and partners. But building versus buying stops being a dramatic choice because they'll do both on a regular basis.

Figure 4-11 illustrates the previous divide between packaged applications and custom code. Figure 4-12 shows how this divide is bridged by composite applications drawing upon the relevant functionality of both. Service enablement will simultaneously drive down the cost of custom development by eliminating the need to develop code from scratch each time out, while also increasing the value of commodity software by raising the possibility of innovation through creative reuse.

FIGURE 4-11. Build versus buy

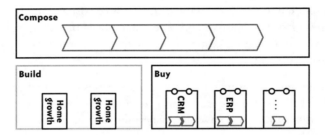

FIGURE 4-12. From build versus buy to build, buy, and compose

Why is an ecosystem of companies and standards so important to ESA?

As ESA adoption spreads, services will begin to proliferate. SAP will provide them, other vendors will provide them, customers will build their own, and so on. As the number of vendors and users expands, it will become increasingly important for commercial vendors to design services that meet their customers' specific needs. SAP has created the Enterprise Services Community (ES-Community) as a way for all sides to give feedback on the design and specifications of new services in order to guarantee the highest quality before delivery. It also provides a setting to ratify services that become de facto standards so that organizations can begin using them to create integration processes.

SAP realizes that it will never create all of the services its customers need. It hopes that by creating a flourishing ecosystem around ESA, specialized developers will step in to fill the gaps profitably and help create a universal inventory of services (see Figure 4-13). You can find more information about the partner ecosystem in Chapter 6.

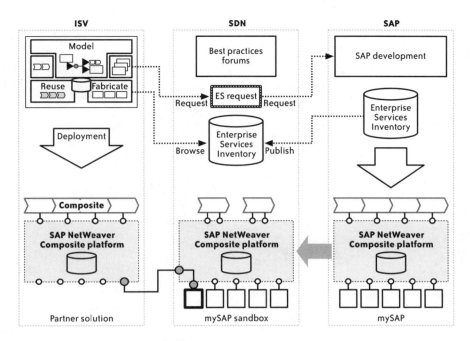

FIGURE 4-13. Empowering partners to build xApps

CHAPTER FIVE

The Structure of ESA

SO FAR, THIS BOOK HAS FOCUSED ON FRAMING THE ISSUE AND EXPLAINING THE CONTEXT FOR **ESA**. **THE** explanation has covered the business value and the general outline of how ESA creates value. This chapter dives deeper into the structure of ESA and covers the mechanisms that will be implemented at every level of enterprise software to make enterprise software simpler to adapt and change and to improve reuse across the board.

The challenge of understanding ESA is that, like mathematics, ESA defines a simple set of operators and primitive constructs that you can apply in many ways to a huge number of problems. Simple examples based on simple assumptions get the idea of ESA across. But the operators and building blocks of ESA are so flexible and powerful that almost any general statement has an exception.

For example, do composite applications consume services or can they also be service providers? Well, most of the time, composite applications are service consumers. They use enterprise services from service providers to do their work, and that's that. But there is no barrier that stops a composite application from being a service provider as well and offering services constructed inside of it to other composite applications. It might not happen often; it may be hard to do, but it can be done.

The concept of business objects offers a similar challenge. Business objects are collections of related functionality and data that bring together and encapsulate something that is important that will be reused. Like enterprise services, business objects can keep track of complex relationships, represent entities such as purchase orders or engines for calculating taxes, start or manage processes, or perform utility functions. In much of our discussion, we talk about business objects as living inside service providers. (It is important to note that when an older application is being used to power enterprise services, it may not have business objects clearly defined, and if they are clearly defined, they may not be created to easily allow enterprise services to be created.) When business objects exist in a service provider, enterprise services can be constructed easily, sometimes automatically, based on exposing the service operations—that is, the function calls—of the business objects as services. If business objects do not exist in service providers, enterprise services must be implemented using traditional methods of writing or generating code and using application programming interfaces (APIs).

But business objects show up in composite applications as well, where their job is to encapsulate important functionality. In composite applications, business objects may be frequently created through *service composition*, the technique of combining many enterprise services to perform a new job or stripping down a complicated enterprise service into just what is needed for the composite. Business objects play a similar role in composites and service providers, but in a different manner with a different emphasis.

The fact that ESA is evolving also complicates the issue. As pointed out in Chapter 1, ESA on SAP R/3 has certain capabilities that are expanded in mySAP releases and will evolve further in the future. What you can do with ESA depends on where you are in this evolution.

This chapter will take a close look at each level of the ESA stack and unmask the personality that lies beneath the technology. Understanding the personalities of the different levels of the ESA stack will enable you to quickly understand ESA and put it to work no matter what the context is.

The purpose of this chapter is to:

- Expand on the explanation of the context of ESA started in Chapter 1
- Explain each level of the ESA stack
- Explain how the levels of the ESA stack work together in composite applications
- Explain how each level of the ESA stack is created
- Explain key technology that supports the ESA stack

While this chapter is intended for technically oriented readers, business-oriented readers will also get a sense of the internal workings of ESA, even if some details seem obscure. The explanations are contained in the following sections:

- "Basics of ESA applications"
- "The ESA stack, layer by layer"
- "The enterprise services layer"
- "The business objects layer"
- "The process orchestration layer"
- "The UI layer"
- "The persistence layer"

One warning to the most technically sophisticated readers: if you expect to find each method of every service explained in this chapter, you will be disappointed. The goal of this chapter is to show the lasting structure of each level of the ESA stack as it has emerged over the last three years of architectural toil. In doing so, we hope to provide the context so that when you are faced with deeply technical literature, you can quickly make sense of it.

Basics of ESA applications

The questions in this section cover the basics of ESA applications to set the stage for the more detailed discussion of the ESA stack that follows. This chapter aims to create a clear understanding of the different ways that the ESA stack supports service consumers, such as composite applications, and the way in which ESA plays a slightly different role inside service providers, which should establish a solid foundation for more learning.

How are applications in ESA different from previous generations?

Figure 5-1 shows the key difference between traditional mainframe/client/server applications and the structure of applications in ESA. In ESA, applications no longer live inside one container in which every layer of the stack resides. Instead, some parts of the stack live in service consumers and other parts live in service providers. Composite applications are the most common service consumers, but the web services standards are so widely accepted and implemented that almost anything can consume a service—for example, a spreadsheet, a portal page, or a mobile phone.

From the service consumer perspective, all that is required is knowledge of the interface of the services that are being consumed, an understanding of what that interface actually does—that is, the semantics of the interface—and the ability to invoke an enterprise service.

The Enterprise Services Repository is the design-time directory of information describing enterprise services interfaces that help people determine what services exist and how to use them. The Enterprise Services Inventory refers to the collection of enterprise services that SAP is initially building and providing to customers.

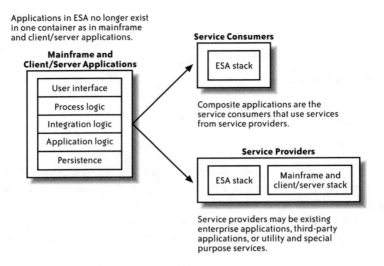

FIGURE 5-1. ESA application structure

Service consumers vary in complexity. The simplest service consumer could just be the user of one service, which would, despite its simplicity, still qualify as a composite application. Composite applications may then add complexity by doing any of the following things:

- Consuming many services.

- Creating new user interfaces (UIs) that take advantage of services for workflow, collaboration, analytics, data management, searching, mobile access, and others.

- Composing new services or business objects out of existing services for use inside the composite applications.

- Implementing new functionality by coordinating the invocation of services to perform some complex task. This is usually called *service orchestration* and can take place at the level of a composite application, inside a service, or inside a business object.

- Creating new services to be used by other composite applications.

- Creating new business objects that store new transactional and master data, thereby extending systems of record.

The service provider's main job is to provide services to service consumers. Service providers generally fall into three categories:

Existing enterprise applications
> In this case, services will be built on top of the Enterprise Services Repository or other mySAP Business Suite solutions using languages such as Java and ABAP to create enterprise services out of APIs. Care must be taken to make sure that services created on top of existing enterprise applications don't have any side effects that may influence the behavior of the other users of the enterprise application.

New enterprise applications

In this case, enterprise applications will be created to be service providers. Most often this means that the enterprise application was created as a set of business objects that work together. Business objects, which were created to be reusable units of functionality, can easily support the creation of enterprise services. Patterns, which will be discussed later, make the transformation even easier.

Special-purpose functionality

In this case, some other functionality—perhaps the information from a system at another company, a radio frequency identification (RFID) reader, a sensor that shows the level of a tank, or an alert coming from an agent monitoring a vital KPI—is made available as a service.

So the key characteristic to keep in mind about the structure of ESA applications is that a service consumer can use services from many providers and a provider can offer services to many consumers. At its best, this creates a situation in which functionality is "loosely coupled" so that parts can be assembled and reassembled to solve new problems.

How are services combined into applications in ESA?

Services represent reusable components, which in themselves are quite powerful, but alone are not enough to achieve the flexibility and rapid development that ESA must provide to create maximum business value. The way services are combined is fundamental to understanding the difference between ESA applications and those of previous generations.

Under ESA, services are combined with various mechanisms for service orchestration. The idea is that instead of using only Java or ABAP code to invoke services, get results, and process the data, tools for Business Process Management, workflow, and process orchestration would be used as much as possible. The more an application can be transformed from Java and ABAP code into process orchestration tools, the easier it will be to change the application. Such tools also increase the number of people who can participate in combining services to create applications. Tools such as SAP NetWeaver Visual Composer, Guided Procedures, and Cross Component Business Process Management (CCBPM) are examples of this technique.

In general, ESA tries to replace coding with modeling as much as possible. We will highlight this as we explain the different levels of the ESA stack.

Can an application be both a consumer and a provider of services?

Service consumers can create business objects that have new functionality coded in Java and ABAP, and can use other services or business objects. These new business objects can support the creation of new enterprise services that can be offered to other applications. In this way, a service consumer becomes a service provider as well. The idea sounds simple, but our understanding of the structure of ESA applications may be helped by walking through an example.

In one of the most popular composite applications, the blocked order list composite discussed in Chapter 11, it is possible to get a list of orders that are being blocked from completing because of credit limits or other issues. This composite was created to allow fast processing of orders that were blocked so that certain orders can be unblocked quickly in special situations. Let's say that a company had a $500,000 credit limit but was acquired by a much larger firm that was scaling up operations rapidly. The orders for that company might skyrocket before the new credit limit based on the credit quality of the new owner was approved. The blocked order composite allows the list of blocked orders to be examined, analyzed, and released for processing if justification can be found. So, how could this composite offer a service?

One natural candidate would be a service to search the blocked order list for the presence of a blocked order for a particular customer ID. This service could then be used on the dashboard for the sales representatives to alert them if any orders were being blocked. They would then be aware of the situation and could help take action to remedy the blocked order if any action was warranted.

Now, if such a service were created for reuse, it would first have to be run through SAP's process for creating, designing, and approving services that would be added to the Enterprise Services Inventory and be described in the Enterprise Services Repository so that it could be used by SAP's development tools. The Enterprise Services Repository, Enterprise Services Inventory, and development tools are described in later chapters.

How does ESA work with event-driven architectures?

ESA, like all forms of service-oriented architecture (SOA), works on a request/response paradigm. Nothing happens until a service consumer invokes a service—that is, makes a request and then waits for the response. While it is theoretically possible that a service could accept a request and always return nothing, most of the time service consumers wait for the service to respond with some sort of information.

Event-driven architectures (EDAs) work completely differently. In an EDA, something happens to start a chain of events. The paradigm is not request/response but fire and forget. The event occurs, some other software system or some person is notified about it, and then all sorts of things could happen. One event could lead to one event or many other events being triggered. Many programs could be listening for the same event. An event could lead to a task being put on someone's worklist. An event could start a composite application that could help a user do the work of reacting to the event. Events could notify systems that were monitoring a business.

SOA and EDA are appropriate architectures for creating software systems that model and automate business activity. SAP has long used events all over the mySAP Business Suite, and now that ESA is transforming how software is structured and created, it is clear that both EDA and SOA will work together. But how?

To understand how EDA and SOA interact, we will delve deeper into how SAP has implemented events and how new forms of architecture and systems are being constructed on top of basic mechanisms.

Core events and business events

Core events are technical in nature and do not really carry much information with them. A core event indicates that a business object has changed its state, and nothing more. For example, Purchase Order Saved is a typical core event. What does it signify? That a purchase order was saved. This purchase order could be new or it could be an existing purchase order that has been changed. More than 2,000 such core events are defined across the business objects of the mySAP Business Suite.

Business events are built on core events. As Figure 5-2 shows, business events start with a core event, but then more information is added to them. The core event, Purchase Order Saved, might become a business event that has the name of the customer, the amount of the purchase order, the product being purchased, and so on. What is stored in a business event is determined by how it is going to be used. In the future, there will be even more types of business events. Business Intelligence events, Knowledge Management events, Database events, and many more types of events are possible.

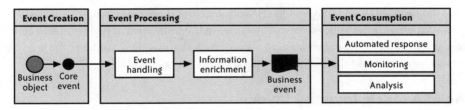

FIGURE 5-2. Core events and business events

It is easy to imagine the many different things you could do with business events. For example, if a business event indicating a new customer was created, a business event could trigger the creation of a task to evaluate that customer's credit quality and set a credit limit, a process that could be supported by a composite application. A *task* is not an event; it is a unit of work performed by a person. Tasks are one important way that ESA will interact with EDA. Composite applications built using ESA will be used to process tasks that are created from core or business events. For example, a composite application created to process a task might have functionality to understand exactly what the task is, inspect and analyze the context, and then take action to properly complete the task. It is also possible that composite apps will monitor business events or analyze information gathered about business events, or wait to be triggered by business events.

SAP plans to implement a form of Business Activity Monitoring (BAM) called Milestone Monitoring. BAM is a general concept that covers many capabilities for automated performance monitoring, such as creating alerts based on KPIs and using events to create a sophisticated model of a business. Milestone Monitoring is a type of BAM in which key business processes are tracked by the SAP NetWeaver Exchange Infrastructure (SAP NetWeaver XI) Business Process Management capabilities for modeling processes. This use of Business Process Management creates a long-running monitor out of a capability frequently used to manage long-running transactions. Business events and alerts are generated when certain thresholds are reached, and then Business Process Management can monitor how long various parts of a process take and can determine whether milestones are met on time. As part of the tracking, metrics about process performance are gathered and delivered into SAP NetWeaver Business Intelligence (SAP NetWeaver BI) for analysis.

For example, monitoring of a Customer Relationship Management (CRM) process might work as follows. When a lead is created, a business event causes a timer in Business Process Management to be set. If a business event indicating an appropriate response to the lead is not generated within, say, two days, an alert is sent to the responsible sales representative. If four days go by, the alert might go to the sales rep's manager. All the while, when people do respond within these thresholds, the actions taken and the results are sent to SAP NetWeaver BI for further analysis.

Milestone Monitoring is just one way that events can be put to good use. Many others are on the way that involve not just monitoring, but also automated responses to business events.

In the long run, EDA and ESA will likely work together in common patterns that will become, in effect, a new integrated architecture. In the short term, it is clear that in certain cases, the fire and forget paradigm allows even more decoupling than the request/response paradigm and that flexibility will be put to interesting uses.

The ESA stack, layer by layer

With the general relationship of service consumers and providers in mind, we can now turn to the idea of how the ESA stack works inside both consumers and providers. Each layer of the ESA stack has been conceived and designed to play a supporting role to create service consumers (usually composite applications) and service providers. Each layer has a specific role to play that promotes flexibility, reuse, and ease of development in concert with the other layers. Before we examine each layer in detail, we will take a look at the challenges each layer must overcome to do its job.

What challenges face the ESA stack?

As Figure 5-3 shows, the ESA stack consists of five layers, each designed to address an enduring challenge that has faced enterprise application architects since the beginning of the industry. The vision of ESA has made those challenges more acute in several ways.

First, one of the promises of ESA is that standard software delivered as a set of services can both better fit the requirements of a business and be recombined to solve many more problems. SAP will recombine services to provide automation of many more processes flavored for industry verticals. This expansion of automation will mean that more UIs will need to be created to assist people who will be playing various roles in these automated

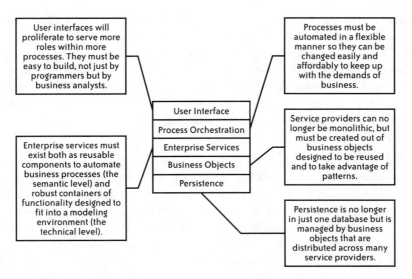

FIGURE 5-3. Challenges facing the ESA stack

processes. More processes automated and more UIs mean that development tools must become more productive and applications must become easier to maintain. Otherwise, the expansion of automation to more processes and more verticals cannot take place.

In addition, some of the tools used to create and configure applications under ESA must become easier to use in order to expand the population of potential application developers from highly technical people using development tools that require knowledge of Java and ABAP, to business analysts who can directly apply their deep understanding of business requirements using simplified modeling environments.

Finding and using services will also be a challenge as the number of services expands rapidly. So will keeping track of the much larger number of processes that are being automated. Figure 5-3 summarizes the challenges facing the ESA stack.

User interface

UIs must become easier to create and maintain. The job of designing and building UIs must be performed not only by highly trained technical employees, but also by business analysts. This will happen through an expanded use of modeling tools for development instead of coding. Patterns will also be used to further automate and accelerate development and to provide common structures in the UI to reduce training time.

Process orchestration

By themselves, enterprise services are not enough to deliver on the ESA promise. They must be combined to create applications in ways that are flexible and that expand the population of developers. For example, ESA would fail if the only way to combine services was to code in Java and ABAP. Instead, process orchestration mechanisms such as Guided

Procedures, modeling in SAP NetWeaver Visual Composer, and CCBPM allow services to be combined via modeling rather than coding. This not only accelerates development but also makes applications easier to change to meet evolving business needs. The job of automating business processes can become a task performed by business analysts and application specialists who are closer to the requirements of the business. This avoids creating a bottleneck and frees up highly skilled developers to address the task of creating new enterprise services that are unique to each enterprise.

Enterprise services

Enterprise services have a dual identity. From the business perspective, enterprise services are units of functionality used to model and automate business processes. Enterprise services may be used to automate whole business processes, process steps, key parts of process steps, or important utility functions. From the technology perspective, enterprise services are building blocks for reusable functionality designed to be used in model-driven environments and to implement patterns that help automate development. The challenge is to design enterprise services properly so that they serve both of these purposes. Some services keep track of relationships, some are focused on processes, and others provide access to important entities such as purchase orders or to engines for complex calculations. Some provide access to important support functions or third-party applications. The domain of enterprise services is vast, and building all of the services that are required is a massive undertaking. The work of SAP's developers, Independent Software Vendors (ISVs), and customers must be coordinated. Once all the necessary services are built, the next challenge is to find them and use them in advanced modeling environments. While enterprise services are process and technology building blocks inside applications, an entire ecosystem must exist to create and support them.

Business objects

Business objects are reusable building blocks inside a service provider or an enterprise application. Business objects are not required to create enterprise services. It is possible to build services on enterprise applications that were not created to support enterprise services. But if business objects exist, then creating enterprise services can be streamlined. The business objects in new service providers created with ESA in mind are designed to simplify and accelerate the job of creating enterprise services.

In the oldest generation of enterprise applications, the architecture was monolithic, meaning that one huge, interconnected program did all the work. As programming became better understood, the idea of reusable objects that encapsulated both data and functionality became the dominant paradigm. Most of SAP's applications, including SAP R/3 and earlier versions, have used the concept of business objects as the main structuring elements of applications to represent real-world business entities. From the beginning, business objects were technical implementations of business ideas.

While many enterprise applications now use objects, most of the objects were designed for internal use in an application. Business objects differ from traditional objects in that they are designed to represent business ideas, support external use, and take into account the processes, process steps, and utility functions they might be involved with creating. If business objects are created according to certain patterns, the process of creating enterprise services according to those patterns can be automated. Higher-level patterns for the structure of UIs or process patterns can then be built on lower-level patterns.

Persistence

In the ideal world of ESA, each business object manages the persistence of its data. The evolving world of ESA will fall short of this ideal for some time, and data will be managed by multiple parts of an application using transactional mechanisms to avoid conflicts. In both of these worlds, data will be distributed across many service providers and the same or similar data may exist in many places. Service consumers, however, will not want to be bothered keeping track of all of this distributed data. ESA provides various solutions to this challenge through Master Data Management (MDM), SAP NetWeaver BI, and SAP NetWeaver Application Server (SAP NetWeaver AS).

As we will see in the following explanation, the ESA stack is supported by many different mechanisms from the Enterprise Services Community (ES-Community) that coordinate the design of services being added to the Enterprise Services Inventory both from inside and outside of SAP. Model-driven development tools use the descriptions in the Enterprise Services Repository to simplify development and replace hardcoding in Java and ABAP. Operational, security, and life cycle management tools help guide ESA applications through the process of design, implementation, operations, and retirement. Specially designed processes for creating implementation roadmaps and new governance models help companies manage the new world of services. Standards are used to simplify and accelerate this process throughout. If this chapter and this book are successful, you will be able to understand all of these dimensions and put ESA to work.

The enterprise services layer

While it is clear from the term that enterprise services are the central element of ESA, it is far from clear what that means in detail. One measure of expertise in ESA is the length of the answer someone can give to the question, what is an enterprise service? The more dimensions that someone can discuss with some degree of substance, the more likely that person will be able to quickly make sense of ESA and put it to work in an organization. This section will take you on a tour of all of the dimensions of enterprise services.

What is the basic structure of enterprise services?

The key to understanding enterprise services is the idea that enterprise services are primarily two things, an interface and an implementation, that are broken into three parts when put into action: the consumer proxy that invokes the service interface; the provider proxy that accepts the invocation of a service, manages the communication with the consumer, and passes the information to the implementation; and the implementation that does the work. Figure 5-4 makes this relationship clear.

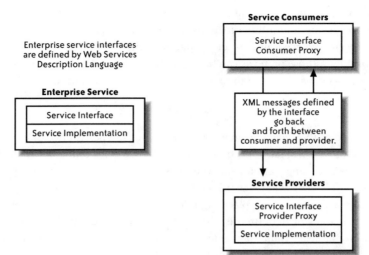

Service Consumers

Service Interface
Consumer Proxy

Enterprise service interfaces
are defined by Web Services
Description Language

Enterprise Service

Service Interface

Service Implementation

XML messages defined
by the interface
go back
and forth between
consumer and provider.

Service Providers

Service Interface
Provider Proxy

Service Implementation

FIGURE 5-4. Enterprise services in consumers and providers

To really understand how all of the parts work together, we will discuss what happens during two phases of design and then look at what happens at runtime.

The first phase to be examined is that of designing an enterprise service. There are two ways that enterprise services are designed: either from the outside in, or from the inside out. Outside-in design happens when process automation is being designed and modeled and an interface to a service that does not yet exist is designed to meet the needs of the process. In this case, the interface is defined in detail, development tools are used to generate the service provider proxy, and then traditional coding methods using Java, ABAP, or other tools are used to create the enterprise service implementation.

In the case of inside-out design, the service implementation exists and the interface must be designed on top of it. Sometimes—for example, when a BAPI or an IDOC is being turned into an enterprise service—the enterprise service interface can be generated from the definition of the BAPI* or IDOC. Other times, when many BAPIs, IDOCs, or other existing functionality are going to be combined to create a new enteprise service, the service interface must be constructed by hand. The details of outside-in and inside-out development are described in Chapter 15.

The second design phase consists of the process of using a service in a service consumer, such as a composite application. In this phase, a development or modeling tool uses the description of the service interface that is stored in the Enterprise Services Repository to generate the consumer proxy code that invokes the service by sending XML messages to the provider proxy that ask the service implementation to do the work.

---

* Not all BAPIs can be enabled as enterprise services.

Now we must consider what happens when a service interface is designed. As Figure 5-5 shows, each service interface consists of a set of service operations.

On the provider side, the XML message for a service operation is accepted by the proxy and then passed to the service implementation for processing. The proxy then sends the response back to the service consumer.

Service operations represent the different functions a service can perform.

On the consumer side, service operations are invoked to perform some function. The proxy translates the information provided to the service proxy into an XML message and sends it to the service provider.

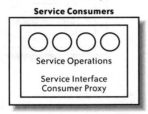

FIGURE 5-5. Service operations

A service operation represents one of the functions of a service. A service operation is like a method on an object in object-oriented programming, or a remote function call to a BAPI or some other function module in ABAP. As part of the definition of a service interface, each service operation must be defined in detail. For example, for a service that can create a purchase order, service operations must exist to create, read, update, and delete the purchase order. Of course, you must also define the data that will be passed to and from the service consumer and provider. We will discuss how this data is defined in the next section.

Perhaps the simplest way to think of service operations is as the inbox and outbox for services. Each service operation defines what, if anything, will be sent into the service and what will be sent back once the processing is done. It is important to remember that service operations can be *synchronous* or *asynchronous*. In a synchronous service operation, the service proxy on the consumer waits for the response before proceeding. In an asynchronous service operation, the service consumer just sends messages that begin the service operation, and then continues its work. Then a response is sent back in another message, when the service operation is complete. Almost all of the interaction for web services has been standardized through the WS-* series of standards.

So, now we come to the subject of what happens between the receipt of an incoming message from a service consumer and the response from the service provider. The answer is that the service implementation accepts the information from the incoming message related to the service operation and then the service implementation does the work, as shown in Figure 5-6.

Service implementations can take many forms.

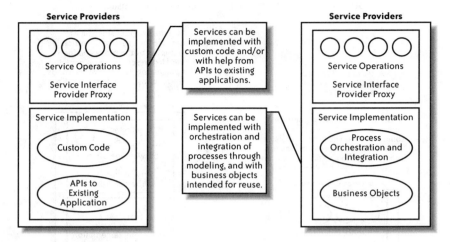

FIGURE 5-6. *Service implementations*

Service implementations are programs, pure and simple. They can be implemented in any language, run on any platform, and do anything that a computer program can do. This separation of how the implementation is performed from the definition of the service is one of the most powerful aspects of enterprise services and services in general. It means that as long as the service works the same way, you can change the implementation without disrupting the service's users. For example, if a legacy mainframe application now is encapsulated as a service, nobody needs to worry about when this application is upgraded to a more modern, lower-cost version because the services hide the implementation and the changes are invisible to the users.

Services, in essence, form a contract between the service providers and the service consumers. The clarity that the definition of a well-defined service provides is being used to formalize all sorts of relationships. IT departments are defining what they offer the rest of the enterprise in terms of services. Companies such as Amazon, Google, and Yahoo! are defining their offerings to developers in terms of services. Suppliers and manufacturers are defining their relationships in terms of services.

In the early days of services, almost all services were implemented as shown in the left side of Figure 5-6. Underneath a service interface was a service implementation that was created through custom coding techniques using Java, ABAP, or other languages. When well-established forms of APIs existed, such as BAPIs and IDOCs, it was easy to generate the code that defined a service's interface for the existing functionality that was used as the service implementation. Many services in use today have been written this way.

But the vast importance of services has changed the way applications are being created to make the creation of services easier, faster, and more flexible. The core problem is this: APIs created for mainframe/client/server applications were created to solve all sorts of different needs. Sometimes these APIs existed to facilitate bulk loading of data. Other times the APIs were created to solve a common integration challenge. Yet other times they existed to support development of UIs. Almost none of the APIs of previous generations was created to provide functionality needed by processes, process steps, and other utilities to support an SOA. The internal architecture of many programs did have reusable components, but these were designed to be reused inside a program, not by composite applications and other service consumers seeking to flexibly automate processes.

When the work of creating services began on top of existing APIs, developers quickly found out how difficult it was to create services using APIs created for other purposes. Sometimes the APIs did not have all the power they needed. Other times they had unintended side effects. When the developers turned to writing new code using the objects for internal use, similar problems arose. For example, it was not uncommon for objects such as sales orders, purchase orders, or invoices to be huge and to have many interconnections to other objects. This was fine for the context of internal use inside an application, but it was too large a granularity to efficiently support services.

The solution to the challenge of creating service providers that could easily support the creation of enterprise services is to organize functionality around the concept of business objects, which are objects that are internal to a service provider and are designed to be reusable building blocks in automating processes and process steps, and in providing utilities to support service consumers such as composite applications. This structure is shown on the left side of Figure 5-6. Inside a service provider, coding in Java, ABAP, and other languages is almost inevitable, but service providers also can use process orchestration and modeling to improve flexibility and reduce the cost of change.

Although this explanation is just a quick introduction to the topic, a clear understanding of the internals of enterprise services goes a long way to reduce the confusion that can sometimes creep into SOA discussions. We will provide this explanation in the next few sections.

What are global data types and how are they related to enterprise services?

Our discussion of enterprise services did not address the issue of how data formats will be standardized, an issue that must be addressed if ESA is to work as efficiently as possible. Let's imagine what would happen without a standard for basic customer information, such as name and address, for example. That would mean the definition of *customer information* would be different from one service interface to another service interface, which means that one of two things would have to happen: either service interfaces would have to be written to accept customer information in many different formats, or the service consumers would have to do the work of translating the customer information into the format used by each service interface. As anyone in the IT business with a little gray hair knows, this is a massive and annoying problem that has been addressed by general-purpose data mapping technology and special-purpose suites of adapters.

Of course, everything would be so much simpler with just a little standardization so that data types in UIs were the same as those in service interfaces and business objects. That is precisely the job of the global data types used in ESA. Based on the data type methodology of ISO 15000-5 and the UN/CEFACT Core Component Technical Specification, SAP's global data types provide a standardized set of data that is described using XML schemas that are stored in the Enterprise Services Repository.

The idea is that whenever possible, people will use standardized global data types instead of making up new ones. The initial collection of global data types will be expanded using SAP's governance process for business content, which is part of the Process Integration Council, an internal standards setting and engineering governance body at SAP. With global data types in place, ESA can deliver a level of efficiency of which previous generations of enterprise software were incapable.

Does ESA have an Enterprise Service Bus or the equivalent?

In addition to the concept of SOA, another concept called the Enterprise Service Bus has become current. While SOA is the general concept of building software by using services, the Enterprise Service Bus is something much closer to ESA: it is the idea of creating a framework for a standard set of services that can be reused to do the work of enterprise computing. One way to think of ESA is as an infrastructure and set of tools for creating an Enterprise Service Bus. Of course, ESA goes beyond just creating the roadways for a service bus. Unlike most other approaches to SOA, ESA provides services to run on the roadways.

Our discussion so far has papered over many of the details of how services will work, and to complete our study of enterprise services, we should provide these details. Figure 5-7 completes the picture of how enterprise services work by adding a new layer, the Enterprise Services Infrastructure, which does quite a few jobs.

The goal of the Enterprise Services Infrastructure is to hide from service consumers all of the details that go into managing secure, reliable, and optimized communication between service consumers and providers. Here are a few of the most important issues that the Enterprise Services Infrastructure addresses:

Reliable messaging
> When a service consumer sends an XML message to a service provider, how does it know that the message was received? New standards for reliable message delivery have been created and are used by the Enterprise Services Infrastructure to perform this task.

Security
> Sometimes it is OK to send an XML message across a network without encryption, but other times it would be a huge problem. The Enterprise Services Infrastructure uses standards for security to address this problem.

Enterprise Services Infrastructure performs many of the jobs associated with an Enterprise Service Bus.

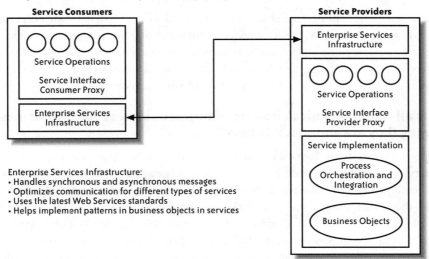

FIGURE 5-7. *Enterprise Services Infrastructure*

Synchronous/asynchronous messaging

A service consumer can call a service synchronously, meaning that the caller waits for a response, or asynchronously, meaning that the caller does not wait and the response is sent later. The Enterprise Services Infrastructure handles the details of these two different types of conversations between service consumers and providers.

Optimizing message traffic

If a service asks that one million rows of a database be returned, the nature and behavior of the messages between the service consumers and the service providers will be quite different compared to a situation in which only one byte is asked for. The Enterprise Services Infrastructure is built to allow different conversations between service consumers and providers to be optimized in different ways. Special care is taken in the Enterprise Services Infrastructure to ensure that UI-related services perform well.

Support for patterns

As we already mentioned, business objects may have methods that are created according to patterns. These patterns may then be reflected in patterns of service operations and may be used to support higher-level patterns for UIs or process automation. The Enterprise Services Infrastructure is aware when patterns are being used and helps optimize their use.

How all of this works in practice deserves a guide of its own, and in fact, senior SAP engineers are working on such guides.

How are database transactions handled in ESA?

Transactions are mechanisms that ensure that all related changes to a database occur either at once or not at all. In ESA, the complexity of implementing transactions is complicated by the fact that data consistency must be ensured across many services that use data stored in different service providers. SAP has developed several approaches to managing transactions that will be made public in future versions of SAP NetWeaver.

This is all rather technical; how do enterprise services get the business meaning they are supposed to have?

So far, our discussion has focused on the form of enterprise services—namely, how enterprise services fulfill their mission from the technology perspective. ESA falls apart, however, if enterprise services are not designed properly to fulfill their business mission—that is, to fill the role of reusable building blocks for processes, process steps, parts of process steps, and key utility functions. Hundreds of thousands of fine-grained services do nothing to help manage complexity and make applications more flexible and easier to build and change. If a service is too granular, it means the service's consumers have to be fiendishly complex. On the other hand, if services are too large, service consumers lose flexibility. A behemoth service can fulfill one purpose but cannot be recombined to meet other needs.

There is no silver bullet that guarantees enterprise services will be designed to the proper level of granularity. Service design is an art, and it is hard to ensure good art. Fortunately for SAP, experience is frequently a process of good art, and SAP has plenty of that. SAP has many processes in place to prevent bad art from creeping into the process of service design. The ES-Community helps customers, ISVs, and systems integrators (SIs) to design services that will be widely used across the SAP ecosystem (see Chapter 6). SAP has an internal process for vetting requests for services from various development departments inside SAP and from the ES-Community and then making sure that all the requests are reconciled and supported by an inventory of services that has a coherent design at the right level of granularity (Chapter 8 includes a description of this process).

Perhaps the most comprehensive guide to the art of enterprise services design is the Enterprise Services Design Guide, which is available on the SAP Developer Network (SDN; *http:// sdn.sap.com*). This guide explains the context for enterprise services design and presents the outline of a three-step process that involves the following:

Discovery
> First, a business-driven analysis reveals the scenarios that might benefit the most from enterprise services. Pain points, opportunities for creating value, and the business drivers of ESA are used to find promising scenarios. The business processes and the existing supporting solutions for these scenarios are then analyzed to determine the requirements for services that would improve support for the business.

Design
> Once a promising business process has been identified, the design process begins. A single service, a system of services, or a program of service enablement may satisfy the

requirements. In any of these cases, a design must be invented, evaluated, and refined in order to meet the requirements outlined in the discovery process. This is usually an iterative process in which the design work improves the understanding of the requirements, which may then be changed in ways that affect the design.

Documentation

The final step of the methodology involves properly documenting the new services and entering them in the Enterprise Services Repository.

The process of designing a single service or a system of services is set forth in the Enterprise Services Design Guide, along with guidance about the issues that are generally involved. One of the most innovative aspects of the process is the recommended way of running a program of service enablement—that is, looking at a large application, many large applications, or even an entire enterprise, and identifying where services might help.

The idea is that generally you find certain patterns for a common way of improving an application by adding enterprise services when a program of service enablement is underway. The Enterprise Services Design Guide calls these patterns *design contexts*. For example, in SAP's program of service enablement, in the user productivity areas are several ways that help users interact successfully with computer software. One of those design contexts involves using a work list–oriented UI design pattern to provide users with self-service functionality and reduce dependence on experts. The design context for this improvement shows how a series of UI elements can be used in various types of screens to enable this work. In other words, the design context is a sort of template for a successful UI that enterprise services can support. A design context explains a lot about how the enterprise services should be designed, which should help us achieve the goals of our methodology: to increase productivity and quality. A design context is not a design, but rather the shape of a design that may apply repeatedly.

As a program of service enablement is carried out, designers know that a design context may apply by using *indicators*, features of a business process that suggest it might benefit from a solution based on the design context. Each design context has its own indicators. One of the indicators for the work-list-oriented design context is when a large group of workers must frequently consult an expert to do certain tasks. This indicator suggests that some sort of self-service could help. (For a more detailed description of the indicators, see Chapter 8.)

The Enterprise Services Design Guide has proven popular with ISVs, SIs, and SAP customers involved in service design, but it doesn't answer one question: how do services fit into general business processes or those of a particular industry? SAP, of course, has had to link business processes to systems that automate them since the inception of the company, and has created an elegant approach that uses SAP Business Maps, solution maps, and business scenario maps to show the process structure of how various businesses translate into SAP solutions. Now, instead of those maps leading to various components of R/3, they lead to services and systems of services that are performing the automation. You can see this approach in action on the Enterprise Services Preview on SDN, which allows solution maps to be navigated down to enterprise services.

How do enterprise services fit into business process modeling?

This question will be answered in more detail in the section "The process orchestration layer," later in this chapter, but the short answer is that enterprise services are the smallest level of container for reusable building blocks for automating processes.

To understand what this means, it is important to understand that modeling of businesses and business processes takes place on various levels. At the highest level, business analysts create the business maps and scenario maps mentioned in the previous answer. These contain various *process components*, which are large collections of processes, such as order processing and order fulfillment. Inside the process components, business processes are modeled in terms of processes and process steps. When we say *modeled*, we mean that the relationships among the elements of the model are described. At the highest level, these relationships may represent a large flow of data. At the lower levels, where the processes are described, the relationships may describe which data is being passed back and forth and which enterprise services are going to be invoked. The most detailed description of automated processes exists inside the enterprise services in the code or in the models used to build the service implementations.

What is service composition? How can you build enterprise services from other enterprise services?

Enterprise services are designed for reuse in many different contexts. But a particular composite application may need only part of one enterprise service or a combination of many. *Service composition* is the task of transforming reusable enterprise services into a single service that meets the needs of one application.

Service composition can take place in service consumers or in service providers, but most commonly, it occurs in composite applications. A variety of different tools can be used for service composition, including the SAP NetWeaver XI Integration Builder and tools that are part of the SAP Composite Application Framework (SAP CAF).

What are the main categories of enterprise services?

Enterprise services are like numbers in that they are generally useful and you can categorize them in thousands of ways. The authors of the Enterprise Services Design Guide created one of the most useful categorizations, and it involves the following four categories:

Component services
> These services keep track of the context—the relationships, data, and external information—related to an important business function. A component service keeps track of relationships that are not represented by simply a data field. For example, a service that provides access to the credit limit for a customer and her existing balance is a classic component service. The service would provide not only the credit limit and balance,

but also access to external providers of credit ratings, information on currently unpaid invoices, and payment history. Such information could be provided by other services consumed by the credit management service.

Process services

These services trigger the execution of a process or a process step and then manage the execution of that process. Process services assume control of execution when called and then orchestrate services or other functionality to carry out consistent execution of a process.

Entity or engine services

These services model and provide access to a business object or engine. An entity service might represent a create order, which makes sure that every time an order is created, all business rules are checked and all data is consistent. An engine service provides access to commonly used functionality such as a pricing or tax calculation engine.

Utility services

These services perform some commonly used functionality for other services or for consumers of services. A service that provides the allowed values for a specific field (a so-called value help service) is a classic example of a utility service.

Services are sometimes categorized by the business benefit they provide or by the ways in which they assist composite applications. There is no official taxonomy of services yet created.

What kinds of enterprise services support the special needs of composite applications?

Composite applications have special needs and must meet higher expectations than previous generations of applications. For example, composite applications manage information that is distributed across many different databases. Previous generations of applications were usually based on a single database. Composite applications are created in an environment in which many applications have search, collaboration, analytics, reporting, and mobility included. Users have come to expect everything they need in one place, and composite applications must live up to these expectations.

Different kinds of services help composite applications to do their job, as shown in Figure 5-8. While the following categories are not the only types of services that support composite applications, they are the most important in terms of meeting special needs.

Master data management

Master data, the data about customers, partners, and other items used repeatedly, must be available for any application to do its job. Composite applications manage master data that is distributed across many different service providers. In such an environment, duplicate data may be stored in different places, data may not be consistent, and no one version of the truth may exist anywhere. SAP NetWeaver Master Data Management is a solution

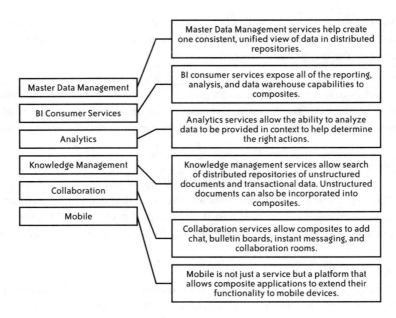

	Master Data Management services help create one consistent, unified view of data in distributed repositories.
Master Data Management	BI consumer services expose all of the reporting, analysis, and data warehouse capabilities to composites.
BI Consumer Services	
Analytics	Analytics services allow the ability to analyze data to be provided in context to help determine the right actions.
Knowledge Management	Knowledge management services allow search of distributed repositories of unstructured documents and transactional data. Unstructured documents can also be incorporated into composites.
Collaboration	
Mobile	Collaboration services allow composites to add chat, bulletin boards, instant messaging, and collaboration rooms.
	Mobile is not just a service but a platform that allows composite applications to extend their functionality to mobile devices.

FIGURE 5-8. Services that support composite applications

that helps manage this challenge by bringing together all of the distributed master data in a coherent form that eliminates duplicates, resolves conflicts among different forms of data, and provides a way to locate all data items quickly wherever they are stored. SAP NetWeaver Master Data Management also provides applications that allow data to be cleaned. Composite applications rely on MDM for quick access to high-quality master data.

Business Intelligence (BI) Consumer Services

SAP NetWeaver BI is a vast part of SAP NetWeaver that uses data warehousing, reporting, OLAP, and a huge menu of adapters to allow consolidation, cleaning, analysis, and reuse of both master data and transactional data. Parts of SAP NetWeaver BI are exposed through standards, such as the XML for Analysis (XMLA) standard that created a query language for OLAP queries that was independent of the implementation. The XMLA standard covers just a portion of the rich and wide pool of functionality in SAP NetWeaver BI, however. SAP NetWeaver BI Consumer Services provides access through services to all of this functionality, not just what was standardized. In addition, SAP NetWeaver BI Consumer Services has advanced techniques to allow data warehouses to be kept up-to-date in near-real time and to optimize the speed of queries. Composite applications benefit from all of this functionality to create a unified view of distributed and possibly inconsistent data, to create special-purpose repositories or data marts to meet the special needs of a particular composite, and to add reporting and analytical functionality to composites. SAP NetWeaver BI Consumer Services allows a composite to present a complete suite of functionality that allows information to be gathered and analyzed in one context, so appropriate action can be taken.

Analytics

SAP xApp Analytics refers to the services built on SAP NetWeaver BI Consumer Services and through other means to create a set of tools to make the job of adding analytic functionality to composite applications as easy as possible. SAP NetWeaver BI Consumer Services provides the backend functionality to get access to the data in SAP NetWeaver BI and to do the number crunching. SAP Analytics provide the building blocks, such as UI building blocks, interactive graphics functionality, reporting, and other flexible information containers, that allow users of composite applications to understand the data presented to them so that they can take the appropriate action.

Knowledge management

SAP's services for knowledge management bring the world of unstructured documents and search into composite applications. Knowledge management services provide for flexible containers that can associate unstructured documents with structured transactional information. Knowledge management search services allow both unstructured and structured information kept in multiple repositories to be searched to create a consolidated set of results. Using SAP's knowledge management services, composite application designers can bridge the gap between structured and unstructured data and create one complete picture in a composite application.

Collaboration

Collaborative functionality such as instant messaging, bulletin boards, email lists, web conferencing, and shared collaboration rooms have become an expected part of modern enterprise applications. The best applications integrate collaborative functionality in the context of an application so that users are not forced to move back and forth between multiple environments to do their work. SAP's collaboration services allow composite applications to bring collaborative functionality into an application context when and where a user needs it.

Mobile

Mobility services allow any type of application, whether an enterprise application or a composite application, to extend its reach to mobile devices. It provides one way of adapting an application that will allow it to support any number of specific devices.

All of the services just mentioned serve a similar purpose: expanding the potential of composite applications to meet any need in the most elegant way possible. With these services, composite applications should be able to bring together functionality from multiple service providers in a way that creates a more comprehensive context to meet users' needs.

What development tools are used to create enterprise services?

Enterprise services are created in many different ways depending on what is being developed and who is doing the development. We will discuss this in more detail later in this chapter and later in the book, but to complete our picture of enterprise services at this point, it is worth examining the different ways enterprise services come into being:

From the inside out

You can use SAP NetWeaver Developer Studio or ABAP Workbench along with the Web Service Infrastructure to make existing functionality such as BAPIs or IDOCs accessible as enterprise services. You can expose an existing BAPI, IDOC, or many other sorts of functionality through an automated wizard. If many services need to be combined or new functionality needs to be added, you can use Java and ABAP coding.

From scratch

You can use SAP NetWeaver Developer Studio or ABAP Workbench to define and code an enterprise service by hand. You can use this technique to create new services that extend the functionality of an existing enterprise application or custom services that may provide functionality unique to a customer.

From the outside in

You can use SAP NetWeaver XI Integration Builder and SAP NetWeaver XI Integration Repository, the precursors to the Enterprise Services Repository, to define interfaces for enterprise services in the context of a process that is being modeled and automated. Once the interfaces are defined, the services are implemented using one of the other methods.

Modeling environments

You can use SAP NetWeaver Visual Composer or the SAP CAF to create enterprise services through various forms of modeling. SAP NetWeaver Visual Composer focuses on the UI but will eventually play a role in modeling guided procedures. The SAP CAF allows modeling of the application logic, business objects, and external services inside a composite.

The common part of all of these methods is the fact that the interface description for the enterprise service is stored in the Enterprise Services Repository, which evolved from the SAP NetWeaver XI Integration Repository.

The business objects layer

If enterprise services are interfaces to reusable functionality for the automation of processes, process steps, parts of process steps, and utilities, business objects are the reusable units of functionality that exist within service providers to help implement enterprise services.

As mentioned so far, the business objects layer exists in service providers and enterprise applications to represent business entities. The newest generation of business objects was constructed with support of enterprise services in mind. So far, this is not a large group of applications. But as time passes and the mySAP Business Suite is enhanced over the next few years, more services will be automatically created from business objects.

Business objects are important for everyone in the SAP universe for two reasons. First, as services are built on top of the mySAP Business Suite, they will be created through a process of modeling. Process components will define groups of processes that are connected. Inside process components, processes will be modeled by describing through a modeling language how the processes will be automated in terms of enterprise services. The structure of enterprise services will then be described in terms of how business objects implement them. Even when the right business object does not exist to support an enterprise service in the next few versions of the Enterprise Services Repository, *notional* business objects—that is, business objects that exist only in the model—will be created in the Enterprise Services Repository to show how business objects would implement the enterprise services if they existed. In this way, business objects of the future will exist as notional objects in the Enterprise Services Repository alongside real ones to start showing developers inside and outside of SAP the future structure of the service providers that will use business objects to implement enterprise services.

The other reason business objects are important is that they are in use inside of composite applications, which have their own needs to create reusable units of functionality. Later discussions of composite applications in this book will show how business objects play various roles in composite applications: as a container for new functionality in a composite; as a way to combine existing services into a more useful form for use in a composite; or as a way to support the implementation of services that will be offered by the composite, for example.

So, what is a business object? It is beyond the scope of this book to explain every detail of how business objects that have been used in the past will work in the future, but we can provide a high-level preview in the following list and summarized in Figure 5-9:

- Business objects are collections of data and methods that act on that data to represent a business entity. Business objects are designed to be reused as much as possible.

- Business objects differ from programming language objects in that they do not have any sort of inheritance.

- Business objects have detailed descriptions of service operations and the data used in service operations that will make it easy to expose them as enterprise services using global data types.

- Business objects may have more structure, such as a state-action model that keeps track of the state of an object, how states transition from one to another, and what actions or methods are possible at each state.

- Business objects may keep track of associations with other business objects.

- The service operations of business objects may be constructed according to patterns that may be exposed in enterprise services and used to support higher-level patterns in UIs and processes.

- Business objects may initiate processes and send the information and instructions to other business objects to continue execution of a process.

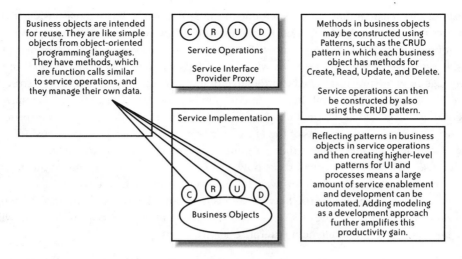

FIGURE 5-9. Business objects and enterprise services

Business objects represent a standardized structure that accelerates the implementation of enterprise applications, service providers, and composite applications. Business objects make it much easier to create and maintain the hundreds of thousands of enterprise services that will be needed in the future.

The process orchestration layer

The process orchestration layer contains the key mechanisms that create the flexibility that ESA must deliver to succeed. Enterprise services are the reusable building blocks built on top of business objects. Process orchestration is the simpler way that these building blocks are combined to solve problems.

The word *orchestration* has many different meanings in many contexts. Some people prefer the word *choreography*, which is sometimes used to mean the same thing. Orchestration became associated with SOA in the past few years because of the idea of web services orchestration, which was an attempt to create a language that could be used to combine web services to automate processes. Eventually, different standards efforts championed by different vendors were combined into the Business Process Execution Language (BPEL) standard. When many people speak of orchestration, they are referring to using BPEL to orchestrate the behavior of web services. But this is only one form of process orchestration as we use the term in this book.

What is process orchestration?

Since programming began, applications have controlled process flow. That is not what we mean by orchestration. We use the term to mean a form of modeling in which a simple set of abstractions is combined repeatedly to help solve a problem. The job of orchestration is to replace coding in Java and ABAP with modeling so that process orchestration is easier and more flexible, and can be performed by more people. As modeling tools have improved, more people have begun modeling. Process orchestration is one form of modeling. Modeling is also used heavily to create UIs and to manage system landscapes among other applications.

For this book, we will expand the notion of orchestration to include not only the high-level orchestration of enterprise services, but also the orchestration of any process using a simplified method, whether it is a guided procedure that is controlling the flow of work through a UI, or a workflow modeling technique in SAP NetWeaver AS. By "simplified method," we mean a mechanism that is much easier to use than Java or ABAP coding but that still has the power to allow a process to be constructed out of building blocks. The building blocks for BPEL are web services; in ESA, they are enterprise services. For guided procedures, the building blocks are callable objects of various sorts, including enterprise services, Adobe Interactive forms, and UI elements such as iViews. For workflow mechanisms in SAP NetWeaver AS, they are Java or ABAP objects. For process components, the building blocks are collections of enterprise services and business objects working together to solve a problem.

No matter what the building blocks are, the orchestration layer has a similar job. It must carry out the following tasks:

- Send and receive messages to and from the building blocks.

- Manage a process's flow of control as it moves from one building block to another. This includes deciding how the flow of control should proceed based on information provided from the building blocks.

- Keep track of any information needed in the context of the orchestration. For some orchestrations, this may mean maintaining the state of a long-running transaction, or it may mean keeping a collection of documents related to a guided procedure.

- Report on the state of the orchestration to other interested parties or to programs that are monitoring the process.

These tasks take on different forms based on the orchestration being implemented.

Why is process orchestration important in ESA?

Without process orchestration, the logic that controls processes must be coded in Java or ABAP. This makes the orchestration process difficult and complex, which shrinks the pool of people who can design and implement processes. Orchestration mechanisms simplify the process of defining an orchestration, usually through some model-driven development technique, which not only allows orchestrations to be created quickly but also allows them to be changed quickly.

Process orchestration also serves as a bridge between IT and business and as a form of documentation. Instead of writing a lengthy requirements document, process orchestration mechanisms can allow business analysts to describe, in an executable form, the automation of processes. The processes described through orchestration mechanisms serve as a highly accurate form of documentation, especially when the orchestration mechanism allows annotations to describe services that may be missing and are needed to complete the automation of a process.

What forms of process orchestration will be used in ESA?

SAP and many other vendors have been pursuing orchestration and a model-driven definition of business processes for many years. When XML arose as a standard and Enterprise Application Integration (EAI) systems were created, Business Process Management systems allowed orchestration based on reusable XML messages. Workflow modeling has existed for years in both ABAP and Java. What has changed in ESA is that now the building blocks for all levels of orchestration have a common element—enterprise services—and many different contexts for applying orchestration have been well understood through trial and error. The different forms of process orchestration in ESA include all of the following:

Frontend process orchestration

Frontend process orchestration is aimed at the UI and will play a big role in the development of composite applications. Frontend processes are conversational and user-centric. Certain types of processes appear repeatedly in UIs, and SAP has created orchestration mechanisms to allow them to be easily implemented. Probably the most important new mechanism is guided procedures, a general-purpose way of walking a user through a series of steps that may be occurring in many different applications. Guided procedures can easily start a user in a portal UI, invoke an interactive form to gather more information, and then use that information to use enterprise services to perform other work, and so on. Standard UI mechanisms show the user's progress through the process steps. Guided procedures can be built through tools that are part of the SAP CAF. SAP NetWeaver Visual Composer will eventually be able to construct guided procedures.

Backend process orchestration

Backend process orchestration is focused on high-volume flows of transactions that do not require a lot of manual processing. This sort of work includes long-running transactions. Backend process orchestration is frequently associated with EDAs and processes that are automated with a management-by-exception model. The CCBPM mechanism of SAP NetWeaver XI is SAP NetWeaver's primary backend process orchestration mechanism. CCBPM can route, map, and process messages sent at high volumes, keeping track of the state of many different transactions that may take place over weeks or months. Backend process orchestration is not focused on UIs primarily, although some UIs are always part of backend process orchestration to help monitor the process underway or to allow exceptions to be handled.

Service composition

Service composition has an element of process orchestration to it. Sometimes this sort of process orchestration takes place in Java and ABAP code, but SAP CAF has a service modeling environment that contains a simple mechanism to model the creation of a new service composed from other services.

Workflow

Workflow automation generally refers to the automation of a set of steps that occur within one application. In the context of ESA, workflows will still be used in service implementations and business objects to help execute a process that moves through a well-defined series of steps. Configurable workflow mechanisms exist for both Java and ABAP, and these mechanisms are powerful enough to invoke functions and enterprise services outside of an application. Primarily, however, workflow mechanisms are focused on automating processes inside a single application.

Process component modeling

Process component modeling helps describe the high-level structure of business processes. In ESA, process components are large building blocks created out of orchestrated groups of enterprise services and business objects. If the other forms of process orchestration reduce the gap between business and IT by making processes easier to model, then process component modeling closes an even larger gap between how the processes are related to business and how enterprise software implements them.

What are the limits of process orchestration?

Like any other modeling-oriented technique, process orchestration provides simplicity, but in doing so, it sacrifices some flexibility. While most process orchestration mechanisms provide some flow control mechanism, frequently this is simpler and less powerful than what is possible in ABAP or Java code. Certain orchestration problems will always be too thorny to be represented in one orchestration mechanism or another. The goal of orchestration mechanisms is not to handle every case possible, but to handle most cases in a simpler manner that does the job and lets more people participate, ending development bottlenecks. In most cases when orchestration mechanisms fail, it is possible to create a service that can do the job that is outside the scope of the orchestration mechanism.

How does process component modeling work?

Process component modeling is the newest form of orchestration, and it plays such a fundamental role in closing the gap between business and IT that it deserves a longer explanation. The other process orchestration mechanisms are primarily intended to accelerate development, but process component modeling actually spans the space between the high-level abstract descriptions of businesses and processes that use business scenarios and solution maps, and the world of enterprise services, as shown in Figure 5-10.

Three levels in process component modeling help bridge this gap:

- Integration scenario modeling, as shown in Figure 5-11, which shows how a group of process components work together

- Process component modeling, which describes how enterprise services are built on top of business objects to perform the work of a process component

- Process component interaction modeling, which describes in detail the interaction between two process components that are communicating with each other

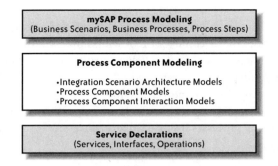

FIGURE 5-10. The role of process component modeling

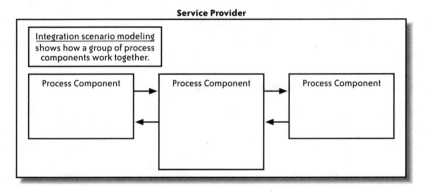

FIGURE 5-11. ESA integration scenario modeling

Figure 5-12 shows process component modeling and process component interaction modeling.

Process component modeling is so important because it attacks at a fundamental level the lack of structure and abstraction that led to the monolithic enterprise applications of the past. Process component modeling provides a tool that allows much of the structure of business that was never formally defined, to be captured and to be made clear and explicit. This sort of transparency has many different benefits, such as making it easier to identify gaps in end-to-end processes, making existing patterns in processes visible, helping to establish standards for solving the same problems in the same way, allowing flexible design based on reusing existing parts, and supporting outside-in development of new functionality based on modeling. Perhaps the largest benefit of this sort of modeling is its role as a communications tool that makes existing functionality clear to all interested parties and provides a tool for managing the growing complexity of business by breaking it down into smaller, more easily understood pieces.

Through process component modeling, the development process becomes much more connected and integrated, and specifications and requirements are communicated through the formal mechanisms of the model rather than through language, which can be less efficient.

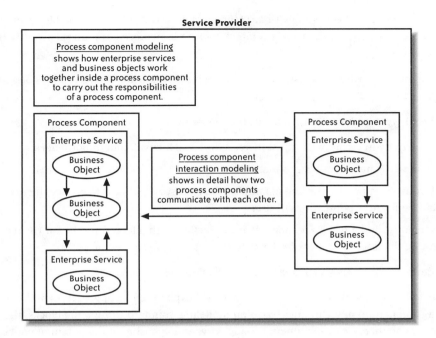

FIGURE 5-12. ESA process component modeling and process component interaction modeling

The UI layer

One of ESA's primary goals is to make standard software more powerful at every level. Using enterprise services and process orchestration, a given set of service providers, leveraged by composite applications, will be able to meet more requirements than traditional forms of enterprise applications. More processes will be automated. More people will be involved as users, not just as experts. More value will result.

Implied in this expansion of value, however, is another expansion, an expansion of do-it-yourself capability. SAP is creating ESA so that standard enterprise software can solve many more business problems. Delivering enterprise applications using enterprise services provides access to the building blocks that allow more processes to be automated. To automate a new process, existing services must be orchestrated and new UIs must be created to serve the needs of each role in the process. But who will do this orchestration and who will create these UIs? SAP, of course, will provide standard business applications built on enterprise services. Third parties will use enterprise services to add their own applications, building on SAP's suite of services. And IT departments will be able to automate new processes much more quickly and easily using enterprise services and model-driven development tools.

This change will involve an interesting transformation of the UI layer. More than 100,000 different UI screens came with SAP R/3. SAP has studied these UIs and discovered patterns that will allow the same functionality to be delivered in fewer than 10,000 screens. But under ESA, many new processes will be automated, which will result in a significant number of role-based UIs. Supply Chain Management (SCM) will be needed for every role in every process. The typical user will interact with many more UIs than is currently typically the case.

SAP will not construct these UIs, however; customers will, using the techniques described in this section.

For the UI layer under ESA, this means the following:

- Productivity in creating UIs must increase to avoid a development bottleneck.
- The new UIs must be easier to maintain to avoid a large maintenance burden.
- UIs must be created according to familiar structures and patterns to reduce the need for training for new populations of users.
- Users must find a way to manage their interaction with a larger number of UIs representing the larger number of roles they may play in automated processes.

In order to succeed, ESA's UI layer must meet all of these challenges.

As the following set of questions and answers will explain, ESA's approach to building UIs uses a combination of techniques based on modeling, standard UI building blocks, the use of patterns to increase development productivity, an expansion of the potential pool of developers, and a reduction in the burden of training and maintenance.

How will the UI layer change in ESA?

The biggest change in the UI layer under ESA is a wholesale introduction of modeling as a development method. SAP NetWeaver Visual Composer will be the primary modeling tool and UI patterns will be used to amplify productivity. The details of these two changes will be explained shortly, but their effect on how UIs will be structured is shown thematically in Figure 5-13.

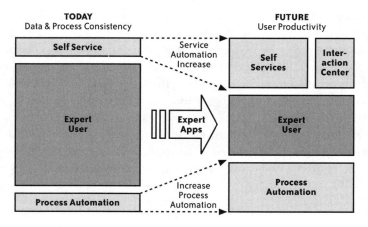

FIGURE 5-13. UI transformation under ESA

The message of Figure 5-13 is that as automation increases, the domain of the expert user becomes smaller as more users are able to meet their own needs. The interaction center box can be seen as a proxy for the way patterns standardize the operation of UIs so that the same common structures can be used repeatedly to solve new problems. Self-service means that users who are now asking others to do work for them through communication with call centers or with experts of some sort will do the work for themselves.

Replacing traditional sorts of coding with model-driven development offers several advantages:

- More than ever before, the UI will be decoupled from the underlying application functionality. Many UIs for different purposes may be powered by the same set of enterprise services.

- Modeling will make UIs more platform independent than ever before. The abstractions combined using visual tools will be captured in a visual composition language that can be rendered into any number of forms.

- Developer productivity will increase while maintenance and training costs will decrease because patterns for standard forms of UIs will streamline the process. Patterns give developers a running start and users a familiar structure.

- Based on modeling, pattern-based UI building blocks, and UIs automatically created from enterprise service interfaces, UIs may be generated on the fly in response to exceptions containing just the right information to allow a user to resolve a problem. While this may be a way off, it is not implausible and it shows the power of modeling and patterns.

These claims are dramatic, but in order to understand them better and to add to their credibility, it is important that we explain how this will happen.

How will modeling be used to create the UI layer?

SAP NetWeaver Visual Composer, shown in Figure 5-14, is a primary modeling tool for creating UIs under ESA. SAP NetWeaver Visual Composer is used to build all sorts of different applications, including UIs for the SAP NetWeaver Portal, analytical applications, and other, more complicated composite applications. Our goal is not to document the detailed workings of SAP NetWeaver Visual Composer, but rather to explain at a high level how it works and why it will achieve the goals of ESA.

The first thing to understand is that SAP NetWeaver Visual Composer will be used in ESA in two ways. Freestyle modeling is what most people think of when they think of modeling. In freestyle modeling, some sort of tool is used to create relationships with modeling primitives. In the case of SAP NetWeaver Visual Composer, the tool is a visual editing environment that runs on the browser, and the modeling primitives are UI elements and enterprise services. The relationships among the elements are captured in a visual composition language. When it comes time to run the UI, the visual composition language is rendered into some executable form. In the case of SAP UIs, iViews that run in the SAP

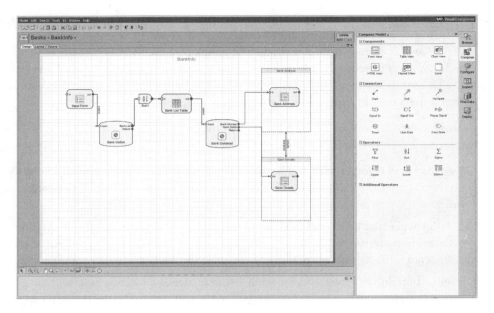

FIGURE 5-14. Visual Composer

NetWeaver Portal are frequently in the executable form, but not always. For example, for some applications the visual composition language was rendered into Adobe's Flex environment for building UIs.

Freestyle modeling starts to meet several of the challenges facing the UI layer. Development using visual methods is generally simpler, which improves productivity and expands the pool of developers from engineers to business analysts. The visual composition language separates the definition of an application from the implementation. The visual composition language can be rendered into many different forms for execution. Basing the application on enterprise services provides a clear separation from the service providers.

But freestyle modeling is not enough to meet all of the challenges. UI building blocks and patterns must be used to amplify the power of freestyle modeling and further reduce the training and maintenance burden, as the next question and answer will show.

What are patterns and UI building blocks?

UI building blocks and patterns complete the journey to a UI layer that meets the needs of ESA. What are they anyway, and how do they work?

As mentioned in Chapter 4, patterns have had a profound influence on software development for many years. For the purposes of UIs, a pattern is a relationship between certain components that is found to be repeated over and over again in various UIs. Patterns are useful because they can become the starting point for development. While developers use single UI elements such as buttons, text fields, and tables and then combine them in freestyle development, a single pattern may contain tens or hundreds of UI elements already connected to solve some common purpose.

For example, the tab pattern is one of the most commonly used patterns; it's used in Microsoft Windows for settings in the Control Panel such as Display Properties. At the top of the window is a set of tabs that represent different sections of an application or web site. When one of the tabs is clicked, the display changes to indicate that the tab is now active. When a UI developer realizes that a pattern may be useful, he may select a pattern and configure it for a particular use. Configuration of the tab pattern may mean determining the number of tabs and the name of each tab.

SAP's approach to UIs has three levels of patterns:

UI pattern elements
> These patterns have the smallest scope and are made up of basic UI elements, such as buttons, tables, trees, and such. They are configurable and reusable and include such elements as forms, lists, and object searches.

UI pattern components
> These patterns are larger in scope than UI pattern elements, and they do more work. Usually they focus on one user task, such as searching for and identifying an object, inspecting and maintaining attributes, or editing data with guidance. UI pattern components usually combine many different UI pattern elements.

Floor plans
> Floor plans are the highest level of patterns. They combine pattern elements and/or components into larger structures that are reused. Three common floor plans will be described later.

Another term, UI building blocks, refers to any one of these levels of patterns that has become part of a common approach to building UIs. For example, one of the most important UI building blocks is called the Universal Work List (UWL), which collects in one place all the tasks assigned to one user or one role.

Patterns then finish the job that modeling started. Patterns not only make developers more productive, they also allow UIs to be constructed out of common elements. Using a core set of common elements reduces the maintenance burden and means that many more UIs can be standardized, which should reduce training time.

Patterns can be implemented in many different ways. They can be collections of UI elements that are assembled using the visual composition language, or they can be implemented in technology such as Web Dynpro.

How will UI building blocks and patterns change the nature of applications?

SAP has created a set of UI building blocks that provide a general structure for organizing the work of a user who must interact with various UIs playing different roles with varying levels of frequency.

These building blocks address the challenges of helping users manage their work when faced with a much larger set of UIs, some of which they do not use that often. The two most important UI building blocks are the control center and the work center, shown in Figure 5-15.

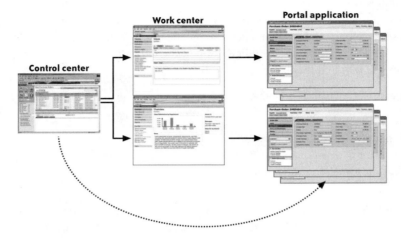

FIGURE 5-15. Control centers and work centers

These UI building blocks work together as follows. The control center is a combination of an inbox and a homepage for all of the work that is assigned to a user. The control center provides access to working content such as alerts, notifications, work items, news, reports, and information. At the heart of the control center is a UWL UI building block, which is a list of all of the alerts and workflow items assigned to the user. From the control center, a user can also see all of the documents, analytical displays, reports, and tasks that are relevant to her work.

It is assumed that each user is assigned a number of roles. For each role, a work center is created that helps organize all of the work that is required for that role. The work center may include information from one or more of the enterprise solutions that help carry out various tasks required by that role. Work centers that are visited often may include many elements from the enterprise solutions to allow frequently performed tasks to be done quickly. Work centers that are used less frequently may provide access to guided procedures that walk a user through the steps of performing a particular process.

Much of the work done by common enterprise applications can be captured using the control center and work center UI building blocks. It is important to remember that the control center and work center are just the first step in a journey SAP is undertaking in an effort to standardize as much of the UI as possible. Such standardization is perhaps the most important strategy to managing the expansion of UIs as more and more business processes are automated.

How will the UI be implemented under ESA?

One misconception related to the transformation of the UI that will take place under ESA is that all existing UIs will have to be rewritten. Fortunately for SAP and for customers, this is not the case. All of the existing SAP UIs created in the SAP NetWeaver Portal or in other manners can participate in the new world of patterns and UI building blocks.

The SAP NetWeaver Portal will remain the center of the SAP UI. Portal iViews will be the container in which all of the UI building blocks, floor plans, and patterns will reside. In turn, iViews from existing SAP solutions will be used as building blocks themselves and will be included in work centers and control centers as needed. Web Dynpro is being used to implement some of the most common and frequently used patterns in a highly optimized manner. And in special cases, such as analytical applications, the visual composition language allows other forms of UIs, such as Adobe Flex, to be used as a platform for UIs.

The persistence layer

Some people who look at the ESA stack are puzzled by the presence of the persistence layer. From one point of view, persistence really should not be visible in the stack because it is handled by enterprise services or business objects. Persistence is not a general-purpose part of the stack, but rather a feature of the underlying technology that helps implement applications. While this perspective has merit, we have chosen to include persistence as a separate layer in order to highlight the differences in how persistence must be managed in ESA.

There are two major challenges related to managing persistence in ESA, and both are related to the fact that data is distributed across a set of service providers.

The first challenge is restoring the single, consistent, unified view of data that was one of the most attractive features of the first generation of enterprise applications. One of the reasons Enterprise Resources Planning (ERP) became so valuable to companies so quickly is that it created a central location for one version of the truth. For small- to medium-sized companies, that is still the case today, but at large companies, that situation did not last long. Soon after the first ERP was implemented, other instances were quickly created. Not long after that, CRM, SCM, and other applications showed up, leading to the current situation of multiple repositories with duplicate and sometimes inconsistent data.

Under ESA, distributed databases are accepted as a fact of life. SAP offers three tools for managing the distributed data and assembling a consistent view of it: SAP NetWeaver Master Data Management, SAP NetWeaver BI, and the forthcoming techniques for distributed transactions. SAP NetWeaver Master Data Management helps create a centralized view of master data as if it were in a single database. SAP NetWeaver Master Data Management also has tools that help identify and correct inconsistent and incorrect data. SAP NetWeaver BI is a full-service data warehouse that can assemble a consistent view of master data or transactional data and offer advanced analytical and reporting capabilities. How both of these tools are used in composite applications is discussed in Chapter 13.

The second challenge is consistently writing data to distributed repositories. In the previous generation of enterprise applications, the transaction mechanisms of the database became the foundation of maintaining a consistent collection of data. Higher-level mechanisms in the applications were built on top of the basic functions of opening a transaction, making series changes, and then committing them or rolling them back. In a world of distributed repositories, this approach will not work. Data consistency must be more actively managed at the application level. If something goes wrong with a series of changes, the application must reverse the changes through compensating transactions. Transaction mechanisms for distributed repositories using services are on the way but are not yet completed.

How will this discussion be continued?

This chapter covered many concepts that are central to understanding ESA, but there is plenty more to cover. If you are interested in more details about these concepts, please see Chapter 12, which explains how the ESA stack is used in composite applications and the development tools used to create them.

CHAPTER SIX

The Enterprise Services Community

NO SOFTWARE COMPANY WOULD EVER CLAIM THAT IT IS SINGLE-HANDEDLY ABLE TO MEET EVERY ONE OF ITS customers' requirements. Instead, software companies work closely with systems integrators (SIs), consultants, hardware suppliers, and the customers themselves both formally and informally to jointly specify and develop extensions, modifications, and new versions of existing software products that can meet customers' evolving needs.

SAP happens to be one of the few software companies today that has the scale and resources to design and build software platforms that serve as the focus of activity for thousands of other companies and, arguably, millions of people. One of the reasons these vibrant ecosystems work is that SAP leverages a wide range of contributions to the benefit of everyone. SAP achieves this through the input of a highly valuable community of customers, Independent Software Vendors (ISVs), and other entities in the IT marketplace. SAP interacts with them through several important engagement models, including the PartnerEdge program, customer influence councils, Industry Value Networks, and now the Enterprise Services Community (ES-Community).

With the ES-Community for ESA, SAP is embarking on its most ambitious effort yet: to foster and engage with this broad ecosystem around enterprise services. SAP recognizes that for ESA to achieve its full potential as an architecture for developing new IT solutions quickly and in alignment with fast-changing business processes and strategies, the SAP ecosystem has to work more effectively than ever. Therefore, SAP has formalized the ES-Community to ensure rapid and focused innovation around ESA.

The ES-Community process is the mechanism for the diverse SAP ecosystem to provide input into the definitions of planned enterprise services, giving customers and partners direct access to the teams within SAP that are defining and implementing enterprise services. The program is new and flexible, and it will continue to evolve over time to meet the needs of the community. SAP sees that the best way to make ESA innovation flourish is to create and nurture an open community process.

What is the ES-Community?

The ES-Community is SAP's new program for enabling partners and customers to provide valuable input and feedback on the definition of enterprise services. This highly interactive program brings together the thought leaders of the community with a clear goal and under a robust legal framework to share ideas and innovations. The community serves as the primary roll-in channel for partners and customers to request new enterprise services from SAP and as the sole licensing mechanism for partners and customers who want to build solutions that take advantage of SAP's platform of enterprise services.

What is the value of the ES-Community?

The ES-Community has a direct impact on the business requirements and technical architecture of the evolving SAP platform by fostering targeted, business-driven feedback from community members. This allows:

- *Customers* to create more cost-effective, interoperable, customizable, and flexible business process solutions

- *ISVs* to leverage the depth and breadth of SAP's platform, thus reducing development time, driving down integration barriers, and freeing resources for innovation

- *SIs* to reuse enterprise services, shifting their focus up the value chain from IT integration to business process integration

- *Infrastructure providers* to tap into SAP's cross-industry platform infrastructure and industry-specific application suites to be more application aware and adaptable to business processes

Figure 6-1 provides an overview of the ES-Community process. This figure illustrates how information flows through the Definition Groups of the ES-Community and into SAP's products, which in turn creates value for the participants of the community.

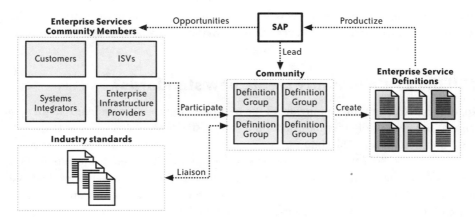

FIGURE 6-1. A high-level view of the ES-Community process

What is a Definition Group? Who can join?

The ES-Community brings relatively small groups of thought leaders together to discuss and design services. These groups are called Definition Groups. There are Request Definition Groups for the request process and Review Definition Groups for the review process.

All Definition Groups have a finite life cycle—they are not standing bodies or long-lived committees. All are required to deliver something of value to the community at the end of that life cycle. Request Definition Groups deliver a request for new services or service changes to SAP. Review Definition Groups deliver final service definitions, an accompanying platform update from SAP with the service implementations, and a test suite for community members to use in certifying products that are implemented to use the services in SAP's platform.

Definition Groups form, by invitation only, out of the diverse membership of the community. A company can have membership in many different groups depending on the interest level and input it can provide. In general, the leaders of the Definition Group will invite the thought leaders of the community, those who have relevant experience in the subject area, and those who have a demonstrated ability to work within collaborative environments to create community value. Having diverse participation within a Definition Group is important, but because these groups have a short, finite life cycle and are tasked with delivering value efficiently to the community, Definition Group leaders will balance the ability to deliver with the desire to be as inclusive as possible.

What does the ES-Community contribute?

The community creates requests for new enterprise services from SAP and provides input and feedback on the service definitions that SAP decides to put into its platform. Both of these outputs focus on the definitions of enterprise services and not on specific implementations, nor on any of the software for running the services. The community is designed to enable discussions around service definitions, leaving the creation of the platform to the product groups within SAP and the creation of products and solutions that consume the services up to the members of the community.

Will the ES-Community create new standards?

No, the service definitions coming out of the ES-Community are not standards in the same sense as the outputs of other industry and technical standards bodies (such as OASIS, the W3C, and RosettaNet). The community creates service definitions targeted at the SAP platform that SAP's customers and partners will adopt broadly. There is the potential for the ES-Community to work through a liaison relationship with other standards bodies as needed. This liaison relationship would enable the community to take advantage of any preexisting standardization work, ensuring that new definitions are not reinventing any preexisting successful innovations.

Most industry standards groups determine a standard in a fairly abstract way that is available for implementation on any platform. At that point, the SAP community has the chance to tweak the standard so that it works as efficiently and effectively as possible with the SAP platform while still meeting the original standard's definition. A typical opportunity for this kind of tweaking occurs when a standard's original definition is purposely vague. By being more specific about how the standard ought to work within the context of the SAP platform, the community creates the best possible version of it for the use of the entire SAP ecosystem.

It's also important to understand that the community provides SAP with feedback and input on more than simply Web Services Description Language (WSDL) files. The community also has the opportunity, through Definition Groups, to review and comment on SAP's business processes, business objects, and even global data types—all of the artifacts, in other words, that support the actual service operations.

How are enterprise service definitions created within the ES-Community?

Services are defined using two relatively similar processes in the ES-Community: a request process and a review process. The request process is used when SAP or another member of the community has an idea for a new service or a request for a change to an existing service. Once the community has completed the request, it is channeled into the internal SAP process for determining what should be added to the platform, and the community is given clear visibility into whether that request is accepted for the platform. The review process is used after SAP has committed to adding a set of services to the platform, enabling the community to provide important input and feedback as SAP is adding the services. This review process also provides early access to the definitions so that community members can begin creating products around the services, and it increases the transparency of SAP's product plans for the services.

What is the organizational structure of a Definition Group?

Figure 6-2 shows the structure of both Request Definition Groups and Review Definition Groups. Note that each member of the group has a particular skill set (i.e., business lead, IT lead, product manager).

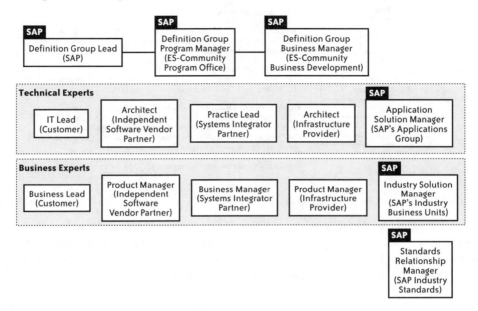

FIGURE 6-2. ES-Community Definition Group participants

How do Request Definition Groups operate?

Figure 6-3 illustrates the process that Request Definition Groups follow. There are three phases to the life cycle of a Request Definition Group. In the first phase, SAP works with customers and partners to propose enterprise services. These proposals are prioritized and approved. SAP then selects community members to form a Definition Group around the proposal. The next phase is a series of workshops and meetings in which the Definition Group builds a detailed enterprise service request. In the third phase, the final proposal is entered into a request pool for reconciliation and prioritization. Once the service request is completed, an evaluation license is made available to all community members.

How do Review Definition Groups operate?

The Review Definition Groups have four phases, as illustrated in Figure 6-4. Once a set of services is approved to be included in the SAP platform, SAP chooses which of those services will most benefit from a community review. The Review Definition Group is then formed around the set of services. The group reviews and provides feedback on a draft that is specific to the deliverables at each stage of the process. In phase 3, the final draft of the service definition is delivered to community members under an evaluation license, and all

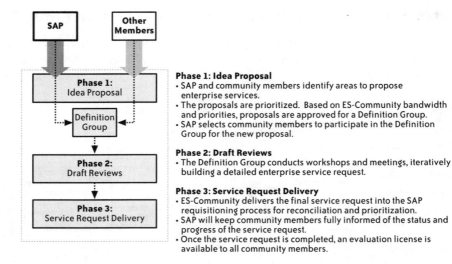

Phase 1: Idea Proposal
- SAP and community members identify areas to propose enterprise services.
- The proposals are prioritized. Based on ES-Community bandwidth and priorities, proposals are approved for a Definition Group.
- SAP selects community members to participate in the Definition Group for the new proposal.

Phase 2: Draft Reviews
- The Definition Group conducts workshops and meetings, iteratively building a detailed enterprise service request.

Phase 3: Service Request Delivery
- ES-Community delivers the final service request into the SAP requisitioning process for reconciliation and prioritization.
- SAP will keep community members fully informed of the status and progress of the service request.
- Once the service request is completed, an evaluation license is available to all community members.

FIGURE 6-3. Request Definition Group overview

members of the community can begin implementing their products and solutions that utilize those services. SAP also hosts an implementation of the service against which members can test their solutions. Phase 4 is the final delivery of the updated or new service, and members can begin certifying their products at this phase.

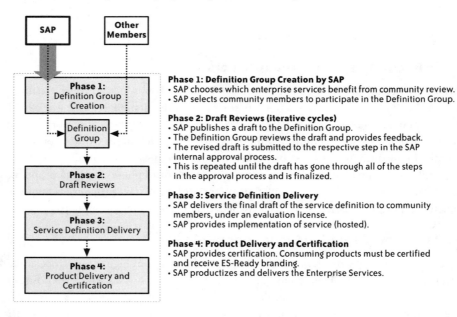

Phase 1: Definition Group Creation by SAP
- SAP chooses which enterprise services benefit from community review.
- SAP selects community members to participate in the Definition Group.

Phase 2: Draft Reviews (iterative cycles)
- SAP publishes a draft to the Definition Group.
- The Definition Group reviews the draft and provides feedback.
- The revised draft is submitted to the respective step in the SAP internal approval process.
- This is repeated until the draft has gone through all of the steps in the approval process and is finalized.

Phase 3: Service Definition Delivery
- SAP delivers the final draft of the service definition to community members, under an evaluation license.
- SAP provides implementation of service (hosted).

Phase 4: Product Delivery and Certification
- SAP provides certification. Consuming products must be certified and receive ES-Ready branding.
- SAP productizes and delivers the Enterprise Services.

FIGURE 6-4. Review Definition Group overview

What is certification? Is it mandatory?

Companies can license enterprise services that SAP ships in its products and makes widely available in order to create products and solutions that consume them. The license to create a consuming product includes a requirement for products that consume SAP enterprise services to pass a set of certification tests, ensuring the product meets the minimum compatibility and conformance requirements of the services. This certification is required for any product or solution that contains SAP's enterprise services.

SAP will also make available, through the ES-Community, an evaluation license on the same services, ensuring companies have the chance to review and evaluate the services before they are available for building a compatible product.

What is ES-Ready? How can partners use this brand?

ES-Ready is the branding available to products that pass the certification tests of the community. It is important to note that ES-Ready is a brand for products, not companies. Furthermore, the branding is available only for a specific version of a given product. If a certified product changes, it must be recertified to receive the branding again.

This branding is designed to ensure community value and create a substantial level of compatibility between the different products that come from the community. It is important for customers to be able to rely on the ES-Ready brand when making key purchases and for partners to receive value from the brand as a clear indication of community participation and collaboration.

How does the ES-Community balance efficiency with open participation?

One of the biggest challenges in designing a process for collaboratively defining services in groups such as the ES-Community is finding a reasonable balance between the competing interests of efficiency and open participation. It is not possible to create a high-quality service definition with very little input, even though it would be very efficient. Conversely, it is not possible to create a high-quality service definition in a timely manner if the process requires input from every member of the community.

In order to balance these competing interests, the ES-Community uses a flexible approach to the Definition Group process. The leaders of each Definition Group are empowered to decide how much participation will yield the highest-quality definition within the time constraints of the collaboration. This means that some groups will be small and very focused and others will be open to all who wish to participate.

What is required to participate in the ES-Community?

First, it is important to remember that only companies can officially become members of the ES-Community. Employees of member companies participate in the activities of the community on behalf of the member, but it is not possible for individuals to become members.

Each company is required to sign a membership agreement that includes a general NDA for the community process. The membership agreement also requires an annual fee to cover the operations of the community, and the creation and administration of the certification tests. Once the agreement is in place, employees of a company can be selected for participation in Definition Groups. A company may be a member of several Different Groups at once depending on its interests and capabilities.

How is intellectual property (IP) treated in the ES-Community?

It is important to state at the outset that any interpretation of legal documents—such as the membership agreement of the ES-Community—must be handled by a member's legal staff. No book can be an authority on specific legal matters such as this.

Some high-level characteristics of the IP framework of the community are worth noting, however. Members of the community do not lose ownership of any of their IP by participating in the ES-Community. If a member chooses to participate in a Definition Group and provides input or feedback that includes any IP that they own, that IP is automatically licensed to SAP so that it can be included in the definition and utilized for the benefit of the community.

How will the ES-Community differ from SAP's other partner and customer efforts?

The ES-Community is different from other ongoing partner and customer efforts in three primary ways. First, the ES-Community is focused on definitions of services and not specifically on SAP products. Other partner and customer programs are geared more toward SAP products and how SAP works with the ecosystem to take those products to market. Second, a robust legal framework supports the ES-Community and enables its members to participate without being overly concerned about how their IP can and will be used. Third, the ES-Community is not a give-to-get program (you don't get more by putting in more). Instead, SAP aims for broader acceptance of the definitions created by the ES-Community by making them widely available and encouraging participation through the community's meaningful impact on the resulting services.

How does participation in the ES-Community benefit customers?

Most of SAP's customers have invested heavily in SAP products and related activities such as training. As a result, they have a strong interest in further development of those products and solutions. The ES-Community presents even more opportunities to directly influence and collaborate with SAP and other industry leaders on the ESA platform. The community provides an excellent way for individual companies to work closely with other thought leaders within and outside of their respective industries—think of it as networking, but at a senior level.

What should a company do to get involved in the community process?

The first thing to do is learn about SAP's comprehensive ESA strategy by reading the articles and documents the company is making available on the SAP Developer Network (SDN) web site (*http://sdn.sap.com*). That ESA strategy is what guides the work of the community. Second, the company should review the membership agreement to ensure it meets with its business and legal objectives. Business development managers from the ES-Community Program Office are available to meet with interested companies about the membership agreement and membership opportunities. Interested companies can contact the ES-Community Program Office directly through its web site (*http://esc.sap.com*) or by email (*esc@sap.com*).

While ESA may be unprecedented in the breadth and depth of its vision, the process by which SAP's customers and partners contribute to the ongoing evolution of the enterprise services in the platform is very clear and concise. The sooner customers and partners sign up, the more quickly they can become involved in shaping the future of the platform. If you're a thought leader in your industry and you want to be able to influence the services in SAP's ESA, the ES-Community is the right place for you to get involved.

CHAPTER SEVEN

Creating a Roadmap with the ESA Adoption Program

As THIS BOOK HAS ELUCIDATED THUS FAR, ESA PROVIDES A TECHNICAL AND BUSINESS BLUEPRINT THAT can help large organizations structure and manage their IT resources in a flexible and efficient manner—indeed, in a way that provides unprecedented agility in business processes with no sacrifice in either IT performance or cost.

But what does an organization need to successfully adopt ESA? What steps must it take to get from here to there to implement this powerful idea in a way that assures achievement of its full potential yet with minimum risk? Where do business managers or the IT team begin, and what path do they need to follow?

Fortunately, as new as ESA is, there are solid, proven answers to these questions. Building on years of experience in helping customers to apply the latest IT methods and concepts, SAP and its consulting partners have worked out a rigorous and field-tested method for adopting ESA. What follows here is a step-by-step description of this adoption process and the thinking behind it. The description will necessarily be general, suited for readers in every industry, but the industry-specific examples that follow will help to illustrate in detail how the process is likely to unfold.

No single set of rules or methods is likely to address every enterprise's exact and specific needs. Those needs are by definition shaped by the pressures peculiar to each enterprise's internal makeup and strategy, its industry, and the business ecosystems within which it operates. High-technology manufacturers and chemical makers, for example, face radically different challenges in business and IT. While there is enough that's common to all enterprises in all industries for an essential ESA adoption process to be developed and put into practice with measurable results, there's no hard and fast rule that customers must adhere to SAP's adoption process. Clearly, some companies will alter the process described here in ways that suit them, and others will find success through using the process more or less as is.

Let it be noted that there's no magic involved, nor the need for any fancy new software or hardware. The first and most important steps in adopting a service-oriented architecture (SOA) are simply serious and fairly involved thinking and analysis—preliminary groundwork that will ultimately pay for itself many times over. Business managers and the IT team will work closely toward a goal of essentially reconceiving how the organization's business processes and IT systems should relate to each other in the context of the higher-level business strategies that they are jointly intended to support.

As SAP has outlined this adoption process, the enterprise will not work toward a "big-bang," all-or-nothing ESA implementation. That would be a mistake and likely a recipe for disaster, as has been proven repeatedly since the dawn of IT. Instead, the initial focus falls on a carefully selected set of business processes, or perhaps even a single process, whose decomposition into a set of enterprise services can yield positive operating results within a relatively short period. Speedy results, in turn, can be used to advertise and propagate the ESA vision throughout the rest of the organization, creating sincere demand for the benefits it has shown it can deliver. Indeed, if all goes well, a self-perpetuating snowball effect will take over and ESA will essentially sell itself to everyone who can use and benefit from it.

The benefits of this step-by-step approach are obvious. Perhaps especially in IT, it is usually better to walk before trying to run. One gain is simply political: if IT is able to showcase a successful, albeit limited, implementation of ESA as quickly as possible, the enterprise will be better positioned to win a buy-in from executives and line-of-business managers. Their support, after all, will be critical to the success of a full-blown, enterprise-wide implementation of the new services-based architecture. The incremental approach also helps lower an organization's exposure to risk because it facilitates change management processes, such as staff training, which are necessary for any successful change-of-technology strategy.

Why the roadmap approach?

An initial roadmap is actually a first scenario that shows how ESA can improve and optimize existing processes. Once a company has successfully created a roadmap, it may discover new areas for analysis, usually based on the priorities facing the business. The goal of creating and implementing roadmaps is to achieve a new level of flexibility so that IT can be transformed from inflexible, brittle concrete to a powerful collection of building blocks that companies can put together to solve today's problems and easily reassemble to solve tomorrow's. Properly defined, enterprise services lead to a faster response to unanticipated business conditions, perhaps with entirely new business processes.

What challenges do companies face in adopting ESA?

The biggest challenge any enterprise faces in moving to ESA is the past—the enterprise's own past, that is. This past often weighs down the present in the quite tangible form of legacy applications and layers of IT infrastructure. Due to various mergers and acquisitions, not to mention the decentralized IT purchasing that may have taken place in years past—departmental computing, data marts, and so forth—it's not uncommon for today's large corporation to find itself running a dozen Enterprise Resources Planning (ERP) systems, and perhaps at least that many Customer Relationship Management (CRM) systems. Generally, such corporations conceived, designed, and implemented these systems without the slightest knowledge or forethought of web services, enterprise services, or composite applications. Yet that doesn't mean they must be excluded from the new service-oriented IT landscape. It just takes a little extra thinking to meld them into a new architecture that's based on enterprise services.

The move from old to new—from understanding and managing IT as a collection of isolated, stovepipe applications, each one a realm unto itself, to running IT as an array of service components that can be snapped together like so many building blocks—cannot be achieved overnight. It requires careful and methodical planning.

There is another problem, too. Many people involved in IT for several years now have recognized the great potential of web services. Web services promise to help make it easier to connect disparate systems, the common wisdom holds, and all that's needed is to impose a few technical standards and this Linux-based system running Vendor X's database will soon be chatting away with that Windows-based system running Vendor Y's database. If only it were that easy. Without the right planning and architecture, the great potential of web services technology will be dissipated and lost as these IT-level services are created in a vacuum and with no foresight into how they might support and become vital elements of a comprehensive, enterprisewide service architecture.

How does SAP help customers adopt ESA?

SAP's program for adopting ESA is a formalized yet flexible methodology that turns the journey toward an SOA into a logical series of steps. Each step involves a team of stakeholders, and together they can streamline and simplify an otherwise complex endeavor and provide an evolutionary path. With careful advanced planning and consideration of all risk factors—technical, economic, political, and so forth—disruptions are kept to a minimum.

The ESA Adoption Program SAP has developed reduces adoption to a series of four sets of activities. It is a cross-organizational approach designed to align business and IT, help customers keep costs in check, and shorten the time needed to create a versatile, powerful foundation on which to build ESA.

The program is divided into four phases, as outlined here and as illustrated in Figure 7-1.

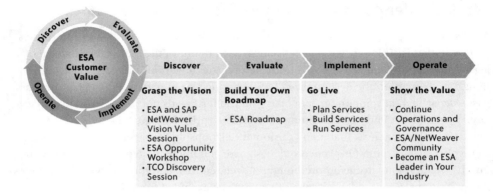

FIGURE 7-1. Phases of ESA adoption

Discover
> The user organization endeavors to grasp the vision of an SOA in general and ESA in particular.

Evaluate
> The goal of this phase is to identify a first set of valuable enterprise services to build, framed as a short-, medium-, and long-term plan.

Implement
> A new composite application is constructed from the services identified in the evaluation phase.

Operate
> The value of the new architecture is showcased internally and externally, allowing other companies to see the new solution.

Each phase is supported by SAP's portfolio of field-tested *enablers*, a dozen or so support services that include a variety of tools, templates, samples, and workshops. Because of the program's flexibility, customers can select these enablers on an as-needed basis and they don't necessarily have to start from the first phase.

No two enterprises will progress along the same path while working through this sequence of steps. Of course, SAP supports customers throughout the process with its consulting services and other aids. But any enterprise that does make the effort will be able to achieve similar gains: a good measure of mid- and long-term planning reliability, a major reduction in risk and complexity, and greater alignment across the customer organization. What's more, that enterprise will have the advantage of being able to leverage SAP's deep

THE SAP NETWEAVER CUSTOMER ADVISORY OFFICE

Helping customers is the job of the aptly named SAP NetWeaver Customer Advisory Office, which ensures that early adopters can leverage newly introduced SAP solutions effectively. The Customer Advisory Office works with account teams to identify customers facing common challenges who are moving forward with new solutions. They work to develop a complete solution from the new product introduction that can be replicated to other customers. The complete solution is then tested to ensure it can scale to other customers. The Customer Advisory Office takes care to coach the account teams and the customers to introduce new solutions at an early stage to ensure successful adoption. The Customer Advisory Office helps minimize the risk of failure for early adopter projects and at the same time speeds up the mass-adoption process for the solution for SAP.

and unmatched expertise in applications, services, business processes, and the modeling of business objects.

The guiding principle throughout is sober-minded evolution, not wildly optimistic revolution. The result will be an in-depth plan, or roadmap, describing in fairly specific terms what needs to be done at each stage of the adoption process, when to do it, and why.

We must emphasize that this four-stage adoption process is *not* intended to yield a complete, enterprisewide plan for adopting ESA. The aim is simply to identify a good starting point or two for trying out ESA and proving its concept in the context of a specific enterprise and its specific IT systems and business strategies. An incremental approach such as this makes it possible to leverage some early successes and thereby encourage other parts of the organization, and eventually all of the enterprise, to get on board and adopt ESA, too.

A key aspect of these sessions, making them particularly valuable, is that they inevitably help IT and business to better align with each other. Each side can describe what it believes as essential and, through give and take, can come to an agreement about how to proceed. Each side can identify the most pressing projects in its pipeline, and can work with the other side to hammer out a prioritized list of what should be done first and what can wait.

What happens in the Discover phase?

As the term *discover* implies, the emphasis in this phase (see Figure 7-2) is on learning and understanding. Line-of-business IT staff gather with SAP consultants in a series of workshops or interactive sessions that are designed to explore ESA's basic workings and its potential for enhancing the organization's business. Typically, IT and business leaders work together, brainstorming on the ways and areas in which an SOA could foster innovation and lower costs for their particular enterprise given its specific IT landscape or set of systems, and its specific business needs and strategy.

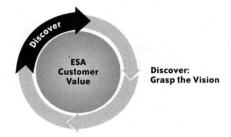

FIGURE 7-2. The Discover phase

The aims of these sessions are to:

- Grasp the value of the NetWeaver platform
- Identify opportunities for applying the enterprise services idea
- Explore the total cost of ownership (TCO) of this approach

In support of these goals, SAP has developed a workshop plan for each session. First, customers can participate in an ESA and SAP NetWeaver Vision Value Session. This provides a basic understanding of two entities: one a concept and the other a product that supports that concept.

Next comes an ESA Opportunity Workshop, in which the customer and SAP advisor/consultants explore the customer's key business challenges and how ESA might help to address them. As we'll see shortly, this workshop can be an eye-opener for many people, revealing the true power of an SOA while showing that this concept is not as new as one might think. The provision and consumption of services are pervasive in today's corporation, even if those services are not always rooted in IT.

Finally, a TCO Discovery Session identifies and validates the long-term economic advantages of SAP NetWeaver. A customer will see, for instance, how ESA can help reduce ongoing development costs, mainly through its ability to enable businesspeople and IT staff to work on relatively high-level, graphical models of business systems that SAP NetWeaver translates directly and automatically into functioning code.

What do the workshops reveal?

Let's look a little closer and see what these Opportunity Workshops strive for. Both IT managers and business managers must gain an understanding of just how new ESA is, how it does what it does, and how it offers a fundamentally new way for large enterprises to apply IT to business problems. Equally critical is a general understanding of the SAP NetWeaver platform and its business value.

Getting comfortable with ESA may require some determined thinking by newcomers. What makes the idea so new, of course, is that it centers *not* on pieces of hardware or software, but instead on the notion of services—self-contained tasks, that is, or building blocks of functionality, that can be called into action by other services or by people through well-defined and stable interfaces.

By definition, each enterprise service that an organization defines and makes available for use will consist of some business logic and a method, or technology, which enables individual workers, business processes, or other enterprise services to gain access to that logic. ESA's goal is to provide a single technology platform—in this case, SAP NetWeaver—for all enterprise services to use in a common, standardized way, a platform that also enables users to identify new services within their set of applications and business solutions. In many cases, enterprise services will combine functions that several disparate information systems currently handle, thus creating a brand-new, higher-level construct.

The first step toward implementing ESA, therefore, is to identify potential areas of enterprise services that promise to be particularly useful to the organization in question. These services won't necessarily map on a one-to-one basis to existing IT resources or business processes. Identifying these potential areas for enterprise services will likely require new thinking and analysis. You can find more information about the design and discovery of enterprise services in Chapter 4.

How about a concrete example?

Good idea. Let's suppose a U.S. manufacturer's high-level business strategy calls for expanding annual sales in the South American market over the next few years, and to achieve that growth, it has decided to rely mainly on indirect channel partners. This goal may appear to have little to do with ESA, but let's take a closer look. An executive in charge of this strategy might explain that the company will depend on indirect sales partners in South America simply because it is not sufficiently familiar with the business and sales culture in South America to succeed on its own. Listen again and you'll understand that this executive is actually concerned with the quality of a specific service—namely, a service whose focus is the selling of goods in South America. The company could decide to provide this service through internal means, setting up offices in South America, hiring and training the appropriate staff, and doing whatever is required to find customers and successfully close sales with them. Instead, however, the manufacturer has decided that South American channel partners can provide this localized sales service more effectively—with a higher level of quality and at a lower cost—than an in-house sales team could manage.

With this choice, however, the company has embarked on a plan that, to be successful, will require a costly and somewhat risky integration of its new South American channel partners into the main body of the enterprise. And more likely than not, setting up and managing that kind of integration is not one of the manufacturer's core competencies. Indeed, the company would do best to treat its sales partners strictly as providers of a service—as transparently as possible, with stable, well-defined expectations of what they are to deliver and how much they are to be paid for different kinds and levels of their services.

The lesson here is that this kind of service-focused analysis of business strategy often yields a clarity that a company's business managers will find tremendously valuable. If a company wishes to have direct power over its South American channel partners, more or less telling them how to do their jobs, then those partners become part of the company's internal business processes. Therefore, the company will have to invest accordingly, perhaps installing a full-blown CRM system to serve them, for example. But if those channel partners are treated as hands-off providers of a service, the manufacturer can safely reduce the investment in such systems by a significant degree.

In precisely this way, through reframing strategic business problems in terms of enterprise services, a company can begin to grasp the nature and ultimate benefits of the ESA approach. Of course, getting to the point where a company can conceive, plan, and conduct business and IT in terms of such enterprise-level services requires serious effort in analysis and planning.

This discovery process will make it clear that ESA is not just another IT concept. A company is most likely already using enterprise services, even though they may not go by that name or be understood in those terms, or it may not contain any obvious IT component. A good example is that of an external warehouse operated by an outsourcer under contract. Typically, this contract will bind the warehouse operator to provide a well-defined set of services at a predefined level of service and at a predefined cost, perhaps with incentives and penalties added to further structure the relationship. What truly matters to the company acquiring this service is that this warehouse service delivers the right goods at the right time, as expected. How or where or by whom this service is executed is less important.

In creating an ESA roadmap, managers who run key business processes can start to understand their business process strategy in terms of services. And they can do a much better job mapping those strategies to ESA, which empowers their business to the full extent possible. That is, by defining an enterprise service as being ripe for ESA, an organization learns about the underlying layers of business solutions and technology and can take advantage of those layers in ESA.

Executives will now be aware, for instance, that they must keep the interface between their organization and any provider of a service as reliable and stable as possible. This is a key concept with ESA, whether the interface faces outward to engage with third-party providers or connects a provider and a consumer that are both internal.

The main goal is to start to understand what changes will be needed to develop ESA, both in terms of manpower and IT elements. This understanding will be at a fairly high level, and the organization will understand that an ESA roadmap is not just another process optimization; it is an architecture that can cause a change in ownership, in moving activities, in creating a service provider organization, in reviewing corporate strategy, and so on. Executives will become aware, for instance, of the need for a vehicle to feed their applications with the enterprise services being created. At the same time, they will see that new skills may be needed. Take the example of that company seeking to boost sales in South America. Although its headcount in sales may shrink because the company is using external providers, the headcount will need to increase in the department that interacts with those new partners.

Are there different types of enterprise services to look for?

By drilling down to an appropriate level of detail, two types of prototype enterprise services may be identified: execution-related services, and those that support Master Data Management (MDM).

In many cases, a particular step of some business process will be standardized enough for it to be treated as an enterprise service. It will then be available for reuse across the enterprise and therefore able to yield economies of scale. For example, looking up the profile of a customer—postal address, phone number, email address, and so forth—is the kind of activity that lends itself to being provisioned as a service.

In some cases, though, a certain business process step may not be standardized across the enterprise. The reasons may vary: for instance, they could include local laws, regulations, or cultural factors. The best that can be done, therefore, is to create an enterprise service that accepts inputs from different sources but makes sure that master data records are updated in a standardized way. Depending on circumstances, this may be as far as the enterprise services concept can be taken in that particular area.

Take as an example the checking of customers' credit ratings. At first glance, this may seem like a perfect candidate for being treated as an enterprise service—well-defined parameters and a task that's typically handled by an outside provider. In Germany, however, legal restrictions might render credit checks to be quite different, in terms of scope and the kind of data returned, from the credit checks typically run in the U.S. As a result, a company operating in those two countries may depend on a different provider of credit-checking services in each locale. But to pursue the enterprise services model as thoroughly as possible, this company might also create an enterprise service that receives the data supplied by each of those services and, in a highly standardized way, makes sure that the data is clean and consistent before permitting it to go any further and update the enterprise's master data records.

How can companies avoid disruptive change?

Short answer: by careful planning.

In its ESA Adoption Program workshops, SAP works closely with each customer to identify its pain points and, in turn, the two or three business processes that make the most sense as the initial places to implement ESA. The customer IT team will work with SAP's consultants to analyze, quite closely, their firm's business processes and IT landscape. This analysis ranges from the organizational model to the specific IT systems to the structure of the business processes. Key to avoiding risk is that the analysis will take into account the interdependencies that may exist between different processes and underlying systems and attempt to evaluate the risks that may arise if any of these systems are significantly changed.

At this point, a company and its senior consultants will work together to select the best initial candidates for enterprise services. They will base their choices on an informed analysis of the potential value that each such service may yield, taking into account all relevant factors. The company must evaluate each process step on its own, using a standard compare-compute-analyze procedure, with the results presented in the form of a matrix that compares effort and benefit.

The goal is not to rush forward at all cost, but to make solid progress while avoiding too much disruption to company activities—to strike a good balance, that is, between costs, both direct and indirect, and the benefits that may accrue. The potential gains to be reaped from creating a new enterprise service may be substantial, but they must be weighed against negative consequences, too. For example, an enterprise may have recently upgraded a particular IT system in a major way, putting its end users through a trying period of testing and retraining. Aware of this episode, consultants might recommend postponing the implementation of any enterprise service that would affect that system and those users, just to avoid additional trauma.

As a company begins to see the first outlines of ESA, revealing in limited but growing detail the people, processes, and information integration that will be involved, it will have an increasingly concrete plan for moving forward. This plan, or roadmap, will show the optimal sequence of enterprise services to be created, one after the other. This development sequence is of critical importance because it will take into account not only logical interdependencies between different enterprise services, but also any preparatory work that a company needs to do before creating those services. For instance, with different partners providing credit-check services in different parts of the world, it's possible that each service would identify the same customer in a unique and different way. Without some kind of data-cleansing mechanism, these disparate customer IDs would pollute the master data record with redundant information. In order to proceed with the relevant enterprise services, the company must ensure that this data-cleansing mechanism is developed and tested before deployment.

To help determine dependencies, evaluate risks, and generate specific action items, a quality consulting organization will rely on the so-called SWOT technique. In a structured manner, consultants will weigh Strengths, Weaknesses, Opportunities, and Threats that each service brings to the table. Done properly, such a thorough analysis takes time but is the best way to identify potential problems before they become serious. Equally important, this analysis can show the owners of business processes, in explicit and concrete terms, just how the move to ESA will directly benefit them.

What happens in the Evaluate phase?

The goal of the Evaluate phase (Figure 7-3) is to design a customer-specific roadmap for reaching ESA. This roadmap will take into account vital details of the customer's IT systems and key processes such as interdependencies, IT practices, and the needs and even moods of the people who work with those systems.

FIGURE 7-3. The Evaluate phase

To help out, SAP offers two workshops: the ESA Enabling Roadmap Workshop, which is project focused, and the ESA Roadmap Workshop, which has longer-term vision and considers how the organization can tap into the full power of ESA. Together, these workshop sessions can provide the customer a point-by-point strategy for working with ESA. Depending on their circumstances, customers may choose to run either workshop or both in their development of a roadmap.

Let's look at them in more detail.

The Enabling Roadmap Workshop is not concerned with enterprise services per se. Instead, its focus is on identifying the customer's current applications, his IT infrastructure, the business processes those systems enable, and ultimately, the opportunities that may exist in this IT landscape for improvements. In this regard, the customer will be on the lookout for areas where two systems may overlap and where consolidation would improve the efficiency of the IT operations.

The ESA Roadmap Workshop adds to this analysis the notion of enterprise services. Its goal is to redraw the customer's IT setup in terms of enterprise services and show what it might look like after that transformation.

Now, after undertaking these two evaluation workshops, the ESA adoption roadmap will finally be ready for review.

What will the customer be able to see with the roadmap in hand?

With the roadmap in hand, the customer will be able to see:

- What needs to be done
- When to do it
- Why to do it

Thanks to the thorough analysis undertaken with guidance from the consulting team, the roadmap defines a route through and around all important constraints and logical dependencies. It details the prep work that may need to be done before certain enterprise services can be created, implemented, and brought into production. The roadmap puts all of this together in a single, well-structured document that can serve as a central point of reference.

The roadmap will need to be revisited from time to time, as the customer and consulting team implement ESA, encounter problems, revise plans, and respond to changing business conditions. Once the company creates the roadmap, it can hammer out a release, or roll-out, strategy—addressing an important question: what is the potential for disruption to daily activities as each candidate enterprise service is brought online? The goal, of course, is to keep disruption to a minimum. For example, a company's credit-check service may entail only the integration of information that can be turned into a service quite quickly. Even if the consulting team doesn't have such a service in its portfolio, the company may be able to use technologies to build the service itself.

An available-to-promise service, on the other hand, would be significantly more complicated because it involves not just checking for availability, but also making a reservation, and that calls for writing data to the appropriate system—a potentially risky operation if the proper controls and data-checking routines are not put in place. The most advanced service would also check on availability by polling partners' systems, too, which requires integration across companies—yet another exposure to risk, given how complicated that kind of integration tends to be. Clearly, an enterprise service of this complexity could not be implemented quickly.

It may be that some steps in a service can be done quickly in a few weeks or so; other more complicated steps may take many months; and one or two steps will require more than a year's work. Companies can perform this necessary ESA work one step at a time, with each step done as soon as possible.

What about the Implement phase?

In the Implement phase (Figure 7-4), customers plan, build, and implement their first enterprise services and then see them go live. This phase does not require a great deal of ESA-specific work, as implementing these services involves standard development procedures. Using SAP NetWeaver's robust set of tools, customers will plan, build, and run an initial set of services.

What happens in the Operate phase?

This brings us to the Operate phase of the adoption process (Figure 7-5), with the focus on showing the value of ESA, learning as much as possible from the preceding activities, and spreading the word about ESA's benefits.

At this point, the main question that customers will ask is simply this: what is the value we have achieved from our first ESA implementation, and how does it compare to what

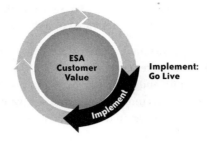

FIGURE 7-4. The Implement phase

FIGURE 7-5. The Operate phase

we expected? Depending on the answers, certain steps in the next round of adopting ESA may be improved. ESA can be used to easily support other business processes by creating new composite applications from existing enterprise services.

Is there more to success with ESA than just analyzing technologies and preparing roadmaps?

Yes, there is. Ultimately, implementing ESA across a large enterprise will depend on sociology as much as technology. It will depend largely on effective communications, for instance: training those in IT and in business units who will directly use and implement the new IT architecture. Stakeholders must be kept informed of what ESA means to them and their particular workgroups and organizations.

SAP has deep experience in addressing these issues, as encapsulated in its Customer Engagement Lifecycle, a set of best practices for planning, implementing, and operating major new IT solutions. The ESA Adoption Program is an ESA-specific variation of the Customer Engagement Lifecycle, since it helps the customer to understand how to define, adopt, and implement ESA.

One particularly powerful approach to fostering positive change in large organizations is to identify individuals who have sufficient understanding and charisma to serve as ambassadors of change. Because of the strong respect they already enjoy from others in the organization, such people can be major influencers, encouraging others to pay attention to the changes underway and to get on board, as it were. Once they've achieved success with ESA in a particular business unit, these "Black Belts," as General Electric famously called them during its campaign to spread the gospel of Six Sigma quality control, will champion the concept and get others interested and motivated to follow suit.

SAP's consulting group, and its consulting partners, can help with this process through formal service offerings. SAP also makes available the SAP Developer Network (SDN; *http://sdn.sap.com*), an online community and web site where ESA is currently one of the most active topics of discussion. Numerous tools, forums, and software downloads are available there. By May 2005, SAP had already created and presented a preview of about 500 enterprise services to its customers through SDN.

SAP's CIO Global Leadership Program provides opportunities for top IT executives to talk about what's on their minds, and here, too, ESA is an increasingly popular topic. Typically, some 30 CIOs are invited to spend a day together, talking to each other and with SAP executives about the ESA Adoption Program as well as about ways to innovate their companies, their experiences with ESA, and best practices and concerns.

How have companies put SAP's ESA Adoption Program to work?

Although ESA is a relatively new addition to the SAP lineup, customers are already reporting success with it. In this section, we will look at three such companies: Manchette Publicité, Wacker Chemie AG, and LHI Leasing.

ESA in action: Manchette Publicité

Manchette Publicité is the advertising arm of the Philippe Amaury media group, the owner of several major newspapers and sporting magazines including *Le Parisien*, *Aujourd'hui en France*, and *L'Equipe*. Manchette designs and sells advertising space in these and other publications, and has been doing so on the Web at its pioneering client self-service portal, *Manchettepub.com*, since 1999. While the portal has proven to be an effective and efficient vehicle—by 2003, 30 percent of its customers regularly used the portal and bookings had increased 70 percent in a single year—Manchette hopes to realize even greater efficiencies by automating the entire process of selling advertising space via a one-stop destination powered by enterprise services.

Manchettepub.com was originally built with the SAP Classified Advertising Management application from the SAP for Media solution portfolio. Customers could create their own ads and enter them into Manchette's system automatically, but the portal lacked interoperability with the functionality embedded in the company's other portals for different publications and for invoicing and payment processes. Manchette's management wanted to fold all of these abilities into a single portal accessible by every customer. After discussions with SAP Consulting, Manchette decided to adopt ESA as the path for doing just that. Each process used in its various portals—from inquiry to ad entry to payment—would be encapsulated using enterprise services as a separate piece of functionality reusable at a granular level.

Accordingly, Manchette decided to overhaul and redesign Manchettepub.com as a self-service, workflow-routed destination site composed entirely of enterprise services. If business conditions changed or a better user interface (UI) surfaced, the site and its services could easily be redeployed as needed, with the added bonus that Manchette's SAP and non-SAP applications could now coexist in the same portal.

With SAP Consulting's participation, Manchette's IT team held a series of workshops during which they analyzed the company's needs and priorities and created a roadmap for the construction of an enterprise services-enabled companion site to Manchettepub.com, named leParisienpro.com (after one of the company's flagship papers, *Le Parisien*). Upon its completion, Manchettepub.com would then be rebuilt using enterprise services and SAP NetWeaver, with Manchette's SAP for Media applications comprising the business logic layer for both. The construction of *leParisienpro.com* took three months, and *Manchettepub.com* is already under reconstruction.

The new portal allows clients to complete artwork and copy templates and check submission deadlines while transaction details are automatically routed to Manchette's accounts payable system for invoicing. Both sets of features have significantly reduced the amount of manual work performed by Manchette staff, a savings that translates to a 50 percent reduction in the cost of selling advertising space. Forty percent of the company's customers now use the portal, a figure expected to rise to 60 percent over the next two years.

Furthermore, Manchette has already reused the enterprise services comprising leParisien-pro.com to create a separate portal for public sector clients legally obligated to place financial notices in the local press. This new site, *Avispublics.com*, was built rapidly, with minimal development effort and cost, by reusing components in *leParisienpro.com*. Two-thirds of Manchette's 70 public sector customers were expected to use *Avispublics.com* by the end of 2005.

This site will be just the first of Manchette's many markets and lines of business to be automated. The company intends to expand from a business-to-business model into the business-to-consumer market with a portal for readers wishing to place their own classified ads from home. The company is even considering becoming an application service provider by marketing its enterprise services platform to other advertising agencies in France. Potential customers will then have the power to reconfigure the platform flexibly, to meet their own unique business needs.

ESA in action: Wacker Chemie AG

Manchette is not the only SAP customer to have had early success in adopting ESA. Wacker Chemie AG is a global chemical manufacturer headquartered in Munich, Germany. Its portfolio of subsidiaries is focused on semiconductor technology, silicone chemistry, polymers, fine chemicals, and polysilicon. As a 2.5-billion-euro-a-year business with 14,700 employees and 20 production sites in Europe, Asia, and the Americas, Wacker has begun looking to enterprise services as the means to integrate its specialized and far-flung operations flexibly.

Wacker's challenges stem from the combination of a strong ERP implementation and a complicated manufacturing environment with highly specialized equipment and the systems that run them. Wacker is using SAP NetWeaver as the platform to integrate its SAP R/3 system and production systems accessed via the Microsoft BizTalk platform within a unified, customized portal interface using enterprise services. Figure 7-6 illustrates this configuration.

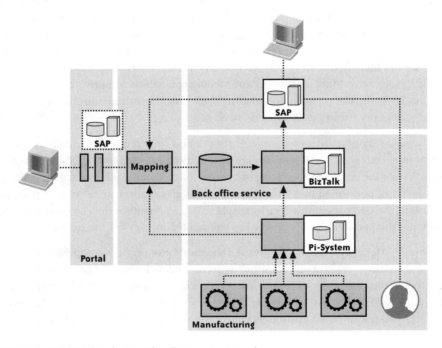

FIGURE 7-6. ESA at Wacker Chemie AG handling maintenance tasks

One example of the company's integration efforts is in the area of maintenance. Wacker tracks the lifespan and scheduled replacement of its manufacturing equipment components in two different places: in its production-level systems and within its SAP R/3 implementation. The former tracks a component's lifespan—i.e., how long it's been in use—and the latter contains a set of parameters and instructions that automatically order a replacement part once a threshold is crossed and that part nears the end of its natural life. The trick for Wacker has been mapping these systems together. Using SAP NetWeaver, Wacker has created a pair of services to map and manage the measurement metrics abstracted from the production environment's applications onto the parameters specified in the SAP R/3 implementation, all within the portal.

As a follow-up along similar lines, Wacker is investigating a solution to the common problem of tank management, included in the new architecture shown in Figure 7-7. A major task in the chemical industry is the storage of liquid chemicals in tanks. Monitoring the status of tanks—how full or empty they are—is the responsibility of Wacker's SAP R/3 system, but the data calculated via process orders and stored in SAP R/3 is often at odds with the reality of tank levels, for any number of reasons. A difference of two or three liters may be acceptable, but at a higher difference, a warning is required. In Wacker's proposed solution, a set of enterprise services monitoring real-world tank levels will be integrated over BizTalk and within another SAP NetWeaver portal with the SAP R/3 data, resulting in an interface that illustrates the difference between the real and "official" amounts in each tank, along with how that difference has changed over time.

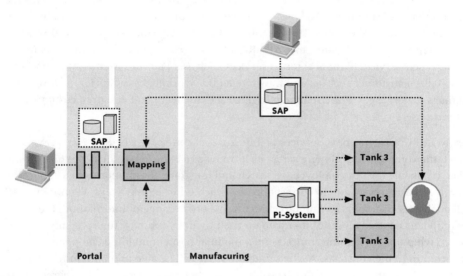

FIGURE 7-7. ESA at Wacker Chemie AG providing tank-monitoring capabilities

ESA in action: LHI Leasing

Bringing innovative new products to market as quickly as possible is a key to success in every industry these days, and that certainly applies to writing leases for retail real estate.

Just ask LHI Leasing, a Munich-based leader in the field, which manages some 1,600 virtual corporations whose combined assets total 16 billion euros. LHI's retail department store customers demand an increasing variety and complexity of financial products, such as structured financing. As LHI moves into the middle market, it needs to quickly update and change standardized contracts and combine them with other products.

Naturally, speed and flexibility in product offerings demand speed and flexibility in IT. However, LHI found recently that its monolithic ERP system just wasn't up to the job. So, LHI turned to SAP for help in adopting ESA and laying the groundwork for a new IT landscape. The goal: long-term flexibility while providing current users with tangible short-term benefits. With help from SAP's consulting organization, LHI worked up the first version of its ESA adoption roadmap in a matter of weeks.

First, a series of workshops were conducted to lay out the concepts and language of ESA for the sake of LHI's business and IT managers. These workshops also served to help the SAP consulting team gain a solid understanding of LHI's business practices. They quickly identified reporting, employee and manager self-service, and knowledge management as business processes that were particularly well suited to early use of ESA and that would be able to produce quick wins for LHI. The SAP consultants also drilled down on specific business scenarios in order to craft a high-level design for LHI's overall enterprise services architecture.

The result was a roadmap sketching out activities over the short and long terms. This roadmap provided a list of potential risks, a management summary, and a three- to five-year timeline for major milestones. The timeline laid out the schedule on which LHI was to implement ESA with the latest mySAP ERP solution, create portals for employee and manager self-service, harness external services such as a FileNet system that generated personalized customer reports, and integrate ad hoc workflow systems for creating new products. Later stages of the roadmap covered the discovery and design of customized enterprise services.

Key to LHI's new enterprise services architecture, of course, will be SAP NetWeaver, which the company is deploying across its intranet and extranet. At first, this platform will make it possible for LHI employees to search and integrate information across applications via a web-based portal and to correspond with each other in new ways. Eventually, LHI will enable its customers to gain direct access to a broad range of information, too, and even update selected pieces of that data on their own. Eventually, the company will be able to whip up new leasing contracts on a modular basis, combining components extracted from old contracts. At the same time, LHI will be able to maintain records of each lease in a form that's easily accessible for yearly financial and regulatory reporting purposes.

The next step will be to work with SAP Consulting in analyzing still more business processes within LHI and identify additional candidates for delivery in enterprise services form. As it implements the roadmap, LHI stands to save considerable expense. With its IT infrastructure resembling a set of reusable services, as opposed to a collection of self-contained applications, LHI will be able to quickly create, try out, and refine new leasing and asset management products to meet every change in business conditions. In short, LHI is on its way to becoming a sort of department store itself, offering just the right product for every customer.

PART THREE

Consuming Services

CHAPTER EIGHT

The Enterprise Services Repository and the Enterprise Services Inventory

I**N MANY WAYS, THE ENTERPRISE SERVICES REPOSITORY IS THE HEART OF ESA. THE ENTERPRISE**
Services Repository is the design-time repository of service objects for ESA. Before we
unpack that more technical definition, let's frame the Enterprise Services Repository and
Enterprise Services Inventory in simpler terms.

A *repository* is essentially a container, as shown in Figure 8-1. According to Wikipedia, a
repository is a central place where data is stored and maintained. SAP offers the container—the Enterprise Services Repository—and its contents—the enterprise service
descriptions defined in the Enterprise Services Inventory (see Figure 8-2)—as part of the
SAP NetWeaver platform.

What is an *inventory*? It's a detailed list of all items that a company has in stock. The Enterprise Services Inventory is a set of services that SAP has provided to its customers. The initial version of the Enterprise Services Inventory includes some 500 enterprise services.
Additional services will be added to the Enterprise Services Inventory over time by SAP
and by customers and partners participating in the Enterprise Services Community (which
is discussed in Chapter 6).

A repository includes:

the container   and its contents

FIGURE 8-1. A repository and its contents

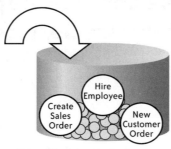

SAP and the Enterprise Services Community
offer the container and its contents

FIGURE 8-2. A simplified view of the Enterprise Services Repository and the Enterprise Services Inventory, which it contains

By providing not only the container—the Enterprise Services Repository—but also the contents—the enterprise services themselves—SAP's approach to service-oriented architecture (SOA) can be seen as dramatically different from that of its competitors. Of course, the Enterprise Services Repository is further enriched with services that your organization may add for your own use. You might also choose to submit the services you create to the Enterprise Services Community for possible inclusion in the Enterprise Services Inventory offered to all customers.

In the first part of this chapter, we will talk about the Enterprise Services Repository; later in this chapter, we'll cover the Enterprise Services Inventory.

Before we delve deeper into the Enterprise Services Repository, however, let us make it perfectly clear: the Enterprise Services Repository, simplified graphics aside, does not contain the services themselves. The service definitions are what reside in the Enterprise Services Repository; the implementation of the services is stored in the development environments (more on that topic in Chapters 15 and 16). What the Enterprise Services Repository includes, however, is vital. It includes everything we need to design services using a model-based approach, reusing data types, message types, and entire operations if desired.

The Enterprise Services Repository is still evolving. As we move through the chapter, we will describe where the Enterprise Services Repository is today, and, where relevant, we will provide you with a glimpse of its future direction. The Enterprise Services Repository is evolving quickly, and it's quite possible that by the time you are actively using it in your own ESA implementation, these features of the future will be a current reality. Having a more complete concept of the Enterprise Services Repository from the outset will help you form your ESA strategy.

In this chapter, we'll describe the Enterprise Services Repository from a number of angles. We'll talk about the nature of the Enterprise Services Repository, its roots, its advantages, and what is in it. Finally, we'll look at the Enterprise Services Inventory: a collection of services that SAP provides to help users get started on the path to ESA adoption.

What is the Enterprise Services Repository?

The Enterprise Services Repository is the design-time repository of service objects for ESA. What do we mean when we call the Enterprise Services Repository a *design-time repository*? This term refers to the process of designing services. There are essentially two methods for creating enterprise services: from the inside out and from the outside in (see Chapter 15 for detailed examples of these two methods). Inside a service is its implementation, the code itself. With inside-out development, you start with code—that is, existing application functionality. You then service-enable this functionality and turn it into a web service using a wizard. Inside-out development is straightforward; you take an existing function like a BAPI and turn it into a web service. It's helpful and easy, but not really anything new.

Outside-in development takes a process-oriented, model-driven approach. Instead of starting with the application, as in more traditional application development, you start with your business, examining your business processes from end to end. You focus on particular business processes that bring you the most value. You then model these business processes and map them to the services you need to bring them to life. You start from the outside—your business needs—and work your way in to the implementation.

This is where the Enterprise Services Repository comes in. To start with, you model data types and service interfaces in the Enterprise Services Repository. Because you're starting in the repository, you can reuse data types and interfaces that already exist. Having a central repository as a starting point enables orderly development, reuse, and enforcement of governance rules. Because you are doing your design work in the Enterprise Services Repository, and because everything you need for designing services is included in this central repository, the Enterprise Services Repository is a design-time repository. Let's qualify that a little. Everything you need for creating services might not be in this repository; you may want to import software components into the repository, for example. The point is that not only is the repository the central starting point for design, but also that it should be. If something you need is not in the repository, you model it there or import it into the repository. If everyone who is creating services works from the outside in, orderly development and reuse become the norm rather than the exception.

Figure 8-3 shows specification time, design time, and implementation time.

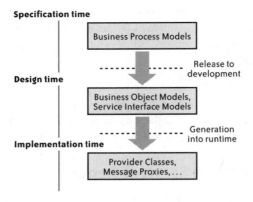

Specification time

Business Process Models

— — — — — — — — Release to
development

Design time

Business Object Models,
Service Interface Models

— — — — — — — — Generation
into runtime

Implementation time

Provider Classes,
Message Proxies, . . .

FIGURE 8-3. The Enterprise Services Repository in relationship to the development process

After modeling data types and service interfaces, you generate proxies in the Enterprise Services Repository, and the action moves to the implementation phase. The generated proxies are code skeletons that a developer will flesh out in the appropriate development environment, whether the ABAP Development Workbench or the SAP NetWeaver Developer Studio for Java (.NET support is coming as well). The Enterprise Services Repository is directly linked to these tools, so work flows seamlessly from one phase to the next. From implementation time, the service moves on to runtime. To be specific, the service is released to the SOAP* runtime, which is part of the SAP NetWeaver Application Server (SAP NetWeaver AS). Note that the tools create all the necessary XML entities for you; you do not need to write XML yourself.

Looking ahead, the Enterprise Services Repository is the design-time repository for ESA, and that won't change. One important change on the horizon, however, is the integration of the ARIS modeling tool into the Enterprise Services Repository. Today ARIS is available as a separate product, but its integration into the Enterprise Services Repository marks a step in which specification time also centers on the repository. We will discuss the integration of ARIS modeling and its implications for the Enterprise Services Repository in more detail later in this chapter.

What are the Enterprise Services Repository's roots?

To understand where the Enterprise Services Repository has come from, you need to understand SAP NetWeaver Exchange Infrastructure (SAP NetWeaver XI).

SAP NetWeaver XI plays an important role in development. Specifically, SAP NetWeaver XI helps with integration scenarios in which messages from different organizations, different XML vocabularies, or different systems are mapped to provide a robust integration that does not rely on custom development efforts.

---

* For details on web services standards such as SOAP, see Chapter 14.

SAP NetWeaver XI includes the Integration Repository, the Integration Builder, and the Integration Server. The Integration Server continues to act as an integration broker, brokering at runtime services that require more complicated integrations or mappings to translate between systems.

The Enterprise Services Repository is an evolution of the SAP NetWeaver XI Integration Repository. This means that the Enterprise Services Repository includes everything that was formerly in the SAP NetWeaver XI Integration Repository and a great deal more. All existing SAP NetWeaver XI business processes, interfaces, and data types are naturally part of the Enterprise Services Repository. The interface to the Enterprise Services Repository is through the Enterprise Services Builder, which is an evolution of the SAP NetWeaver XI Integration Builder.

What are the advantages of the Enterprise Services Repository?

Having a central repository offers several distinct advantages, including:

- Orderly development
- Reuse
- Ease of development
- Model-driven development
- Service orchestration

Let's look at each advantage in more detail.

Orderly development

Having a central repository based on structured data makes development an orderly process rather than a free-for-all in which applications are developed only to solve a particular problem.

Consider how development has been done in the past. A developer looks at a problem and invents a way to solve it. There are nearly as many ways to solve problems as there are developers, so inevitably this method leads to a lack of uniformity and transparency. Reading another person's code can be tricky at best.

Development from the outside in is a more disciplined approach that promotes reuse. Starting with a central repository reinforces governance rules.

From a development perspective, there's another feature of the Enterprise Services Repository that isn't often noted. You can think of the Enterprise Services Repository as the mother of all development tools, ensuring orderly development. How does it do that? In addition to everything else we've discussed about the Enterprise Services Repository so far, the Enterprise Services Builder provides inherent support for software logistics features such as versioning, as well as a robust change management system. The repository includes an object history for each object it contains.

The Enterprise Services Repository helps companies promote governance such as adherence to standards like global data types, and it brings about uniformity. Looking ahead, the Enterprise Services Repository will include business objects, which are larger units of functionality. In brief, a business object is an identifiable business entity, such as a sales order or a purchase order. Business objects feature a certain uniformity in the types of operations they offer, including creating, deleting, and updating. This homogeneity in turn creates transparency. If everything is framed in the same way, a developer who has worked on one part of a system can easily work on another part. A future version of the Enterprise Services Repository will incorporate business objects as a key larger building block for enterprise services.

The Enterprise Services Repository is the centerpiece of ESA in an effort to shift from one-off solutions and brittle integrations to a robust SOA that provides business value and flexibility to change in response to market conditions without fear that making a change in one area will break integrations in other areas. An orderly approach ensures that development is disciplined and structured in ways that maximize business value.

Reuse

The presence of a central repository also enables reuse of its elements. When you are modeling, you can scan the repository to see if any elements can be reused or adapted. This in turn fosters orderly, robust, efficient development. And of course, it saves time as well.

In the Enterprise Services Repository, you can efficiently design services that reuse data types and even entire service interfaces. You can also ascertain what is missing and model the entities that you need to create.

By having all service objects available in a common repository, you can avoid reinventing the wheel and maximize reuse. All service interfaces are registered in the Enterprise Services Repository.

For example, consider a common feature that is typically handled through two completely different applications: taking an order. A business partner might send an order electronically, with essentially an application-to-application/business-to-business connection. For smaller partners, you might offer a self-service user interface (UI) or a telephone ordering system where employees in turn feed the data to a similar UI. Despite the similarity in the data exchanged, such applications are typically created as entirely different programming efforts. With the Enterprise Services Repository, a large portion of the process can reuse the same data types and service interfaces. When the process or data elements change, the reuse inherent in the repository ensures that the changes are minimal, and certainly duplication of effort is eliminated.

In addition to reuse, services can be adapted and repurposed. The repository makes it possible to see what is there and what you need to add, easily. And what you add becomes another part of the repository that someone else can reuse.

Because of the adherence to open standards, services created in other systems can also be reused by importing them into the repository; data types and service interfaces are created automatically when you do the import.

Ease of development

Let's focus for a moment on how the Enterprise Services Repository and related tools ease development by doing your work for you. Developing enterprise services involves the creation of XML files, including Web Services Description Language (WSDL) files. With the Enterprise Services Repository approach, all XML entities are generated for you; there is no need to write XML or even tweak it unless you want to. By abstracting this complexity, those involved in creating enterprise services can retain a business focus and not be caught up in these details unless there is a specific need to tweak the generated XML. Because ESA is solidly built on open standards, tools can generate XML for you without intervention. And as we will see in Chapter 15, flexibility is not hindered by this automatic generation. Four styles of WSDL are generated automatically, though one style, the document style, will be chosen most frequently to maximize interoperability. Further, model-driven development, as described next, involves generating proxies of services that once again ease development work by providing a starting point for implementation.

Model-driven development

Having a central repository enables a new approach to application development: model-driven development, in which you start with business processes rather than with application code. The central repository grounds these models in reality, tying them to service objects and data types in the repository.

One of the fundamental principles of ESA is that you start with business processes and create strategic services that will support these processes. As we will see later in this chapter, in the section "What is the Enterprise Services Inventory?," you can move from solution maps and drill down to individual services in the repository. This is ultimately a description of the outside-in approach: starting with business processes and moving in toward the fine-grained details of implementation.

Today when creating services from the outside in, you model data types and service interfaces in the repository. In the future, the Enterprise Services Repository will incorporate ARIS models, allowing more specification work to occur in the repository as well. (As mentioned earlier, ARIS is available today as a separate product.)

Service orchestration

The Enterprise Services Repository also plays an important role in service orchestration. The Enterprise Services Repository represents a central modeling layer, which guides implementation from high-level business models right down to callable enterprise services. No matter whether you are reusing services or business objects from SAP applications, those created by a third party, or your own custom development, the repository acts as a central hub for coordinating all of these activities and ensuring uniform development, order, and efficiency.

What tools do you use to access the Enterprise Services Repository?

You use the Enterprise Services Repository directly through the Enterprise Services Builder. The Enterprise Services Builder provides a variety of editors for working with different repository objects. Repository objects are related to various open standards (for example, service interfaces use WSDL). The System Landscape Directory serves as a central information repository for your system landscape. A system landscape consists of a number of software and hardware components that depend on each other with regard to installation, software updates, and demands on interfaces. Software component versions can be imported into the Enterprise Services Repository from the System Landscape Directory (see Figure 8-4).

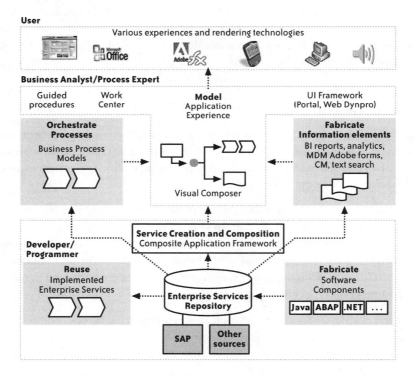

FIGURE 8-4. The Enterprise Services Repository's role in composition

The Enterprise Services Builder is the tool for creating and editing service objects, models, and interfaces contained in the Enterprise Services Repository. While the Enterprise Services Builder is the tool for interacting with the Enterprise Services Repository for both creating and composing services, sometimes developers need to see what is in the Enterprise Services Repository from their development environments. The Enterprise Services

Browser provides a window into the Enterprise Services Repository from development tools such as the ABAP Development Workbench and SAP NetWeaver Developer Studio.

Using the Enterprise Services Browser, you can browse the objects in the Enterprise Services Repository and generate proxies for them. The WSDL descriptions of these objects are then retrieved from the Enterprise Services Repository and form the basis for generated proxies for those objects. Although the Enterprise Services Repository can be accessed in this way through the Enterprise Services Browser, in order to create or modify objects in the repository, you launch the Enterprise Services Builder.

If the Enterprise Services Repository is at the heart of ESA, don't less technical people use it, too?

Modeling data types and creating service interfaces is typically the province of developers. That's why you will find detailed descriptions of these processes in Chapter 15. As we have described throughout this book, ESA allows a much broader group of people to consume enterprise services, compose new applications using enterprise services, and even create new enterprise services. We've mentioned how developers and programmers use the Enterprise Services Repository through the Enterprise Services Builder. Figure 8-4 shows all the touchpoints that leverage the Enterprise Services Repository. Users interact with the repository through a variety of interface types, as shown at the top of this figure. These interfaces are constructed by business analysts using a variety of tools, including SAP NetWeaver Visual Composer. The repository also plays a role in the orchestration of business processes and in analytics. We've already highlighted the role of the Enterprise Services Repository in service creation and composition.

The role of the Enterprise Services Repository in all these areas will become clearer as you read further in this book. This chapter marks the beginning of a deeper dive into the full implications of consuming and composing services, tasks that are the province of business experts. Chapters 9 and 10 will delve into specifics about consuming services, including a discussion of Project Mendocino, which uses service consumption to provide robust integration of SAP application functionality through Microsoft Office. Chapters 11 through 13 provide important details about how business analysts can use existing services to compose new applications, through the SAP Composite Application Framework (CAF) at the center of Figure 8-4. We don't want to steal the thunder from those critical chapters here, but rather to show you visually that all of these approaches to service consumption, composition, and creation are ultimately tied back into the Enterprise Services Repository.

What is in the Enterprise Services Repository?

Now it's time look at the contents of the Enterprise Services Repository in more detail. Figure 8-5 provides an overview of what is in the Enterprise Services Repository, including service objects, integration objects, and process models.

Let's look at each element in a bit more detail.

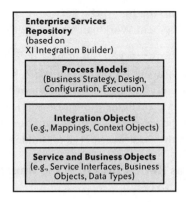

FIGURE 8-5. What's in the Enterprise Services Repository

Data types

Data types are the lowest-level element from which we construct services. Data types are used in business objects and they are used in interfaces. They are very basic building blocks.

How did the focus on standardizing data types for reuse come about? Like many companies, SAP discovered over time that the definition of a given data type in one software module might differ from a similar data type in another module. In an effort to standardize both internally and externally and therefore achieve greater interoperability, SAP chose to adopt the UN/CEFACT standard for global data types. This international semantic standard ensures maximum reusability and ease of integration. As a result, developers can't just create data types on a whim. Instead, creating a data type is subject to a governance process, where standards personnel work to figure out whether the proposed addition is redundant with other data types. (For more details on ESA governance, see Chapter 17.)

The use of global data types ensures standardization and interoperability. To describe global data types, another open standard is used: XML Schema Definition (XSD). XSD allows for cardinality, default values, and facets. Data types can be nested. They can be created using the data type editor or imported from XSD documents. They can also be exported from the repository as XSD documents.

Message types

Message types are XML entities that describe the messages the service will send over the wire. Message types are the design-time representation of the messages that are exchanged at runtime.

Operations

You can think of an *operation* as what the service does. Operations are the specific actions that the service can perform at runtime. An operation can be synchronous or asynchronous. A synchronous message waits or blocks until it receives a response (a telephone call is synchronous, as an example). An asynchronous message is sent and may receive no response at all (an email message is asynchronous). More germane to ESA, you can think of an order sent from a business partner electronically as an asynchronous message.

Service interfaces

Service interfaces are the metadata description of messages and operations used at runtime.

Currently, service interfaces have one operation per service. In an upcoming version of the Enterprise Services Repository, they will offer multiple operations per service.

Service interfaces have a direction attribute that defines them as outbound, inbound, or abstract (a category used for business processes or canonical interfaces).

A service interface represents a large part of what makes up a WSDL document (it will get its binding and address data at runtime). As such, the service interface is completely independent of the language in which the service is implemented and the platform on which it runs.

The WSDL for a service interface is shown in Figure 8-6. The exported WSDL document can be published either to a Universal Description, Discovery, and Integration (UDDI) server (whether to a public UDDI server on the Internet or to a private UDDI server running on SAP NetWeaver AS) or exchanged with partners in another way (such as HTTPS or encrypted email).

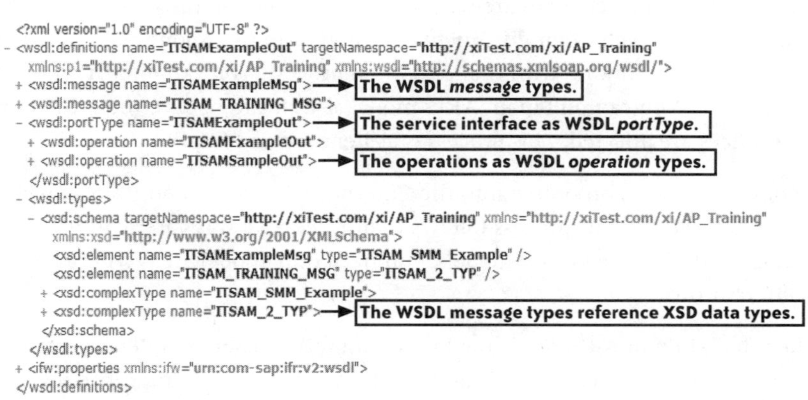

```
<?xml version="1.0" encoding="UTF-8" ?>
- <wsdl:definitions name="ITSAMExampleOut" targetNamespace="http://xiTest.com/xi/AP_Training"
    xmlns:p1="http://xiTest.com/xi/AP_Training" xmlns:wsdl="http://schemas.xmlsoap.org/wsdl/">
  + <wsdl:message name="ITSAMExampleMsg"> ───▶ The WSDL message types.
  + <wsdl:message name="ITSAM_TRAINING_MSG">
  - <wsdl:portType name="ITSAMExampleOut"> ───▶ The service interface as WSDL portType.
    + <wsdl:operation name="ITSAMExampleOut">
    + <wsdl:operation name="ITSAMSampleOut"> ───▶ The operations as WSDL operation types.
    </wsdl:portType>
  - <wsdl:types>
    - <xsd:schema targetNamespace="http://xiTest.com/xi/AP_Training" xmlns="http://xiTest.com/xi/AP_Training"
        xmlns:xsd="http://www.w3.org/2001/XMLSchema">
      <xsd:element name="ITSAMExampleMsg" type="ITSAM_SMM_Example" />
      <xsd:element name="ITSAM_TRAINING_MSG" type="ITSAM_2_TYP" />
      + <xsd:complexType name="ITSAM_SMM_Example">
      + <xsd:complexType name="ITSAM_2_TYP"> ───▶ The WSDL message types reference XSD data types.
      </xsd:schema>
    </wsdl:types>
  + <ifw:properties xmlns:ifw="urn:com-sap:ifr:v2:wsdl">
  </wsdl:definitions>
```

FIGURE 8-6. A service interface in a WSDL document

Integration objects

We mentioned that the Enterprise Services Repository has evolved from the SAP NetWeaver XI Integration Repository. The presence of integration objects and mappings in the Enterprise Services Repository relates to its ongoing role in helping facilitate flexible integrations among business partners. The Enterprise Services Repository aids in creating integration scenarios, mapping from the data types used by one business partner to another and automating translations between two systems or two XML vocabularies, such as RosettaNet, an XML standard for the high-tech industry.

Mappings are among the integration objects used in integration scenarios. Message mappings transform the sender message to the form of the receiver message. You can create message mappings using a graphical mapping editor (which generates Java code), using Java programs, ABAP Objects classes, or XSLT stylesheets. Interface mappings register a pair of interfaces for use in an integration scenario and specify the message mappings to be used at runtime.

Process models

As mentioned earlier, dynamic process models will be added to an upcoming release of the Enterprise Services Repository with the integration of the ARIS modeling tool. ARIS models further enable a top-down or outside-in approach to development. Once ARIS is integrated into the repository, you will be able to use this tool to create high-level ARIS models that drill down into more detailed process models.

What are some of the benefits of visual modeling? For one, models make development easier and prototyping faster. They expand the audience of people who can participate in the development process, allowing business analysts, whose expertise lies in the area of business processes, to help create these models instead of having to leave all of the development to "code jockeys." These models are dynamic; they drill down to more detailed integration models that in turn drill down into services. Unlike static models, they do not get out of sync over time; changes are reflected in the model, so the model can be used for creating a test plan as well as for documentation and training. Additionally, since the models are dynamic, working with them is a fluid process. You can import and export models as needed. You can pull in an ARIS model as a starting point, then drill down and see what services are affected. This process is as iterative and fluid as you need it to be.

Further, once ARIS is incorporated into the Enterprise Services Repository, it will include SAP-specific content. If your process follows that of the SAP software, you have a good starting point with these reference models; you need only model areas where your process takes a different turn.

While the integration of ARIS modeling into the Enterprise Services Repository is a future focus, modeling is still the basis of the design-time process in the Enterprise Services Repository today; you model service objects as you create enterprise services from the outside in, as described in Chapter 15. Those who are also interested in visual modeling may want to start taking immediate advantage of ARIS modeling, which is available today as a standalone tool.

Business objects

Another important element that is coming in a future release of the Enterprise Services Repository is *business objects*. In brief, a business object is an identifiable business entity. Business objects are conceptually clear to businesspeople as logical units, such as a customer or a sales order. What is clear in the mind of business experts has been less clear in software in the past. Business objects follow a consistent structure and have logical relationships with other business objects (a purchase order is associated with a customer, for example). Like a purchase order, a business object has subelements known as *business object nodes*. Business objects reuse existing data types. Business objects can be used in predictable ways to ensure orderly development and generate enterprise services that are guaranteed to perform basic functions such as modifying a purchase order, creating a purchase order, or deleting a purchase order. Because business objects are strategic building blocks, the creation of new business objects must be subject to a governance process (governance in ESA is the topic of Chapter 17).

All entities in the repository link together in a hierarchy, and you can navigate through the repository to find just the element you need for any given task. Further, the availability of a common repository enables smooth and consistent development, all the way from high-level graphical process models to services and right down to the definition of global data types.

What is the role of namespaces in the Enterprise Services Repository?

Given that the Enterprise Services Repository serves as a common repository for all service objects, how can we ensure that two objects are not duplicated? After all, we could certainly have multiple objects with the same name. How can we prevent naming collisions?

To ensure that each object in the repository has a unique name, objects are named through a combination of component version, namespace, and name. Namespaces ensure that when a component is named, it can definitively point to a single entity. Each object in the Enterprise Services Repository is uniquely identified by the triple of software component version, namespace, and name. During the modeling process for data types and service interfaces, we supply a namespace to prevent any naming collisions.

To be registered in the repository, a software component version must exist in the System Landscape Directory. The software component version then becomes an object in the Enterprise Services Repository that can be edited (if it is configured to be editable, that is).

For each software component version, we specify whether its Remote Function Calls (RFCs) and IDOCs can be imported. Since accessing these entities entails logging in to a remote system, credentials must be supplied if this access is permitted.

For each software component version, multiple namespaces can be defined. This allows development objects to be segregated into different areas. These namespaces are defined by either a URI or a URN, according to the W3C's XML Namespaces specification.

Now that we've looked at the Enterprise Services Repository and what it contains, we will direct our attention to the "content" that SAP provides for the repository: the some 500 services that comprise the Enterprise Services Inventory.

What is the Enterprise Services Inventory?

As we mentioned at the beginning of this chapter, the Enterprise Services Repository can be thought of in one sense as a container for descriptions of enterprise services. The Enterprise Services Repository is a directory, just like a phone book. And like a phone book, it is not filled with what it describes, but rather with information about what it describes. A person's phone number is not a person. Nor is the information in the Enterprise Services Repository describing the interface for a service the same as describing the service itself. The concern of this portion of the chapter is the services themselves, described in a way that a business analyst can understand. That's what makes up the Enterprise Services Inventory.

The Enterprise Services Inventory is a comprehensive set of business-level enterprise services created by SAP, though as we will see, the Enterprise Services Inventory is open and customers and partners may request services be built by SAP or submit services for inclusion in the Enterprise Services Inventory. (The process of adding to the Enterprise Services Inventory happens through the Enterprise Services Community, described in Chapter 6.)

The Enterprise Services Inventory is a key differentiator for SAP. It's one thing to say to customers, "Create an SOA," or even to provide the tools for doing so. In the case of SAP, the Enterprise Services Inventory represents a collection of enterprise services that come ready made. These services have been created by SAP and are secure and scaleable. The first version of the Enterprise Services Inventory, including 500 services, was made public as a *preview* in June 2005. Registered users can access it via the SAP Developer Network (SDN; *http://sdn.sap.com*). We describe the ESA Preview System in detail later in this chapter. Not only can the services in the Enterprise Services Inventory be used by customers and partners as is, but they can also be adapted. Sometimes the service that meets your needs might be similar to a service in the inventory. In these cases, the Enterprise Services Inventory provides a starting point for adapting a service that meets your needs perfectly and saves you time versus developing that service from scratch.

The actual list of what services have been implemented will change quarterly or even faster as new services are created and added to the inventory. This book is not a good place to list available services. SDN is a good place to do that. Instead, in this section we will explain in greater detail the sorts of services that will end up in the Enterprise Services Inventory, and some processes that are used for creating them. Is this a bit on the technical side? You bet, but if you cannot get a little technical now and then, why bother to write a book about ESA at all?

What does the Enterprise Services Inventory provide for each service?

Each service in the Enterprise Services Inventory includes not only the high-level description of the service but also information about that service so that organizations using open standards can consider whether to incorporate a particular service into their SOA. Each service in the inventory has an implementation-independent service definition. It includes information about providers or implementations of that service, with specific details. The inventory includes details relevant to consumers of services, such as scenarios and processes in which the service might be used. In fact, it provides a cross-reference listing of all the processes in which a given service is used.

What kinds of services are part of the Enterprise Services Inventory?

A wide range of services will become part of the Enterprise Services Inventory. A service can be considered a candidate for the Enterprise Services Inventory if it supports one of four key business drivers:

User productivity
> Various role-specific UIs communicate with the backend applications through services. This results in services with fine granularity—for example, for data validation. Service calls are usually handled synchronously.

Next business practices and process innovation
> New processes can be implemented on top of existing applications, and existing processes can be extended by composite applications. The granularity of these services is therefore coarser. Synchronous and asynchronous service calls are possible.

Process automation and efficiency
> Business partners can exchange information directly between applications so there is less manual interaction. This results in services with coarser granularity. The information is included in one service call, which, typically, is asynchronous.

Deployment flexibility
> Customers adapt business processes according to their organizational structure. For example, they outsource a specific payment process to an external payment service provider. This results in services with finer granularity. Service calls are mainly asynchronous.

Services fit into a variety of scenarios. Some services are utility services that are required for almost every application, such as pressing the F4 key to get context-sensitive help information. Other services follow a UI process, such as employees changing their address. Still other services implement application-to-application communications, enabling a business process behind the scenes.

But how do services become part of the Enterprise Services Inventory? Figure 8-7 provides a view of the service definition and alignment process used to bring services into the Enterprise Services Inventory.

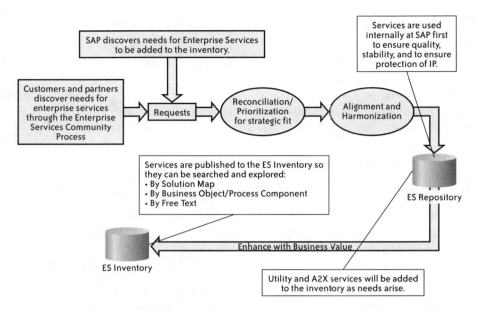

FIGURE 8-7. *The Enterprise Services Inventory service definition and alignment process*

As Figure 8-7 shows, once the ideas for services arrive, they are prioritized and considered for their strategic fit and their harmonization with existing services. Their alignment with the business drivers listed earlier is examined. SAP also considers whether the service in question is relevant for the outside world and is appropriate for externalization. At this stage, a series of steps is taken to ensure quality, scalability, and protection of intellectual property (IP). If it is determined to be a strategic enterprise service, it is published as part of the Enterprise Services Inventory.

The request for creating a particular service might come from SAP internally, or it might come from a customer or partner through the Enterprise Services Community. Regardless of from where the request came, the impulse for creating a service at all is generally motivated by one of three reasons:

- You are interested in creating one service to solve a problem.

- You want to create a system of services to help with composite application development.

- You want to run a program of service enablement to get widespread benefits from services.

The next two questions in this chapter describe a progressive methodology to identify meaningful enterprise services as a part of service enablement. The information that forms the basis of the answers to these questions comes from the internal SAP engineering documents that were used as the foundation of the more accessible Enterprise Services Design Guide, available on SDN. If you are new to the world of services and want to create a service or a system of services, you might be better off going to SDN and reading the design guide. But if you are the equivalent of an SAP sports fanatic, read on. The section later in this chapter titled "What is the Enterprise Services Preview?" will be of interest to everyone.

What methodology has SAP created for service enablement?

A program of service enablement is not about building services. Service enablement is actually a design process in which scenarios, processes, and applications are analyzed and the opportunities for creating services are discovered and evaluated. In the first part of a program of service enablement, many ideas for services are invented and evaluated. In the second part, the services are actually built.

All sorts of things happen in service enablement, and the SAP process we will describe is supported by existing analysis such as business scenario maps. The process of service enablement we will describe has two parts:

- Analysis of different scenarios to find opportunities for creating services
- Evaluation of the scenarios for services with respect to a set of indicators that are associated with well-designed services

This process is described in Figure 8-8, which is one of the most elegant and eclectic process graphs you will ever see. A quick look at Figure 8-8 indicates that it is not like other process graphs. An exclusive or operator is used to indicate that the process may begin in one of three ways. Below, the and operator indicates that the process flow splits and moves in parallel. These primitives for flow control come from the sort of logic used in designing circuit boards, but they are used here to describe a procedural model. While some might find this approach obscure, for the right reader this graphic is an elegant and efficient mode of communication.

The starting point for our service identification example is the SAP solution maps. We then select a business scenario by following this process:

1. Do first-pass prioritization of the business scenarios to be investigated further.

2. From this list of prioritized business scenarios, pick one selected scenario.

3. Analyze the business scenario using the procedure model described earlier.

Table 8-1 describes the key tasks in the procedural model. The idea is that scenarios for services are invented and then are evaluated with respect to indicators. Table 8-1 outlines the key tasks; Table 8-2 describes the performance indicators mentioned in the "Process step" column in Table 8-1.

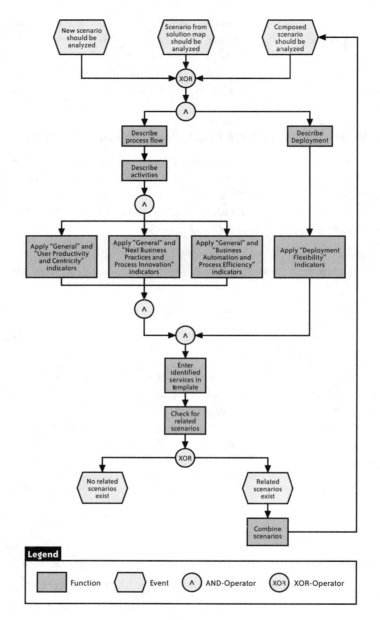

FIGURE 8-8. Procedural model for service discovery

TABLE 8-1. Step-by-step description of procedural model for service discovery

Process step	Description
Describe process flow	Describe the as-is business process flow with process steps of the selected business scenario. For each process step, the description should include the role of the one who does something during the process step and the outcome or deliverable of the business process step (e.g., design specification).
Describe activities	For each business process step, describe the activities performed during the process step.
Apply general, user productivity, and centricity indicators	Focus on optimization of activities or tasks that are performed by users in one or more roles during a process step. Services discovered by this approach try to improve user productivity. Think of enterprise services that enable a user to achieve the tasks faster, cheaper, or with better quality than today.
	Take each indicator, analyze the process flow and the description of the activities to identify services, and review the services identified from similar analysis of other indicators. In the example that follows, we will see that applying more indicators on a business scenario can lead to better enterprise services discovery.
Apply general and next business practices and process innovation indicators	Focus on next business practices and process innovation.
	Focus on the gaps between available scenarios and their specific usage.
	In terms of optimizing the services by applying more indicators, the statements from the previous step apply.
Apply general and business automation and process efficiency indicators	Focus on business automation and on making the processes efficient.
	Focus on frequently used business scenarios, business processes, or process steps that create considerable value or consume considerable resources.
	Combine knowledge of business processes with knowledge of typical system landscapes and investigate processes that cross one or more system borders within or across companies to discover services.
	In terms of optimizing the services by applying more indicators, the statements from the previous step apply.
Apply process innovation indicators	These indicators help identify services that facilitate composite applications.
Describe deployment	Describe the deployment situation.
Apply flexible deployment indicators	Start with the first flexible deployment indicator and use the deployment diagram to identify services.
	These indicators could also influence already identified services, so they should be double-checked.
Enter identified services in a template	After all indicators are applied, enter the identified enterprise services in a service template.

Process step	Description
Check for related business scenarios	In our example, we will combine more than one business scenario (New Product Development and Introduction, Procure-to-Pay, Order-To-Cash). We show in the example that we found services that we wouldn't have found if we looked at the business scenarios separately. Therefore, think of possible business scenarios that could be related to the selected business scenario. If there are no related scenarios, finish the enterprise services identification.
Combine business scenarios	If there are related business scenarios, pick one of them and start the service identification process again, but this time take the combination of the business scenarios into consideration.

The indicators are the key to this process. The indicators help service designers determine if they have discovered a scenario for a service or if they are barking up the wrong tree. If certain indicators apply, it is a clue that a certain type of opportunity for a service may have been found. Table 8-2 lists the indicators.

TABLE 8-2. Indicators to identify enterprise services

General indicators	
Indicator 1	Complete processes or process steps with frequent high execution time or frequent high execution costs are potential candidates for being supported by services.
User productivity and centricity indicators	
Indicator 2	Frequent changes or custom development could indicate the need for a service.
Indicator 3	Information logically linked and often needed by users is distributed throughout disparate systems.
Indicator 4	Business know-how is decentralized, but the decentralized users need support from central users to get their business done. There is a high call or request rate to expert users that results in repeated information retrieval from application systems or the application of well-defined business rules—i.e., tasks that could be automated.
Best practices and process innovation indicators	
Indicator 5	Information is manually transferred from paper into applications or between applications.
Indicator 6	All needed input parameters for performing a specific activity are already available in a system, not necessarily in the system implementing this activity.

TABLE 8-2. Indicators to identify enterprise services (continued)

General indicators	
Business automation and process efficiency indicators	
Indicator 7	Important data from external (technical) sources or functionality is needed within the process in general or enables the automation of the respective task.
Indicator 8	In some cases, an application might reach a "steady state" even though a process is not completed—i.e., the application has finished processing data but has not triggered the events that logically follow in the business process. In such cases, manual intervention is usually necessary to get the process going again.
Indicator 9	A process is crossing a (potential) borderline to other applications, other systems, or external organizations.
Indicator 10	Industry standards such as CIDX and RosettaNet can be an indicator for services that optimize the communication between applications.
Indicator 11	A given business process needs external synchronization to a B2B scenario, without including details of a specific standard.
Indicator 12	There are different variants of a given business process where major parts are stable and only single activities may vary.
Indicator 13	A solution often receives data from various other solutions.
Flexible deployment indicators	
Indicator 14	A solution is often deployed multiple times within one company, with data exchange between the solutions.
Indicator 15	Check the relevance of the business process for outsourcing—for example, whether business process outsourcing (BPO) providers offer outsourcing services for a given business process or whether customers are asking for interfaces to BPO providers. The outsourcing borders, interfaces, and messages exchanged among BPO providers, the enterprise, and third parties are indicating the possibility for an enterprise service.

Using the procedural model and the indicators, therefore, a large group of people can analyze many different scenarios and processes, and it's likely that the descriptions of opportunities for creating services will be understandable to each other. This process for service discovery creates a common language for a large team to use to communicate about a program of service enablement. If the communication for a large group can be harmonized, great things can happen.

How do the indicators and the procedural model work in practice?

A concrete example will help you see how the indicators and procedural model work in practice. Consider a business scenario that describes the purchase of a new component in the context of a development project.

First, here is a short overview of the scenario, including the process flow and the deployment.

Scenario for purchasing a new component

In the development and launch of new products, companies risk huge sums developing ideas into prototypes and, finally, into products and brands for consumers. This cross-functional activity touches many departments, including product management, supply management, manufacturing, invoicing, and finance. Best practices for new-product development involve creating a set of increasingly demanding gates that each idea must pass through to move to the next stage. Figure 8-9 illustrates this scenario.

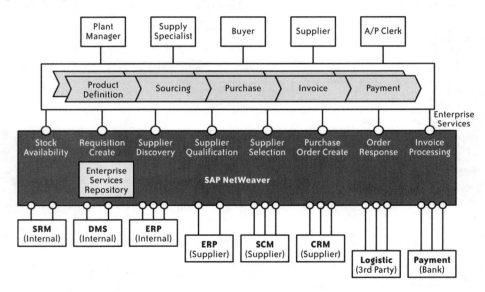

FIGURE 8-9. Purchasing a new component

Process flow

Figure 8-10 shows the high-level process flow of our example. Table 8-3 describes each step of this process in detail. We kept the example simple. That means that the process flow does not show every possible case of the scenario.

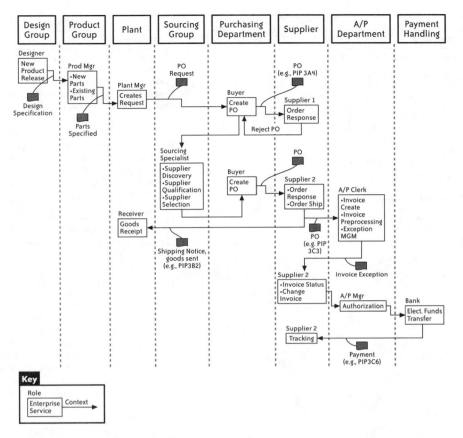

FIGURE 8-10. High-level process flow, with roles

TABLE 8-3. Process flow activities

Process step	Role	Artifact	Description of activities
Design new product	Designer	Design specification	The designers design a new product. Their output is a design specification.
Specify needed parts	Product manager	Part specification	Considering the design specification, the product manager specifies the needed parts for the new product and creates a part specification.
Check for new parts	Plant manager	PO request	Considering the part specification, the plant manager differentiates new parts from parts already used by the company. For new parts, she directly fills out a form for a PO request and sends it to the sourcing specialist by internal mail.

TABLE 8-3. Process flow activities (continued)

Process step	Role	Artifact	Description of activities
Check stock availability	Plant manager	PO request	For parts already in use, the plant manager checks in the plant for needed parts using a search function of her application. If the needed parts are not in this plant, she logs into applications of other plants and uses their search function. If she finds the needed parts, she does not create a PO request. Otherwise, she creates a PO request by filling out a form and sending it to the purchasing department by internal mail.
Create PO for existing parts	Buyer	PO	The buyer creates a PO for needed parts.
Evaluate supplier	Source specialist	Evaluation results	Considering the PO request, the source specialist starts searching for the right supplier for new parts using the Internet, and the telephone and the Yellow Pages. After he has all the information he needs, he creates a short list of suppliers and sends them a request for quotation (RFQ). For the RFQ, the source specialist needs to attach some information about the part. After unsuccessfully searching for that information, he calls the product manager to ask for the location of the information. Now he can attach the information to the RFQ and send it out. He waits for the offers of the suppliers. After he receives all the offers, he selects a supplier for the new parts. He writes down the supplier on an evaluation result form.
Create PO for new parts	Buyer	PO	Considering the evaluation results of the source specialist, the buyer enters the data of the new supplier into his system. The buyer then enters the data of the PO request in his system and assigns suppliers to the needed parts. He prints the PO for each supplier and checks whether a manager has to approve the PO. A confirmation is needed if the sum of a PO exceeds a defined amount. If a confirmation is needed, he sends the PO to his manager by internal mail and waits for the confirmation. After the manager approves the PO, he sends it back to the buyer by internal mail. The buyer faxes the POs to the suppliers, getting confirmation from a manager first, if necessary.
Execute order	Supplier	Invoice, goods	The supplier receives the order and starts to execute it.

TABLE 8-3. *Process flow activities (continued)*

Process step	Role	Artifact	Description of activities
Goods received	Receiver	Goods, receipt	The receiver receives the goods and enters the receipt into his system.
Invoice received	A/P clerk		The A/P clerk receives the invoice by mail, fax, or email.
Payment authorized	A/P clerk	Payment	If the payment is not related to the receipt of the goods and the invoice is correct, the A/P clerk authorizes the payment. If the payment is related to the receipt of the goods, the A/P clerk calls the receiver and asks whether the goods have been received. If the goods haven't been received yet, the A/P clerk calls the receiver every day until the goods have been received.
Payment received	Supplier		The supplier receives his payment. The process ends.

Deployment

Figure 8-11 shows the current system landscape and application deployment of our model company.

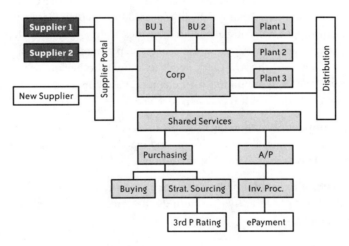

FIGURE 8-11. *System landscape of an example company*

Service identification by applying the indicators

Using the process flow with the process steps and the deployment diagram, we can now take the indicators from Table 8-2 and apply them to our scenario.

Applying general indicators

The most relevant general indicator is Indicator 1, which says what we should look for: "Complete processes or process steps with frequent high execution time or frequent high execution costs are potential candidates for being supported by services." In our example, the process step "Evaluate Supplier" has a high execution time because the sourcing specialist has to perform many activities manually (e.g., search for suppliers, call suppliers). We suggest building a role-specific UI to support him with the supplier discovery and qualification. The UI would call a service that provides all the necessary information about suppliers needed to select a defined part.

Applying user productivity and centricity indicators

To apply these indicators, concentrate on the process steps that are not performed automatically and therefore need human interaction. Analyze the activities of those process steps and apply the following indicators.

Here's how we would apply these indicators in this case. Indicator 3 says what we should look for: "Information logically linked and often needed by users is distributed throughout disparate systems." Since each plant has its own system, it is sometimes necessary to log on to every plant to search for parts. We suggest building a service that searches automatically across the relevant plants.

Indicator 4 also applies. It states: "Business know-how is decentralized, but the decentralized users need support from central users to get their business done. There is a high call or request rate to expert users that results in repeated information retrieval from application systems or the application of well-defined business rules—i.e., tasks that could be automated." In the example, to go from the process step "Invoice Received" to the process step "Authorize Payment," the A/P Clerk needs to know whether the ordered goods have been received yet. We suggest building a UI element, based on a service, so that the A/P Clerk can see whether the goods have been received.

An example of automatically applying business rules could be to check an incoming electronic invoice. If a corresponding PO is found and matches the invoice, the invoice can be posted automatically without manual intervention.

As we will see later, this is only the first approach to optimizing the interaction between the Receiver and the A/P Clerk. By considering other indicators, we will optimize this interaction even more.

Applying best practices and process innovation indicators

Indicator 5 states: "Information is manually transferred from paper into applications or between applications." In this example, the sourcing specialist is using a web site of a third-party service provider to get information about potential suppliers and their products, such as performance ratings. He uses copy-and-paste to get that information into the vendor master record of his Enterprise Services Repository system. We suggest a service in which the Enterprise Services Repository system calls the service provider upon request, automatically retrieving the most current data.

Applying business automation and process efficiency indicators

To apply these indicators, we concentrate on process steps where human beings are involved but don't need to be, or where human beings just trigger the next process step.

Indicator 6 states: "All needed input parameters for performing a specific activity are already available in a system, not necessarily in the system implementing this activity." In our example, during the "Evaluate Supplier" process step, the Source Specialist needs to attach further information for an RFQ. The Source Specialist needs to know where the information is and attach it manually. We suggest a service that aligns the information needed for the RFQ automatically so that the Source Specialist doesn't need to know exactly where he can find the information.

Indicator 7 states what we should look for: "Important data from external (technical) sources or functionality not supported by an existing enterprise service and is either needed within the process in general or enables the automation of the respective task." Consider our discussion of Indicator 4. There we suggested a service for the Receiver that allows him to enter the goods received. But considering this indicator, we can optimize this step even more by using bar coding or radio frequency identification (RFID) technology. Using this technology obviates the need for the Receiver to enter the goods received because this entry will be done automatically. We suggest that we define a service in such a way that goods receipt is automatic via bar coding or RFID technology.

Considering the next indicator will optimize our interaction between Receiver and A/P Clerk even more.

Indicator 8 states: "In some cases, an application might reach a 'steady state' even though a process is not completed—i.e., the application has finished processing data but has not triggered the events that logically follow in the business process. In such cases, manual intervention usually is necessary to get the process going again." Indicator 4 led us to services that make it needless for the A/P Clerk to call the Receiver every day to ask for the goods received. Indicator 7 led us to services that obviate the need for the Receiver to enter the goods received. Still, the A/P Clerk has to use his service to check whether the goods are received. Now this indicator leads us to a service that informs the A/P Clerk as soon as the goods are received and shows him the invoice he needs to authorize. We suggest you do not build a service that allows the A/P Clerk to look for goods received, but that you redefine the service from Indicator 7 in such a way that it notifies the A/P Clerk as soon as the goods are received and shows him automatically which invoice to authorize.

We have seen how we can optimize a process by considering more indicators. In doing this, we might start out with fairly simple, atomic services and move to more sophisticated, composite services. We can identify services after considering a single indicator, but we may have to redefine them after we have considered more indicators.

Indicator 9 states that we should look for "A process crossing a (potential) borderline to other applications, other systems, or external organizations." When an invoice is received, information from multiple backend systems may be necessary to automatically process the rules mentioned earlier to determine whether the invoice can be accepted. This information may reside in several systems, and the update of, for example, the PO that the invoice belongs to may happen in a different system. Retrieving information and updating the status of the PO are suitable services.

Indicator 10 states that industry standards (such as CIDX and RosettaNet) can be an indicator for services that optimize the communication between applications and industry standards. For purchasing, the industry standard CIDX should be used. We suggest building a service that takes the data needed for purchasing and transforms it in the format used by CIDX.

Indicator 11 shows us that a given business process needs external synchronization to a B2B scenario without including details of a specific standard. During the process step to create the PO, the Buyer has to wait for a confirmation from the supplier in order to know whether the supplier has accepted the order. After the Buyer gets the confirmation, he informs others that the order is in progress. We suggest a service that accepts an electronic order confirmation in a suitable B2B format and creates the appropriate notifications. If the supplier rejects the order, the Buyer will also be notified.

Indicator 12 asks us to look for different variants of a given business process where major parts are stable and only single activities may vary. During the process step "Create PO," the Manager of the Purchasing Department has to approve a PO if it exceeds a certain amount. Therefore, we suggest building a UI element that informs the Manager about such POs and provides him with the appropriate actions (accept/reject/get more details). This leads to services for getting the relevant PO information and changing the status.

Applying flexible deployment indicators

To apply the following indicators we now consider the deployment diagram shown in Figure 8-11.

When Indicator 13 looks for a solution, it often receives data from various other solutions. Figure 8-11 shows that the company has three instances of the operational system for its plants and one corporate finance system so that many transactions in the operational systems need to be mirrored in the corporate finance system. We suggest a service in the financial application that can receive relevant accounting information from the operational systems.

Indicator 14 looks for a solution that often is deployed multiple times within one company, with data exchange between the solutions. If the company actually is running local financials in addition to corporate financials, we could create a service in the corporate system that periodically receives aggregated financial information from the local systems.

Indicator 15 asks us to "Check the relevance of the business process for outsourcing. The outsourcing borders, interfaces, and messages exchanged between BPO Provider, enterprise, and third parties are indicating the need for services." As we can see in our deployment diagram, the company has outsourced its payment process. We suggest building a service that provides the outsourcer with the data he needs to fulfill the payment after the A/P Clerk authorized a payment. That means that the A/P Clerk only needs to authorize the payment; the rest, such as collecting the data and transferring it to the right format for the outsourcer, is done automatically by the service.

While this example moves quickly, it does provide a real-world instance of how a program of service enablement might work. Having described how we do service discovery, we now turn our attention back to the Enterprise Services Inventory.

For each service, what does the Enterprise Services Inventory provide?

Each service in the Enterprise Services Inventory includes information about that service so that organizations using open standards can consider whether to incorporate a particular service into their SOA. Each service in the inventory has an implementation-independent service definition. It includes information about providers or implementations of that service, with specific details. The inventory includes details relevant to consumers of services, such as scenarios and processes in which the service might be used. In fact, it provides a cross-reference listing of all the processes in which a given service is used.

What is the Enterprise Services Preview?

An important facet of the Enterprise Services Inventory is the ability to search for and discover enterprise services in a variety of ways. Services can be located by drilling down through a solution map, by searching for a particular business object or component, or by freeform text searches. You can also review a categorized index of the services in the Enterprise Services Inventory and discover services in this way.

To get a feel for outside-in development, sign on to the ESA Preview System on SDN (*http://sdn.sap.com*). Essentially, this system provides access to a PC-based tool, called Solution Composer, which you can use to create and modify solution maps for your own business processes. We've often written in this book and in this chapter about a methodology of looking at enterprise services that starts with business processes and drills down to services. The Solution Composer makes this process very concrete, literally providing the drill-down from industry to solution map to business scenario group, all the way down to service and the WSDL for that service, as shown in Figure 8-12.

You can view solution maps for a generic business context or for specific industries. Using these maps, you can drill down to see individual business processes and view enterprise services that comprise parts of these processes.

Typically, you start with a business solution map and drill down into an end-to-end scenario, such as sales and marketing. You can see particular processes relevant for that business scenario, such as Sales Order Management. By drilling down further, you can see the related enterprise services described on a business level. Registered users can click on a service operation and view the technical service implementation in WSDL.

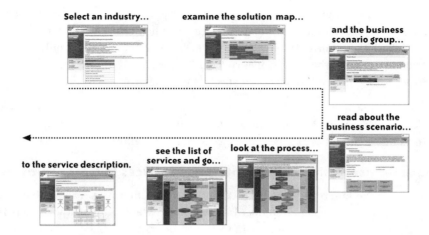

Select an industry... examine the solution map... and the business scenario group...

read about the business scenario...

look at the process...

see the list of services and go...

to the service description.

FIGURE 8-12. *The ESA Preview System: a presentation of enterprise services along processes*

With that overview in mind, let's take a look at the Enterprise Services Inventory in the ESA Preview System, which is available at *http://sdn.sap.com*. You must register to access it. The ESA Preview System appears as an option on the left side of the screen, as shown in Figure 8-13. (Note that you must log in to see the option and that you may have to expand the ESA node to display it.)

FIGURE 8-13. *The ESA Preview System, reachable through the SDN homepage*

Clicking on ESA Preview System displays an introductory screen that offers not only access to the preview, but also a variety of supporting documents for your review. Under Quick Links on the right side of the screen, click on *Browse service definitions* to display the ESA Preview System shown in Figure 8-14.

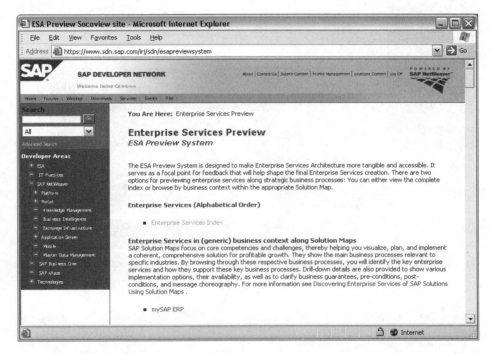

FIGURE 8-14. The ESA Preview System

From here you can take one of two paths: you can either click on Enterprise Services Index to view a categorized list of all the services, or you can drill down through solution maps. Selecting mySAP ERP displays the solution map shown in Figure 8-15.

This solution map covers a comprehensive range of business scenario groups divided by category. Business scenario groups listed here include those for analytics, financials, and human capital management to name a few. Select *Human Capital Management* to display Figure 8-16. This is where all human-resources-related functions can be found.

The body of this screen describes the area of Human Capital Management and the challenges facing today's HR professionals. On the upper part of the screen, the options Search and See Also appear. Under See Also, click on *Enterprise Services in Human Capital Management* to display the screen shown in Figure 8-17. The enterprise services are grouped by business scenario.

The enterprise services for Human Capital Management fall into three business scenarios: Recruiting Talent, Workforce Process Management, and Workforce Deployment. Subcategories for Workforce Process Management include Benefits Management, Time and

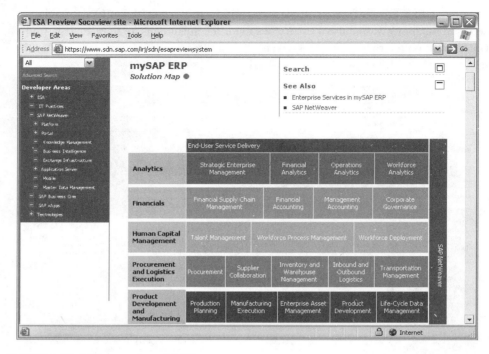

FIGURE 8-15. Solution maps for mySAP ERP

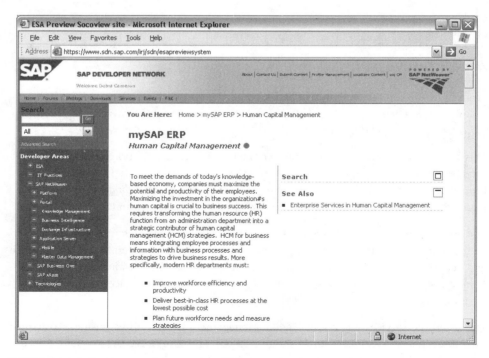

FIGURE 8-16. Drilling down into the Human Capital Management business scenario

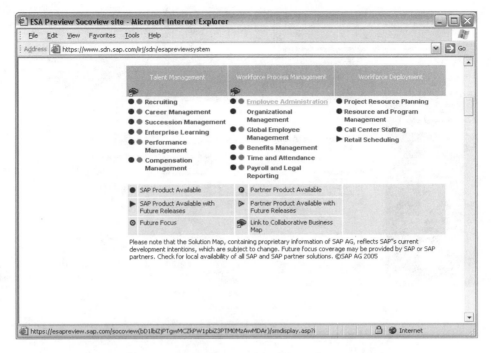

FIGURE 8-17. *Categories of enterprise services for Human Capital Management*

Attendance, and one that is important to everyone, Payroll and Legal Reporting. We will drill down into the Employee Administration area, so click on *Employee Administration* to display Figure 8-18.

The Employee Administration business process includes a Personnel Management enterprise service. Clicking on this service reveals the related service operations, as shown in Figure 8-19.

Under See Also, you can click on "Where used" to see where else this service is used. Numerous enterprise services operations are listed. We'll choose the second one in the list, *Employee List of Manage Query Response*, shown at the bottom of Figure 8-19. This service operation provides a list of the employees who report to a given manager as of a certain date. Clicking on this operation displays the screen shown in Figure 8-20.

Now we have drilled down to the level of a service operation. The final drill-down step is to click on one of the WSDL files, either the Inbound Interface WSDL or the ERP Inbound WSDL. At this point, you will be asked to authenticate because this crosses the boundary from the Enterprise Services Inventory into the Enterprise Services Repository, from which the WSDL will be retrieved. After successfully authenticating, the WSDL file for the enterprise service is shown, as in Figure 8-21. On the left side, you can see where this service fits into the mySAP ERP hierarchy, which mirrors our drill-down process.

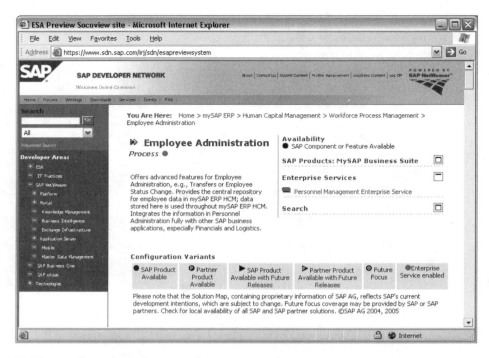

FIGURE 8-18. The Employee Administration business process

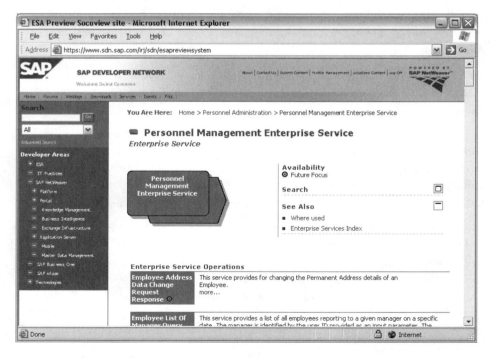

FIGURE 8-19. The Personnel Management enterprise service

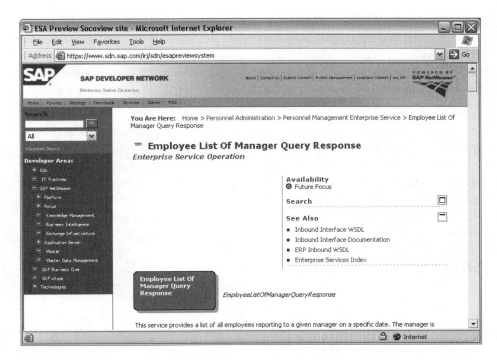

FIGURE 8-20. *Employee List of Manage Query Response enterprise services operation*

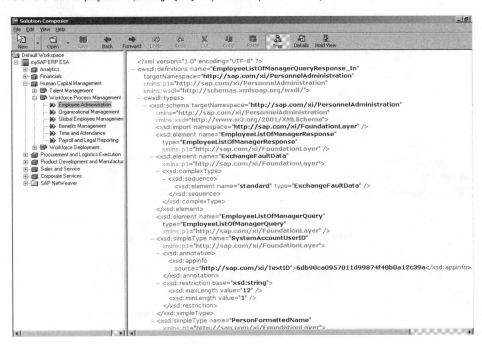

FIGURE 8-21. *WSDL excerpt from the Enterprise Services Repository, viewed through the Solution Composer*

As you can see, we start with looking at the business and move, from the outside in, all the way down to the technical details of the WSDL file. Not everyone will need to see this level of detail, but by starting with a business view, the many people in the organization with business expertise can look at business processes and see how they map to enterprise services, drilling down as far as they desire, from the Enterprise Services Inventory right down into the Enterprise Services Repository.

The Enterprise Services Repository, and the project to fill that repository with useful services, the Enterprise Services Inventory, are at the heart of ESA. This chapter described the strategic importance of the Enterprise Services Repository and how it is connected with the Enterprise Services Inventory. An understanding of the Enterprise Services Repository will inform your work with enterprise services whether that work involves consuming existing services, composing services, or creating services, and will help you formulate your ESA adoption strategy.

ESA in action: Elsag

Elsag's story shares much in common with the example we used earlier for service discovery. Like the real world, Elsag's situation was even more complex.

Elsag is the strategic IT solutions arm of the Finmeccanica Group, an Italian aerospace, defense, and transport giant composed of more than 100 subsidiaries and 51,000 employees located across Europe. Elsag applies its IT expertise on behalf of customers operating in each of those areas—including its corporate siblings—and in the telecommunications, utilities, and banking industries. The company has embraced enterprise services as a means to integrate disparate sources of data and improve process efficiency at both its customers and its siblings.

One of Elsag's largest customers is Fincantieri S.p.A., a shipbuilding firm that is a key supplier of the Italian navy. Fincantieri asked Elsag to create a solution for a maintenance and supply chain problem troubling its client. Each of its vessels is built using components from hundreds of contractors—Fincantieri provides the hulls, and others supply armaments, communications systems, etc.—involving considerable overlap and integration. But due to security and competitive reasons, there is little to no communication between the inventory systems of each supplier.

So when the navy needed to make maintenance requests, the challenge usually became "from whom?" Navy technicians needed to know exactly which combination of suppliers were responsible for which parts of the systems in question or else considerable time and energy would have to be spent in the error-prone process of asking likely suspects whether a needed part was theirs and starting over when, more likely than not, it wasn't.

Fincantieri asked Elsag to implement a two-step solution that could combine the figuration scheme of each ship—the tree describing the components' relationships to each other—with each component's supplier in a single window. The first step would create a consolidated bill of materials covering every component aboard each ship by linking the backend systems of each supplier and integrating them into a single window. The second step would allow navy engineers to send a maintenance request to any supplier using an interactive form available from that window.

Elsag engineers used SAP NetWeaver to create a web application that could communicate with each supplier's SAP R/3 implementation via enterprise services. Using SAP NetWeaver, Elsag created enterprise services to provide access to remote function calls that query the inventory tables within the production modules of each supplier's variation on R/3 (see Figure 8-22). The web application then collected the data and presented it using an iView in a single portal interface.

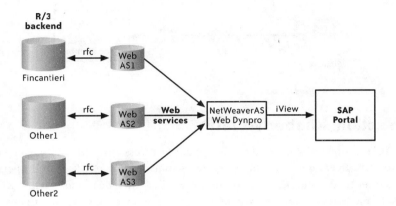

FIGURE 8-22. Elsag ship maintenance solution

This first step has already successfully been implemented, saving countless hours of what was previously a trial-and-error process. With a complete bill of materials available at a glance, navy technicians are able to quickly identify needed parts and contact the respective suppliers. Elsag hopes to streamline this process further in the project's second phase, in which a single form in the portal interface will automatically pass maintenance requests to the appropriate supplier without prompting from the user. To do this, Elsag will write new enterprise services, passing the request along to the appropriate R/3 module. All of the underlying functionality will be invisible to the user.

Elsag also used web services to centralize the treasury of its corporate parent, the Finmeccanica Group. Prior to Elsag's solution, each of the Group's 100+ subsidiaries maintained its own accounts for the conduct of operations. While flexible, this financial structure also required each unit to keep cash on hand that could be better put to work elsewhere in the Group and made it difficult to negotiate favorable lending terms with the Group's banks and to monitor the performance and spending behavior of each subsidiary. Because the Group's banks communicated directly with the Group's management, and because each subsidiary continually needed to request additional funds, the Group decided that a centralized corporate treasury would be the more effective solution. In order to centralize the treasury in principle without having to drastically change business processes or rewrite millions of lines of code, Elsag was asked to create a solution that could distribute funds to the Group's subsidiaries from the treasury on a just-in-time basis.

In practice, this meant using enterprise services to connect the Group's SAP R/3 system— which consolidates the holding company's accounts with data arriving from the Group's banks—with each subsidiary's own financial planning unit, as shown in Figure 8-23. Elsag used SAP NetWeaver to create a portal application, which managers at each company use to request funds from the central treasury. This way, the Group is able to leverage a single R/3 implementation across all of its subsidiaries while at the same time maintaining centralized control over its finances.

FIGURE 8-23. Elsag's centralized financials

ESA in action: Kimberly-Clark

Kimberly-Clark is one of the world's largest manufacturers of health and hygiene consumer products. Every day, 1.3 billion people use one of the products from its personal care, consumer tissue, and B2B lines of business, which include brands such as Kleenex, Scott tissue, and Huggies diapers. With 60,000 employees working in more than 100 manufacturing plants worldwide, nearly half of Kimberly-Clark's $15 billion in annual revenues stem from sales in 150 countries besides the United States.

Kimberly-Clark's management was quick to recognize the inherent flexibility and other advantages of ESA, but because of the company's size and global scope, it has chosen to follow a cautious roadmap toward strategic adoption of enterprise services. Instead of rushing down a piecemeal, project-driven path, the company and its IT architects have chosen to first develop the skill sets, business process maps, governance structures, and repositories necessary for wholesale and wholehearted adoption.

The central event of Kimberly-Clark's timetable is the arrival of the Enterprise Services Repository from SAP. Only with the Enterprise Services Repository, the company feels, will enterprise services achieve the degree of flexibility and reusability that justifies the level of investment necessary to convert its business processes into service-enabled composite applications.

But it hasn't been idle. Kimberly-Clark has already mapped thousands of business processes in simple PDF form for eventual translation into ARIS or other application modeling tools. There is already a standardized modeling methodology and governance structure. The next step is to begin designing governance procedures for an enterprise services environment in which a central authority would manage the services shared by multiple applications. Kimberly-Clark also has the advantage of an unusually close bond between the business and IT sides of its operations; it's taken relatively little time for both sides to discuss the advantages of evolving toward ESA and the necessary steps along the way.

Kimberly-Clark intends to make the jump to using the SAP Solution Manager to model its business processes within the IT toolset. The timing will depend on finding an appropriate business driver or a project large enough to drive the transition. The company is also organizing its IT department to create both a shared services group fluent in using SAP NetWeaver Developer Studio and Web Dynpro capabilities, and to teach its business analysts the skills necessary to think of functionality in terms of combinable, reusable services.

Along the same timeline, the enterprise architecture team and IT will embark on convincing the rest of Kimberly-Clark that enterprise services are a business solution, not a technology solution. Kimberly-Clark's plans for upgrading business solutions such as Customer Relationship Management (CRM) and Supply Chain Management (SCM) will offer opportunities to begin testing and experimenting with the creation of enterprise services and composite applications.

But the one thing that won't happen is sudden, systemwide, dramatic change. Even after Kimberly-Clark adopts ESA with the arrival of the Enterprise Services Repository, the company expects the cost of moving its employees en masse to new applications and interfaces to remain too expensive to justify the effort. Why? Because adapting change in business processes requires extensive efforts concerning retraining and rolling out the capabilities to the business clients. There will always be advantages to moving slowly.

ESA in action: CSA International

CSA International is a leading provider of product testing and certification services for electrical, mechanical, plumbing, gas, and a variety of other products. Recognized in the United States, Canada, and around the world, CSA International certification marks appear on billions of products worldwide.

CSA International is a division of CSA Group, an independent, not-for-profit membership association serving business, industry, government, and consumers. CSA Group employs more than 1,200 people across North America and has international offices in India, China, and the Netherlands. In addition to CSA International, CSA Group consists of three divisions: the Canadian Standards Association, a solutions-based standards organization providing standards development, application products, training, and advisory services; QMI for management systems registration; and OnSpeX, a provider of consumer product testing, inspections, and advisory services for retailers and manufacturers.

As an increasingly global player, CSA International faces a growing competitive environment in both its traditional and emerging markets. CSA International recognized early on that in a globally competitive arena, service and speed would be key differentiators.

To that end, CSA International has embraced ESA as a means for accelerating its internal processes and publishing its final reports. The organization intends to wholeheartedly embrace enterprise services in its next upgrade cycle to mySAP ERP 2005, the next iteration of SAP NetWeaver, and Documentum 5.3, all of which are slated to include features provided as enterprise services, more advanced modeling tools, and a fully functioning Enterprise Services Repository.

In advance of these upgrades, CSA International has already mapped its business processes to spot inefficiencies in its certification processes and plans to leverage ESA to service-enable these processes and continue to build on its client- and employee-focused portals for accessing documents. Services will take the form of previously existing functionality recast in easier-to-use interfaces and more efficient incarnations, streamlining how clients conduct business with CSA International in a global marketplace.

A number of service components have already been developed in support of this vision and are in use today. For example, a service-enabled version of a third-party DRM application CSA International has used to secure its PDF documents can now be easily extended to help ensure that client information remains secure when distributed globally via the Web. Service-enabling a "shopping cart" traditionally available within CSA's Online Store (*http://www.shopcsa.ca*) paves the way for extending online purchase of services across CSA Group's different lines of business. Additionally, reusable UI services are starting to be developed that hold the promise to compose applications that both speed application deployment and maintain the look, feel, and usability of electronic service offerings for clients and process-oriented portal workspaces for employees.

CHAPTER NINE

Project Mendocino: A Product Based on Consuming Enterprise Services

ON ANY GIVEN WORKDAY, INFORMATION WORKERS AT COMPANIES AROUND THE GLOBE CAN BE FOUND performing the same task: planning time off for a vacation. It starts with opening a calendar program, most likely Microsoft Outlook, and scanning for available dates. Appointments get moved forward or back, and eventually a week—or two—gets cleared for takeoff. After emailing a manager for approval, the next step for many employees is to log on to the company's enterprise system, find the HR workspace, scroll down to the correct section, and ultimately submit a vacation request. This process is often tedious.

Even if the vacation request screen has a nice-looking user interface (UI), employees still have to use two different tools with two different views of reality, and often the conversion from the calendar to the vacation request form is done by hand. This laborious task of updating information in one system that is not automatically reflected in the other also increases the probability of erroneous data being entered. Completing just one simple vacation request requires all these additional steps. If these steps were part of planning the vacation itself, a travel agent could be called on for assistance. Unfortunately, there is no travel agent to call on when problems are encountered during the request-for-leave process—instead, a power user who understands the system is all too often called on for support. Figure 9-1 illustrates the problems caused by the disconnect between desktop applications and enterprise applications.

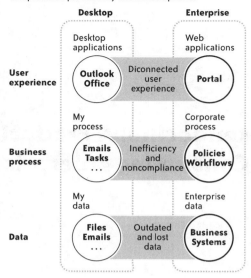

Compromised productivity and noncompliance

FIGURE 9-1. The disconnect between desktop applications and enterprise applications, leading to compromised productivity and noncompliance

What if an employee were able to access the HR system without ever knowing it? Instead of navigating the intranet labyrinth, information workers could simply enter a week-long vacation request into Outlook—the same desktop application used daily anyhow—and have that request translated into data that can be integrated with the enterprise system and automatically directed into the appropriate workflow process for payroll and management. That, in a nutshell, is the goal of Project Mendocino: to take the simple enterprise processes that are used every day and make them transparent to the end user.

SAP and Microsoft joined together to leverage the openness of the ESA blueprint with the .NET architecture of Microsoft's Office applications suite. The result is Project Mendocino, a solution that extends and automates the business processes from mySAP ERP within the familiar and commonly used Microsoft Office UI. Project Mendocino provides role-relevant displays of information while retaining process context as well as the collaboration and analytic tools for which SAP is famous. By simply taking the information that is already being gathered through desktop tools on a daily basis and reusing it by pushing it forward into underlying enterprise systems, SAP is creating tremendous value, increasing efficiency, and lowering total cost of ownership (TCO).

Project Mendocino is an extension to the enterprise portal, which will always be needed to gain full access to more advanced SAP business applications. But most of the time, information workers only require quick access to simple processes, such as billable time entry or budget monitoring. Project Mendocino eliminates the reliance on power users and business application experts while also seamlessly connecting business process applications with commonly used productivity applications.

Project Mendocino's capabilities include:

- Personalization
- Object synchronization
- Report distribution
- Alerts and notifications
- A form-based approval process
- Offline functionality

Through these capabilities, employees and managers realize greater efficiency and flexibility through self-service processes. These processes take the form of Project Mendocino applications, which in the initial release include:

- Time Management
- Budget Monitoring
- Leave Management
- Organization Management

Project Mendocino consumes the underlying functionality of transactional applications through services and offers new ways to use the system. It represents one of the first in a new wave of products from SAP that uses ESA to extend the reach of transactional applications to where they will make the most difference for businesses—in this case, the information worker's desktop.

What is the goal of Project Mendocino?

The goal of Project Mendocino is to improve the way information workers interact with business processes by closing the gap between desktop productivity tools and enterprise business applications. The expected results are more efficiency and less inconsistency. Information workers will no longer have to switch between enterprise tools and desktop applications. The tools that information workers use today are unstructured and unlinked to backend processes. Now those tools are linked to underlying business processes so that transactions in the Enterprise Resources Planning (ERP) system can be triggered directly from the desktop, as shown in Figure 9-2.

As a result, less time will be wasted searching for such information as the amount of vacation time accrued or budget outlays. No one will have to enter the same data into two different systems, thus making it less likely that erroneous information is passed along. Automated processes mean that investments in best practices within the enterprise applications are utilized to the fullest. One result is that companies will be better able to comply with corporate and industry regulations. By dovetailing all of these capabilities into the simple UI of Microsoft Office, businesses can reduce reliance on power users and increase workplace efficiency.

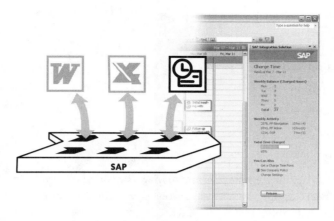

FIGURE 9-2. Exposing SAP tools through Microsoft Office

Project Mendocino delivers other significant benefits, including:

Higher productivity

By providing easy access to enterprise applications, Project Mendocino removes the need for redundant tasks and enables information workers to participate directly in automated processes.

Better decision making

Project Mendocino eliminates information inconsistencies between desktop and enterprise applications, providing information workers with a solid foundation for decision making.

Audit traceability and transparency

By facilitating consistent and proper use of corporate processes, Project Mendocino reduces personal, ad hoc workflows and mitigates the risk of noncompliance with corporate workflows and policies.

Fast user adoption

Project Mendocino's familiar UI is instantly usable by all information workers, which leads to a higher degree of business process automation across the organization.

By exposing selected business process functions and data from mySAP ERP 2004 through Microsoft Office, Project Mendocino leverages the openness of Microsoft's .NET infrastructure with ESA. This enables information workers to perform corporate-driven tasks such as time management, budget monitoring, organization management, and leave management through their desktops, using features such as:

- Extended application menus

- An SAP-specific smart panel

- Business analytics delivered through Microsoft Excel

- Smart business documents in Microsoft Word

- Outlook synchronization between Microsoft Exchange and SAP processes

Microsoft and SAP will sell and support Project Mendocino. An early version of the product was available to select customers in December 2005. General availability is slated for the third quarter of 2006, when it will also receive its official product release name (Project Mendocino is a code name).

How does Project Mendocino use ESA?

Project Mendocino is one of the first examples of an ESA product you can touch. While several tools use ESA in conceptual ways that are sometimes hard to grasp, this tool is based on consuming services in tangible ways that every information worker can benefit from. Project Mendocino shows how ESA can be applied to the user experience through familiar desktop applications. For some users, it will deliver functionality that supercedes the need to work directly with any line-of-business or backend applications. By exposing functionality and giving information workers an easy way to update data that normally resides only on the back end, Project Mendocino embraces the revolutionary potential of ESA.

Project Mendocino is a prime example of how SAP is using services, exposed from ERP, in new ways that create enormous value. And these services can be used together, even though they may have been written for a system that was not designed specifically for ESA. This fulfills one of SAP's short-term goals for ESA adoption: to create simple services that work on top of the applications already used by organizations. In the future, the entire stack that encompasses ERP, Customer Relationship Management (CRM), and all other mySAP solutions will evolve to use business objects as the underlying form of an application. Instead of having a monolithic set of applications, SAP is creating a collection of business objects that can be applied in flexible ways. By the middle of 2007, there will be even more services to choose from than the ones used to support Project Mendocino.

From a purely architectural standpoint, there are a variety of insights here for anyone contemplating the bigger picture of ESA. One is that ESA follows the "model once, run anywhere" model. Instead of hardcoding multiple solutions that apply to different domains, ESA employs business objects that are modeled in a way that allows them to handle different solutions. Project Mendocino is just one of many client-side solutions that ESA will enable. Ultimately, an organization that invests in the ESA infrastructure will be able to leverage it in many different ways.

To understand how this is possible, it is important to become familiar with the new stack defined by ESA.

Project Mendocino overlaps with nearly every part of the new stack:

UI
> Project Mendocino utilizes the familiar Microsoft Office desktop interface. This is achieved not by hardcoding the UI, but rather, by modeling the UI in the backend and deploying it to the client.

Process orchestration

Project Mendocino uses a communications hub referred to as the Mendocino extensions to route data to and within the ERP system.

Process integration

Using the Mendocino extensions, Project Mendocino translates data from Microsoft Office applications such as Excel into a format that is easily understood by existing ERP tools and their respective enterprise services.

Process workflow

All of the normal workflow processes within mySAP ERP take place within the context of Microsoft Office's desktop tools.

Distributed persistence

The ability to cache data for working online or offline also plays a part in Project Mendocino's functionality.

Other applications being created by SAP will use different parts of the stack to enable different solutions. But certain services created for Project Mendocino will indirectly benefit all ESA users by increasing the total pool of objects in the Enterprise Services Inventory. Every service and application being created for Project Mendocino is designed in a global way to be used by other applications within the ESA environment. Timesheet entry services are part of the Cross Application Time Sheet (CATS). These enterprise services will be used by many applications that rely on timesheet recording and account assignment.

Project Mendocino applications

Project Mendocino provides applications that support four primary business processes (see Figure 9-3) through data accessible on the desktop. They include:

Time management

The Outlook calendar can be used for recording time on projects, cost centers, and other accounting objects into the SAP CATS, streamlining time entry while ensuring time-reporting compliance.

Budget monitoring

Reports from mySAP ERP can be scheduled for delivery in the Outlook inbox and users can work with them online or offline.

Leave management

Leave requests can be entered as calendar items, and approvals can be routed automatically based on enterprise-defined processes.

Organization management

Up-to-date information about employees, open positions, and organizational structures is integrated from SAP software into the Outlook contacts area and Microsoft Office documents.

Project Mendocino and its associated applications do not replace other UI strategies or solutions that SAP has in place already. Rather, access to these other UIs, most dominantly

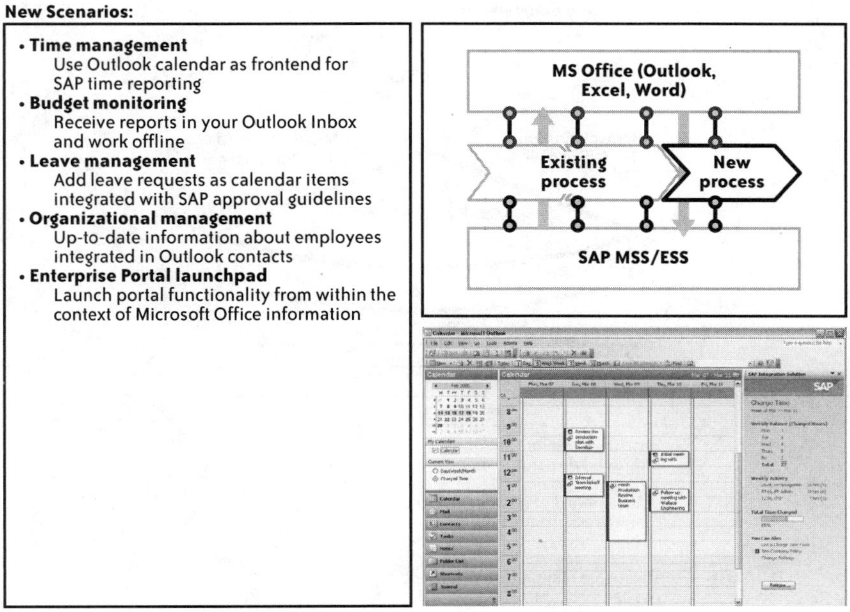
New Scenarios:
• Time management
Use Outlook calendar as frontend for SAP time reporting
• Budget monitoring
Receive reports in your Outlook Inbox and work offline
• Leave management
Add leave requests as calendar items integrated with SAP approval guidelines
• Organizational management
Up-to-date information about employees integrated in Outlook contacts
• Enterprise Portal launchpad
Launch portal functionality from within the context of Microsoft Office information
MS Office (Outlook, Excel, Word)
Existing process
New process
SAP MSS/ESS

FIGURE 9-3. Project Mendocino version 1.0

the SAP Enterprise Portal, is made easier for the user, and certain processes are frontended within Microsoft Office. A financial controller, for instance, has a full-featured and flexible solution within existing SAP applications and for the purpose of his tasks, a financial controller will not see a lot of benefit from working inside of Microsoft Office or Outlook other than having access to reports, approval processes, and self-service scenarios.

As with any other technology, organizations must determine which business scenarios deliver the most value from within Project Mendocino. The unique advantages of this technology cannot be applied in every use case. Managers and cost center owners, for example, will benefit greatly by having access to information, alerts, notifications, and reports in a simple environment that is already used on a regular basis. Project Mendocino also alleviates the need for expert users who are in charge of providing a whole group with information in the system on an as-needed basis, thus creating bottlenecks in productivity (see Figure 9-4).

Project Mendocino makes it easier for information workers to perform corporate-driven tasks through the following features:

Report distribution

Analytics and transactional reports from SAP are preformatted and customized for reading as spreadsheets in Microsoft Excel. Information workers can personalize the spreadsheet templates, format reports, and subscribe to new reports right from the desktop suite.

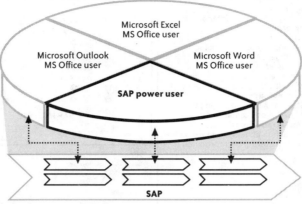

Project Mendocino empowers all users

Microsoft Excel
MS Office user

Microsoft Outlook
MS Office user

Microsoft Word
MS Office user

SAP power user

SAP

Synchronized information
Improved decision-making

In the context of business processes
• Improved productivity
• Compliance

Through a familiar user interface
• Instantly usable
• Prevalent process participation

FIGURE 9-4. Project Mendocino alleviating overdependence on expert users

Alerts and notifications

Microsoft Outlook can trigger event-based alerts and notifications that work through backend mySAP ERP applications. Information workers can preset monitoring thresholds, receive actionable items, and view reports as email attachments as well.

Form-based approval process

Customized forms from within Microsoft Office guide information workers through processes for performing common business tasks that require approval by authorized users. This facilitates consistency and reduces data entry errors. It also ensures compliance with administrative directives and corporate regulations.

Offline capabilities

All of the functions available through Project Mendocino applications can also be performed while offline. When the user goes back online, all data and forms are synchronized automatically with the backend systems.

Personalization

Role-based access through Outlook allows information workers to access and modify only the transactional data, SAP report templates, and subscriptions for which they are authorized based on their role within the organization.

SAP chose to include the aforementioned applications in Project Mendocino because they provide several organizational benefits, including:

Improved decision making

With up-to-date information and the capability to drill down into information sources in critical business applications, information workers can access the most recent, consistent views of information within the context of a business task. For instance, when a manager drills down into employee compensation details in Outlook, relevant personnel budget information is simultaneously retrieved from the back end and displayed. This enables managers to make better business decisions more efficiently. At the same time, the traceability and transparency of information throughout the enterprise help satisfy regulatory compliance requirements.

Enhanced productivity

Because processes supported by mySAP ERP are embedded into Microsoft Office applications, the complexity of advanced tasks is reduced and the transparency of simple tasks is increased. In addition, costs associated with training will be minimized because the product runs within the Microsoft Office environment that employees already use on a daily basis.

Intuitive access to enterprise processes

By initiating business processes through the familiar Microsoft Office interface, a higher degree of business process automation occurs across the organization, thus allowing organizations to realize greater value from investments in SAP software and Microsoft Office applications.

What is the goal of the Time Management application?

An ideal time management solution enables a knowledge worker to record the time spent working throughout a week or month without the need for timesheets, memorization of billing codes, manual data collection from multiple business systems, and questions about cost centers. Information workers could arrange a meeting online or offline using a familiar desktop application, such as Microsoft Outlook, and be automatically prompted with questions that facilitate account charges. Outlook would prompt the worker with the most recently charged account selected as the default, and a list of other relevant accounts. If the meeting was extended within the calendar application, the billing updates would be performed automatically. Pertinent information such as the total number of hours billed to each account, and unaccounted hours, would be accessible as well. Managers would be alerted to approve a charge and ensure budget compliance. Quick reference links would let employees view detailed statistics and company policies. Essentially, the solution would provide easy access to the task's relevant information, eliminate time spent searching for information, and enhance the decision-making process.

Project Mendocino's Time Management application, shown in Figure 9-5, is capable of performing every one of those tasks. One of the biggest benefits of the Time Management application is that it allows information workers to keep track of project time without the overhead of filling out a timesheet. Time recording activities can be initiated directly from an Outlook calendar appointment. Information workers can review and edit data if necessary and preset time recording defaults in their Outlook preferences for frequent activities.

The information worker also has access to the Time Management application when offline. When her system goes back online, the data will be automatically submitted into the system of record.

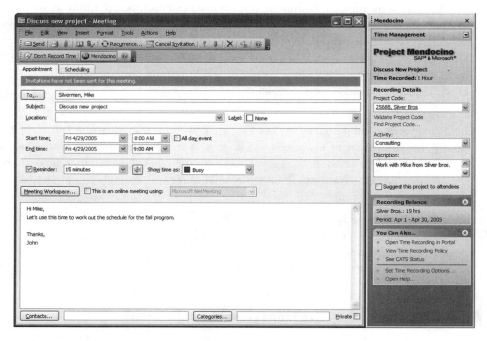

FIGURE 9-5. The Time Management application

The Time Management application extends the standard Outlook appointment object to include a means of logging time and selecting a charge code to go with it (see Figure 9-6). This is known as an *appointment object with time logging entry*. Information workers can log whole days to a charge code or assign multiple appointments in a single day to different charge codes. The information worker can also select a view in Outlook that displays only appointments that are associated with a particular project code. Likewise, all meetings that are not yet associated with a charge code can also be viewed and managed. And the information worker can define a default project code that will be assigned to times with no meetings or unassigned meetings in the calendar.

The SAP action pane also carries time-logging contextual information, such as an overview of the available charge codes. This also gives each user a way to view data related to his timesheet, such as total percentage of time logged to a particular project.

So what happens when an employee goes into the calendar and begins deleting or archiving a meeting from two months ago? The SAP system controls the data, so even though the appointment might be erased from the individual user's calendar, it does not disappear from the database if it has been approved, unless the user explicitly asks for this. This ensures that the correct business functionality is accomplished while also giving the user the ability to use her calendar program in a personalized manner.

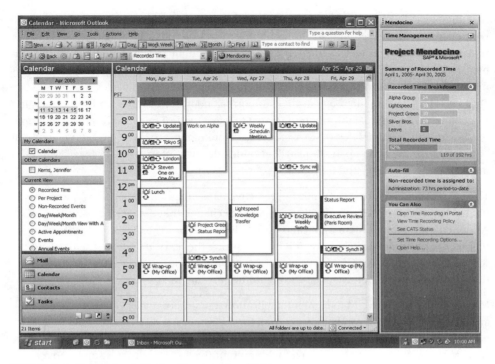

FIGURE 9-6. Charging time in the Time Management application

What is the goal of the Leave Management application?

Every time an information worker requests leave using Microsoft Outlook, it triggers a workflow that is fully incorporated with backend services through ESA. The employee puts in a leave request, and the manager will approve or deny it. To these two information workers, the process appears as nothing more than entering information in the familiar Microsoft Outlook interface, but the emails are actually controlled through workflows that are accessible through ESA.

But that is only the simplest form of leave management. What use is a leave time request and approval without the relevant contextual information to go with it? How much leave has been accrued, for instance? Until the day an information worker decides to request leave, the amount of vacation time he has accumulated is immaterial. So, for instance, if an information worker is getting married, he knows that a particular number of days are allotted but has no clue how many—or, for that matter, where to find the information inside the system. With Project Mendocino, the contextual information regarding leave days is delivered within the Outlook calendar appointment. An information worker can click on the appropriate link in the Mendocino action pane and find out that marital leave is five days. Microsoft Office supplies the environment and Project Mendocino provides the functionality to enable this transaction.

Within the Outlook calendar, information workers can create, monitor, and view all calendar-specific activities. The leave request object looks similar to the appointment/

meeting object in the Outlook calendar. This object is the primary way that information workers will enter leave requests through the Outlook calendar. Information workers can request whole days, as well as fractions of a day, depending on the leave types configured by the customer (a half-day vacation, for example). The Leave Management system allows information workers to create leave requests from several different places within Outlook—by selecting the range in the Outlook calendar, for instance, or by choosing it from a menu. Contextual information related to leave request types as they are configured on the employee self-service (ESS) system (vacation, maternity leave, jury duty, etc.) will be available in the action pane. This will also include such information as leave entitlement, leave availability, and leave taken.

The Leave Management system fills in predictive data such as the approving manager's name. But the information worker will be able to change that data if necessary as well. And the Leave Management application capabilities will be available offline. When back online, the system executes the action by submitting the leave request to the backend server. Leave request information originating in Outlook is synchronized to ensure that the data is updated when changed through other means, such as ESS.

Managers use the Leave Management application in a different way than employees do, and Project Mendocino can be personalized for their needs, too. The approving manager has the ability to approve or reject a leave request from within Outlook, for example. This is achieved by presenting the manager with an intuitive interface that is similar to a meeting request approval. Employees are then notified within Outlook that the leave request has been approved or rejected. Approving managers can also view leave status for entire teams through the team calendar. A manager can create reports through her access to the team's leave status.

What is the goal of the Budget Monitoring application?

When a manager wants to be notified about emerging budget issues, she can easily set an alert: "Please notify when term costs are exceeding 50 percent or if I have a single posting to the account exceeding $10,000." That is the most basic level of control required on any budget management tool. But the Budget Monitoring application in Project Mendocino, shown in Figure 9-7, incorporates a much deeper level of reporting. It includes the ability to be notified by the system about the current status of a team's budget use, its cost center, and the cost-specific projects. These reports can be customized and triggered for regularly scheduled delivery to an Outlook inbox.

When a manager selects a report template, or is in the viewing mode of a report, she can define the delivery schedule and frequency of delivery through the action pane. These settings are stored for each user and are reported in the Mendocino Server as personalization values. The reports are then distributed to Outlook.

A manager will even be able to initiate a budget transfer (as shown in Figure 9-8), posting an adjustment directly from a received alert through integration with forms or by drilling down into the SAP Enterprise Portal. When authorized, an information worker could then

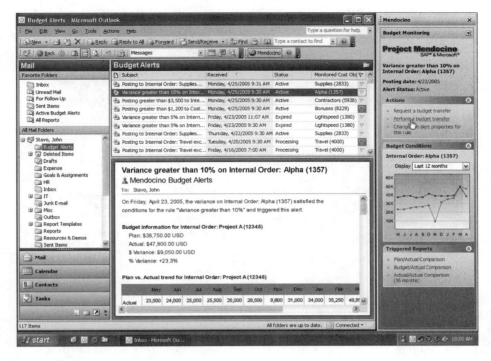

FIGURE 9-7. The Budget Monitoring application

have the ability to make a budget transfer or trigger a workflow to the area controller from there.

There are several ways to view reports in the Outlook folder, including through a role-based list. Within the report view, the user will be able to:

- See a catalog of all reports that originate from ERP systems based on his role
- Configure the report execution parameters in Outlook
- Add personalized report templates from the catalog
- Schedule report delivery, recurring and nonrecurring, or based on the data change in the process chain
- Use "run report now" or "refresh/update" functionality

Project Mendocino delivers reports in multiple formats: text only, data only (XML), formatted (MHTML, native *.xls* files), or any mixture thereof based on user preferences. Project Mendocino can even map the incoming data to a user's local XML template, which is based on Excel templates, allowing for formatting according to the individual user's needs.

The Budget Monitoring application provides managers with all the time-critical information required to effectively monitor their budgets. This happens via alerts and notifications in the Office environment, as well as with ongoing financial reports, allowing managers to

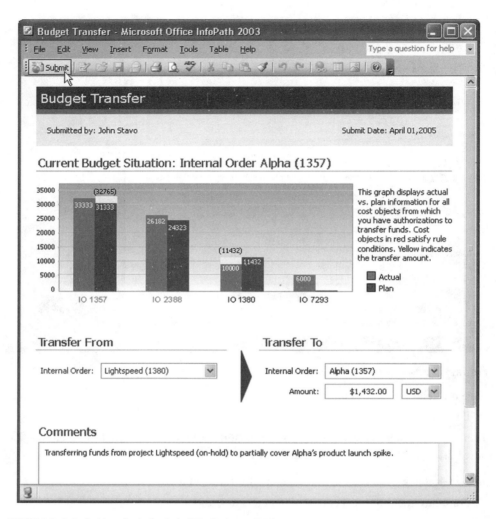

FIGURE 9-8. Budget transfers in the Budget Monitoring application

recognize critical postings and variances, and to take immediate action on them. Managers have access to information such as the company's budgeting and budget handling policy as well as extensive analytics. Access to some of this data may require drill-down functionality to the SAP NetWeaver Portal, which is seamlessly integrated.

The administrative user also has specific abilities that are enabled by the Budget Monitoring application. An admin can define existing reports in the underlying system and make them available for distribution to end users based on roles (this is known as a *reporting catalog*). When defining the reporting catalog, the admin user first defines which report to make available. Then he defines the selection parameters, delivery mechanism (HTML, Excel, etc.), and frequency for it to be made available to the end user. A list of basic Budget Monitoring report templates will be included in the standard delivery of Project Mendocino. Reports that are defined by the admin user for distribution are executed by the backend server. Upon creation of the report, the report will be converted to an Outlook item and enriched with metadata.

What is the goal of the Team Management application?

The Team Management application provides contextual personnel and organizational information to the Project Mendocino user through the Microsoft Office environment. It allows managers to use the Outlook Contacts view to browse and display contact details about team members and subordinates. For managers, Team Management also displays additional contact information supplemented by personnel data gathered from the Human Resources backend system. This includes compensation data (salary, compensation ratio, etc.) and related files (e.g., employee files). Adding an information worker's HR-related file from the Outlook client to a related component in the file management system is as simple as dropping an email or document into a corresponding folder with the team member's name. The information provided and activities enabled depends on SAP security and the user's structural relationship to the contact (My team, My data, Colleagues, etc.).

Information workers can display organizational data, such as org charts, alongside contacts data and have it supplemented by related data from the Human Resources backend system.

The Project Mendocino architecture

When the goals of Project Mendocino were first formulated, it became clear that two very different architectures needed to be brought together. On the one side was the client application, which requires local data storage. On the other side was the mySAP ERP environment. The different technologies in this case made it very easy to select web services as the interface technology, since both technologies added web services support in their last releases. However, simply connecting these two worlds using web services did not offer a comprehensive enough solution, in this case. The goals required more extensibility—SAP wanted to enable a model-driven environment on the client side. The model-driven environment is what allows Project Mendocino to push additional screens and updates to the user without the need to continuously run through an installation and reinstallation for every change in business needs.

On top of that, Microsoft Office currently works in online as well as offline modes—and that capability had to be maintained in Project Mendocino. The users had to be able to trigger activities while being offline and have them automatically resynchronize once their machines went back online.

Microsoft and SAP also realized that the system components involved—Exchange Servers, Microsoft Office, and mySAP ERP systems—are of such a high value to customers that massively updating those environments would not be acceptable. There is no reason to expose the existing system landscape to any unnecessary disruption.

SAP and Microsoft weighed these requirements carefully and realized the need for a communications hub that would sit in the middle of the two existing environments. The hub is used to collect various configurations from the backend system, determine the objects that should be exposed, and decide which activities the user can trigger and how all of that ties together in the UI. That communications hub is the Mendocino extensions.

The Mendocino extensions then had to be connected with the Microsoft Office client and the mySAP ERP system. The result is that there are three primary parts to Project Mendocino's architecture (see Figure 9-9): the Mendocino extensions, the Microsoft Office Add-On, and mySAP ERP.

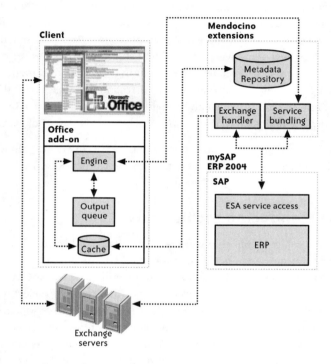

FIGURE 9-9. Project Mendocino architecture

What makes up the Mendocino extensions?

The Mendocino extensions are implemented in .NET as well as by using Java 2 Enterprise Edition (J2EE) technology. The Mendocino extensions sit between the client and the mySAP systems and enable these two to talk with each other. On top of that, the Mendocino extensions include the application description in the form of metadata and cater the metadata to the client.

The major components of the Mendocino extensions include:

- Metadata repository interface and storage
- Exchange handler
- Service bundling

- A number of so-called "Pluggable Services" to interact with existing technology that enables user roles, authentication, security, and reporting
- A set of tools for configuration and customization

What is the Office Add-On?

The Microsoft Office Add-On enables communication between the local Microsoft Office client with the Mendocino extensions and the mySAP system through a metadata portal and storage interface.

The major components of the Office Add-On include:

- Runtime engine
- Output queue
- Caching mechanisms

We will discuss these mechanisms in more detail next.

How is data routed through the Project Mendocino architecture?

A typical Microsoft Office user often creates status reports of one kind or another. Using Mendocino, this process is accelerated since the Office interface already shows which reports an information worker can subscribe to, and offers templates for creating new ones. Perhaps a budget report needs to be delivered every Monday morning at 8:00, to be used in a staff meeting at 10:00 a.m. Later, as the inbox overflows with reports, that might need fine-tuning. Now the user wants an alert only after reaching 80 percent of total budget consumption. All of these sorts of activities can be done using the local client—in this case, Microsoft Office combined with Project Mendocino.

The client's Office Add-On is responsible for representing the UI based on metadata and other kinds of desktop information. For this purpose, the client Add-On is separated into three major parts: engine, output queue, and cache.

The runtime engine interprets metadata in order to understand which business object is being exposed (a budget report or time entry, for example). Through these exposed objects, the Office Add-On is able to create subclasses of the existing objects within Microsoft Office—a time entry would then be treated as a subclass of an appointment object. These cases are exposed through the UI within the action pane environment. In addition to describing objects, the metadata also describes the UI as well as actions that can be triggered from within the UI. This additional metadata, available on the client side, includes both generalized personalization data as well as some master data. The generalized personalization data, for example, determines which fields become available in the action pane. The master data, for example, determines which project's budget is being assessed or the default status report profile.

The caching component ensures that metadata, master data, and additional files and objects are being kept available locally and are up-to-date. The cache is able to store this data on the local client without the need to continuously synchronize and resynchronize with the backend ESA services. And by inserting a validity period into that, Project Mendocino can always keep the data cache up-to-date with regard to changes from the backend system. It's not so much a push of the updated information but more of a pull from it. This also dramatically speeds up the end-to-end communication by preloading some of the data that the underlying system will request.

The Office Add-On includes features that allow for offline processing. This is being enabled through the output queue component. The output queue component is invoked when a user triggers an activity, such as saving a time entry. It then takes the selected business object and triggers activities in the underlying mySAP system through either synchronous or asynchronous web services calls. Those web services calls then come into the SAP environment within the Mendocino extensions, through the service bundling component. This component allows Project Mendocino to compose multiple underlying web services into a single one for, say, performance improvement, or for using the result of a first call for a second call.

The Mendocino extensions handle all of the communication between the client and the underlying mySAP ERP system. They gather the context and define the objects that are being exposed to the end user. So the Mendocino extensions invoke the relevant underlying ESA services to talk to the underlying applications within the mySAP ERP environment. In some cases, the responses might actually not be handled synchronously, but asynchronously. For this, the Mendocino extensions communicate the data back to the local client by means of the Exchange handler. This completes a simple round trip of data from the UI within an action pane to the mySAP ERP system and back.

The metadata that is available on the client resides within the Mendocino extensions. This server also acts as a consolidation engine. Most businesses have an IT landscape using a number of different SAP systems—an SAP Business Information Warehouse (SAP BW) system, mySAP/ERP, CRM, Supply Chain Management (SCM), or any number of other solutions that might not even be coming from SAP. The Mendocino Server coalesces one or multiple backend systems. It takes the metadata from various underlying systems and combines it based on the user and the user's role within the organization, and pushes it down to the client.

Remember that the client might not always be online, and Project Mendocino must be careful in the way it communicates information back to the client. Additional queuing and caching may be required in the Mendocino extensions. The data is communicated from mySAP ERP into the Exchange handler, which properly formats the information into an XML document—a format that the client can then understand.

In the case of a report, that means converting it into an HTML-based email, maybe with some kind of attachment. It also requires flagging the report with specific metadata that is not visible to the end user but is attached to the email body to enable certain kinds of processing once it reaches the client environment. The client interprets the metadata and dynamically combines it into the UI before presenting the final budget status notification to the end user. The rules gathered from the backend system are converted into metadata that the client can understand, and the gap between the two systems is bridged.

Project Mendocino is role sensitive. This means that the information which is being presented and the actions available to the end user depend on the user's role within the organization (whether the user is an employee or a manager, for example).

What are the system requirements for using the Project Mendocino architecture?

The client runs on Microsoft Windows XP with Microsoft Office 2003 installed. The Mendocino extensions require Microsoft Windows Server 2003 or higher and Microsoft Exchange Server 2003 or higher, including Active Directory 2000. There are no additional installation, software, or hardware requirements for existing Exchange Server landscapes.

What is the primary function of the Office Add-On?

The Office Add-On, also known as the client, represents the UI based on metadata. It uses the master data for drop-down menus or business rules and then triggers activities in the underlying SAP system through either synchronous or asynchronous web services calls. The metadata descriptions of the various applications are interpreted through the engine, which supports integration with various kinds of host software. The engine also provides:

- Outlook integration
- Personalization
- Excel integration
- InfoPath integration
- Metadata-defined forms

The web services calls from the Office Add-On are relayed into the SAP environment (this occurs within the Mendocino extensions, through the service bundling component).

The engine on the client loads assemblies and metadata from the cache and interprets the metadata descriptions of applications to:

- Execute service calls
- Execute business logic
- Construct and display the UI based on metadata
- Interact with host software

The runtime engine uses an Outlook services library (using the standard programming features of Outlook) to allow the integration of the following features and services:

Action pane
   The Mendocino action pane will mimic the behavior of the Office programmable task pane.

Toolbar buttons

Custom buttons can be added to the application-level toolbar. Buttons will trigger the execution of metadata-based actions.

Context menu items

Custom context menu items can be added to folder and item context menus. Menu items will trigger the execution of metadata-based actions.

Outlook events

Selected standard Outlook events and behaviors will be extended to automatically activate metadata-defined actions.

Custom Calendar views

Outlook tabbed forms and action panes will be defined via metadata.

Contact management

Additional tabs will be added to contact objects for server-maintained data.

The engine's metadata form definition component is the primary way to customize Project Mendocino forms and dialogs. Administrator users, using a metadata definition, can customize the action pane, custom dialogs, or Outlook custom forms. This level of customization also enables easy text replacement and UI localization.

The cache is responsible for maintaining the proper metadata on the client machine. It is based on the user's role and supplies the functionality to store a user's metadata based on user role and data instances, stores metadata in a secure manner, and provides access to metadata while disconnected from the Mendocino server. Furthermore, the cache includes deployment capabilities (described later) to have application assemblies proactively delivered to a user's machine. Last but not least, the cache provides offline data retrieval for Mendocino. It allows for the switching of access to data to the offline store or to the online Mendocino server, depending on hints from either metadata parameters or other configuration information. The cache component also provides the first-time provisioning and deployment of reference data, reference data expiration refresh rules, and storage of data locally.

The third component of the client, the output queue, provides the functionality to allow users to initiate actions while offline, which are then invoked whenever a connection becomes available. Queued actions will be serviced as soon as possible. If online, these calls are serviced in short intervals of time; if offline, the calls are stored for invocation later. The output queue is used only for asynchronous calls. To support this functionality, the output queue provides interfaces to be able to flush the "queue" when the backend server is available. Calls made by the output queue to the service bundling component in the backend system will generally respond synchronously with acknowledge confirmation.

Mendocino will support deployment of applications to the client machine as complete units containing the metadata, assemblies, additional required client components, and reference data required to execute the application. This will occur automatically through a deployment mechanism and includes upgrade control in the form of versioning.

What are the functions of the Mendocino extensions components?

The Mendocino extensions include components for the metadata repository, Exchange handler, and service bundling.

The metadata repository stores the metadata, authorizes access, and enforces consistency of the stored data. The metadata storage component is a relational database built on top of SQL Express 2005. This metadata describes the objects that are exposed within Microsoft Office and their related UIs and associated actions. This metadata is being pulled by the client based on the user and the role(s) of the user within the organization.

The Exchange handler provides an application-friendly and user-friendly view of messages in Microsoft Exchange. It addresses the conversion of standardized messages from the backend server into Outlook objects such as IPM.Note. The Exchange handler provides an independent layer to different versions and formats of messages so that the calling components do not have to care about versions and formats of Office objects and command messages for the client Add-On. The Exchange handler provides interfaces to the most important objects within Microsoft Office, including email (IPM.Note), email attachments, the calendar, tasks, and contacts.

The service bundling component hides the implementation details and distributes the incoming calls to the Mendocino-specific web services or ESA services, or any combination thereof. Which of these is chosen during the implementation depends upon the methods that can best support the respective use cases within the applications. The service bundling component also implements a method to resolve any Mendocino IDs toward SAP item IDs where necessary. It is anticipated that the vast majority of these services will be executed synchronously for functionality such as data validation and displaying information in action panes. In case of asynchronous calls, the service bundling component will always reply with an acknowledgment confirmation and then route the reply through the Exchange handler back to the client. An example of such an asynchronous call can be found in team management when requesting all organization contacts for a given user.

In addition to the described components, the Mendocino extensions also include pluggable services. The pluggable services enable integration with preexisting technologies for functionality such as user roles, authentication, security, and reporting. Since these capabilities are not Mendocino specific, customers will be able to deploy any of these services from various vendors supporting these standardized interfaces. It is also possible to reuse existing solutions already installed on site.

How is security handled in the Project Mendocino environment?

The challenge with authentication in Project Mendocino is the need to separate the authentication from the authentication within the system. For authentication to the system, Project Mendocino is able to reuse the authentication of the local user in the Windows environment. This is generally implemented using Windows NT LAN Manager or Microsoft Active Directory, which most people are familiar with. Within Project Mendocino, SAP security experts are also developing a module that is able to take the user token from the Windows environment and map it to the proper SAP user. In doing so, Project Mendocino is able to issue a single-sign-on ticket for the client to communicate in a secure way with the web services on the SAP side.

Once authentication is secured, standard SAP guidelines and principles take effect. To this extent, access is granted based on authorization profiles associated with the user in the underlying SAP system. Each profile is associated with, for example, a handful of cost centers out of all the cost centers that exist in the underlying system. An information worker may have access only to his own personal information based on service scenarios, while a manager will be granted access only to her organizational unit within the entire system, and so on.

How will Project Mendocino change in the future?

Today, Project Mendocino is bringing two very different worlds together: the client user experience and the SAP environment. That required a number of enhancements in many of the underlying modules exposing all of the enterprise services, such as enhancements to the reporting functionality and the alerts and notification functionality. SAP continues pushing forward to get all of those pieces in place until eventually it seamlessly becomes part of NetWeaver.

By making almost all of Project Mendocino's baseline functionality an integral part of NetWeaver, SAP can ensure that the total cost of ownership for our customers will continue to get lower while at the same time providing more services. It will allow SAP to open up the Project Mendocino suite of applications to application developers outside of SAP to create their own metadata and push that out to the client to provide the same user experience for their relevant applications as well. The next release of Project Mendocino, which is targeted for the third quarter of 2007, will feature these capabilities as well as improved tools that can be used by third-party application developers along with those at SAP. Project Mendocino will be split into two different tracks over time: the underlying infrastructure (the framework and the tools) and the application layer.

Some of the additional applications under consideration for enhancement include employee self-service and manager self-service applications and CRM scenarios. Just as Project Mendocino can make an internal meeting request, it will soon be capable of scheduling a customer meeting as well. And once that meeting is scheduled, a travel request and the budget for that request will be triggered, too. A contact within Outlook could be a customer contact, even a business partner at the customer site. An Excel spreadsheet can be used for reporting in the current release, but future releases will offer scenario analysis as part of a customer's supply-chain modeling. The Project Mendocino architecture offers additional possibilities with regard to exposing additional business scenarios, such as use on mobile devices, as well.

Without question, Project Mendocino is poised to increase user productivity by giving users a familiar environment that is seamlessly linked to SAP backend functionality.

ESA in action: Agile Solutions Ltda

SAP customers are eagerly anticipating Project Mendocino. One such customer is Agile Solutions Ltda, which is adding this application to its in-process ESA adoption plan. Agile is a pioneering systems integrator (SI) and custom solutions developer in Latin America, the first in the region to create composite xApps with SAP NetWeaver for its customers. Founded in Brazil in 1999, today Agile Solutions has annual revenues of $35 million and 600 employees located in Chile, the U.S., India, and Australia. Its customers include the commodities giant BHP Billiton, Codelco, Samarco Mineradora, Empresas CMPC, Masisa, and Concha y Toro. Despite its deceptively small size, Agile Solutions is one of the world's leading creators of composite applications, and it is currently developing some of the first composite applications based on Project Mendocino.

Agile Solutions's development philosophy in the dawning age of ESA is to focus almost exclusively on the business objectives of its customers, the functionality needed to meet those objectives, and then building the composite application containing that functionality, drawing upon whatever systems and resources are at hand to complete the task.

This has meant that Agile Solutions has tended to downplay discussions of architecture with customers and describe the benefits of composites and ESA in purely business-focused terms. The first customer of its xApps was Agile itself, which implemented the SAP xApp Resource and Portfolio Management in 2002 to integrate its own project work-flows. Agile Solutions knew its project management execution was embodied in Microsoft Project and that its data was stored in SAP R/3. What was important was that the two systems be integrated—not how, precisely, that would be done. Now Agile Solutions is able to share the status of projects with its customers and partners via an online portal. The portal offers a unified view of the data from the underlying applications, incorporating customers' and partners' feedback and knowledge into the development process.

In practice, Agile Solutions's development strategy demands aggressive timetables and huge skill sets on the part of its developers, who may be called upon to write iViews in Java, services and interfaces in ABAP, and similar tasks in non-SAP applications, all in the service of a single composite application. While Agile Solutions has found it is key to always keep a complete picture of the desired application in mind (just as an architect stays focused on the image of a house), peeling the needed layers of functionality away from their original applications (the metaphorical bricks of the architect's house) calls for developers capable of understanding and transforming each layer. As ESA and the service grid evolve, this process will become simpler, and Agile Solutions's methodology—to focus on the goal and what it takes to achieve it, rather than what is easy to do within the existing technology—will become easier over time.

In the case of Project Mendocino, Agile Solutions is once again using itself as a test bed for new functionality—in this case, a series of knowledge bases that will offer suggestions to and guide future users of Project Mendocino when they make mistakes or confess to the system that they are stuck in a process. To do this, Agile Solutions will create a knowledge base containing insights from its own implementation of Project Mendocino and then test its suggested solution on its own developers during their second, third, fourth, and fifth customer implementations, and so on, incorporating more insights each time.

The resulting composite application will hide the deep functionality from the user and offer context-specific advice instead, essentially automating the search engine concept to deliver knowledge at the precise moment and the necessary level of understanding.

Thanks to the reusability of enterprise services-enabled composites, Agile intends, as a next step, to recycle the application to train new employees in its development process, and to manage business knowledge to create new solutions for customers in fields such as medical diagnostics, where the system could suggest tests or medications in response to user-submitted systems in a predefined process using pattern recognition and search engines.

CHAPTER TEN

ESA at Work: Examples from the Field

IN MANY WAYS, THE POWER OF **ESA** MUST BE UNLOCKED THROUGH THE IMAGINATIONS OF ENTERPRISE architects and business process designers. It is in the trenches of business, while battling to survive and succeed, that the best ideas emerge. This chapter is devoted to illustrating how at a variety of levels, ESA is transforming processes, scenarios, and even entire industries in the hope that further inspiration will result. The examples in this chapter rove through many different industries such as consumer products, chemicals, and logistics service providers. The processes covered include service management, vendor-managed inventory, and manufacturing execution. Each of these examples represents the sort of innovation that ESA can unleash.

ESA in consumer products

Consumer product (CP) manufacturers are among the most familiar faces on the front lines of ESA adoption. They face one of the most challenging and competitive landscapes of any manufacturing-based industry. Retailers led by Wal-Mart have consolidated distribution and pricing power, all but dictating the cost structures in which manufacturers must operate. The same pressure forces them increasingly to outsource and offshore their operations, straining their supply chains, while consumer demand—which goes hand in hand with consumer boredom—calls for ever-proliferating numbers of spinoffs from successful products and brands. This leads to even more strain on product development, supply chains, and manufacturing systems, as the classical model of relatively stable business processes buckles under unpredictable demands—a buckling felt by the underlying IT as well.

In its many conversations with customers in the CP industry, SAP has been told again and again that they understand that ESA represents a paradigm shift and is not just another upgrade; that the functionality once packed into a black box is about to be freed from that box—i.e., your classical enterprise application. But they have questions of their own, as it turns out. Yes, they understand that ESA will be a platform, but will it be *the* platform, and what will it mean for the IT landscape that exists today? They're not afraid of re-rendering their current applications as enterprise services, but they want a detailed roadmap to adoption, and they are demanding real-world examples (not just the theoretical benefits) of how ESA will solve what is rapidly becoming their biggest IT challenge: reconfiguring their landscapes to keep up with business processes that are anything but stable.

And there are such examples. Procter & Gamble (P&G) invented the concept and practice of Vendor-Managed Inventory (VMI) in the mid-1980s, effectively differentiating itself with an innovative supply chain process. As shown in Figure 10-1, the evolution of VMI continued to create a competitive edge for P&G, and its first wave of retail partners, until widespread adoption throughout the CP industry ultimately made VMI a critical but non-differentiating task that could be outsourced successfully to third parties.

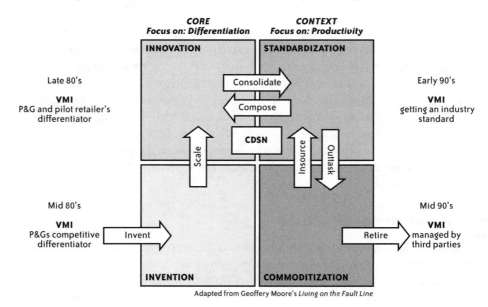

FIGURE 10-1. Business process life cycle for Vendor Managed Inventory (VMI)

Seeking to leverage more than a decade's worth of investment in its VMI processes, however, P&G sought to reinvent them by decomposing components of the underlying applications and recombining them as composite applications driving its "Responsive Replenishment" process, in which data from even the point-of-sale helps to trigger replenishment at its retail partners automatically.

There are other examples as well. One CP manufacturer uses enterprise services to gain a competitive advantage by extending the reach of the global purchasing process to its large supplier base. The result is a standardized purchasing process enabling collaboration partners to manage purchase orders throughout the entire supply chain more efficiently. This process provides business value to both the manufacturer and suppliers by streamlining manufacturing cycle time on the one hand and jointly tackling critical out-of-stock situations on the other. In this example, enterprise services added to a foundation of mySAP ERP, SAP Business Information Warehouse (SAP BW), and third-party purchasing applications lay the groundwork for business process innovation.

Store-specific pricing

As SAP continues to extend the functionality of its packaged applications using enterprise services and composite applications (its xApps), opportunities to create xApps using ESA principles have already emerged. One lightweight xApp created in just days for SAP's customers in the retail industry uses guided procedures, a handful of simple interfaces, and analytic tools to make a key feature of their Enterprise Resources Planning (ERP) systems available to managers at the individual store level.

These managers were all but barred from accessing the sales, pricing, and margins data—to name just three of more than 100 fields and parameters—residing in their company's ERP system. The complexity of that application, coupled with the potential for confusion and misuse if hundreds of middle managers were granted access to an industrial-strength application they were ill-equipped to use, had kept control over pricing consolidated in the hands of category managers at corporate headquarters.

However, the store managers were also the ones closest to the front lines of the business—the ones responsible for monitoring the prices of their immediate competitors and the effect of price changes on their own business. This led to tension between store managers who understood local conditions and needed the flexibility to respond, and category managers who possessed ultimate responsibility and access to analytical tools but were unable to focus on a store-by-store basis. In many cases today, the store managers simply override prices listed in the point-of-sale system, which has the unfortunate side effect of creating inconsistent price information in relevant process steps and obscuring the reasons for local markdowns.

The xApp that SAP has created sought to resolve this tension by using enterprise services to create a solution, which would offer store managers the analytical tools they needed to examine competitors' prices, and would do so within a simple interface that could pass their findings to a category manager for ultimate approval. As illustrated in Figure 10-2, the process begins with a store manager selecting items for comparison within the xApp, which then generates an Adobe form that is passed to a junior store employee who is responsible for gathering the relevant price data from competitors (window shopping, in other words), and then entering that data in the form. At that point, the guided procedure processes within the application pass the form back to the store manager, who is then able to analyze the competitive pressure against his current prices and margins, calculate new prices, and measure their impact on margins.

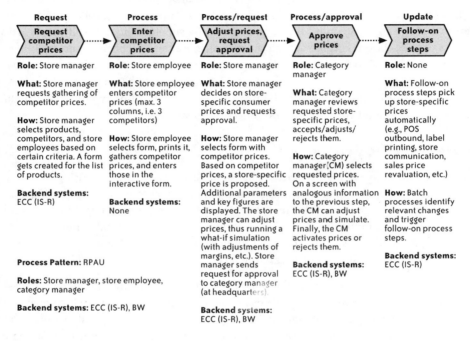

Request	Process	Process/request	Process/approval	Update
Request competitor prices	**Enter competitor prices**	**Adjust prices, request approval**	**Approve prices**	**Follow-on process steps**
Role: Store manager	**Role:** Store employee	**Role:** Store manager	**Role:** Category manager	**Role:** None
What: Store manager requests gathering of competitor prices.	**What:** Store employee enters competitor prices (max. 3 columns, i.e. 3 competitors)	**What:** Store manager decides on store-specific consumer prices and requests approval.	**What:** Category manager reviews requested store-specific prices, accepts/adjusts/rejects them.	**What:** Follow-on process steps pick up store-specific prices automatically (e.g., POS outbound, label printing, store communication, sales price revaluation, etc.)
How: Store manager selects products, competitors, and store employees based on certain criteria. A form gets created for the list of products.	**How:** Store employee selects form, prints it, gathers competitor prices, and enters those in the interactive form.	**How:** Store manager selects form with competitor prices. Based on competitor prices, a store-specific price is proposed. Additional parameters and key figures are displayed. The store manager can adjust prices, thus running a what-if simulation (with adjustments of margins, etc.). Store manager sends request for approval to category manager (at headquarters).	**How:** Category manager (CM) selects requested prices. On a screen with analogous information to the previous step, the CM can adjust prices and simulate. Finally, the CM activates prices or rejects them.	**How:** Batch processes identify relevant changes and trigger follow-on process steps.
Backend systems: ECC (IS-R)	**Backend systems:** None			**Backend systems:** ECC (IS-R)
Process Pattern: RPAU		**Backend systems:** ECC (IS-R), BW	**Backend systems:** ECC (IS-R), BW	
Roles: Store manager, store employee, category manager				
Backend systems: ECC (IS-R), BW				

FIGURE 10-2. Handling store-specific consumer prices

Store-specific prices are passed once again, this time to the category manager at headquarters, who is able to run her own analysis of the new prices and their estimated margins, and then accept or reject the store manager's request, at which point the guided procedures pass the final ruling back to the store manager.

The entire process used enterprise services derived from ERP core components (ECC-ISR) and SAP BW analytical tools to create tailored features at the appropriate level of sophistication for users at each step. These include simple services for reading master data, reading the relevant inventory of articles, reading relevant vendors, reading relevant competitors, and one for creating new, store-specific consumer prices. The ERP backend then integrates any new prices with dependant processes, seamlessly incorporating data about items priced manually.

ESA in CRM: service request processing

As SAP continues its work to enhance its classic suite of packaged applications with enterprise services, new opportunities to extend their flexibility and versatility via xApps created using ESA principles are already starting to emerge. One such xApp was created in just 10 days by SAP's solution management team to fill a gap in functionality in mySAP Customer Relationship Management (mySAP CRM).

Most Customer Relationship Management (CRM) service applications were originally envisioned as tools for managing in-house teams of service representatives. But just as the business vision has changed for many companies, so has the assumption that CRM roles will remain internal. The outsourcing of these duties to third parties has increased the strain on the underlying IT, leading to difficulties in incorporating those parties into the smooth workflow enjoyed by internal participants. As mySAP CRM is currently configured, a matter as simple as arranging a repair visit by a third-party technician requires manual notification and confirmation of the appointment and inevitably concludes with the third party having to file a paper bill that then needs to be input into the CRM system. What is an otherwise automated system begins to be exposed as inefficient and error-prone when external services are required.

SAP set out to solve this problem by creating an xApp that simply extended a business process that involved the CRM Customer Interaction Center (CIC), Workflow Management (WFM), and CRM Service. The resulting composite application collects all the relevant information to allow external service providers to handle the job in question. Fields containing all of the pertinent details—the date, time, duration, and location of the appointment, along with the name of the customer in question, the point of contact, the order number, etc.—are entered into the xApp, which then automatically generates Adobe forms containing this data and emails a PDF file to the external service provider.

These forms are linked to the CRM backend. Later, after the repairs have been completed, the service provider enters final confirmation data—how long repairs took, what parts were needed, the cost of those parts, etc.—and sends it to the CRM backend. The confirmation data is also used to start the billing process for the service provider, replacing the paper forms that the provider previously had to complete by hand and submit by mail and which in-house staff then entered into the system. Every field on the form corresponds with a field in the CRM application; the Adobe forms act as the intermediary, and the xApp smoothly automates and integrates the entire process.

Behind the scenes, enterprise services culled from mySAP CRM supply the xApp's underlying functionality. Figure 10-3 illustrates both the new business process steps created by the xApp, and the corresponding enterprise services, shown near the bottom. "Service order list" generates a list of service orders for a specific business partner (for example, all open service tickets for an external service provider). "Service order detail" shows all relevant data for a single service order and "send/receive message" creates the framework for passing the Adobe forms to the external service provider via email. "Confirmation create" enables the user of the Adobe forms to create and send confirmation data to the backend.

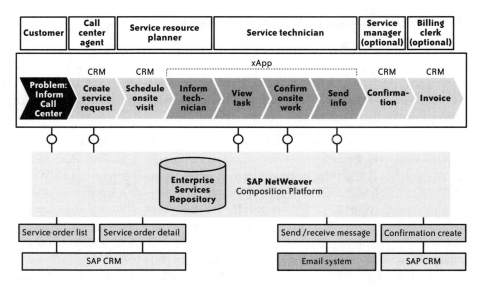

FIGURE 10-3. CRM: service request processing

The benefits of this xApp were immediately evident to its creators. The automated process replaced an ad hoc exchange of emails and phone calls, thus reducing errors, increasing productivity, improving data collection, and accelerating the customer billing process. More important, it acts as a model for future lightweight applications, which can literally be assembled and configured in days, and are capable of bridging the gaps between the fixed business processes supported by packaged applications and the increasingly flexible markets facing most companies today.

ESA in the chemical industry: e-VMI at Solvay

The chemical giant Solvay has already begun using ESA principles and essential technologies to transform its essential business processes, especially those pertaining to its supply chain. Up to 60 percent of total costs in the chemical industry derive from materials and logistics, which is why manufacturers place such value on the effective handling of material shipments.

Scenarios for inventory management at business partner sites or VMI aren't new, but they still pose a challenge to suppliers such as Solvay, which try to reconcile long-term supply forecasting with real-time usage data arriving from the actual storage tanks. A truly effective VMI solution would mesh these complementary streams of data together and automate the resupply process. An accompanying portal could make the entire process transparent to Solvay, its customers, and the third-party handlers actually tasked with driving the delivery trucks to its customers' plants.

Solvay used SAP NetWeaver as the integration platform, and the SAP NetWeaver Exchange Infrastructure (SAP NetWeaver XI) framework, to do just that, creating a process it has dubbed "e-VMI." This process combines forecasting and real-time data, displays both in an external portal, and automates delivery by eliminating paperwork and assigning loads to specific drivers, who identify themselves and confirm receipt of shipments using biometric data. This is another opportunity for business process improvement, as automation along role-based lines yields faster and more reliable dispatch handling. Standard processes are simplified and employees can concentrate on exceptions.

In VMI, a chemical customer essentially outsources the management and replenishment of its raw materials to the manufacturer, which then faces a pair of supply chain challenges: when the customer begins to run low and needs replenishment, how long does the manufacturer need to resupply its customer with a product that's in stock? And if it's not in stock, how long will it need to manufacture more, and how much warning will it need to ensure the customer doesn't run out? The former depends on careful measurement of the customer's daily usage; the latter is a matter of accurately forecasting long-term consumption patterns (which may fluctuate seasonally, for example). Combining the two into a single, smoothly meshed process is not an option in traditional VMI solutions, which tend to focus on long-term forecasting.

In Solvay's e-VMI process, illustrated in Figure 10-4, forecasting data is retrieved from Elemica, an electronic marketplace used by the industry, and is passed via SAP NetWeaver XI messaging to its SAP Advanced Planner and Optimizer (APO) system. Simultaneously, telemetry data recorded by sensors in its customers' tanks is encoded into SAP NetWeaver XI messages and is passed to the APO, where the sources are reconciled to yield a strategy for daily replenishment and for longer-term manufacture.

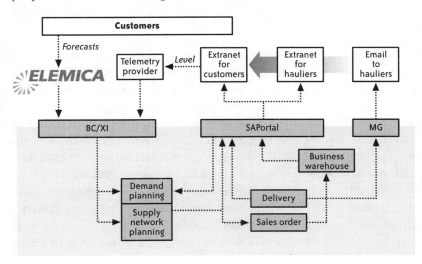

FIGURE 10-4. e-VMI

There, the two are reconciled to aid the manufacturer in knowing when to replenish its customers with supplies in stock and when it's time to produce a new batch. The APO is then integrated with an external portal used by the customers to confirm the data, and to check the status of replenishment shipments. The drivers hailing those shipments also use the portal to check the status of their next assignments, information that is passed to the manufacturer's warehouse to prepare those shipments before the drivers arrive. Upon their arrival, each one receives a retina scan to confirm their identity, and to confirm that replenishment is now en route—data that is once again encoded as SAP NetWeaver XI messages and is passed back to both the portal and the manufacturer's APO system.

ESA for logistic service providers

SAP's solutions for logistic service providers (LSPs) have focused increasingly on using enterprise services to recompose once-innovative, now-standard processes into new, differentiating ones. An industry that began with warehousing and forwarding freight on behalf of its clients began to evolve as early as the 1980s into an externalized supply chain, adding value by essentially adding services and increasing the scope of these services with each iteration. It's no longer enough for UPS to simply deliver coffee machines; these days, the company is prepared to install the machine and replenish the grounds inside on a daily basis if the customer is willing to pay for it. The flip side of these constantly expanding offerings is the need to develop new business processes and implement them.

Meanwhile, supply chains now circle the globe and include multiple tiers of suppliers, contract manufacturers, and service providers such as the logistics companies themselves. Connecting each of these fluid and rapidly changing participants to each other is an incredible strain on applications built along monolithic lines. Enterprise services offer a solution through their ability to begin recomposing commodity supply chain processes such as "track and trace" into differentiating ones, such as "supply chain event management."

"Track and trace" refers to the technology invented by FedEx to track packages via the now-familiar systems of unique IDs and sensors. As illustrated in Figure 10-5, what began as a differentiating, core process very quickly became an industry standard adopted by DHL and UPS, and ultimately became a commodity. Today, SAP is creating enterprise services that nearly encapsulate this functionality, and which will be added to the Enterprise Services Repository. But the next step, as seen in Figure 10-6, is to recompose those services from a supporting contextual technology into a differentiator—a composite application capable not only of tracking and tracing packages, but also of alerting the appropriate parties at both the logistics provider and the customer in case of exception—i.e., supply chain event management. That will be done using enterprise services, which continually locate the shipment and react, based on the location, to a predetermined rule set regardless of whether its location and condition at that moment in time demand an alert.

LSPs are poised to take this capability a step further with radio frequency identification (RFID) tags and other real-world awareness technologies. With consumer product manufacturers such as P&G and retailers such as Wal-Mart currently deadlocked on which side should cover the investments in tagging and software, LSPs may step into the breach, offering to cover those costs in exchange for integration with their customers' enterprise

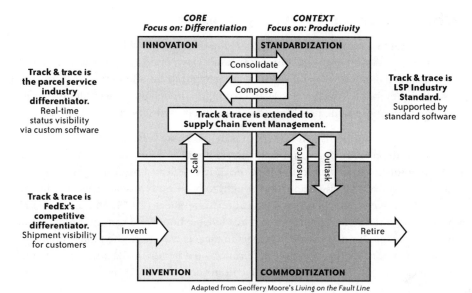

FIGURE 10-5. Process example: track and trace

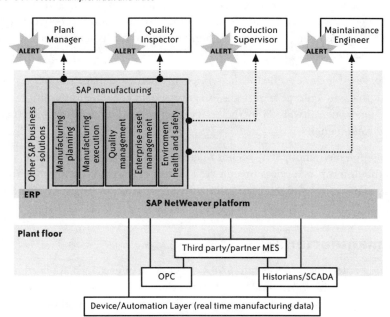

FIGURE 10-6. People and application integration

systems—a tradeoff necessary to keep track of what, exactly, is in all of those boxes. This idea, in essence, is a higher-value implementation of track and trace, one that might be made possible through an ESA-driven integration of existing ERP software, supply chain processes, and new technologies such as SAP Auto-ID Infrastructure.

ESA for professional service providers

When it comes to creating solutions for professional service providers—a job description that includes everything from consulting, tax, audit, law, and IT services to hospitality—SAP often plays a dual role. Not only is it creating applications and enterprise services that firms such as Deloitte & Touche choose and configure on behalf of their clients, but it is also encouraging those same providers to develop their own services for use within ESA.

One example of the former is SAP's work in providing base services for professional firms—e.g., automatically time-capturing billable hours and invoicing clients. The traditional pain points for these applications are the time-to-bill and confirming the accuracy of the data in question. SAP engineers have sought to solve both problems by creating enterprise services derived from the Cross Application Time Sheet (CATS) and using them in a composite application. This application records billable hours and can then link that data to a portal-based application in which project managers can check the total number of billable hours so far, or link it to a mobile application on a laptop or BlackBerry—an application which can also be used to record billable hours on the road. Using enterprise services, all of this data can be aggregated faster and with greater accuracy than current packaged solutions allow. Using enterprise services, it's relatively simple to take a standardized service for time-capturing and creating customized interfaces for both the manager juggling two or three projects per week and the attorney whose attention flits between 100 clients each week, all while billing his time with pinpoint accuracy. In both cases, the enterprise service is the same, and it's reusable.

Conversely, when it comes time for the service provider to manage its own expenses, it's not difficult to create enterprise services integrating data generated by credit card charges to expense reporting software or by the reservation systems of an outsourced travel agent or online ticketing engine.

In terms of implementation, SAP intends to create services for time recording, which will appear in the Enterprise Services Inventory: a service calling time data from either SAP or third-party applications and a service calling the list of projects the user is scheduled to work on.

ESA in manufacturing

Incorporating enterprise services into SAP's classic suite of packaged applications highlights new opportunities to extend their functionality. One immediately obvious opportunity for manufacturers in nearly every industry is the reconciliation of classical enterprise software—ERP, Supply Chain Management (SCM), and the like—with traditionally incompatible shop-floor automation and execution systems. Only by linking the business processes of the larger enterprise to the actual point of manufacture will these companies be able to realize the larger vision of adaptive manufacturing—i.e., the ability to respond with maximum speed and flexibility to sudden changes in their supply chains or in the business logic of the greater enterprise.

SAP's solution to this challenge is SAP xApp Manufacturing Integration and Intelligence (SAP xMII), formerly known as Lighthammer, which uses SAP NetWeaver XI and industry standards such as S95 to connect these incompatible systems. It does so using a layer of enterprise services deployed as connectors, on top of which reside analytical tools capable of extracting real-time data from plant automation and Manufacturing Execution Systems (MES) used to drive a broad range of KPIs for alerts and performance dashboards.

Using these tools, it becomes possible to visualize processes—order statuses, yields, start and stop rates, etc.—and merge that data with KPIs and business processes stored in ERP systems. As the integration of these systems continues, it becomes possible to create entirely new business objects storing KPI data or production orders that link to and automatically update the corresponding data in each system. The xApp and its corresponding services can be used as an integration and visualization toolbox; it is a composite application that concentrates all of the underlying functionality conveniently in one place.

Just as important, it provides all of these things through role-based interfaces designed to deliver the appropriate amount of information to each user at critical moments. For the plant manager, that may take the form of an alert warning of a massive disruption when a critical process fails; for the shop-floor manager, it's a detailed readout of real-time KPIs. In both cases, this functionality previously existed but was disconnected and packaged inside of inflexible interfaces. Now, using enterprise services as the foundation, it's possible to use SAP xMII as the connection and platform upon which to aggregate and reaggregate data generated on both sides—production data from the floor and business performance data arriving from analytical engines elsewhere in the company—in new business processes that will yield competitive advantage.

ESA in the chemicals industry

The chemicals industry is more or less split in two along the lines of its business models: specialty manufacturers racing to develop their next hit product—the secret ingredient in a new form of fuel, or paint, or plastic—and commodity manufacturers reliably producing massive amounts of bulk ingredients for industrial consumers a few links down the supply chain. Chemical companies in both camps are looking to ESA and enterprise services as a method for integrating their increasingly far-flung operations in an era of global consolidation. While specialty manufacturers are seeking help in managing their product portfolios and accelerating the pace of new-product development, commodity manufacturers are looking to maximize the efficiency of their operations further by finally linking their enterprise applications with the automation and execution systems on the shop floor.

SAP has already begun using enterprise services to create xApps that serve all of these needs. SAP xMII connects ERP applications to the shop floor using SAP NetWeaver XI and industry standards such as S95 to deploy a layer of enterprise services as connectors, on top of which reside analytical tools capable of extracting real-time data from plant automation and MES and running it through a range of KPIs. The next step is to begin recomposing functionality already in place to create new roles and processes—alert mechanisms and digital dashboards that will drive the management-by-exception model described in Figure 10-6.

In tandem with that effort, SAP is also working with IBM to create an xApp connecting and managing the many laboratory information management systems (LIMS) found inside most chemical manufacturers. LIMS are essential for monitoring production and guaranteeing the quality of the final product. An xApp connecting these systems to each other and to ERP, SCM, and other enterprise applications could accelerate the development of new products by connecting managers on the business side to real-time data emerging straight from the labs.

Chemical manufacturers are even applying enterprise services–driven integration efforts to their supply chains. Composite applications designed to support supply chain event management are able to track ships anywhere in the world—recording and updating data on their position, condition, cargo status, etc.—and trigger alerts on the other side of the globe should one drift off course…or begin to spring a leak.

PART FOUR

Composing Services

CHAPTER ELEVEN

SAP xApps Composite Applications for Analytics

SAP XAPPS COMPOSITE APPLICATIONS FOR ANALYTICS ENABLE PEOPLE TO TAKE EFFECTIVE AND TIMELY action based on a thorough understanding of a business process and its context. By building on the ESA approach, SAP xApp Analytics help businesspeople leverage relevant information from wherever it resides, provide the analytic tools to gain a deeper understanding, and then offer the means to perform the necessary tasks or to collaborate with others.

SAP xApp Analytics fulfill ESA's mission to put more powerful, flexible, and role-based solutions in the hands of a larger population of users. In the past, users too often had to perform a context switch in order to take advantage of analytic functionality, or they had to rely on experts to do the analysis for them. The need to analyze a customer's credit profile or the patterns in past orders would arise, and to access information or to perform any analysis, businesspeople would have to leave the enterprise application in which they were working and do research and analysis using a reporting environment or an OLAP tool. Taking action required accessing an enterprise application, oftentimes not the same one as before, all the while being the "human integrator:" remembering key figures, actions, information, and people who need to be involved.

SAP xApp Analytics use enterprise services and standard application programming interfaces (APIs) to access relevant data and functionality. They can be standalone solutions or embedded in enterprise applications. Either way, a seamless, comprehensive environment is created that combines the process automation, information, and functionality in an enterprise application, building and utilizing SAP NetWeaver capabilities to manage processes, manage security, extend customized applications, manage master data, and of course, consolidate and normalize information from a wide variety of sources. SAP xApp Analytics also may use SAP NetWeaver capabilities for knowledge management and collaboration. With everything unified, businesspeople do not have to switch from one solution to another, and they don't need to be "human integrators" but instead can focus on improving their understanding and getting the job done. Because the analytic functionality is tailored to the needs of a user participating in a process, SAP xApp Analytics allow people to do their own analytical work and rely less on experts.

Model-driven development—where IT and power users do not write code, but rather assemble models—within SAP NetWeaver Visual Composer that leverages existing functionality through services makes SAP xApp Analytics faster and cheaper to create and easier to modify and evolve as business requirements change.

This chapter will provide a tour of SAP xApp Analytics. In doing so, the way that ESA creates value will spring to life.

How do SAP xApp Analytics help business users?

Getting the right information from enterprise applications—Enterprise Resources Planning (ERP), Customer Relationship Management (CRM), and Supply Chain Management (SCM), among others—and into the hands of the people who need it, has sometimes proven costly and difficult. One result is that organizations have had to invest in special environments such as data warehouses, ETL processes, and specialized OLAP tools to satisfy analytic needs.

These past approaches, while excellent in their own right, required a different user type and created a new cottage industry of business analysts whose mission was to interpret business data for business users. This slowed the organization's ability to respond, because the business intelligence tools that reported on historical data were disconnected from the business applications and frontline information workers who apply it on a daily basis.

Perhaps the biggest drawback was that the information being delivered was arriving too late to be of real value. An enterprise would be in the middle of a sale to a key customer and would have no idea whether the customer was actually profitable or what kind of product they should sell. Like driving a car while looking in the rearview mirror, these opportunities appeared only after the fact and did not help enterprises to anticipate opportunities or swerve away from hazards.

The ability to understand processes and receive timely, actionable information in context, with the ability to perform deeper analysis, has long been a desire of every enterprise. For example, knowledge workers responsible for sales do not need generic reports, but rather, information on whom their best customers are and what products they most want to buy. Today's enterprise needs the ability to gather the *complete* process information in the *relevant* context, and give users the ability to take *appropriate* actions: complete, relevant, appropriate, timely, and actionable—key requirements for any solution!

SAP xApp Analytics not only help you find your best customer, but also bring you information about his current and past behavior. Then they let you take action on the information: do you want to sell him product A, B, or C, with what discount, and with what payment terms? On top of that, SAP xApp Analytics show you the probability of success in selling one or the other of those three products, or they recommend potential cross-selling options.

The following examples of SAP xApp Analytics illustrate how the ideas behind these solutions work in practice. These represent just a small sample of more than 100 different analytic composites delivered to the market.

SAP xApp Analytics for credit management

One of the clearest examples of the value of analytic composite applications is the application of xApps to the credit management challenge. In the normal course of business, credit managers within a company monitor accounts receivable to determine how much their customers owe. If a customer's balance due rises higher than the customer's credit limit, the order may be blocked and put on a blocked order list. SAP xApp Analytics for credit management improves the process of evaluating a customer's credit, getting a sense of whether the customer might pay the outstanding bills in the future, and communicating how to resolve orders put on the blocked order list.

In the past, credit management was frequently a role of the accounts receivable department. Today it is generally an independent role located between the accounting and sales departments. The credit check is executed in credit management, but the required information for credit decisions is spread out all over the company.

The process of monitoring all of these receivables and business activities with the customer is very complex. First there are the incoming orders for a given customer. Then there are the outgoing materials, goods, or shipments to the customer in the logistics system. Open invoices from the business accounting system have to be monitored as well. The set of required data includes incoming orders, shipments, open invoices, and credit management, all generally provided from a set of heterogeneous systems, and all with their own data formats.

So, the credit manager's goals are to:

- Reduce risk by preventing the company from doing business with high-risk customers
- Improve business efficiency by quickly identifying good and bad customers
- Enable revenue growth by not slowing down sales order processing
- Implement best business practices by automating credit checks

The tasks involved in credit management, shown in Figure 11-1, include:

- Reducing the risk of shipping products and not receiving payment for them
- Releasing or cancelling sales orders that are blocked due to a failed credit limit check
- Setting the credit limit for a customer
- Performing scoring and risk assessment for new and existing customers

To do this, a manager needs to know:

- When a sales order is blocked (Order System)
- The customer's payment behavior (Accounts Receivable)
- The customer's risk class and credit limit (Credit Management)
- The customer's external ratings (e.g., D&B)

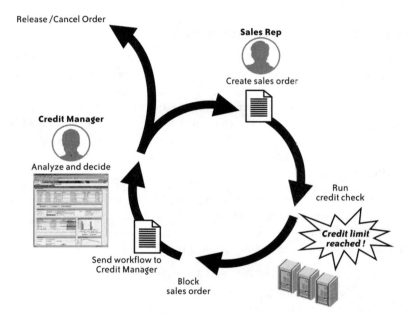

FIGURE 11-1. Credit management process

Credit management is an important risk control process because a company might have to wait 30 or 60 days after delivering goods to receive payment from a customer. During that time, that customer may be placing more orders. The risk is that if the customer goes insolvent or bankrupt, the payment will never be made. This risk has to be managed carefully to balance the exposure to a customer versus the potential insult of refusing to accept more orders from that customer.

The Analytic xApp for credit management brings all the information from all relevant systems into one composite application so that credit decisions can be managed quickly and effectively. Figure 11-2 shows the way the information from a variety of locations is gathered in one place to serve the needs of one role.

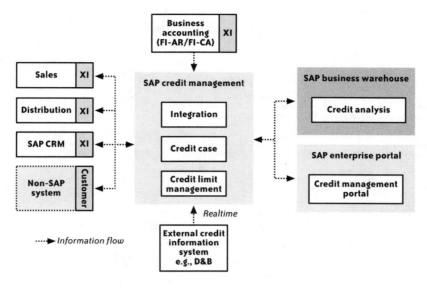

FIGURE 11-2. SAP credit management

One of the key parts of the Analytic xApp for credit management is the way it helps credit managers work with others in the company to properly resolve orders that end up on the blocked order list. Blocked order list functionality supports the credit manager in deciding whether sales orders that are blocked due to a failed credit limit check should be released or canceled. To come to such a decision, the credit manager needs to have an overview of the most important customer master data and KPIs.

Without the Analytic xApp for credit management, the credit manager may have to log in to several different systems to determine how many open invoices the customer has, whether the total dollar amount on the open invoices exceeds the customer's credit limit, which blocked orders should be released, whether the customer owes too much, and whether the customer is having trouble paying invoices. Communication between the sales, credit, and finance departments is very time consuming. The result can be ineffective or slow credit management, which could result in allowing too much or too little exposure to customers.

The blocked order list functionality draws data directly from the ERP system and puts it into a table showing the orders that are blocked due to credit limit reasons (see Figure 11-3). Clicking on a customer's name reveals that customer's payment history. This may show that the customer has had a payment problem for many months. Alternatively, it could show that the customer has a seasonal business and has problems every April but that his business always picks up in June, so he starts paying bills in July once cash starts flowing in. The credit manager now has more information regarding whether to release the order, cancel the order, or recheck the credit limit.

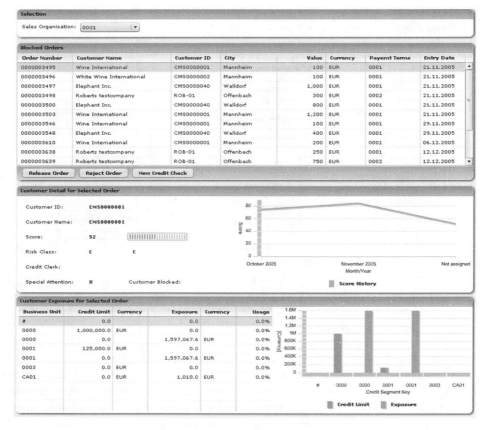

FIGURE 11-3. Blocked order list—screen view

Only after bringing all of this data together into one view can the correct decision be made in a timely fashion. If a manager decides to release the order—he overrules the system and says, "OK, I'm taking the risk to deliver the goods to the customer because he promised that he would pay us in seven days"—one of the key advantages of the Analytic xApp for credit management is that it allows credit managers to interact with the backend system. It provides the possibility to override the system.

The Analytic xApp for credit management also provides an enterprise service to search the blocked order list that can be used to enhance and enrich other applications. For example, the blocked order list enterprise service allows a sales representative's work center to show an alert if any of his assigned customers show up on the blocked order list. The sales representative can then participate in the process of resolving the blocked orders.

SAP xApp Analytics composite application for campaign management

SAP xApp Analytics composite application for campaign management provides an analysis of marketing projects. It is used to pull planning data from the backend CRM system and compare that data with the company's actual progress, telling the user whether target margins are being achieved. The Analytic xApp for campaign management lists all campaigns that have commenced within a specified time, presenting the user with an analysis of planned versus actual costs, revenues, margins, responses, activities, and campaign details, as shown in Figure 11-4. Analytics integrate with the backend system at the transactional level and allow marketers to reject campaigns that are not performing well. Campaigns that the marketing planner rejects are also synchronized with the CRM backend system automatically. This allows the marketer to continue his work without logging into another system. The marketer can be sure the decision is reflected in the relevant business processes.

FIGURE 11-4. Market campaign analysis—screen view

SAP xApp Analytics composite application for corporate governance

SAP xApp Analytics composite application for corporate governance enables Sarbanes-Oxley Section 404 (Sarbox 404) compliance. An Overview application supplies all of the most essential Sarbox 404 compliance data at a glance, including internal control issues resulting from assessments, statistical key figures and the progress of control/process design assessments (see Figure 11-5). Further, a separate set of applications delivers detailed displays concerning control design assessment, process design assessment, and control effectiveness. The Issues Analysis application shows internal control issues and associated remediation plans. And the Sign-off application monitors the status of sign-off activities within a selected area of responsibility. These apps visualize Management Internal Controls (MIC) statistical and detailed data in an intuitive, transparent manner using colorful graphics and animations. The end users involved require virtually no training.

FIGURE 11-5. Corporate governance—screen view

In a real-world example, this project delivered six business applications for governance, regulatory, and compliance management on top of MIC capability to SAP AG—and it took just five weeks from conception to completion. In the process, additional areas for Sarbanes-Oxley reporting were identified, and an additional two custom-based analytic applications were developed and deployed to support SAP's own reporting needs in the area of compliance.

How hard is it to deploy SAP xApp Analytics?

In late 2005 and early 2006, a handful of customers went live with SAP xApp Analytics. In a few weeks, these customers defined, customized, and deployed analytic xApps, a process that is almost impossible with any other approach. One early adopter of SAP xApp Analytics deployed seven applications in just four weeks—two were custom projects—and rolled them out to 1,000 users.

What are the different parts of an analytic composite application?

SAP xApp Analytics combine business know-how, process know-how, and software know-how into a form that amplifies the power of existing data and functionality. In practice, this means this work is accomplished by knitting a composite application out of five parts: the user interface (UI), process logic, and services from transactional enterprise applications and those for analytics and collaboration.

Everything starts with the needs of the enterprise, department, team, and organization. What are the critical metrics or success indicators? Where does this data reside, and would enterprise services, web services, APIs, or periodic data "dumps" be the appropriate way to go?

The business logic comes next. What information needs to be presented to the actual user at what time, what action options are appropriate, and would these interactions be with backend SAP processes, third-party applications, or homegrown tools? Will this process span intradepartmental efforts or cross over partner, supplier, and customer boundaries? This business logic, available options, and analytic guidance are developed, customized, simulated, and deployed using SAP NetWeaver Visual Composer, a model-driven development environment that enables and accelerates development. The powerful, simple, model-driven nature of SAP NetWeaver Visual Composer means that the population of people who can create or modify an analytic composite application can grow beyond developers and can include business analysts who are experts in the business processes that need further automation. ESA makes the SAP NetWeaver Visual Composer design tool possible.

The key part of SAP xApp Analytics is the process logic. For some applications, so little process logic is required that everything may be handled through UI navigation. The only process is moving from page to page. More advanced analytic applications may use mechanisms such as guided procedures that can coordinate functionality and UIs from many different sources. For example, a guided procedure that you can create with the Guided Procedure Design Time plug-in for SAP NetWeaver Developer Studio could begin by asking the user to fill out an Adobe Interactive form. Then it could take that information and partially populate an interface in ERP that the user could complete. Next, it could invoke an enterprise service from SAP or a third-party web service, and so on. Guided procedures enable flexible and configurable process automation. In fact, that is one of the key differentiators of a composite application: these applications include their own business logic, and sometimes they include data representations, not just a common UI.

Enterprise services from transactional enterprise applications enable SAP xApp Analytics to use their data and functionality. These services provide access to functionality for changing data or kicking off processes. In this way, analytic applications can perform actions within the process context of enterprise applications without requiring a context switch from one solution to another. Analysis and action can occur within one environment.

Analytic enterprise services provide access to analytical functions from SAP NetWeaver Business Intelligence (SAP NetWeaver BI) to perform data analysis through OLAP and other advanced techniques. SAP NetWeaver BI offers services based on standards, such as XML for Analysis (XMLA) for performing OLAP queries. Later in 2006, the Enterprise Services Inventory will contain services that support SAP xApp Analytics, and an increasing number of analytic services will be offered in the future. Analytic services provide a means for users to ask and answer all the questions they need within the context of the business process being supported. The information being analyzed may reside in a data warehouse or in the enterprise applications. The analytical functionality in SAP xApp Analytics focuses on the business process being served.

Collaborative enterprise services allow access to parts of SAP NetWeaver in order to put workflow items on the work lists of others, send email or instant messages, and provide access to shared spaces such as collaboration rooms and other collaboration tools.

Finally, in SAP xApp Analytics, UIs are constructed using SAP NetWeaver Visual Composer. The multifaceted nature of SAP NetWeaver Visual Composer is one of the reasons the initial deployments of SAP xApp Analytics went so fast. Business analysts could do the work for themselves. Developers were not a bottleneck. During internal SAP experiments using business analysts to create composites, SAP found that productivity increased dramatically when business analysts had an initial application from which to start.

The power of SAP NetWeaver Visual Composer suggests a new relationship between IT and the business side. For SAP xApp Analytics, perhaps the paradigm will become one in which highly skilled IT developers create sample applications, interfaces, and enterprise services that are the starting points for business analysts who apply those frameworks to many different problems. Who knows; SAP NetWeaver Visual Composer might be the tool that will allow CIOs to become CPIOs, or chief process innovation officers.

All of these elements work together, to make analytic composites a powerful force for delivering ESA's promised value.

In which application and process areas are analytic composites being created?

SAP xApp Analytics are being applied to every industry area and every broad area of functionality. However, some areas are on the front burner.

Consumer products, high technology, life sciences, utilities, and analytics for applications such as CRM, finance, and human capital management are among the most important focuses for the first wave of analytics because these areas have such a quick and dramatic impact on productivity and they reduce dependence on expert users.

For specific industries, and for general applicable functionality, analytic composites are being developed to fill gaps that may exist in or between enterprise systems, or to provide innovative ways of solving well-known challenges. In all cases, analytic composites may be focused on serving new requirements created by recent developments in industries or regulatory environments.

How do ESA and SAP NetWeaver help create analytic composites?

Although this chapter already touched on many of the mechanisms used to construct SAP xApp Analytics, a more thorough discussion will help illuminate the power of both analytics and ESA.

For example, we pointed out how SAP NetWeaver Visual Composer and the Guided Procedure Design Time xApp are used to create UIs and guided procedures, and we mentioned how these model-driven development tools improve productivity and enable business analysts to participate because development is easier. One of the most important ways that development is accelerated is through use of patterns or templates. Patterns are structures that occur repeatedly. Pulldown menus are a pattern, and tabs on web sites are patterns. Patterns build on the power of modeling to accelerate further development. In order to have a consistent and logical series of applications, SAP supplies commonly used patterns that will support several different composites. One pattern is called Analyze and Take Action. This pattern occurs in applications that consolidate information and then offer a variety of ways to respond. Another pattern is called Request Process Approve Update. In this pattern, a request for information is made, and then the information is processed, the results of the processing are approved, and the systems of record are updated. When a development environment implements a pattern, it means a large portion of the application's development has already taken place when the developer starts to work. The job of development becomes modifying and enhancing the pattern's basic behavior.

Another key ability for SAP xApp Analytics comes from SAP NetWeaver's portal functionality. Because the portal is the primary UI technology for the mySAP Business Suite, it is possible to embed new applications such as analytics at almost any place in the existing UIs. The iView container functionality allows the UI to be customized, reorganized, and substituted as needed. Of course, SAP xApp Analytics can also run as standalone applications just as easily when appropriate. SAP xApp Analytics will also be able to take advantage of all of the other UI mechanisms SAP NetWeaver offers, such as Project Mendocino integration with the Microsoft Office suite and SAP NetWeaver Mobile, which extends solutions to mobile devices.

As mentioned earlier, the workhorse of analytics is enterprise services that provide access to data and functionality from transactional enterprise applications. Most of the services that SAP xApp Analytics use come ready made in the Enterprise Services Inventory, whose interfaces are described in the Enterprise Services Repository. In some applications, however, special requirements arise for enterprise services that would serve a unique purpose in a specific analytic composite application. In such cases, it is possible to use the ABAP Development Workbench or the SAP NetWeaver Developer Studio development environment for Java to create your own enterprise services. New services can be based on combinations of existing services, a process known as *service composition*, or they can be ABAP or Java code that performs a unique task or provides a gateway to external functionality. This ability to extend existing services and create new ones greatly expands the functional range of SAP xApp Analytics and of composite applications in general.

Of course, because they are composite applications, SAP xApp Analytics have all of the functionality from business intelligence, Master Data Management (MDM), knowledge management, and all the other help for composites that we describe in Chapter 13.

What are the benefits of SAP analytics?

Several themes are present in the examples just mentioned. First, there is the idea of role and process orientation. Each Analytic xApp ties together previously disconnected information and functionality into a form that lets the user take action to advance an automated process—to overrule a blocked order and increase a customer's credit limit, for example.

The second theme is consolidation. Context, process, and information gathered from disparate places are consolidated into a unified form in SAP xApp Analytics. Unlike previous forms of reporting that also consolidated such information, analytics use the unified context as a starting point to add deeper analytical functionality and put process insights, along with the means to take action, at the user's fingertips.

The third theme is accessibility. Analytics are simple to use, yet full of powerful capabilities. This is amplified by the ability to embed these applications into an enterprise application in order to better support a process. In this way, analytics enhance existing enterprise applications with analytic functionality in a seamless fashion.

The fourth theme is improved decision making, leading to faster and smarter actions. With ready access to more relevant and timely information about decisions conveniently at hand, as well as the means to take action, the speed and quality of decisions should be improved.

The fifth theme is speed of development and associated cost reduction. The number of analytic composite applications is growing rapidly because they can be built and modified quickly. SAP xApp Analytics use application patterns that give developers a solid foundation to build upon. In a recent experiment, SAP trained a team of business analysts to create SAP xApp Analytics. The business analysts built more than 100 such applications in just three months. Most of the development time they spent on each application did not concern coding, but rather, choosing and gathering the right services, data, and functionality from systems of record.

The ease and speed of development and deployment are perhaps the most important aspects of SAP xApp Analytics. Without them, analytics would be interesting but impractical. Today analytic functionality is available to only about 25 percent of employees in an enterprise. Because SAP xApp Analytics are affordable to create and deploy, analytics should be available to virtually everyone in the enterprise, from heavy-duty information consumers to occasional users. ESA makes the expansion of analytics practical and unlocks the door to the host of business benefits outlined earlier.

CHAPTER TWELVE

The Architecture and Development Tools of Composite Applications

COMPOSITE APPLICATIONS ARE THE VEHICLE THROUGH WHICH ALL OF THE ELEMENTS OF **ESA** COME together to create value. The idea of composite applications is wonderful: flexible solutions constructed out of services, knit together with process modeling, and made accessible with easily constructed and adaptable user interfaces (UIs). Making this idea work in practice requires that many things interact precisely. The goal of this chapter is to explain the mechanisms that will make composite applications work in the real world of IT.

The architecture of composite applications

This chapter is divided into two major sections. In the first section, we'll describe the architecture of composite applications in detail. In the latter half of the chapter, we'll describe the development tools you use to create composite applications.

What is the purpose of composite applications in ESA?

The world of composite applications in ESA goes far beyond generic definitions of service-oriented architecture (SOA) and composite applications. At the most basic level, a composite application is an application based on services provided by other applications. Using this broad definition, everything from a portal that consolidates information from several

281

applications to an Asynchronous JavaScript and XML (AJAX) application that brings together services from many web sites qualifies as composite applications. But this definition leaves the door open for many different kinds of messes. Composite applications under this broad definition could have rigid UIs, hardcoded process logic, no systematic approach to defining services, and complex development tools. Under ESA, for composite applications to create value, our definition must be more detailed and exact.

Let's start with the UI layer. A composite application under ESA must not only have a UI layer but must have one that is easy to create, modify, and maintain. As the number of processes that are automated grows, so will the number of roles that people play in those processes, which will lead to an increased demand for UIs. If UIs are not easy to create and if the population of potential developers and modifiers of UIs is not somehow increased, then ESA cannot work. So for a composite in ESA, UIs must be easily created, adapted, and maintained, which in practice means they must be developed with modeling tools that use patterns.

The same idea holds for the process orchestration or choreography layer of a composite. If a composite combines services from service providers using spaghetti code that is undocumented and hard to maintain, the ESA promise will not be fulfilled. Changing such an application would be a slow process that could be performed only by experts. An ESA composite must perform process orchestration of enterprise services in a manner that allows the behavior of the application to be created, adapted, and maintained as easily as possible. In practice, again this means using model-driven development techniques that expand the pool of potential developers. Patterns at the process level also amplify productivity.

The service layer offers another challenge. It is possible to think of the application programming interfaces (APIs) of existing enterprise applications as services. What's wrong with using them to create composites? The problem is that first, they were not built to be reusable services, so frequently an API call has to work with several other API calls to do some useful work. Second, it may take time to figure out how an API call works and whether it has side effects. Third, API calls tend to be rather fine-grained. Each API call does a very specific thing. Tens or hundreds may need to be understood thoroughly to accomplish a particular task. A composite in ESA must be created using enterprise services at the right granularity—the right size to be a useful building block in automating processes. If the services are too small, the application using them becomes too complex. If the services are too large, they become hard to understand and cannot be easily recombined to solve new problems. Designing enterprise services is an art that relies on deep knowledge of business processes. To make ESA succeed, SAP is bringing all of the experience gained in the last 30 years of enterprise software development to this challenge.

Let's imagine that it would be possible to create services at the right level of granularity quite quickly. Another set of problems would then arise: how can you find the right service? How can you tell what a service does? How can you tell which other services are related to a particular service? Even if all of the previous problems were solved, development would not be easy or even possible without a mechanism to easily find services, understand what they did, and use them in development tools. For ESA to work, an Enterprise Services Repository must exist to fill this need and to allow developers to navigate and understand a large repository of services.

If we take a close look at services, another challenge appears. What if the customer data required by one service is different from the format used by other services? Or, even worse, what if four or five different formats for customer data are in use in a set of services? How will the translation and mapping between these forms take place? If you extend this challenge to all types of data used in enterprise applications, the translation and mapping tasks could become huge. In ESA, composite applications must use a standard set of global data types to solve this problem.

Finally, in order for development of composite applications to be possible, a large collection of enterprise services must exist and be ready to use. No matter how many tools are available for development, without an existing set of services that represent the core processes of an enterprise, composite applications cannot be created at a sufficient scale to solve a large number of problems for companies using enterprise software. Without a repository of enterprise services, composite applications are merely an invitation to a huge amount of greenfield development using a new paradigm. With a fully populated Enterprise Services Repository, composite applications become a dynamic force for evolving a business.

So, with a clear picture of how composite applications in ESA have to overcome many more challenges than the generic definition of composites, we can quickly understand the role of composites in ESA. Simply put, composites in ESA are the way that each layer of the architecture comes together to create business value. Composites in ESA are built to overcome the likely challenges that stand in the way of rapid evolution and process flexibility. Whether it is the ability to quickly create a new application based on existing parts or to fine-tune composites provided by a vendor, composite applications built according to ESA standards transform the nature of IT from a bottleneck into a strategic weapon. That is their most fundamental and most important role.

What is the architecture of composite applications?

How, then, do composites live up to the higher standards that ESA requires of them? The most condensed answer is that composite applications do their job through a well-designed separation of duties in each layer that allows for recombination and reuse of building blocks. Second, the construction of the building blocks in each layer relies on modeling amplified by patterns to simplify development. But how exactly does this work? Figure 12-1 gives us a complete picture.

This view of composite applications identifies the building blocks in each layer and begins to show how they work together. Our tour will start at the top of the graphic at the work center and move down to the service provider.

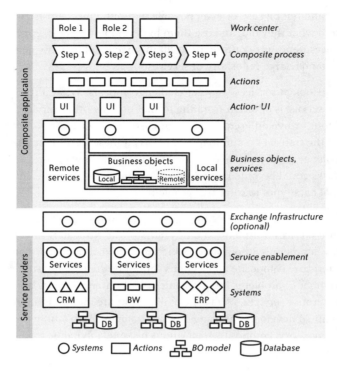

FIGURE 12-1. Anatomy of a composite application

Roles and work centers

Composite applications use patterns and building blocks in the UI to meet as many needs as possible. A user may play many different roles in many different processes. For each role, a work center exists to provide the information and functionality needed to do the work of that role. Without the standardization and common approach that a work center creates, each UI would become a training burden. Work centers may include application components such as iViews, guided procedures, analytic views, and search capabilities, all working together to help the person playing a specific role to do his job. One central element of work centers are task lists that provide the user with a clearly defined unit of work to be done. These tasks are supported by business objects in the composite or in the service provider. The work center assembles a task-specific view of certain functionality from one or more business objects so that the user can just worry about the capabilities relevant to the task. Any single user may work with a large collection of work centers. A control center provides a summary of all the work centers for a user and helps keep track of what is going on in all the work centers. (You can find a more detailed explanation of the UI layer in Chapter 5.)

Let's imagine a team management work center that a manager would use to carry out all of the tasks and activities related to a group of direct reports. The starting point for this work center would be a list of tasks that are related to the team. The list could include requests for vacation, approval of changes in benefits, or creation of new positions. Each task in the list would be supported by an activity in the work center that would be constructed to take into account how frequently a user would perform the task. Frequently performed tasks might look like a complex UI with all the functionality on one or two pages so that all the work could be performed without having to move too frequently from page to page. Tasks performed rarely would probably be implemented as guided procedures that were constructed to walk a user step by step through a process and provide assistance about what should be done in each step. A guided procedure for creating a job opening might have actions for entering a job description, approval of the job description by upper management, and assigning a hiring expert from HR to fill the job. Activity in the team manager's work center would then result in activity in other work centers playing different roles. Upper management's task list would receive any job description approvals. The task list of hiring experts in HR would get the task of hiring for a newly created job description. The control center would show an aggregated list of all of the tasks from each work center with urgent tasks highlighted, along with important information gleaned from each work center as needed.

If we take a step back from this functional description, a surprising thing occurs. We are no longer dealing with the UI as an undefined realm of unlimited flexibility. The constructs of work centers using activities, tasks, and actions built around roles provide a reusable approach to meeting the interface needs of many different applications and linking the activity of one role to another. In this manner, the work center pattern serves to reduce a huge amount of the complexity and therefore the maintenance burden. The pattern makes development much easier than starting from scratch. Developers do not worry about designing the structure and context for the UI and the information flow. Instead, they focus on how to fit the work at hand into a well-understood structure. Simplified tools based on this pattern allow business analysts to build and modify work centers.

One should remember that the work and control centers are just the beginning of SAP's use of patterns in composites. As we will discuss shortly, patterns will be used not only at the UI layer but also at the process orchestration layer. And more patterns at every level will be added as they are discovered and implemented.

Composite processes and business activities

The next level down from work centers in Figure 12-1 contains composite processes. Composite processes are those that walk a user step by step through the actions needed to perform a task or business activity. *Composite processes* is the generic name for the sort of automation provided by SAP's guided procedure mechanism. These processes are composite in that they use actions that may come from a variety of different sources. The first step or action in a composite process (or guided procedure) might invoke an Adobe Interactive form. The next action might use an iView from the mySAP Customer Relationship Management (mySAP CRM) system. The next might use an external web site or a UI built specifically for a composite.

The guided procedure mechanism allows the order of the steps to be changed on the fly if need be, for new steps to be created, or for new users to be assigned to tasks to handle special situations. Guided procedures help users through any sort of repeated activity, whether it be the normal set of steps to do the work of a task in a composite or a set of steps designed to handle exceptional conditions.

Guided procedures are created using model-driven development techniques. When they show up in a work center, they use UI patterns that show the user a visual representation of the step-by-step process.

Actions

The term *action gallery* encompasses the actions and action-UI levels of Figure 12-1. Actions are reusable abstractions of either UIs or service calls that simplify the flow of a process and associated data from step to step. An action consists of a UI or service call and the corresponding import and export parameters that specify what data is coming into that step from the previous one and what data is coming out of that step to the next. Within the guided procedure, a process flow is built out of these actions by bringing them in the right sequence and defining the data flow via the import and export parameters. Within each process step, exactly one action is executed.

Actions decouple process steps from services and UIs to allow business experts to model processes on a nontechnical level and extend steps with additional process-relevant information such as attachments or additional actions related to the steps.

Why do we need actions for guided procedures anyway? The reason is to conceal messy details involved in invoking UIs or other callable objects in a guided procedure and to provide the opportunity to add additional functionality if needed. Specifically, actions allow:

- Decoupling of the interface from implementation
- A separation of the language of business experts (Action) from the language of developers (Callable Objects)
- Reuse of one Callable Object in several different scenarios
- Addition of attachments, info actions, or permissions, which are handled on the Action level

The simplicity of actions makes it easier for business analysts to engage in process modeling.

Composite application business logic and abstraction layer

It should be clear that the mechanisms described so far—work centers, composite processes, and the action gallery—could automate a wide variety of processes, which is of course why these mechanisms were created. Composite applications must also be able to create new functionality, which is the purpose of the business objects and services layer in Figure 12-1.

Business objects in composites are used to encapsulate reusable functionality, the same role they play in service providers. And, just as in service providers, business objects may have services created on top of them. Such services would be called *local services* if they were going to be used by just one composite and were not going to be published for reuse by others. The term *remote services* refers to those provided by other service providers. Through a process known as *service composition*, business objects themselves can be constructed out of existing services.

The business objects and services layer is not required for every composite. It frequently appears, however, because many remote services may need to be recombined into a simple-to-use local service. Or the composite may need its own persistent data. Or some external functionality may not be available as a service and the composite may need to use an API to convert that functionality into a service. In general, the more complex the composite, the more development will occur in the business objects and service layer.

Service providers

The Exchange Infrastructure and service provider layers in Figure 12-1 show how the composite application can use remote services. The service providers expose enterprise services for reuse. Service providers also can present functionality for reuse using the Web Service Infrastructure, services based on messages defined in SAP NetWeaver Exchange Infrastructure (SAP NetWeaver XI), BAPIs, or in other ways, but as time passes, enterprise services will become the most common method.

What are the main categories of composite applications?

Composite applications come in several different forms. It is useful to understand the differences when analyzing how to put a particular composite to work in your organization.

The first thing to understand when examining a composite is the level of complexity. Some composites are very thin and have just a UI that combines services from several different service providers. In this way, simple composites are similar to portal applications. But as more of the mechanisms of composites are added, they become more complex. Using the work center patterns and guided procedures adds another level of complexity. Adding business objects and services adds another. Sometimes you may read of a distinction between lightweight and heavyweight composites. The more that is implemented in the stack in Figure 12-1 and the more functionality in each layer of the stack, the heavier the weight of the composite.

The second distinction that sometimes is useful to consider when analyzing composite applications is the difference between frontend and backend composites. While there is no hard dividing line, frontend composites are focused on user interaction and collaboration using the work center and other patterns. Frontend composites are conversational and user-centric. But imagine instead that a composite had almost no UI layer but a huge amount of development of business objects and services, all knit together by Business Process Management modeling techniques. This is a different, more backend kind of composite. Backend composites are process-centric. They are focused on processing huge volumes of messages or managing complex, long-running transactions. Backend composites are key to the creation and development of event-driven architectures (EDAs) that greatly increase automation and only occasionally require user intervention.

Composites of any weight will appear most frequently in one of three ways:

- As custom composites built by SAP, Independent Software Vendors (ISVs), or companies for their own use using SAP NetWeaver

- As xApps, packaged composite applications that are sold by SAP or ISVs as separate products

- As part of the mySAP Business Suite solutions, which will use composite applications to extend their functionality

Other categories of composites will no doubt be invented, but knowing these categories can be useful in discussions of how to put composites to work.

How are processes modeled in composite applications?

The big picture of composite applications and ESA in general starts to make more sense and become more exciting when the hierarchy of modeling is more clearly understood. So far, we have talked about how in composite applications, UIs use guided procedures, a form of composite process automation created through modeling. SAP NetWeaver XI offers another modeling tool known as Cross Component Business Process Management (CCBPM), which is used most frequently in more complicated backend applications.

Guided procedures cover the simpler user-centric sort of modeling, and CCBPM handles more complicated process-oriented modeling that has less user involvement.

Another sort of business process modeling is used inside both service consumers and service providers to perform tasks that usually start and finish inside one application. These mechanisms, which exist both in ABAP and in Java, are grouped under the term *business workflow*.

In ESA, modeling is used at every level to simplify development, improve communication, and bring more people into the process. The modeling we have discussed so far in this chapter is focused on modeling of processes that are being automated inside an application. This sort of modeling is known as *process execution modeling*. It is important to keep in mind that modeling in ESA also takes place at a higher level of process components and process configuration.

Process architecture modeling is the highest level. In process architecture modeling, the larger processes of a business, such as order to cash, are broken into process components. The relationships between the process components are specified (integration scenario models), as are the interactions between them (process interaction models). The behavior of each process component, of the structure of the processes, process steps, enterprise services, and business objects, is also modeled (process component models). (Chapter 5 has a more detailed explanation of this sort of modeling.)

Another sort of modeling called *process configuration modeling* is used in the SAP Solution Manager to help configure processes that exist in SAP products.

How do composite applications use patterns?

The patterns we have discussed so far have to do with the UI. The work center pattern is a general structure for how a certain type of UI works. It turns out that patterns also appear in the processes automated in composite applications. The process patterns simplify development and amplify productivity the same way that UI patterns do, but they apply the internal structure of the application.

Patterns at the process level are continually being discovered, but there are three that will likely show up frequently in the first generation of composite applications:

- Analyze, Take Action (ATA)
- Multi-User Guidance (MUG)
- Single-User Guidance (SUG)
- Request, Process, Approve, Update (RPAU)

The ATA pattern starts with a dashboard presentation of information that allows problems to be noticed. Once the problem is discovered and analyzed, the application allows action to be taken to fix the problem.

The MUG pattern is used to guide many users working together through the steps of a complicated process. Each step can come from a different source, and the users are provided with a lot of hand-holding and contextual information to help guide them through the process. SUG is similar, but as the name suggests, SUG guides a single user through a process.

In the RPAU pattern, a request for information is sent out. Once the information is collected, it is processed or enhanced and then approved so that updates to systems of record can occur.

Warranty registration is a perfect example of a process that fits into the RPAU process pattern. The request would be a warranty card or online form filled in by the user. This information could be brought into the system and then enhanced with other information. The enhanced information could then go through a quality control step to be approved before it is used to update many different backend systems.

Another version of the RPAU process pattern for updating store-specific prices in the retail industry is shown in Figure 12-2.

UI patterns and process patterns are only the beginning. Many more patterns will be applied at all levels of composites as time goes on.

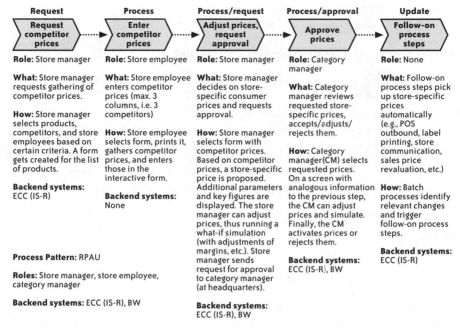

Request	Process	Process/request	Process/approval	Update
Request competitor prices	**Enter competitor prices**	**Adjust prices, request approval**	**Approve prices**	**Follow-on process steps**

Role: Store manager

What: Store manager requests gathering of competitor prices.

How: Store manager selects products, competitors, and store employees based on certain criteria. A form gets created for the list of products.

Backend systems: ECC (IS-R)

Process Pattern: RPAU

Roles: Store manager, store employee, category manager

Backend systems: ECC (IS-R), BW

Role: Store employee

What: Store employee enters competitor prices (max. 3 columns, i.e. 3 competitors)

How: Store employee selects form, prints it, gathers competitor prices, and enters those in the interactive form.

Backend systems: None

Role: Store manager

What: Store manager decides on store-specific consumer prices and requests approval.

How: Store manager selects form with competitor prices. Based on competitor prices, a store-specific price is proposed. Additional parameters and key figures are displayed. The store manager can adjust prices, thus running a what-if simulation (with adjustments of margins, etc.). Store manager sends request for approval to category manager (at headquarters).

Backend systems: ECC (IS-R), BW

Role: Category manager

What: Category manager reviews requested store-specific prices, accepts/adjusts/ rejects them.

How: Category manager(CM) selects requested prices. On a screen with analogous information to the previous step, the CM can adjust prices and simulate. Finally, the CM activates prices or rejects them.

Backend systems: ECC (IS-R), BW

Role: None

What: Follow-on process steps pick up store-specific prices automatically (e.g., POS outbound, label printing, store communication, sales price revaluation, etc.)

How: Batch processes identify relevant changes and trigger follow-on process steps.

Backend systems: ECC (IS-R)

FIGURE 12-2. The RPAU process pattern: store-specific consumer prices

Development tools for composite applications

Distribution of the ESA stack across service consumers and service providers has had a significant impact on the role and structure of development tools. In the mainframe and client/server eras, each developer had a top-to-bottom slice of the application stack to work with, from UI to persistence. A single developer or team would craft the UI and create the process logic and the persistence to support it.

In ESA, this situation has changed dramatically. The idea of one developer creating an application no longer applies in a world of service providers and service consumers. Developers create components and building blocks or use those created by others, or both.

In addition, the developer population has changed. In ESA, the people doing development and modification are no longer just highly skilled engineers. Business analysts and others with more understanding of requirements but less technical skill have been added to the mix.

Accordingly, the development tools used in ESA to create composite applications and the supporting building blocks have changed. This section looks at the new development tools and how they interact with each other.

What development tools are used to create composites?

The goal of composite application development in ESA is to allow the developer to ignore implementation complexities and instead focus on using the simplified abstractions created by modeling environments to specify an application's behavior. When this is accomplished, development becomes a much simpler task.

But in the current state of the art, and probably for the foreseeable future, no one modeling environment will serve every need. Traditional development techniques based on ABAP and Java will still be required and will play an important role. What has changed and is vital for composite application developers to understand is the way that a division of labor has been created among the development tools used for composites.

Four development tools are used to create composites:

- SAP NetWeaver Visual Composer for modeling UIs
- Guided Procedures design time for modeling user-centric composite processes
- The SAP Composite Application Framework (SAP CAF) for modeling application logic
- ABAP Development Workbench and SAP NetWeaver Developer Studio for creating enterprise services and advanced logic at any level

Each tool works inside the SAP NetWeaver environment and builds upon various underlying technology, such as SAP NetWeaver Portal, the Web Dynpro development and runtime environment for creating UIs, SAP NetWeaver Application Server (SAP NetWeaver AS), SAP NetWeaver XI, and many other such platform components.

But while composite applications couldn't work without the foundation SAP NetWeaver provides, the most important job for this section of the book is to explain to composite application developers when and where to use each tool mentioned. The starting point for the explanation is Figure 12-3.

Figure 12-3 shows a more detailed view of the programming constructs and SAP NetWeaver components used to create a composite application than Figure 12-1 did with its focus on logical layers.

SAP NetWeaver Visual Composer is focused on modeling UIs that are rendered into the portal layer and the SAP NetWeaver Visual Composer runtime. It is possible to create entire applications using SAP NetWeaver Visual Composer if they do not require advanced application logic. In the future, it will be possible to create simple guided procedures using SAP NetWeaver Visual Composer.

The Guided Procedures design time is a server-side modeling environment through which guided procedures, shown in Figure 12-3 in the process layer, can be modeled and created. If any Java code is required in the callable objects of a guided procedure, this can be done in the SAP CAF.

The SAP CAF Core plug-in for SAP NetWeaver Developer Studio allows modeling of business logic. CAF Core has an environment that allows modeling of entity services, external services, and application services. Each service is constructed as much as possible by modeling, with coding filling in when needed. The CAF Core environment is needed most when a composite application has complicated application logic. CAF Core also allows for

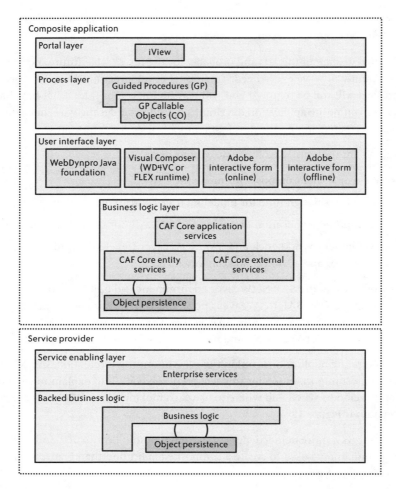

FIGURE 12-3. Composite Application Architecture

service composition, the technique of creating services based on functionality provided by other services.

ABAP Development Workbench and SAP NetWeaver Developer Studio play two roles in developing composite applications. First, they are used for service enabling. These tools are used to create enterprise services in service providers. In addition, when the requirements of any layer of a composite become more complex than the modeling environment can handle, ABAP Development Workbench and SAP NetWeaver Developer Studio can be used to create code that uses SAP NetWeaver components to create an application that solves the problem.

Can every development challenge be met through modeling?

Modeling involves creating a set of abstractions and relationships between the abstractions that can be combined and recombined to express an application's behavior. Even when models are constructed using visual tools, some sort of composition language is used to represent the relationships that are expressed visually. Once a model is constructed, the composition language is used as the basis of a compilation or interpretation process in which an executable form of an application is rendered.

The challenge for designers of modeling environments is to create abstractions and relationships that are simple enough so that productivity is increased but are complicated and powerful enough so that useful applications can be created. In any modeling environment, it is always possible to find certain requirements that cannot be satisfied in terms of the model. In these cases, to meet these requirements, developers must resort to coding in ABAP or Java using traditional methods and SAP NetWeaver components. If almost every application requires such coding, a modeling environment has perhaps not been properly designed. The experience of composite application developers with SAP NetWeaver Visual Composer, Guided Procedures, and CAF Core has been quite positive. Many, many applications can be completely represented in terms of the modeling environment.

What role does SAP NetWeaver Visual Composer play in creating composites?

SAP NetWeaver Visual Composer is the primary UI modeling tool for developing composites. In the future, SAP NetWeaver Visual Composer will be also have the capability to model guided procedures to perform service composition. SAP NetWeaver Visual Composer's use of modeling and patterns will increase productivity and allow a much larger number of UIs to be created and maintained at scale and at reasonable cost. Perhaps the largest impact that SAP NetWeaver Visual Composer will have is to enable business analysts to participate in developing and modifying composite applications.

SAP NetWeaver Visual Composer will also be an important part of creating special-purpose environments or factories to build certain types of applications. One of the first such uses of SAP NetWeaver Visual Composer is as an environment to create SAP xApp Analytics.

What role does the Guided Procedures design time play in creating composites?

The Guided Procedures design time is a development tool that allows modeling of guided procedures. Guided procedures maintain contextual information that is passed from one step to another in a process. Each step in a guided procedure is an action that can be executed by a callable object, which can be anything from an iView in SAP NetWeaver Portal, an Adobe Interactive form, a call to a web service, or special-purpose code. Guided procedures allow for alteration of the order of process steps during execution. In future releases of SAP NetWeaver, Visual Composer will also be able to model simple guided procedures, but the Guided Procedure Design Time will still be useful for modeling more complex processes.

What role does the SAP CAF play in creating composites?

The SAP CAF is the first tool created for composite application development. The SAP CAF was created as SAP was first grappling with what role composite applications would play in ESA. Because of this, the SAP CAF focused on many different areas, including patterns in the UI, service composition, process orchestration, and modeling. Many of the ideas that are now prominent in composite applications, such as the work center and control center patterns and guided procedures, had their origins in the SAP CAF, making it challenging to understand what the SAP CAF is and how it is used.

But as xApps were understood and new tools such as SAP NetWeaver Visual Composer arrived, the SAP CAF's role changed. Now the SAP CAF is focused on modeling advanced business logic that uses entity services, external services, and application services. Each service is modeled to a greater or lesser extent. Construction of some of them, such as application services, always requires coding in Java. Entity services are business objects that add local persistence to a composite. External services provide gateways to enterprise services outside of the composites and offer the opportunity for service composition. Application services contain the advanced process logic that may be required in a composite. As part of its modeling of services, the SAP CAF also allows for incorporation, through services of SAP NetWeaver, of capabilities that can support composite applications, such as functionality for business intelligence, knowledge management and collaboration, and other services mentioned in Chapter 13.

The SAP CAF is usually required only in more advanced composite applications that add quite a bit of functionality in the business process layer.

What roles do the ABAP Development Workbench and SAP NetWeaver Developer Studio play in creating composites?

The ABAP Development Workbench and SAP NetWeaver Developer Studio are focused on creating service implementations. The most highly skilled developers will spend their time building services that will then be used by others who will use simpler tools to finish the job of creating composite applications. In this way, the deep technical skills of developers and engineers will be leveraged as much as possible.

ESA in action: Asian Paints

Composite applications are playing an important role in companies' transformation efforts. This is certainly the case at Asian Paints, where the internal transformation strategy focuses on the creation of composites.

Asian Paints is India's largest paint manufacturer and is among the top 10 decorative coatings companies in the world, with annual revenues approaching $600 million. The company serves more than 30,000 customers in 65 countries in Asia, the Middle East, the Caribbean, and Africa. With a supply chain that includes 29 production plants located in 23 countries and a handful of global subsidiaries, Asian Paints has invested heavily in IT in recent years to automate its most important business processes, including manufacturing, distribution, and inventory control.

In 2000, the company began to migrate its core custom-developed legacy systems to the prepackaged Enterprise Resources Planning (ERP), Customer Relationship Management (CRM), and other enterprise applications contained in the mySAP Business Suite. Asian Paints also adopted SAP NetWeaver as its toolkit for integration, as well as the platform for its next generation of enterprise services. With the migration nearing completion, the company has begun drafting the blueprint for the companywide strategic adoption of ESA. Its goals revolve around both internal and external integrations. Internally, the company intends to connect its new enterprise applications with its existing supply chain, R&D systems, and portal interfaces to support the development of new composite applications. Externally, Asian Paints hopes to connect the internal systems of its supply-chain partners to its own and thus optimize the flow of data and business processes up and down the chain.

Asian Paints currently exchanges data with partners via XML messages, but the relative absence of business semantics and standards at both ends forces both companies to transform the data to match their own systems. In an enterprise-services-enabled environment, Asian Paints envisions a scenario in which data is automatically passed back and forth and is reconciled to each system, instead of simply pushed by the company to its suppliers. It is hoped that this approach will lower the cost and time involved to bring on new suppliers and improve the capabilities of current interactions.

To get there, Asian Paints intends to deploy several components of SAP NetWeaver, including Integration Broker and Business Process Management from SAP NetWeaver XI, over the next 18 months. With those serving as the foundation, the company plans to begin building composite applications aimed at streamlining partner interactions (e.g., stock supplying and customer ordering), automating compliance, and supporting its painting services business over the next three to four years.

The company expects its biggest challenge to be encouraging its partners to adopt their own enterprise services over the same span to maximize the level of integration with Asian Paints's infrastructure.

ESA in action: Zuger Kantonalbank

Composites can dramatically improve user productivity and reduce errors. This was the focus of consulting firm CSC's creation of a highly simplified and guided composite to help Zuger Kantonalbank's personnel achieve maximum productivity with a minimum of effort.

Zuger Kantonalbank is the leading bank in the Swiss Canton of Zug and plays an important role in the region's day-to-day business. With 2004 revenues of 333 million euros and more than 400 employees, the bank is one of the largest employers in the region. Although small by international standards, Zuger Kantonalbank offers a range of banking services, including mortgage lending, electronic banking, and corporate finance; manages total assets of more than $6 billion; and handles approximately 115,000 customers in a given year. Considering the size of its staff and the scope of its operations, the bank is constantly looking to improve employee productivity.

To that end, the bank asked the consulting firm CSC to create an interface solution that would integrate all of the relevant processes involved in maintaining customer accounts and creating new ones. Before it could tackle the technical challenges, however, CSC had to resolve and balance the competing needs of employees with different roles, responsibilities, and training across the organization. Each group seemingly had its own limited window of functionality, whether it was a branch's financial advisor struggling to open new accounts or a back-office power user managing the life cycles of those accounts. New employees introduced to the bank's ad hoc collection of portal functionality regularly made errors while entering data and overall productivity was depressed by the amount of time employees spent in the back of branches battling interfaces instead of up front working with customers.

CSC's mission, then, was to create a new portal and composite application that could abstract the functionality underlying all of its previous interfaces and reconstitute it in the form of a streamlined set of business processes. A handful of role profiles would assign the appropriate functionality and complexity to each user, so the back-office experts would have the wide latitude they required and the productivity of new hires would be increased by processes automated using guided procedures designed to walk them through activities and keep errors to a minimum. Beyond the interface issues, the portal would help the bank standardize and automate its usual business processes, provide support for regulatory compliance issues, identify errors and duplicate data, reduce the integration gaps between the underlying enterprise applications, and generally provide a more modern and efficient solution on behalf of its employees.

CSC chose SAP NetWeaver and its SAP NetWeaver Portal component as the integration platform and portal environment, respectively, for its enterprise services–based approach. Zuger Kantonalbank had previously installed mySAP Banking as its ERP solution, and this became the source of many services called by CSC's composite application.

CSC's solution effectively wrapped functionality summoned from the SAP enterprise applications (via enterprise services invoked by ABAP calls) within a loosely coupled, highly reusable composite application that had an additional layer of interface design on top that was unique to Zuger Kantonalbank. The loose coupling between layers meant that the bank could flexibly redesign the workflow within the portal whenever and however business conditions required. It also meant that CSC could offer its composite application as a service to its midsize banking clients in Switzerland.

CHAPTER THIRTEEN

Supporting Composite Applications

COMPOSITE APPLICATIONS REPRESENT A NEW WORLD FOR APPLICATION ARCHITECTS AND DEVELOPERS, a world in which many long-standing assumptions no longer apply. We have dedicated most of this book to examining the transformation that ESA brings to the world of enterprise software to serve the needs of business more effectively. In this chapter, we look at how a set of capabilities that falls under the umbrella of information management helps to address the challenges of creating a new generation of productivity-enhancing composite applications that are the key to increased flexibility. We will also examine how SAP NetWeaver Mobile provides a way to extend composites or any other sorts of applications to mobile devices.

How are composite applications different from the previous generation of applications?

To understand how composites are different, a high-level examination of traditional development practices will be useful. In the past, both in the mainframe era and in the client/server era, developers approached application development with a top-to-bottom perspective on the application stack. The same developer or team controlled the application being constructed—from the user interface (UI) through the application logic down to the database. The developer, in essence, controlled a vertical slice of the application stack.

Development generally proceeded by gathering requirements and then designing that vertical slice of the stack to create an application that met users' needs. If other parts of the existing code were needed, developers would check with the people who created those parts, often sitting down with them to understand how those parts worked and could be reused. Eventually, standard application programming interfaces (APIs) and frameworks such as CORBA and DCOM were created to promote reuse of certain types of functionality, but even then, knowledge of other developers was crucial to finding out how things really worked or how to perform certain tasks correctly. Also, almost all applications of the mainframe- and client/server-era applications were built on top of a single database. Development took place using various toolkits and application constructs designed to enhance the power of people writing code in third-generation computer languages such as ABAP, C, C++, and eventually, Java.

This development paradigm created a huge amount of amazing software that led to the modern world of business applications, such as mySAP ERP and the mySAP Business Suite, as well as offerings from other vendors. Of course, as time passed, many different methodologies and divisions of labor were created to control development processes, but teams generally focused on the vertical slices of the stack.

In the ESA world, developers and architects control horizontal slices of the stack. Coding in third-generation languages is replaced as much as possible by modeling. Enterprise services that were carefully constructed for reuse are the fundamental building blocks, not APIs or undocumented internal functionality. The database is no longer visible. Data used by a composite application is controlled by services.

The division of labor has changed as well. Modeling makes development simpler and allows business analysts to create and configure certain types of composite applications. Developers or business analysts who create composites are in control of the UI, which can be modeled through SAP NetWeaver Visual Composer, and of the process logic, which can be modeled and implemented through guided procedures and other ways discussed throughout this book. The services layer is in the control of developers who are experts in third-generation languages. These developers, both those at software vendors and those in corporations, focus their time on creating services that can be provided to composite application developers. The data used by a composite may be located in several different service providers.

In other parts of the book, we discuss helpful tools, such as the Enterprise Services Repository, that provide a comprehensive environment to search for services, understand their interfaces and how they work, and then use them from development tools such as SAP NetWeaver Visual Composer. Chapter 12 covers how development tools are used to create composites. The key question facing us now is how composite application developers deal with the fact that data is distributed in databases located in not one but several different service providers.

What are the challenges facing composite application developers and architects?

Perhaps the most challenging difference between composite applications and those of previous generations is the way data is distributed throughout several service providers in most composite applications. Much of what we discuss in this chapter deals with how application developers have new responsibilities in this new world and how information management helps.

Data is only the beginning of what composite application developers must face, however. They need to turn that data into information and then into knowledge. Other challenges include the fact that composite applications are being created in a world of demanding users who expect the highest levels of functionality, integration, and ease of use. In other words, composite applications must live up to higher expectations than previous generations. For example, analytics, collaborative functionality, and mobile versions of key applications are no longer an innovation but a must-have for many users.

To better understand the challenges facing composite applications, let's imagine that we have gathered requirements from users and are ready to start exploring how we will create an application to meet their needs.

The first stop may be the Enterprise Services Repository. By searching through the directory, developers identify the services that meet the needs of the application. Once they find a service, they can look at its interface and see how it fits into the process component models of the applications that use it. The models in the Enterprise Services Repository also may show the business objects that each enterprise service uses. OK, so now we have the services. What's next?

The next question we may ask concerns the data. Where is the data that we need? How can we access it? Does the data exist in more than once place? What services can provide access to the data? (Perhaps these would have been the first group of questions many developers would have asked, but in a service-oriented world, we prefer to start with services.) In order to build applications in an ESA world, developers must have a catalog of data that maps where data is in all the service providers and helps to reconcile differences between them. It is also important that data inconsistencies be identified and cleaned (information quality) and that data can be moved around and synchronized easily when needed (information synchronization). What about a central repository of certain types of data consolidated from all of the different service providers? That certainly could come in handy. Somehow, composite application developers must be able to understand and manage the landscape of data.

Once the data has been identified, it can be used to meet the needs of the application. One of those increasingly important needs is not only to create, read, update, and delete data, but also to provide tools to analyze the data in the context of a process and to take action with appropriate functionality. In other words, composite developers need tools for extracting meaning—that is, analytics in the broad sense, not just data analysis, and the means to do something about it. Analytic functionality can range from simple reporting to advanced interactive environments for advanced analysis using OLAP. The means to do something involves using the appropriate enterprise services.

But doing something may mean working with others. Composite applications must not send users back to email when they need to get help from others, but instead should provide ways to engage others through collaborative functionality ranging from assigning tasks that can be managed to real-time, secure instant messaging to use of collaborative rooms or workspaces, blogs, Wikis, and bulletin boards.

Collaboration often leads to communication that is captured in documents: what about documents, anyway? Composite applications must be able to incorporate unstructured documents into their functionality so that users are not sent to some other filesystem or search engine to find the documents related to the applications, which may exist in many different repositories. Documents related to the composite application should be managed within the composite. So should the ability to search for relevant documents—both documents that reside within the composite and documents that reside outside of it.

Given the distributed and real-time nature of most enterprises, mobile access has become vitally important not just for composites, but for all applications that are central to an organization's productivity. When called for, composites must be able to be used from mobile devices.

While other challenges face composite application developers, if most applications had ways to address these challenges, the developers would be empowered and the applications would be powerful.

What is information management and how will it help?

Information management is an umbrella term we are using for a group of capabilities focused on helping companies manage and extract the most possible value from the information assets that they create in the course of doing business. In providing these capabilities, information management solutions also can help meet the challenges facing composites that we just outlined. In our discussion of information management in this chapter, it is important not to lose sight of the fact that each solution we will discuss has a life of its own and solves many problems outside of serving the needs of composite applications. We added mobile access to this discussion because unified access to information from anywhere becomes increasingly important to support the knowledge worker efficiently.

Our definition of the information management umbrella includes the following solutions:

SAP NetWeaver Master Data Management (MDM)
    Provides a unified environment for managing distributed master data

SAP NetWeaver Business Intelligence (SAP NetWeaver BI)
    Provides functionality to support access and analytics for data distributed in many databases, including BI Consumer Services and the BI Accelerator

Knowledge Management and Collaboration (KMC)
Provides the ability to search and manage distributed repositories of unstructured information as well as collaborative functionality

SAP NetWeaver Mobile
Provides mobile access for enterprise applications

These capabilities play an important role in helping developers create composite applications, but of course many other parts of ESA and SAP NetWeaver provide help as well. Project Mendocino helps extend composite applications into the Microsoft Office environment, and the services provided by the Enterprise Services Inventory provide more functional muscle. Global data types help keep data in a consistent format across many systems and services and given the central role that composite applications play, many more methods for accelerating their development will likely be created in the future.

The rest of this chapter will explain the different parts of information management and SAP NetWeaver Mobile and will discuss how they help meet the challenges of composite application development.

SAP NetWeaver MDM

Master data, when properly managed, can be an important model of an enterprise that allows a company to answer different questions about its business, including the following:

- Who are our largest customers?

- Who is our largest supplier?

- What raw materials do we buy the most?

- Are activities for purchasing appropriately consolidated?

There is an old joke about an economist stranded on a desert island with an engineer, a physicist, and a can of food. After the engineer and physicist explain their approaches to opening the can, they turn to the economist for his approach. "First, assume we have a can opener," the economist replies.

In the ESA world, with many systems containing potentially redundant or overlapping information managed by different service providers, it can be dangerous to make any assumptions about the quality, consistency, or understanding of the data landscape. Assuming that all data is clean, consistent, and well-understood is not that useful. But what can be done?

SAP NetWeaver MDM is a solution aimed directly at the problem of managing the quality of master data distributed across many systems. SAP NetWeaver MDM provides tools to analyze and clean data, create maps of the data in each repository, construct a centralized model that resolves inconsistencies, and transport and synchronize data as needed.

When you can understand what data resides where and move it around as needed, the task of developing composite applications becomes much easier. And while someday all master data may be created and maintained perfectly across all potential service providers, for the foreseeable future SAP NetWeaver MDM will be an important function in most large-scale corporate computing environments. This section will explain the basics of SAP NetWeaver MDM and will discuss why it is important to composite applications development.

What is master data?

Master data is data that lasts from one transaction to another in a business. If you are a customer of an online bookseller, your name, address, email, and any other data used each time you buy a book is master data. The list of the specific books that you are buying is *transactional data*—data that is specific to that order or transaction.

What is SAP NetWeaver MDM?

A clear view of master data is crucial to understanding a business. For example, if a business has five systems that are used to track sales and customer records stored in each, how does the business determine, for instance, which customers give it the most business? The business can determine the right answer to that question if the records that identify each customer in each database are mapped to a master record that provides a consolidated view of the information about a customer and an index of where all the data is located. In this way, when information about a specific customer is needed, the right records in each system can be looked up and the answer determined. The master record and index have to take into account the different ways information is looked up in each distributed database. One system might use the customer's Social Security number and another system might use the customer's credit card number, phone number, or some other identifier. The index has to map all of these different identifiers to a specific system.

What happens, though, if some of the data is bad, incorrect, or duplicated? For example, what happens if several records exist in one system for the same customer with different identifiers or misspellings? It would be impossible to get a comprehensive view of that customer until that data was cleaned. Once the data was cleaned and mapped to a central index, wouldn't it be nice if the business could access the data as if it were consolidated into a central repository? And wouldn't it be nice if the business could distribute clean subsets of the data to different applications? The answer to these questions is yes, and SAP NetWeaver MDM helps all of this to happen, as we will explain.

The first way SAP NetWeaver MDM helps is by providing a rich client interface for browsing and cleaning all the master data in the various enterprise applications in use at a company. From the ESA perspective, these enterprise applications can be thought of as service providers, but from the SAP NetWeaver MDM perspective, they are systems containing transactional and master data. SAP NetWeaver MDM allows the master data from each system to be transferred to SAP NetWeaver MDM, where it can be checked for duplicates, analyzed, mapped, and modeled. If the enterprise applications have facilities for providing access to the master data, it may be possible to correct errors from SAP NetWeaver MDM, but frequently it is necessary to use the master data management facilities of the enterprise applications to make corrections.

The second way SAP NetWeaver MDM helps is through a flexible modeling environment that allows a master record to be created to consolidate all of the information for a customer, supplier, or other element of the master data. It is in constructing this master record that the differences in indexes to the records are resolved, as well as the differences in values used in each database. For example, if one system uses A,B,C for certain values and another uses 1, 2, 3, the mapping to the master record puts these on the same scale.

The collection of all the master records for all customers becomes a powerful central repository that service providers and composite applications can use for analysis. Enterprise applications that are service providers can look in the central repository when a new customer is being created to see if that customer is already known to the company; if so, all of the information collected about that customer can be accessed and utilized. Composite applications can use a central repository to access in one place all that is known about a customer. Central repositories of master records can be created for not only customers, but also suppliers, materials, parts, and anything else kept in all of the enterprise applications.

The third way SAP NetWeaver MDM helps is by moving data back and forth between the central SAP NetWeaver MDM repository of master records and the systems of record corresponding to the enterprise applications. It can then move master records from the central database in SAP NetWeaver MDM back to the enterprise applications or to other locations that may need it. For example, a supplier may need to maintain information about parts to help fulfill orders.

Clean and consolidated master data has tremendous business value. At General Electric, whose consumer and industrial appliances division already uses SAP NetWeaver MDM, all of the product data has been loaded into the system. When one of the executives there sat down and began playing with the SAP NetWeaver MDM client, he found the system to be so intuitive that a light bulb above his head appeared almost immediately. He said, "I just found every single product we make that is stainless steel. I've never been able to do that before." The executive did that by clicking a mouse. In the past, he would have had to call the IT department; the IT department would have had to run some analytics, and eventually a report would have been created. This is but one example of the value that is created by having your data accessible and in one place. Other examples include being able to analyze global spending across all suppliers, and being able to populate public repositories of master data used for global data synchronization in the consumer products industry.

One way to categorize the value SAP NetWeaver MDM provides is to think of two related concepts: *information quality* and *information synchronization*. Information quality covers all the functionality provided to analyze and clean data and to keep errors from creeping back in. Information synchronization covers all of the functionality related to moving data back and forth from a central repository and synchronizing data across many systems.

What are the key capabilities of SAP NetWeaver MDM for information quality?

Preserving information quality through SAP NetWeaver MDM is an operational process that requires constant attention. Challenges include managing data spread across multiple systems and functions, and improving the quality of the data as it spreads, instead of having it deteriorate slowly over time. The solution is to have an organized process for inspecting data and finding the places where there are mismatches, determining where changes are required, and finally, approving those changes.

The data management task falls not on the occasional user who wants to look up, say, a particular SKU, but on a data management specialist. This person's job is to ensure that the consolidation process is occurring correctly (this should not be the job of the IT department because that arm of the organization is not familiar with the data). But imagine that you have one million customer records and 10 master data management specialists. Are they going to check addresses one record at a time? These specialists must be able to make decisions about 100 records or 1,000 records at a time, and that means they need to be able to find those 1,000 records.

Realizing the importance of the data specialist's role, SAP NetWeaver MDM includes rich client tools for managing data. This environment provides a powerful interface capable of looking at tens of thousands of records simultaneously, thus allowing for volume data maintenance. At the same time, SAP NetWeaver MDM includes thin-client portal components for remote data specialists who are doing data entry on an occasional basis.

The key idea to understanding SAP NetWeaver MDM's capabilities for information quality is that they excel at end-user productivity with an ease of use corresponding to desktop applications such as Word and Excel, unlike traditional technical programs for information maintenance. The master records in SAP NetWeaver MDM's central repository reside in memory so that access to them is virtually instantaneous. This makes SAP NetWeaver MDM's rich client able to sift through thousands of records at once. Algorithms for locating duplicate records and performing other cleaning and analysis functions execute immediately.

SAP NetWeaver MDM has several features that are unique among data management solutions. It uses highly flexible object models for data management that allow for:

- Predefined object models for customer, product, employee, and supplier

- An infinitely configurable schema for user-defined object models

- A rich repository for handling simple to complicated data taxonomy and hierarchies

These capabilities mean that the model of the central master records is flexible enough to handle the steady flow of new data sources that is common in most heterogeneous computing environments.

SAP NetWeaver MDM also provides, for the benefit of external composite applications, a duplicate check service for when a new item is being created. SAP NetWeaver MDM will automatically suggest that the user run a routine to check for duplicates in other systems that may contain the same item under a slightly different designation. This service checks whether an item is new or already exists in the master data.

There are other ways to use SAP NetWeaver MDM beyond operational data cleansing. Say you are looking for a subset of customers that fit the profile for an acquisition campaign you want to run. You run a query, but the results don't bring back enough customers that fit the initial parameter. With SAP NetWeaver MDM, you can look for the next best match based on demographics or other types of information that fit your search. In fact, sophisticated search capabilities allow users to search for and even find the proverbial needle in a haystack. These search capabilities allow users to find information that may have been miscategorized, entered in a different dimension or unit of measure, and so on.

This capability illustrates why SAP NetWeaver MDM is useful to the world of composite applications. It provides services that allow business applications to access data as well as to search and identify master data. Customer Relationship Management (CRM) needs a catalog; Supply Chain Management (SCM) needs one, and Enterprise Resources Planning (ERP) needs one, too. SAP NetWeaver MDM can drive the management of those catalogs, and composite applications such as analytics leverage the services within SAP NetWeaver MDM to help find and visualize that master data.

Moving forward, SAP NetWeaver MDM will perform more sophisticated tasks, starting with create, read, update, and delete functions. This will allow for composite applications that store and read data directly from SAP NetWeaver MDM instead of replicating it into another repository. Future versions will also include functionality for using SAP NetWeaver MDM's quality management capabilities (validations, duplicate checks) through enterprise services.

What are the key capabilities of SAP NetWeaver MDM for information synchronization?

Information synchronization means moving information around a system landscape efficiently and effectively to achieve a business purpose. SAP NetWeaver MDM has facilities for handling several different types of information synchronization scenarios that are common in enterprise computing.

Master data consolidation is the process of bringing master data from a distributed set of systems into a central repository where it can be analyzed and cleaned. Master data consolidation uses cleansing, de-duplication, normalization, and taxonomy management functions for information quality as the data arrives in the central repository of master records. As part of the consolidation, all of the interactive capabilities for consolidation and quality analysis are brought to bear.

Master data harmonization is the automatic synchronization and distribution of globally relevant master data. SAP NetWeaver MDM has both automated and interactive distribution capabilities that ensure that as data changes in one application, other business applications that depend on that data are updated with a consistent view of key data as it changes in real time. This enables decision making based on the most accurate data. Master data harmonization takes advantage of SAP NetWeaver MDM's capabilities for matching and merging, tracking changes, ID mapping, and staging information.

Central MDM is a scenario in which master data for all participating enterprise applications is managed in one central repository. The ability to create master data is effectively turned off in each application. When new master data—say, for a customer—must be created, an interface to the central repository is used and the master record is distributed to the enterprise applications that need it. This form of MDM can help ensure that all systems are always updated with clean and consistent reference data.

Global data synchronization is a comprehensive solution for distributing master data for use by partners that is an important part of the consumer product industry. Using global data synchronization, consumer product companies can publish enriched trade item data for exchange with retailers via data hubs (e.g., 1SYNC, which was formed from a merger of UCCnet and Transora). This allows business partners to use this information to communicate with the company that publishes the information and with each other, which enables seamless and error-free integration with backend ERP systems. SAP NetWeaver MDM's implementation of global data synchronization is certified by 1SYNC, the leading data pool for the consumer products industry.

The *content management capabilities* of SAP NetWeaver MDM include tools for intelligent image management, print publishing including layout and production design, product taxonomy and hierarchy management, staging, and data analysis.

With these capabilities, you can move data to where it needs to be and be sure that its quality is maintained.

How does SAP NetWeaver MDM help development of composite applications?

Now that our tour of SAP NetWeaver MDM's capabilities is complete, a clearer picture emerges of how SAP NetWeaver MDM enables both the development of composite applications and the core value of ESA.

What value can be provided from an inventory of services if the data that they are managing is incorrect or inconsistent? How can analytics have any meaning without high-quality data? How can you build a composite application if you cannot find the data that you need? How can you create interfaces for mobile devices if you cannot stage and synchronize data and move it back and forth with precision?

SAP NetWeaver MDM, in essence, helps restore the consistency and data quality that existed when an entire enterprise could be run from a single database. SAP NetWeaver MDM helps create and maintain a consistent view of normalized, harmonized master data that then can be used within a composite application. SAP NetWeaver MDM also provides the centralized services for maintaining and managing master data.

Eventually, much of SAP NetWeaver MDM's functionality will be available to composite applications as enterprise services. The first such service will be the unified key mapping service that allows the index of master records to be consulted so that master data can be located wherever it resides. Composite applications will be able to use the unified key mapping service to navigate all available master data. In future releases of SAP NetWeaver MDM, services for finding duplicate data, controlling distribution and synchronization, and performing other functions will become available.

SAP NetWeaver MDM will play a key role in supporting *information composition*, the process of finding the information needed and consolidating access to it in a single service for use in a composite. In the future, it is likely that SAP NetWeaver MDM's capabilities will be put to use in creating a distributed network of data in which ownership of each portion of data is clearly assigned to one service provider that manages the data and distributes it to other service providers that may need it.

SAP NetWeaver Business intelligence

SAP NetWeaver BI comprises a vast area of functionality that serves many different business needs. A large part of SAP NetWeaver BI is devoted to extracting data from many different sources, cleaning it, and normalizing it so that it can be used to model and analyze a business. This sounds similar to the role of SAP NetWeaver MDM, but SAP NetWeaver BI focuses primarily on transactional data—that is, the data that keeps track of every transaction, every purchase order, every invoice, and so on. Every instance of any activity that goes into a business may find its way into the data warehouse that is at the center of SAP NetWeaver BI, which can make for huge data volumes. Searching through such vast databases can require massive computing power.

Explaining all of what SAP NetWeaver BI can do could fill several books. Our purpose in this chapter is to look at the way that SAP NetWeaver BI is being used to help make composite applications work better.

What are the core functions of SAP NetWeaver BI?

The core functions of SAP NetWeaver BI include solutions and technologies that cover all of the following IT scenarios.

Enterprise data warehousing

Enterprise data warehousing (EDW) enables customers to create and operate a data warehouse that works enterprisewide. This methodology encompasses integration of heterogeneous systems, supports various system topologies and their development, and describes a layering methodology for highly flexible information access. An EDW approach also facilitates both strategic analyses and operational reporting. Data integration is achieved via physical as well as virtual means (the latter with real-time access to underlying systems and databases).

The IT scenario of EDW comprises two scenario variants, which cover the design time (modeling/implementation) and runtime aspects of a highly flexible, reliable, robust, and scalable SAP NetWeaver BI solution.

The scenario variant for *modeling* the EDW mainly addresses implementation and modeling issues. It includes everything from data modeling (creating InfoProviders) to source definition and transformation to data distribution, and it facilitates metadata management.

The scenario variant for *running* the EDW mainly addresses administration and monitoring issues. It includes data flow control, administration and monitoring, performance optimization (using the highly innovative concept of high-performance analytics), and information life cycle management, and it also facilitates user management.

Enterprise reporting, querying, and analysis

Enterprise reporting, querying, and analysis provide processes and services to serve all business users' needs with regard to information consumption. This comprises reporting, ad hoc querying, interactive analysis, dashboards, analytic applications, and list views, from design-time and runtime perspectives.

The design-time processes are increasingly integrated into an overall strategy for the SAP NetWeaver design time. The runtime environment will utilize the Java platform and open standard technologies to provide a flexible and extensible infrastructure. It can be closely embedded into the operational context. All information that a user gets through reporting, querying, or analysis is actionable—i.e., you can print it, attach it to a workflow, distribute it through broadcasting, give feedback on it, and so on. A host of scenario variants will cover the different possibilities of how to define, design, deploy, embed, and interact with SAP NetWeaver BI data by using the different tools and capabilities of the Business Explorer (BEx) Suite.

Business planning and analytical services

Planning in SAP NetWeaver BI provides the features needed to build planning applications that are tailored to the needs of strategic or operational planning. The focus of the scenario is to integrate planning functionality deeply into the analytical environment of SAP NetWeaver BI in order to leverage an optimal combination of planning and analysis capabilities.

The capabilities span from simple manual data entry to SAP Business Information Warehouse (SAP BW) to the design of integrated business planning scenarios that support the integration of planning for all application areas (financial, CRM, SRM, and PLM, for example).

The scenario addresses different types of users: administrators, business analysts, and planning contributors. They are involved in different scenario variants.

Data quality

SAP NetWeaver BI also plays a key role in ensuring data quality, which is a prerequisite to any effective analysis. If the data is incorrect, any analysis will be as well. Starting with Extraction, Transformation, and Loading (ETL) capabilities—through which data is transferred from enterprise applications to an operational data store and then is followed by advanced functionality for matching records and normalizing data—SAP NetWeaver BI can locate many errors and inconsistencies in both master data and transactional information. Data can then be corrected in the data warehouse so that analysis can proceed, and then the corrections can be propagated to the enterprise applications.

The data warehousing capabilities at the heart of these scenarios represent one of the oldest and most mature areas of enterprise computing. Data warehousing is often exciting because in this area, results from academic and computer science research frequently find practical application.

In its early days, data warehousing was primarily a batch-oriented function. Data would be loaded from enterprise applications into the data warehouse in overnight extractions. Reports were often run in batches and were distributed in the morning. As technology advanced, special database structures such as star schemas and InfoCubes were developed that allowed rapid computation of complicated queries that fell under the OLAP domain.

The current challenges facing SAP NetWeaver BI involve figuring out how to cope with an explosion of data as increasing quantities of information are stored and new data sources such as radio frequency identification (RFID) arrive, with an increasing demand for access to information from an expanding population of users, and with the continuing challenge of increasing speed and reliability.

In the midst of all of these challenges, SAP NetWeaver BI is being asked to play an additional role: that of supporting the development of composite applications in the context of ESA. In a fundamental way, every one of SAP NetWeaver BI's core functions helps support composite applications and ESA in one way or another through consolidating information, modeling business activity, and making it easy to access and analyze information and create actionable insights. But there are three specific areas in which SAP NetWeaver BI is being transformed that are particularly helpful in empowering composite applications:

- Making the functions of SAP NetWeaver BI available through services
- Improving the performance of interactive analysis through the SAP NetWeaver BI Accelerator
- Embedding analytics supported by SAP NetWeaver BI and enterprise services into composite applications and any other applications as needed

How is business intelligence becoming service enabled?

By opening up the functionality of SAP NetWeaver BI through enterprise services, composite applications are able to take advantage of a huge trove of functionality for manipulating and analyzing large volumes of data.

One of the most important ways that SAP NetWeaver BI is becoming service enabled is through the XML for Analysis (XMLA) standard. This standard allows programmers to specify and execute OLAP queries through a web services interface. While this allows composite applications to gain access to all that OLAP has to offer, it is just the beginning of what SAP is doing to open up SAP NetWeaver BI through services.

Although it is a crucial part of SAP NetWeaver BI, OLAP is only one of many different capabilities. In fact, SAP has created a set of services called SAP NetWeaver BI Consumer Services that provide access to many additional capabilities that will be of use to composite applications. For example, one of the services offered allows the top 10 results of queries to be retrieved, so instead of getting the entire volume of data, the service gets just the first 10 items. Another lets a user specify alerts to be triggered if certain thresholds for indicators are exceeded. For example, if actual sales dropped more than 20 percent below projections, an email alert could be generated. The thresholds and alerting mechanism could be controlled through services.

At design time, when applications are being created, SAP NetWeaver BI Consumer Services will be used in the Web Application Designer to provide validation of item attributes or command parameters. In the Report Designer, services will also be used for data validation and for accessing metadata. The BEx Analyzer will use services in its design mode.

At runtime, SAP NetWeaver BI Consumer Services will be used in composite applications written in Java, in the BEx Analyzer, for information broadcasting, in Web Dynpro, for custom portal applications, and for interactive planning.

While SAP NetWeaver BI Consumer Services were initially created as an internal mechanism for SAP developers, they are likely to become part of the Enterprise Services Inventory at some point in the future once more experience has been gained in using them.

What is the SAP NetWeaver BI Accelerator?

The SAP NetWeaver BI Accelerator is a technology that speeds up the SAP NetWeaver BI query runtime through use of compression, indexing, and parallel processing that combine the use of search engine technology with a scalable hardware architecture based on blade servers. The BI Accelerator makes queries 10 to 100 times faster on average, which means that analysis becomes far more interactive even when huge volumes of data are being analyzed.

The SAP NetWeaver BI Accelerator works by compressing and indexing InfoCubes and bringing them in through a large in-memory cache spread across a gang of blade servers. As the data enters the BI Accelerator, a process of dictionary-based compression takes place, which reduces the size of the data so that more of it can be stored in memory. The

BI Accelerator then indexes the data by column rather than by row using Text Retrieval and information EXtraction (TREX) search engine technology, which dramatically speeds up processing. Then the index is stored in memory and is spread across the gang of blade servers so that processing can take place in parallel. Figure 13-1 shows the BI Accelerator architecture.

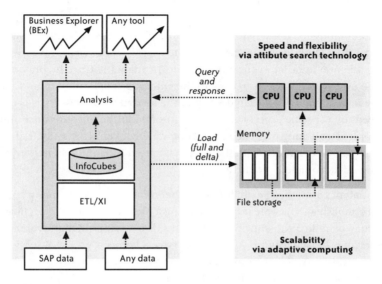

FIGURE 13-1. The SAP NetWeaver BI Accelerator

One of the most convenient aspects of the BI Accelerator is that it works invisibly alongside existing SAP NetWeaver BI functionality. No changes are needed in the queries, in the construction of the InfoCubes, or in the applications that use them.

The BI Accelerator helps improve performance and user satisfaction in scenarios that involve queries across many millions or billions of records. Data volumes of this magnitude are common in the retail, utility, and telecommunications industries. The need for speed is crucial to scenarios such as call centers, where operators must have quick response times for good closure rates. The BI Accelerator also may avoid the need to improve performance by adjusting the structure of the InfoCubes, which can be a time-consuming and difficult process.

For composite application developers, the BI Accelerator functionality of SAP NetWeaver means faster response times so that users can have a more pleasing experience and can work through more queries in a shorter amount of time.

How will SAP NetWeaver BI help embed analytics into composites?

While adding services and making queries faster are a tremendous help to composite application developers, perhaps the most profound impact that SAP NetWeaver BI will have is through embedded analytics. Composite applications known as SAP xApp Analytics will be the first wave of embedded analytic applications released to the market. The idea of embedded analytics is to bring all of the power that SAP NetWeaver BI offers to consolidate, analyze, and understand information, to combine it with the ability to take action that enterprise services offer, and then to insert that analytic capability directly into applications in the context of a process in an enterprise application.

Too often in the past, using analytic functionality has involved a context switch. A user would be in an enterprise application managing a process for evaluating the credit of a supplier or attempting to choose which order should be fulfilled in a time of scarce resources, and then to perform some analysis, the user would have to leave the enterprise application and enter another application to perform analytics. Once he understood the situation, the user would have to go back to the enterprise application to do something about it. The idea of embedded analytics is that the analytic functionality is prepared to meet the needs of a specific process and then is inserted inside the enterprise application so that no context switching is needed and action can be taken right away. Data from SAP NetWeaver BI can be combined with data extracted from ERP and other enterprise applications to provide a complete picture.

Embedded analytics also offer flexibility in another dimension. While many enterprise applications establish a rich context for supporting a process, in the modern business environment it may be difficult to anticipate all the needs of an information worker. Because SAP xApps composite applications for analytics have a large collection of services from which to choose, it is possible to empower users to assemble the information they need at runtime instead of having to limit the choices at design time.

ESA makes embedded analytics possible through composite applications based on enterprise services, as shown in Figure 13-2. SAP NetWeaver Visual Composer allows SAP xApps composite applications for analytics to be created quickly and modified easily. SAP NetWeaver Visual Composer is a modeling environment that simplifies development. This allows business analysts who have a hands-on understanding of the sort of analytics needed at various steps in a business process, to create and adapt analytic applications. Modeling is combined with the use of application patterns that capture common structures of analytic applications to further accelerate development.

As Figure 13-2 shows, the UI created by SAP NetWeaver Visual Composer uses a layer of analytic services to access SAP NetWeaver BI, potentially with the help of BI Accelerator functionality. The layer of analytic services includes XMLA and BI Consumer Services as well as other services created to provide access to SAP NetWeaver BI functionality or to enterprise applications as needed.

Through embedded analytics, the trip from information to action becomes as short as possible.

SAP NetWeaver Knowledge Management and Collaboration

Composite applications exist in a world of high expectations. As each new generation of enterprise applications has arrived, the bar for user satisfaction has been raised. In 1990, it

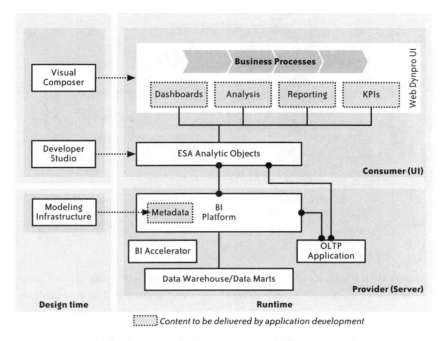

Content to be delivered by application development

FIGURE 13-2. *Service-oriented business intelligence*

was possible to launch enterprise applications successfully without any email integration. Today, no company would ignore email integration where appropriate. Users want a rich environment and rebel when their needs are not served.

Knowledge management and collaboration (KMC) features are quickly becoming a must-have for enterprise applications. The divide between the structured world of transactional applications and the unstructured domain of documents, presentations, spreadsheets, and email is closing rapidly. To succeed, composite applications must offer KMC functionality when users need it. In this section, we will examine the KMC functionality that SAP offers to composite application developers.

What is Knowledge Management and Collaboration?

KMC is an umbrella term for a specific set of functionality offered in SAP NetWeaver. *Knowledge Management* refers to the capabilities for managing documents, such as storage, retrieval, indexing, searching, versioning, and editing. *Collaboration* is functionality for creating virtual spaces called Collaboration Rooms, through which users can communicate. Documents can be uploaded to Collaboration Rooms, group calendars can be displayed, and bulletin boards can store comments. Other features include ways to collaborate in real time through instant messaging or web conferencing (the latter is greatly enhanced by the integration of SAP partner products such as WebEx).

Figure 13-3 depicts the high-level building blocks of KMC.

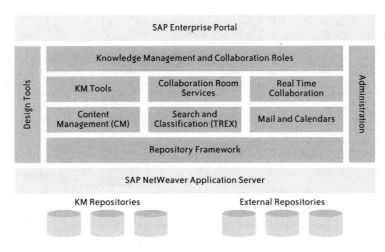

FIGURE 13-3. KMC building blocks

In SAP NetWeaver 2004s, KMC functionality is available through publicly available Java APIs. In the next version of SAP NetWeaver, KMC functionality will be accessible as enterprise services.

What Knowledge Management capabilities can help composite applications?

Using Knowledge Management functionality within composite applications avoids the sort of context switch that we mentioned earlier in this chapter. When Knowledge Management functionality is embedded in a composite, a user can access word processing documents, presentations, spreadsheets, and audio, video, and image files that may be relevant without having to leave the application. Instead of having to sort through a filesystem or some other repository to find the information, or to use a search engine in another interface, the user can find the information nearby. Such seamless integration can be achieved because all of the parts of Knowledge Management are made to work together to provide such an experience. A review of the different functional elements will help us understand what composite applications can do with Knowledge Management.

The Repository Framework is the foundation of Knowledge Management, and it consists of an interface that allows Knowledge Management to access arbitrary repositories so that the documents inside it can be managed, indexed, and searched. To enable access to the repositories (such as a fileserver, an SAP document repository, or a third-party document management system), a connector—technical term: repository manager—per repository type has to be coded once. SAP and its partners deliver a set of ready-made connectors for repositories. In addition, standards such as WebDAV and HTTP are supported, and customers can implement their own connector by using the aforementioned Knowledge Management APIs.

Besides connectivity to external repositories, Knowledge Management also provides its own repository, the Content Management repository, that can be used to store and version documents. For the user, documents from both the external and the Knowledge Management repositories will appear with the same look and feel in the user's UI—for instance, within SAP NetWeaver Portal or a composite that is using Knowledge Management. Furthermore, Knowledge Management provides a range of services on all the documents connected to it, such as classification-based navigation, subscribing to documents, rating, and feedback. Part of the content management features are so-called XML forms that allow for templated creation of HTML content and publication into a web environment.

TREX is the SAP NetWeaver search engine, and it is used to provide search functions wherever needed, which creates the opportunity for a new kind of search, which we will discuss shortly. TREX is also used extensively within Knowledge Management for indexing, searching, and analyzing the content of documents. TREX is not directly available to composite application developers, but instead must be used through the Knowledge Management API that allows control of the storage, indexing, classification, versioning, and searching of documents in repositories.

Until Knowledge Management is exposed through enterprise services, embedding these capabilities in composites in SAP NetWeaver 2004s must be accomplished by using the Java APIs provided by Knowledge Management. Composite application developers can create their own enterprise services to provide the access they need to knowledge management functionality.

Two features that may be part of future releases of SAP NetWeaver are so powerful that they are worth mentioning. The first is the idea of a general-purpose attachment container that could be used in composite applications as a way to collect and refer to a set of relevant documents—for instance, from a purchase order. Once an attachment container is created, documents can be stored in it or referred to from it, providing a convenient way to manage unstructured information in an application.

The other feature is called enterprise search. Right now, TREX is used in many of the solutions in the mySAP Business Suite to index and search for information that is stored in documents and objects inside applications. It is not currently possible, however, to perform *one* search and find every piece of relevant content in all repositories and all business objects in the mySAP Business Suite within *one* consolidated search result list. Enterprise search solves this problem and creates a single federated search that allows one search request to find all relevant information wherever it may reside.

What collaboration capabilities can help composite applications?

At certain points in most business processes, automation reaches its limit, and the people helping the process along must become human integrators. This can happen when an unanticipated problem arises or for any number of reasons. Frequently the enterprise application records significant activity and important actions taken, but the real action shifts to email, instant messaging, or documents that are circulated, often within a restricted group of people such as a project team. For most complicated processes, human integration will always play an important role. Collaboration technology offers the opportunity to integrate collaboration of all forms into composite applications so that people can work with each other more easily without a context switch.

Collaboration Rooms are the central element for collaboration offered by SAP NetWeaver. Collaboration Rooms are flexible workspaces that can contain documents, threaded discussion forums, calendars synchronized from other programs, email lists, and rosters of team members. Portions of other applications that may be relevant to the work of a virtual team may also be included. SAP NetWeaver collaboration features also include lean instant messaging and web conferencing, as well as the ability to connect third-party synchronous collaboration products such as WebEx and Lotus Sametime. The ability to manage tasks through universal work lists and by sending tasks back and forth is another form of collaboration offered by SAP NetWeaver.

How can KMC help composite applications?

In times of information overload, finding the right information at the right time becomes mission critical. When email, cell phones, and instant messages compete for attention, effective techniques for collaboration can ease the burden of keeping track of so many channels.

When a new project first gets underway, the participants are full of hope and excitement, and more importantly, all of the essential information about those aspirations is filed in one central location. As the project evolves and grows, those essential files migrate and propagate. They are updated, revised, and spread through attachments, emails, discussion boards, and of course, the shared drive. Eventually, many of the important project details become so disparate that they are hard to find, if they are not lost altogether. Through KMC functionality, composite applications have a chance to break this cycle.

Using the KMC functionality just described, much of the context switch to and from email, search interfaces, and other related functionality can be avoided. Composite applications can become comprehensive environments for providing all of the elements needed to automate a process, including the ability to manage documents and to collaborate, which should increase user satisfaction and productivity and enable new forms of automation. As KMC becomes increasingly service enabled, deeper and more comprehensive integration will be possible.

SAP NetWeaver Mobile

SAP NetWeaver Mobile offers composite applications the ability to extend their functionality to mobile devices. SAP NetWeaver Mobile is a comprehensive platform that provides an architecture for two-way synchronization of information from a server-based application onto a mobile device. Through such synchronization, the client running on the mobile device, which SAP NetWeaver Mobile also supports, can run in connected or disconnected mode and have changes synchronized when connectivity is restored. SAP NetWeaver Mobile also provides the infrastructure through which thousands of mobile devices can be managed effectively. When needed, SAP NetWeaver Mobile provides a mechanism to bring composite applications anywhere users want to take them.

ESA in action: Arla Foods

Arla Foods, like many companies, faced data challenges. One of its goals in adopting ESA was to create a global master data repository, a feat it has since achieved. Arla Foods is the largest dairy producer in Europe, generating more than 10 billion kilograms of fresh milk and nearly $8 billion in revenues each year. The company employs nearly 25,000 people worldwide, although most are located in its home markets of Sweden, Denmark, and the United Kingdom. Arla Foods is also one of the world's largest cooperative companies, composed of the 11,600 dairy farmers who are also its core suppliers. Cooperative members dominate Arla's board of directors and inform the company's strategic mission—to sell members' milk and process it into dairy products, which can command premiums and maximize profits for the members. To achieve its current size, Arla Foods and its predecessors executed dozens of mergers and acquisitions, leading to a very complex IT environment.

In hopes of resolving this heterogeneity and creating a flexible framework for future acquisitions, Arla embarked on the "One Arla" project five years ago with the goal of integrating nearly 170 customer, employee, producer, and vendor systems and solutions around a single SAP platform (see Figure 13-4). Arla's early solution to this challenge—which has MDM and application integration aspects—was to use SAP NetWeaver Exchange Infrastructure (SAP NetWeaver XI) to create proto-enterprise services beginning in 2002.

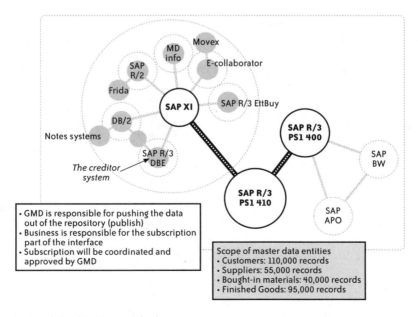

FIGURE 13-4. Arla Foods' MDM system landscape

First, Arla created a single global master data repository filled with harmonized customer, supplier, and partner information. Then, using SAP NetWeaver XI, Arla created approximately 150 interfaces—40 of which are designated "mission critical"—to pass data from the repository and across a system landscape that includes Arla's own SAP R/3 implementation and customers' own systems. Whenever a customer's profile changes, for example, an XML message updates the record in the global master data, followed by a flurry of messages to any other applications currently using that profile, keeping every incarnation of that data in sync with the global master data.

By standardizing the data types contained within these interfaces as XML messages, Arla has already evolved into an enterprise-services-like environment, and currently has an IT application integration team building simple composite applications from the interfaces. One example is myWorkPlace, an employee portal built using the SAP NetWeaver Portal component that integrates Arla's email, invoicing, and other systems into a single UI.

Arla anticipates a full transition to ESA over the next few years when it upgrades from SAP R/3 to mySAP ERP and does the same with supporting systems. The evolution of the service grid—in the form of standardized, commercially available enterprise services—will afford Arla the opportunity to replace the functionality of legacy applications with service-enabled functionality, increasing its flexibility for absorbing and reconciling new systems from acquisitions while lowering total cost of ownership (TCO). The overarching benefit of ESA for Arla will be the replacement of its homegrown, service-oriented environment with a universal, standardized, and less costly one that will still leverage its experience with the underlying IT.

PART FIVE

Creating Services

CHAPTER FOURTEEN

Web Services Basics

ENTERPRISE SERVICES ARE WEB SERVICES. FOR THIS REASON, TO COMPREHEND WHAT **ESA** CAN DO FOR
you, you have to understand the basic principles of web services.

What are web services and why do we care?

To understand the benefits of web services and even what they are, it helps to think back
a bit to life before the advent of the Web. It was very difficult for diverse kinds of computers to communicate; they each had their own protocol stacks and translation was tricky.
The Web offered a lowest-common-denominator approach, making text its foundation
with HTML and sending it over one standard protocol, HTTP. This created a revolution.
Suddenly web browsers running on any platform could communicate with web servers on
any platform, and they didn't need to know or care where those resources resided.

In essence, web services create the same type of revolution, but this time for programs.
Integrating disparate applications is the bane of the IT professional. Integration work
requires using specialized application programming interfaces (APIs) or complex standards
such as DCOM and CORBA to communicate between applications. Further, when applications are upgraded, the integrations typically break and must be refactored.

Web services strip this process down from programmatic remote procedure calls to simple text messages, which are exchanged between systems. With the help of web services, integrators do not need to know or care whether the application they will be interoperating with is written in Java, C++, C#, Perl, or ABAP. It simply doesn't matter, as we will see.

Here's a formal definition of web services:

> Web services are self-contained and self-describing application functionalities that can be processed through open Internet standards.

Web services are, in essence, small, modular applications that communicate using a text format and open Internet standards.

Their modularity is important because we can create and expose services slowly and organically with a gradual adoption plan. We can expose existing application functionality as services, allowing reuse instead of reinventing the wheel. Their small scope allows us to respond quickly to changing business conditions, introducing new services as needed. We will unpack the more formal definition further as we go, but this is enough to get you started.

What are some examples of web services?

Web services, as the term says, provide a service. It might be a price check, an inventory status check, a stock quote, or an airline reservation. Examples of web services include:

- Intelligent product catalog searches
- Product availability checks
- Pricing inquiries
- Customer credit checks
- Order status checks
- Vendor-managed inventories
- Demand forecasts, stock replenishment
- Dynamic auctioning and bidding
- Publishing and analyzing financial reports
- Electronic bill presentment and payment
- Matching vacancies and job applicants' profiles
- Postal service address checks
- Universal Description, Discovery, and Integration (UDDI) registration and discovery
- Automated web searches (Google)

What are services?

Services are callable entities or application functionalities accessed via the exchange of messages. To facilitate this exchange, a web service has a clearly defined contract or interface. This interface defines:

- What actions are performed
- The structure of request, response, and fault messages
- The URL of the service
- The technical means to access the URL

What is service-oriented architecture?

According to Eric Newcomer and Greg Lomow in their book *Understanding SOA with Web Services* (Independent Technology Guides):

> A service-oriented architecture (SOA) is a style of design that guides all aspects of creating and using business services throughout their lifecycle (from conception to retirement), as well as defining and provisioning the IT infrastructure that allows different applications to exchange data and participate in business processes regardless of the operating systems or programming languages underlying those applications.

Simply put, SOA is a system architecture based on services. Although older styles of SOAs include those that use DCOM or CORBA, today when people speak of SOAs, they mean SOAs based on web services and the standards that go along with them.

Why is service orientation better than object orientation?

Object orientation is a powerful programming paradigm in which applications expose functionality through well-defined interfaces called methods. Details are hidden from the calling application. However, the calling application must be written in the same language as the object it is trying to access. If it's not, we need a translator program, as shown in Figure 14-1.

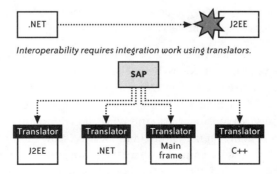

FIGURE 14-1. Object orientation and interoperability

Web services provide a standard way to communicate between services, which may be written in different languages, as shown in Figure 14-2.

FIGURE 14-2. *Service orientation and interoperability*

What are the main components of web services?

The easiest way to understand the main components of web services, which are providers, directories, and consumers, is to think about a real-world example.

You can think of nearly everything a business does as a service. What do you do if you are looking for a service, such as auto repair? You look it up in a service directory, such as the Yellow Pages. You as the potential service consumer look in a directory for a service provider. Using the information in the directory (in this case, a phone number), you then contact the provider, who performs the service you requested, as shown in Figure 14-3.

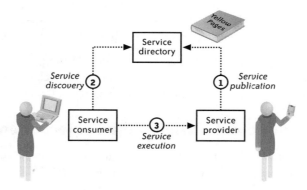

FIGURE 14-3. *Web services mirroring real-world services*

If you think of what happens step by step, first the service provider publishes business information in the directory, then you find or discover the service, you contact the provider, and the provider executes the service for you.

Web services mirror this structure. A provider of a web service writes a service or exposes functionality as a service (the service itself may be written in any language) and then writes a description of that service in the Web Services Description Language (WSDL). The WSDL might be passed directly to a business partner, or it could be published in a UDDI directory. The web services consumer uses the WSDL description to either construct or configure a client, depending on the nature of the service. Now it is time to execute the service. The client and the server must translate their programmatic calls into SOAP messages that handle the execution. Figure 14-4 shows this process.

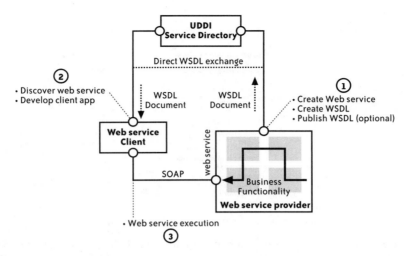

FIGURE 14-4. Basic web services components

Although conceptually it is clear what each web services standard is doing, let's examine the main web services standards in more detail now, starting with the standard that underpins the web services standards: XML.

What is XML?

XML is the Extensible Markup Language. It is the universal format for structured information on the Web.

XML is a markup language similar to HTML. Both are simple to write and use and both can be read by humans and by intelligent clients. Both are text formats.

To understand XML and how it differs from HTML, let's step back and consider what we know about HTML:

- HTML separates data from presentation.
- HTML describes how data should look when it is viewed in a browser.
- HTML uses a fixed tag set.
- HTML tags relate to formatting: how to make text look bold, how to display tables, how to define styles for displaying information, and so on.

XML, on the other hand, separates data from meaning. XML's characteristics include the following:

- XML has no fixed tag set.
- XML has no fixed semantics.
- Instead of tags to describe what data should look like, XML tags define the data itself.

Figure 14-5 shows an XML snippet.

```
<?xml version="1.0" ?>
- <PurchaseOrder>
    <date>1999-05-20</date>
  - <shipTo>
      <name>John Smith</name>
      <street>123 Maple Street</street>
      <city>Mill Valley</city>
      <state>CA</state>
      <zip>90952</zip>
    </shipTo>
  - <lineitems>
    - <Item>
        <product>Lawnmower</product>
        <price>148.95</price>
      </Item>
    - <Item>
        <product>Birdbath Deluxe</product>
        <price>249.95</price>
      </Item>
    </lineitems>
</PurchaseOrder>
```

FIGURE 14-5. An XML-based purchase order

The root element of a purchase order document may have the tag `<PurchaseOrder>`. The tag describes the data it contains. A `<price>` element holds the price of an item.

Because the tags define the items that they hold and because XML data is always structured, simple parsers can retrieve the data from an XML document.

What is XML schema?

XML data is structured. We can define what a complete purchase order looks like and then compare the documents we receive to that document. This is known as *validation*. One way to specify a document's structure is with the XML Schema Definition (XSD) language. XSD is an XML vocabulary used to articulate rules for business data. Example 14-1 shows the XML schema used in a web service that retrieves an address.

EXAMPLE 14-1. An XML schema

```
<xsd:schema
   targetNamespace="http://sap.com/demo/WS/GetAddress/prepared"
   xmlns="http://sap.com/demo/WS/GetAddress/prepared"
   xmlns:xsd="http://www.w3.org/2001/XMLSchema">
<xsd:element name="Request_Message" type="Request"/>
<xsd:element name="Response_Message" type="Response"/>
<xsd:complexType name="Request">
<xsd:sequence>
<xsd:element name="Employee_Id" type="xsd:string"/>
<xsd:element name="Address_Type" type="xsd:string"/>
<xsd:element name="Date" type="xsd:string"/>
</xsd:sequence>
</xsd:complexType>
<xsd:complexType name="Response">
<xsd:sequence>
<xsd:element name="First_Name" type="xsd:string"/>
<xsd:element name="Last_Name" type="xsd:string"/>
<xsd:element name="Care_of_Name" type="xsd:string"/>
<xsd:element name="Street_Name" type="xsd:string"/>
```

EXAMPLE 14-1. An XML schema (continued)

```
<xsd:element name="House_Number" type="xsd:string"/>
<xsd:element name="Name_of_City" type="xsd:string"/>
<xsd:element name="Zipcode" type="xsd:string"/>
<xsd:element name="County" type="xsd:string"/>
<xsd:element name="Country" type="xsd:string"/>
<xsd:element name="Email_Address" type="xsd:string"/>
<xsd:element name="Telephone_Number" type="xsd:string"/>
<xsd:element name="Status" type="xsd:string"/>
</xsd:sequence>
</xsd:complexType>
</xsd:schema>
```

Based on this document, a program given the correct inputs can construct a valid XML message to call this functionality in an SAP system.

What are XML namespaces?

The fact that XML as a standard does not dictate semantics means that we can define any document structures we wish. I may decide on a certain structure for a purchase order, but if you decide on a different structure, we will need to translate each other's messages or else we will not be able to communicate.

The flexibility that XML provides by allowing us to create any tags we want can also lead to problems. An XML document can be constructed from multiple sources. Since these different sources may use tags with the same names, conflicts are possible. Consider the seemingly innocent tag, <Order_Number>. Do we mean the order number used when we purchased the item or the order number assigned when we sold the item? Without further definition, such a common term can be ambiguous. The basic solution to this problem is to use an XML technology known as namespaces.

We declare XML namespaces and then preface a tag with the namespace name. In this way, we remove all ambiguity about which tag we are using.

The schema in Example 14-1 uses namespaces. In the beginning of the file, we see the namespace declaration, using the xmlns element:

```
<xsd:schema
    targetNamespace="http://sap.com/demo/WS/GetAddress/prepared"
    xmlns="http://sap.com/demo/WS/GetAddress/prepared"
    xmlns:xsd="http://www.w3.org/2001/XMLSchema">
```

What is SOAP?

SOAP (which once stood for Simple Object Access Protocol but is now known simply by its rather catchy acronym) is an important web services standard that describes the message structures passed at runtime to call a web service.

A SOAP message is an XML document that describes the operation to be performed and the parameters to pass to the application. Optionally, a SOAP message can include other information that describes how a recipient should process the SOAP message.

A SOAP message, which is always an XML message, wraps the service call in a SOAP envelope, as shown in Figure 14-6. A SOAP envelope includes an optional header area for additional processing information such as quality of service or processing restrictions that have meaning only if the service application is coded to process those headers. A SOAP envelope also includes a mandatory body section that describes the functions to be called and the parameters that are passed to the service.

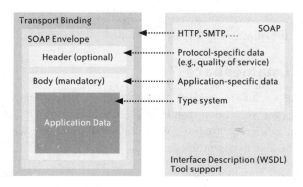

FIGURE 14-6. SOAP structure and features

A strength of SOAP as a code wrapper is that a SOAP message is a text file that is generally passed via HTTP or HTTPS and therefore can cross corporate firewalls. Other interoperability standards such as CORBA, DCOM, and RPC cannot cross firewalls and are therefore not suitable for web services.

Figure 14-7 shows a simplified representation of a SOAP request being exchanged via HTTP. The HTTP header starts with a POST request, followed by the path to the applications, /Accounts/Savings/ and the HTTP version. The second line specifies the host that is processing this request. The next two lines in the HTTP header show the SOAP HTTP binding.

The body of the HTTP request contains the SOAP message. It begins with a mandatory envelope element followed by a SOAP header containing the transaction element. This element has some meaning to the application processing the web service call but no general meaning to the SOAP standard. A body element describes the action to perform—namely, deposit—and an account number, currency type, and amount for the action. This SOAP message allows us to pass an application instruction over the Internet—namely, to deposit $200 to account 112233 and to do it in a way that can cross corporate firewalls. This service may generate a response SOAP message that indicates success or failure.

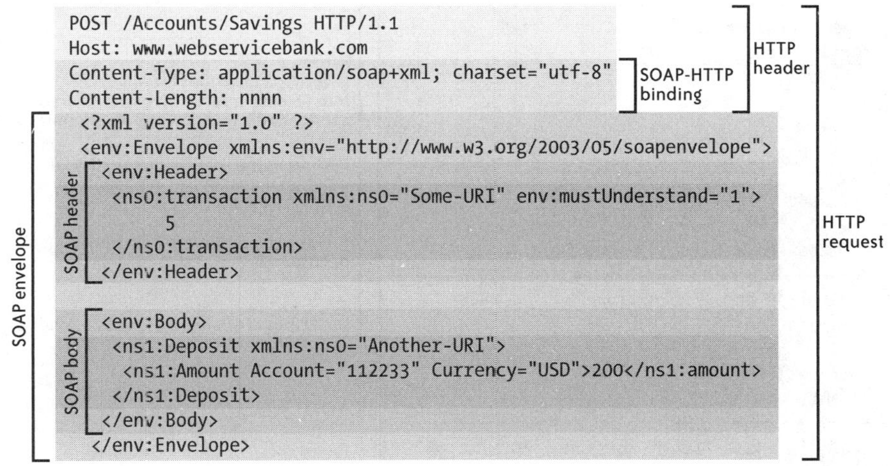

```
POST /Accounts/Savings HTTP/1.1
Host: www.webservicebank.com
Content-Type: application/soap+xml; charset="utf-8"    ] SOAP-HTTP
Content-Length: nnnn                                     binding
  <?xml version="1.0" ?>
  <env:Envelope xmlns:env="http://www.w3.org/2003/05/soapenvelope">
    <env:Header>
      <ns0:transaction xmlns:ns0="Some-URI" env:mustUnderstand="1">
         5
      </ns0:transaction>
    </env:Header>

    <env:Body>
      <ns1:Deposit xmlns:ns0="Another-URI">
        <ns1:Amount Account="112233" Currency="USD">200</ns1:amount>
      </ns1:Deposit>
    </env:Body>
  </env:Envelope>
```

FIGURE 14-7. Sample of a basic SOAP message over HTTP

What is WSDL?

While SOAP is used as the format of the exchanged message, WSDL is used to describe the callable web service. WSDL is the XML vocabulary for describing web services, where they are located, and how they can be called. Using the WSDL description of a web service, we can code a client typically with at least some code generation to reduce the amount of hand coding that must be done.

WSDL documents describe the what, how, and where of web services, as illustrated in the simplified WSDL document shown in Figure 14-8. First, consider the what. A port type describes the abstract interface, which is the web service to be called. A port type can have one or more operations. An operation describes the functionality to be called, and the input, output, and fault message types associated with it. The different messages are built from built-in or custom data types. The data types themselves are defined using the XSD language.

To describe how to call a web service, a binding specifies the transport protocol for exchanging messages, such as HTTP, HTTPS, SMTP, FTP, and so on. The service can be bound to multiple protocols if the service provider can accept them. Finally, a WSDL port details the specific network address at which the service can be found.

Example 14-2 shows an actual WSDL document for a GetAddress function.

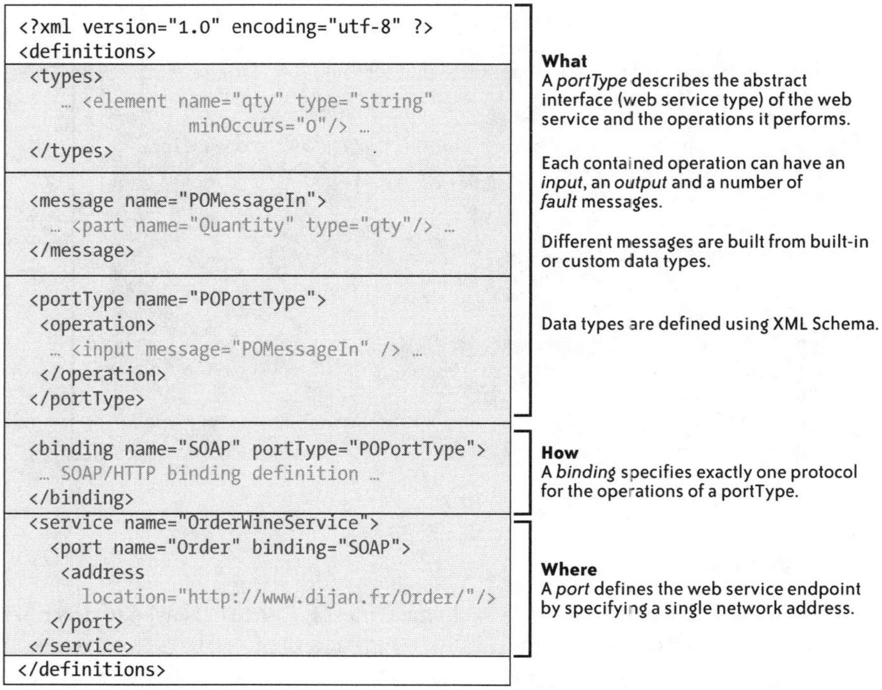

```
<?xml version="1.0" encoding="utf-8" ?>
<definitions>
  <types>
    … <element name="qty" type="string"
              minOccurs="0"/> …
  </types>

  <message name="POMessageIn">
    … <part name="Quantity" type="qty"/> …
  </message>

  <portType name="POPortType">
   <operation>
    … <input message="POMessageIn" /> …
   </operation>
  </portType>

  <binding name="SOAP" portType="POPortType">
   … SOAP/HTTP binding definition …
  </binding>

  <service name="OrderWineService">
    <port name="Order" binding="SOAP">
     <address
       location="http://www.dijan.fr/Order/"/>
    </port>
  </service>
</definitions>
```

What
A *portType* describes the abstract interface (web service type) of the web service and the operations it performs.

Each contained operation can have an *input*, an *output* and a number of *fault* messages.

Different messages are built from built-in or custom data types.

Data types are defined using XML Schema.

How
A *binding* specifies exactly one protocol for the operations of a portType.

Where
A *port* defines the web service endpoint by specifying a single network address.

FIGURE 14-8. A simplified WSDL document

EXAMPLE 14-2. A WSDL file

```
<?xml version="1.0" encoding="utf-8"?>
<wsdl:definitions
   targetNamespace="http://sap.com/demo/WS/GetAddress/prepared"
   xmlns:http="http://schemas.xmlsoap.org/wsdl/http/"
   xmlns:soap="http://schemas.xmlsoap.org/wsdl/soap/"
   xmlns:tns="http://sap.com/demo/WS/GetAddress/prepared"
   xmlns:wsdl="http://schemas.xmlsoap.org/wsdl/"
   xmlns:xsd="http://www.w3.org/2001/XMLSchema">
<wsdl:types>
<!-- XSD schema types shown in Example 14-1 -->
</wsdl:types>
<wsdl:message name="Request_Message">
<wsdl:part name="parameters" element="tns:Request_Message"/>
</wsdl:message>
<wsdl:message name="Response_Message">
<wsdl:part name="parameters" element="tns:Response_Message"/>
</wsdl:message>
<wsdl:portType name="Z_WS_Address_Test">
<wsdl:operation name="Z_Get_Address">
<wsdl:input message="tns:Request_Message"/>
<wsdl:output message="tns:Response_Message"/>
</wsdl:operation>
</wsdl:portType>
<wsdl:binding name="Z_WS_Address_TestSoapBinding"
              type="tns:Z_WS_Address_Test">
```

EXAMPLE 14-2. A WSDL file (continued)

```
<soap:binding style="document"
              transport="http://schemas.xmlsoap.org/soap/http"/>
<wsdl:operation name="Z_Get_Address">
<soap:operation soapAction=""/>
<wsdl:input>
<soap:body use="literal"/>
</wsdl:input>
<wsdl:output>
<soap:body use="literal"/>
</wsdl:output>
</wsdl:operation>
</wsdl:binding>
<wsdl:service name="Z_WS_Address_TestService">
<wsdl:port name="Z_WS_Address_TestSoapBinding"
           binding="tns:Z_WS_Address_TestSoapBinding">
<soap:address
   location=
   "http://iwdfvm1035.wdf.sap.corp:8000/Z_WS_ADDRESS_TEST?sap-client=100"/>
</wsdl:port>
</wsdl:service>
</wsdl:definitions>
```

The WSDL file describes the web service: how to format the messages that will be exchanged to implement the service and the network location for accessing the service.

What is UDDI and how does it relate to SAP?

How does a potential client get the WSDL file? Essentially, there are two options. We can pass the WSDL file itself (or its location) to our partners, or we can publish the WSDL in a directory so that potential clients can find the service. The Yellow Pages, or directory, for web services is a somewhat complicated protocol named Universal Description, Discovery, and Integration, or UDDI. The UDDI registry includes metadata that can be used to search for services by name, ID, category, type, and so on.

UDDI registries can be public or private, can be used for test or production, and can be used in marketplaces or public exchanges. The registry is a structured database of organizations, the services they offer, and the technical descriptions—namely, the WSDL documents—for those services. In a sense, UDDI is a sort of DNS for web services.

SAP's UDDI registry at *http://uddi.sap.com* allows SAP and other organizations to publish service descriptions of their associated WSDL files. For corporate use, SAP NetWeaver includes a UDDI server. Chapter 8 describes the Enterprise Services Repository. Although the Enterprise Services Repository includes WSDL files, that is its only UDDI-like function. The Enterprise Services Repository includes everything needed for creating enterprise services, and WSDL files are a vital but small subset of what the Enterprise Services Repository contains.

How can we ensure that web services will interoperate?

Given the proliferation of standards and the importance of web services to the future of e-commerce, it is important to have a method to guarantee interoperability between organizations at different levels. The Web Services Interoperability Organization, or WS-I, is tasked with accelerating the adoption of web services by reducing the cost associated with standards adoption. WS-I promotes collections of technical standards called profiles that are used for web services between organizations. The initial profile, called WS-I Basic Profile 1.0, includes HTTP, XML, XSD, SOAP, WSDL, and UDDI. Companies know that if another company complies with the basic profile, interoperability is assured via open standards. WS-I also provides documentation and test tools for working with services and the basic profile.

What about web services security?

Security is a paramount concern for web services, especially since XML is essentially text. Many layers of security can be applied to XML exchanges. For example, HTTPS can be used to encrypt the data stream on the wire. Message-level security provides another level of security and encryption that can be very useful. To achieve this more granular level of security, WS-Security describes how to include encryption and digital signature headers in SOAP messages. WS-Security is one of many WS-* protocols or standards. These standards address many advanced web services requirements, such as reliable message exchange, stateful interaction, message exchange profiles, and so forth. Most of these are in the process of being developed or are not yet widely adopted.

Web services are no longer new technology; they are the basic building blocks of SOAs. Nonetheless, having an understanding of web services basics will serve you well as you delve deeper into the details of enterprise services development. With this understanding of web services in mind, Chapters 15 and 16 examine methodologies for creating web services—and enterprise services—using SAP NetWeaver.

CHAPTER FIFTEEN

Creating Enterprise Services in ABAP

THIS CHAPTER DISCUSSES HOW TO CREATE SERVICES IN **ABAP. F**IRST, WE'LL ADDRESS SOME DEVELOPER concerns regarding enterprise services creation and compare web services with enterprise services. The chapter moves on to describe two methodologies for creating services in ABAP. It then explores the capabilities offered by the SAP NetWeaver Exchange Infrastructure (SAP NetWeaver XI). The chapter concludes with a brief look at the future of creating enterprise services.

Can I start creating enterprise services today, or should I wait?

Companies can begin developing enterprise services right away, and here is why. Creating enterprise services doesn't require a big-bang approach. It is an incremental process and can be as simple as turning some piece of needed functionality into a web service. One of the reasons that there is wide industry agreement on the topic of service-oriented architecture (SOA) is that it doesn't require scrapping today's investments in favor of a new architecture. Instead, the systems and functionality you have today will become the basis for your SOA. Even more important, taking a step back to consider your essential business processes and beginning to service enable them allows you to move incrementally toward a full-blown SOA.

Another concern often raised is interoperability. SAP is a founding member of the chief standards-setting body for web services, the Web Services Interoperability Organization (WS-I), and it adheres to its standards, including Basic Profile 1.0 (Basic Profile 1.1 will be supported in a future release of SAP NetWeaver). By ensuring that enterprise services interoperate with web services created by anyone in the industry, maximum interoperability is achieved.

You might also be concerned about whether the enterprise services you create will work with your installed applications. If you have SAP NetWeaver, you can begin creating services today, no matter what version of R/3 you are running, for example. Another advantage to starting now is that the services you create today will continue to work when you upgrade your applications. As we have said before, ESA is a roadmap; get started with enterprise services creation as soon as you can.

How do web services and enterprise services compare?

On a technical level, enterprise services are web services, based on open standards. An enterprise service must be a web service in order to be callable, whether internally or by business partners, customers, or vendors.

Enterprise services, like web services, work from the standpoint of the service provider and the service consumer. The goal is to abstract all the internal details so that the provider and consumer are completely decoupled in terms of implementation. A service consumer should not need to know any details about how the service provider implemented the service on the back end; all the necessary data should be exchanged in a standard, serialized format. There can be no object references that would break the loose coupling of the provider and the consumer. Service providers and service consumers are completely separate; the provider might be a Python application running on Linux and the consumer might be a .NET application running on Windows Server 2003. Although we will talk about service providers and consumers in ABAP and Java in this chapter and the next, it's important to realize that providers and consumers are completely hardware, programming language, and operating system agnostic.

What enterprise services add is business functionality. A one-off web service might be strategic, but designing an enterprise service asks you to look at your most important business processes and turn those into one or more enterprise services. Consider the cancellation of a sales order. This is not a single granular event, but a series of events, a process that has implications for numerous backend systems. Canceling an order entails not just deleting an order; it starts a workflow, perhaps canceling orders for materials, canceling a production request, and so on.

Furthermore, since they are designed to serve enterprise needs, enterprise services must be high-quality, stable, scalable, robust, and secure.

Reuse is another important feature of enterprise services, and that involves separating business logic from presentation logic. The service layer should be implemented without any knowledge of the usage scenario (user interface [UI] or remote communication), allowing the same service to be deployed in a variety of scenarios, including some that the developer never envisioned. Further promoting reuse is the ability to search for relevant services by various criteria.

What are two ways to create services in ABAP?

When creating services in ABAP, there are essentially two ways to approach the problem. You can start at the back end, with an existing application, and say, "I want to service enable that particular piece of functionality." This approach quickly gets some services that you need up and running. In SAP parlance, this approach is called creating services from the inside out because we start with the implementation and move out toward the interface.

Creating services from the outside in is the opposite approach; you start with the interface and work in toward the implementation. While creating services from the inside out entails starting with a piece of application functionality, creating services from the outside in asks you to start with modeling. Creating services from the outside in, starting with modeling, is the preferred—one might say the ultimate—approach to creating enterprise services. The process as it stands at this writing involves modeling data types; at the end of this chapter, we'll look at the direction this process will take in upcoming releases of SAP NetWeaver, where modeling becomes more important and entails working with business objects, as discussed in Chapter 5.

Obviously, creating services from the inside out and the outside in starts from different places; the semantics of the terms imply as much. But they also differ in other important ways. Services created from the inside out follow the message response pattern, which is synchronous. Services created from the outside in can be synchronous or asynchronous, not requiring a response from the service consumer; as a result, such services are even more loosely coupled and more flexible.

What does it mean to create services from the inside out?

Creating a service from the inside out takes a piece of application functionality and makes it available as a web service. That piece of application functionality might be a remotely enabled function module, a Remote Function Call (RFC), or a BAPI. It might be application functionality that you or a custom programmer has created, or a function of SAP's software.

For example, in looking at the IT landscape, managers might request a service to retrieve employee address data. But wait, you might say, there's a Get Address function in our SAP HR system. If we could simply turn that into a web service, we could solve the problem at hand. Creating services from the inside out provides an easy way to turn that functionality into a web service in short order.

Creating services from the inside out is a straightforward process, as shown in Figure 15-1. You start with a piece of existing functionality, you start a wizard to generate the web service, and finally you activate (in ABAP terminology) or deploy the service (if it is Java based). Generating the web service creates all the necessary deployment artifacts, including the Web Services Description Language (WSDL) file, automatically for you. Having created the service, you can test it using SAP's Web Service Homepage.

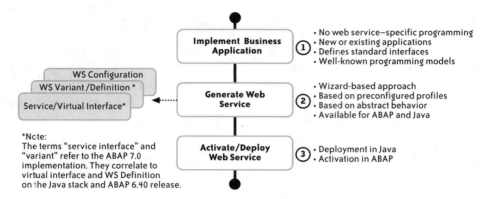

FIGURE 15-1. Steps for creating a service from the inside out

How do you create a service from the inside out using ABAP?

For our first example, we'll service enable a *remote-enabled function module* in the ABAP Function Builder.* Remote-enabled function modules are entities that can be provided to the outside world; they are callable from outside the application.

To start the wizard, we locate the function module that we want to service enable and then select Utilities → More Utilities → Create Web Service → From the Function Module, as shown in Figure 15-2.

Selecting this option starts the Web Service Creation Wizard, shown in Figure 15-3. The wizard provides an overview of the process on the left side of the screen. In the center of the screen, you can see the function module that will be service enabled; this name (Z_EMPL_PRIVATE_ADDRESS_QUERY) will become the default throughout this example, but we will have a chance to change it.

Pressing Continue displays the next screen, shown in Figure 15-4.

First, specify a name for the service definition and a description, then select the endpoint type. The endpoint type defaults to the function module since we started the wizard while viewing a function module. We press Continue to display the screen shown in Figure 15-5.

---

* You can also start service creation from transaction SE80 in the ABAP Development Workbench.

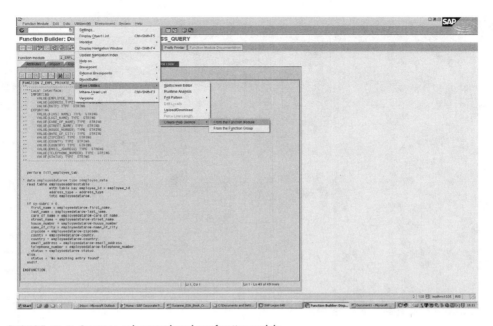

FIGURE 15-2. Creating a web service based on a function module

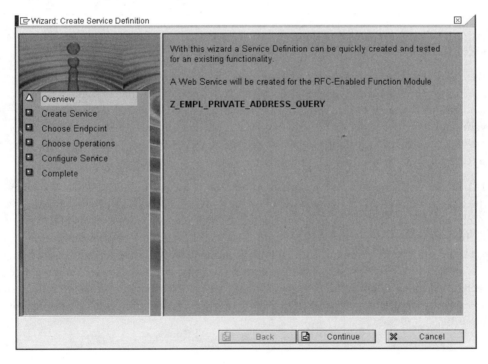

FIGURE 15-3. The Web Service Creation Wizard

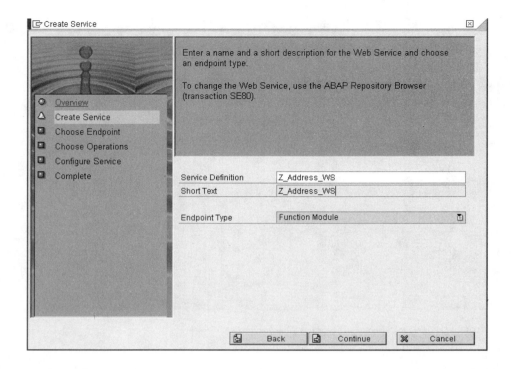

FIGURE 15-4. *Naming the web service*

Here the wizard confirms which endpoint we want to service enable, defaulting to the function module where we started the wizard. The checkbox for the mapping of names (shown in German in Figure 15-5) allows you to map ABAP-style names to a more conventional style by removing the underscores and turning uppercase letters to lowercase. This determines how the names appear in the WSDL file. We press Continue to display the screen shown in Figure 15-6.

This screen configures the web service using profiles. These profiles include details such as the type of authentication the web service will use. We assign a SOAP profile, choosing either secure SOAP or the basic authorization SOAP profile. Secure SOAP offers HTTP authentication using SAP logon tickets and X.509 certificates.* The basic authorization SOAP profile is more common, with HTTP basic authentication (username and password). It is also possible to choose a profile that offers no security, which makes sense for a public web service, for example. You can change these options later, but this pulldown provides an easy way to specify the features desired for your web service while you are running the wizard.

---

* For details, see Gerlinde Zibulski and Peter McNulty's article, "Securely Consume Web Services—With No Coding," *SAP Insider*, Jan-Feb-Mar 2006.

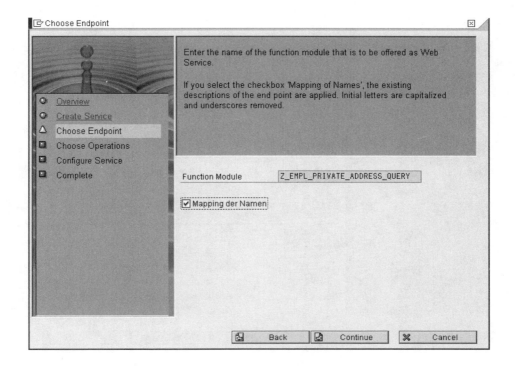

FIGURE 15-5. Choosing an endpoint

Selecting the checkbox releases the web service to the SOAP runtime immediately after completing the wizard. You can also release the service manually using the transaction WSCONFIG. We press Continue to display the final screen in this wizard, as shown in Figure 15-7.

Pressing Complete on this screen creates objects for the interface and web service description, and releases the service to the SOAP runtime.

A Create Object Directory Entry pop up appears where we are prompted to save the service definition objects; if they are local objects, save them in the temporary directory.

We are also prompted with a Customizing Request pop up where you can specify that this service be moved from the test system to the production system, for example. We click OK to continue.

In the Object Navigator, enterprise services are found in a folder under the Function Modules folder. Opening the Enterprise Services folder displays the Service Definitions folder. In this folder, you can see the object we created.

At this point, we can tweak the service definition and interface in a couple of different ways. To start, we select the service definition we created and edit that object, selecting the Interface tab. You can change the names for the fields in the interface, perhaps customizing them for a partner. By default, the interface for the web service includes all the

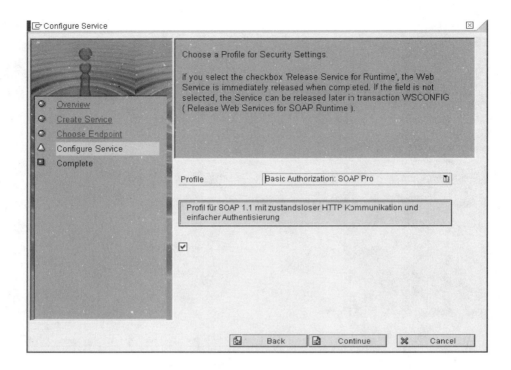

FIGURE 15-6. Choosing a profile

same parameters as the function module on which it is based. But in many cases, this is not optimal. Perhaps the order entry function module has 45 fields, but only 10 of them are relevant for a particular partner. Each field in the interface has an associated Exposed checkbox. Deselecting this checkbox hides a given field. You can also customize the defaults for the fields in the interface. If you were customizing a service for a given partner with whom you do a lot of business, you might streamline the process for them by filling in their name, customer number, and shipping address as defaults.

To test the web service, we move to a transaction called WSADMIN, which displays the Web Service Administration for SOAP Runtime screen, shown in Figure 15-8.

From here we can display the Web Service Homepage, which lists all the available services. We select the service we created and click the Web Service Homepage icon. A Settings for WSDL Generation pop up appears, asking for a WSDL style; we choose Document Style. For ABAP developers, the integration with the ABAP Development Workbench here is a plus; you need not log out of ABAP to take these steps.

The Web Service Homepage appears. We authenticate with username and password, and then the overview page for the web service will appear. From this screen, you can see the URL for the WSDL document, review the features assigned to the web service, and see the service's Universal Description, Discovery, and Integration (UDDI) status. The SAP

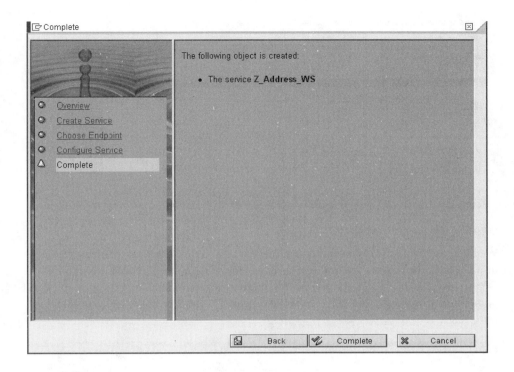

FIGURE 15-7. Completing the web service

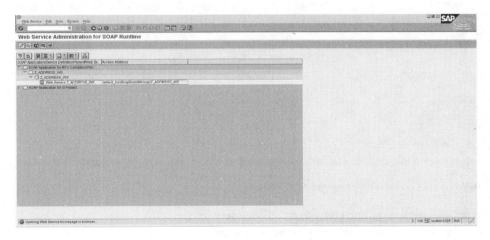

FIGURE 15-8. Web Service Administration (WSADMIN)

NetWeaver Application Server (SAP NetWeaver AS) includes a UDDI server. Currently, it supports UDDI 2.0; UDDI 3.0 support is featured in an upcoming release.

We press the Test button to display the test page, which lists the operations for the web service (in this case, there is one); we select the operation and click Test. The interface appears, as shown in Figure 15-9.

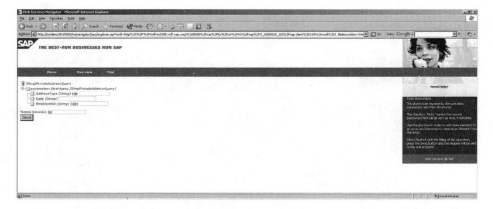

FIGURE 15-9. Testing the web service

We fill in the fields and click Send. The request is sent to the SOAP runtime and the screen displays both the request and the response, as shown in Figure 15-10. This is a test of the web service, not just a test of the function module (which can be done through the development environment). The call goes to SOAP via HTTP and the appropriate response is returned.

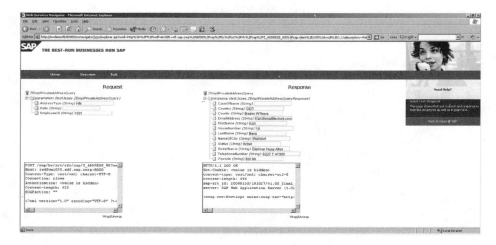

FIGURE 15-10. The results from testing the web service

So far, this section outlined how to create web services using the wizard. Next we will describe how to create services from the outside in.

What does it mean to create services from the outside in?

Outside-in development essentially involves modeling, generating stubs, and providing the implementation for the web service. While development from the inside out starts with existing application functionality, outside-in development starts at a business level, looking at critical business processes and modeling them into services that implement those processes.

While SOA sounds like it is all about services, ESA is, at a higher level, a blueprint for being process oriented rather than service oriented. It asks you to take a step away from the IT landscape and really consider the essential processes that bring you business value. These processes, rather than applications or even services, ultimately form the basis for ESA. From that standpoint, outside-in development is not dependent on any existing applications, not even SAP applications.

How do you create a service from the outside in using ABAP?

Before we dive into the steps for creating a service from the outside in, let's be clear about who is doing the creating. In this chapter, we discuss creating services from the outside in from a developer's perspective. To create a service from the outside in, you start in the SAP NetWeaver XI Integration Repository. As we start developing services from the outside in, we use more of the principles of ESA, such as abstraction from programming languages, hiding the implementation details, and reusing data types where possible.

Figure 15-11 shows the XI Integration Repository and its relationship to the XI Integration Builder.

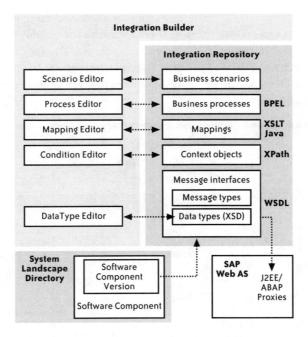

FIGURE 15-11. SAP NetWeaver XI Integration Repository and Integration Builder

The three major steps in this process are modeling the message interface in the SAP NetWeaver XI Integration Repository, generating a proxy from that model, and finally providing the implementation.

In the XI Integration Builder, software component versions are listed down the left side of the screen as a means of structuring the content. You can browse the repository to find out what interfaces exist. If two interfaces have the same name, the system can use the associated namespace to resolve any conflicts, definitively determining which one is intended. Typically, when you are developing, you will create a new namespace to separate your services from others that might have the same name.

Modeling a message interface in the repository requires three smaller steps:

1. Create the data type, using XML schema.

2. Create the message type, an XML entity that describes the message that will be sent over the wire.

3. Create the interface that uses the message type to describe the request and the response.

Although each step involves XML, you don't have to write the XML. Instead, the XML entities are automatically generated for you based on your work in the XI Integration Builder.

In the hierarchy for the namespace you create, you'll see Interface Objects, which include all the elements needed to define a service from the outside in. We start by creating a new data type. In our example, we'll create data types for a Get Address application. First, we create the input data type, which includes three elements: the employee ID, date, and address type, as shown in Figure 15-12. As you can see, you also specify the type. In this case, all three elements are defined as XML Schema Definition (XSD) strings. Also note on this screen that the elements can be defined in mixed case rather than uppercase, as is the convention with ABAP.

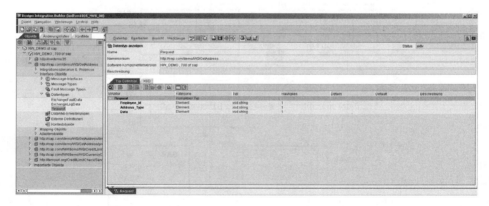

FIGURE 15-12. Creating the input data type

Next, we create an output data type that has several elements, including first name, last name, street name, and zip code; they are also of XML type string, as shown in Figure 15-13.

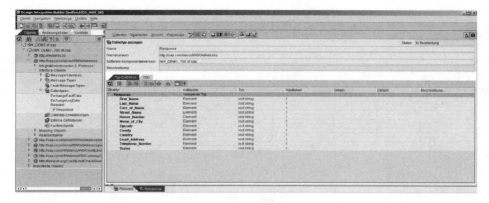

FIGURE 15-13. Creating the output data type

Creating the message type is the next step. The message type defines the request and response messages that will be sent over the wire. We create the input message type, as shown in Figure 15-14. To specify the data type, we drag-and-drop the input data type from the lefthand panel to the field. Similarly, we drag-and-drop the namespace to fill in that field. Creating the output message follows the same process.

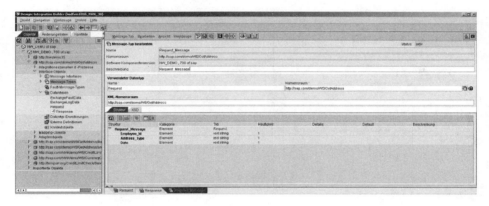

FIGURE 15-14. Creating the input message type

The final step is to create the message interface. Creating a new message interface displays a screen similar to Figure 15-15.

This service is synchronous, so both input and output message types must be specified.

At this point, we are finished modeling the interface. Now we use the transaction SPROXY to generate the proxy.*

---

* Note that in order for this integration to occur, the system has to be preconfigured accordingly on the SAP NetWeaver XI side (in the system landscape directory) and in the ABAP backend (using transaction SM59, RFC Destinations).

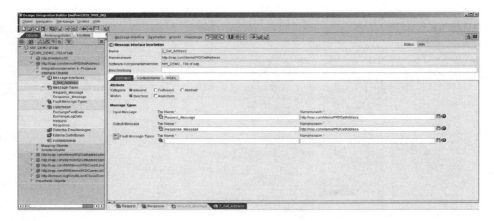

FIGURE 15-15. *Creating the message interface*

SPROXY displays a view of the Integration Repository that we just used for modeling the message interface. Double-clicking on the message interface we created, Z_Get_Address, brings up a pop-up box where we specify that we want to generate a proxy for this service, which displays the screen shown in Figure 15-16.

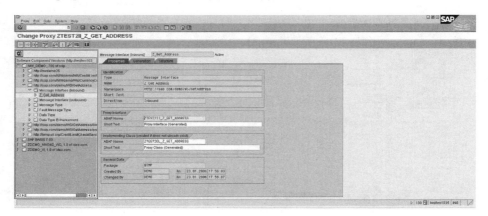

FIGURE 15-16. *Generating the proxies*

Generating a proxy creates all the entities you need. Save the proxy, and then activate it. The next step is to create the implementation in the backend system using the ABAP Development Workbench. The class and proxy have already been given ABAP names; all that remains is to implement the class itself in the ABAP system. Double-clicking the class name displays the method of the class in the Class Builder. Double-clicking the method allows you to insert the implementation coding, as shown in Figure 15-17. The developer must write the implementation for the class and insert it here. (In this case, we had the implementation ready in advance and just pasted it in.)

Having created this functionality—from the outside in—the next step is to enable it as a web service using the Web Service Creation Wizard. This is essentially the same process

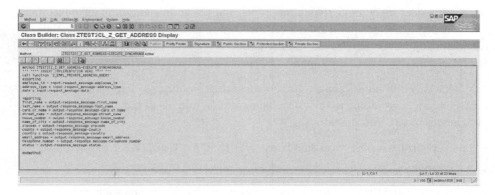

FIGURE 15-17. Inserting the implementation

described earlier, with one difference: in this case, you choose ESIRepository Service Interface as the endpoint instead of Function Module. Since running the wizard is essentially the same procedure described earlier, we'll spare you the details, but you can see the process of outside-in development at work: first you model the interface in the Integration Repository, generate a proxy from that, insert the implementation for the class, and finally service enable the newly created XI endpoint using the Web Service Creation Wizard. In an upcoming release of SAP NetWeaver, this final step will no longer be necessary.

What is SAP NetWeaver's role in creating enterprise services?

SAP NetWeaver provides the technological foundation for creating enterprise services. Earlier in this chapter, when describing development from the inside out and the outside in, we highlighted some of the features of SAP NetWeaver. This section explores some of the additional capabilities of SAP NetWeaver with respect to enterprise services.

Enterprise services are often created to work with business partners. A large part of this effort entails implementing industry-specific XML vocabularies. In addition to supporting open standards for web services, as described in Chapter 20, SAP NetWeaver provides comprehensive support for implementing partner interfaces using specialized vocabularies. NetWeaver is composed of many modules that perform different functions, but most web services support is offered in the Web Service Infrastructure of SAP NetWeaver AS and the process integration functionality of SAP NetWeaver XI.

What is the role of the SAP NetWeaver Application Server?

SAP NetWeaver AS is foundational to all of the rest of SAP's applications. SAP NetWeaver Portal is Java code that runs on top of SAP NetWeaver AS. Even the mySAP Business Suite, which is written in ABAP, runs on SAP NetWeaver AS.

Although it does much more than a traditional app server, in addition to all of its other functionality, SAP NetWeaver AS is a certified Java 2 Enterprise Edition (J2EE) 1.3-compliant app server that provides all the standard app server features, including load balancing, security, and database support via Open SQL.

SAP NetWeaver AS allows companies to extend their solutions by exposing and integrating web services according to their development skills and needs independent of the technical environment. This includes:

- Full support for web services standards (WSDL, SOAP, UDDI, WS-I, and so on)
- An efficient development, testing, and error correction cycle
- A consistent architecture and identical feature sets for the two development environments used in SAP NetWeaver (ABAP and Java)
- Support of web services development for creating new applications and for service enabling existing applications and standard SAP interfaces

SAP NetWeaver AS offers developers comprehensive support on the client side, from client proxy generation to integration with dynamic and comprehensive UIs created with Web Dynpro. The Web Service Framework supports both ABAP and Java and offers all the tools needed to enable standard interfaces (BAPIs, RFCs, Enterprise JavaBEans [EJBs], and Java classes) as web services, as described in this chapter and in Chapter 16.

What is SAP NetWeaver XI's role as an integration broker?

While web services can interact directly with SAP NetWeaver AS, in many cases, it is preferable to use a service intermediate called an *integration broker*. The integration broker can, for instance, handle transformations and therefore map from one service format to another. The integration broker also allows for routing of messages to different or multiple systems based on simple or complex criteria. Figure 15-18 illustrates the role of SAP NetWeaver XI as an integration broker.

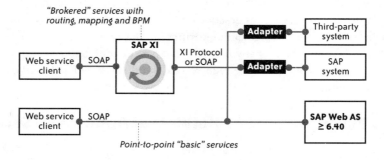

FIGURE 15-18. *SAP NetWeaver XI as an integration broker*

SAP NetWeaver XI allows for the creation of value-added web services that decouple the service layer from the application. It includes a shared repository of integration knowledge that provides transparency to an organization's integration environment. It supplies monitoring and alerting capabilities and provides mapping and routing tools. For connections to applications that are not web services enabled, SAP NetWeaver XI has an extensive library of application and technical adapters based on J2EE Connector Architecture (JCA).

SAP NetWeaver XI has a built-in business process engine that allows for the orchestration of multiple services into complex, stateful interaction patterns. Business processes are modeled using the Business Process Execution Language (BPEL).

SAP NetWeaver XI includes business packages for implementing industry standards for intercompany business processes. For instance, the SAP Business Package for RosettaNet includes the XML structures used by the standard, the business processes that implement the structures, called Partner Interface Processes, or PIPs, of that standard, the mappings to convert the RosettaNet structures to the corresponding IDOC structures in the mySAP ERP system, the adapter for sending and receiving messages in the RosettaNet Implementation Framework, or RNet protocol, and adapter templates to simplify RosettaNet implementation.

What steps are involved with web services brokering using SAP NetWeaver XI?

Because of the services offered by the SAP NetWeaver XI runtime, client applications can accept inputs in whatever format partners can provide, and they can enable easy and flexible integration with business partners. When a message is received at the SAP NetWeaver XI server, the message header is examined, and all valid configurations for that message are executed.

The main steps in this process are logical routing, mapping, and technical routing, as shown in Figure 15-19.

In logical routing, SAP NetWeaver XI determines the business system and interface that are to receive the message, examining all possible valid receiver messages and interfaces. Messages may be split into multiple messages and routed to multiple receivers. Receiver determination and interface determination may be done separately.

As a simple example, perhaps a partner sends a purchase order in an arbitrary format. In logical routing, SAP NetWeaver XI might determine that the recipient of the message should be our production R/3 system and that the purchase order should be processed by an ORDERS05 IDOC.

In the mapping step, SAP NetWeaver XI determines the target message format or formats and executes the appropriate transformation logic to create a message in the appropriate format or formats for the receiver. For example, we use SAP NetWeaver XI to transform the arbitrary PO format of the sender to the IDOC structure. The mapping is designed in advance using one of several mapping design technologies and is executed at runtime.

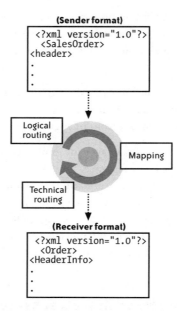

(Sender format)

```
<?xml version="1.0"?>
  <SalesOrder>
<header>
      .
      .
      .
```

Logical routing

Mapping

Technical routing

(Receiver format)

```
<?xml version="1.0"?>
  <Order>
<HeaderInfo>
      .
      .
      .
```

FIGURE 15-19. *Web services brokering with SAP NetWeaver XI*

In the technical routing step, we determine how to physically pass the message to the receiver, including the appropriate technical sending channel and any security and encryption desired. For example, using an IDOC, we would specify TRFC as the transmission protocol and the specific RFC destination that should be used. Essentially, this service enables the IDOC interface without having to do any coding in R/3.

How can services be adapted to reflect changing customer needs?

Consider a bank that offers credit check services to small and large customers. The small customers, such as a travel agency, require only simple credit checks for their customers, similar to checking the credit limit on a credit card for a family wanting to book a vacation. Larger customers have more complex credit checking needs, for lending for construction projects, for example. For this purpose, the bank has a mainframe risk management system.

A simple web service using SAP NetWeaver AS can handle the smaller customer's needs. For the larger customers, a brokered web service run through SAP NetWeaver XI can map the capabilities of the mainframe-based system to a web service. Figure 15-20 shows this architecture.

As time goes on, the travel agency begins offering tours and as a result, it sometimes requires a more complex credit check. By routing the requests through SAP NetWeaver XI, the bank can offer this service to its customer with simple reconfiguration of SAP NetWeaver XI, as follows:

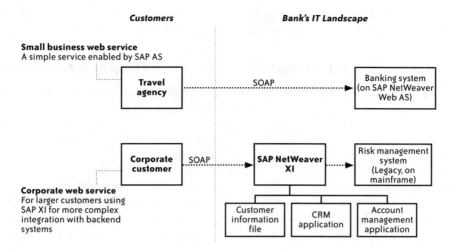

FIGURE 15-20. Separate processes for different customers

- The travel agency must be configured as a message sender or receiver in the SAP NetWeaver XI Integration Directory.

- Web services requests from the travel agency must be routed to the correct receiver system and interface based on the content of the message.

- The channel for exchanging the messages must be configured—in this case, SOAP-based messages.

- XML messages received from the travel agency must map the sender to the receiver interface.

The reconfigured system is shown in Figure 15-21.

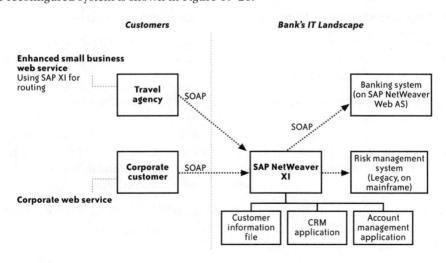

FIGURE 15-21. Changing the business process

For more details about this example, see "Flexible Adaptation of Business Processes" by Martin Huvar and Sven Leukert, *SAP Insider*, Oct-Nov-Dec 2004.

What does the future hold for creating enterprise services?

Web services, although simple and standardized, are not by themselves enough for building a robust, reliable SOA that meets enterprise-level needs. The problem is exacerbated by the fact that the staff who administer enterprise applications and the developers maintaining the corporate web site and creating web services are typically in two different groups.

What is needed is a cohesive blueprint for an SOA that provides integration with enterprise applications and is adaptable to constantly changing market conditions. To be service oriented really means to be process oriented. That's what ESA is all about. It's an architectural blueprint for an SOA that is fully standards based and provides business value, with services modeled from key business processes.

This section briefly explores the future of creating enterprise services. We'll start by digging into the conceptual details of SAP's architectural vision for ESA, concepts that are foundational to creating your own ESA adoption roadmap.

What are business objects?

ESA is built on business objects, described in Chapter 5. Business objects are unique, identifiable business entities. Examples of business objects include a sales order, a purchase order, and a business partner. A business object is a logical building block, composed of numerous data elements, some of which are, in turn, based on the UN/CEFACT standard for global data types, ensuring wide interoperability with customers and partners.

What are the steps one takes to develop enterprise services?

Development of enterprise services can be broken down into two categories: modeling and implementation, as shown in Figure 15-22. The first part, modeling, is completely platform and language independent.

Modeling starts with a business process. During process modeling, in which you use a high-level tool based on ARIS, you identify the business objects and services you will use. You then go to the Enterprise Services Repository where you model the business objects and the services. Once modeling is complete, you create the UI. If the UI does not behave as desired, you can go back to the Enterprise Services Repository and make some changes. The next step is to create the implementation on the backend system.

How will the process change from what we have today? For one thing, modeling becomes a more visual task. Today modeling relates primarily to data types; in the near future, visual modeling tools will be integrated into SAP NetWeaver.

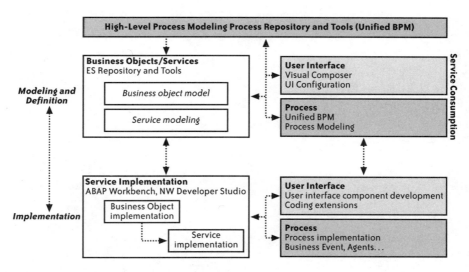

FIGURE 15-22. Typical enterprise services development steps

Modeling occurs in the Enterprise Services Repository, using the Enterprise Services Builder, which is an enhancement of SAP NetWeaver XI's Integration Builder that is slated for an upcoming release. All business objects must be modeled in the Enterprise Services Repository. The data types, data structures, and interfaces described in the Enterprise Services Repository are based on XML standards, including XSD and XML namespaces. (In fact, this adherence to XML standards is evident in the outside-in approach to development available today and described earlier in this chapter.)

The process of creating enterprise services continues to evolve with SAP making the development process both simpler and more robust, providing the infrastructure needed for a scalable implementation of ESA.

In this chapter, we examined how to create services today using SAP NetWeaver, both from the inside out and from the outside in. At various points in this process, you can glimpse the principles of ESA at work: we've seen abstraction that hides the arcane details of XML from the developer, reuse of data types, and modeling as a development methodology. These tools and technologies help us to make ESA a reality, starting today. Nothing that you do today working toward ESA will be wasted effort. However, the next generation of tools will bring ESA even more into focus, helping you to create a full-blown ESA that enhances the agility of your business.

CHAPTER SIXTEEN

Creating and Consuming Services in Java

SAP NetWeaver provides extensive support for Java developers. In this chapter, we'll look at creating services in Java and at using Web Dynpro to create a service consumer for the ABAP web service we developed in Chapter 15. But before examining these tasks and the Java development environment, let's look at a larger question: how SAP supports Java itself.

Today, SAP NetWeaver includes a Sun-certified Java 2 Enterprise Edition (J2EE) 1.3-compliant application server. The next release will conform with J2EE 1.4. SAP NetWeaver supports all major Java standards, including Enterprise JavaBeans (EJBs), the J2EE Connector Architecture (JCA), JNDI, and JDBC. Furthermore, since 2001, SAP has been an active participant in the Java Community Process. SAP NetWeaver uses a model-driven approach to development that makes heavy use of application metadata to simplify and expedite the development process. This declarative, model-driven environment significantly reduces development efforts and makes it easier for business analysts to create business solutions using a code-free environment such as SAP NetWeaver Visual Composer.

What development tools are available for Java developers?

SAP NetWeaver Developer Studio provides Java developers a standards-based and fully featured development environment. It is based on Eclipse, a popular open source development environment, and it provides support for the full range of J2EE development tasks. Since SAP NetWeaver Developer Studio is based on Eclipse, developers can enhance it using custom plug-ins, which are available from many Independent Software Vendors (ISVs). Like Eclipse itself, SAP NetWeaver Developer Studio helps organize development by offering various perspectives, including the following:

- The J2EE perspective supports the development of entities defined by this standard, such as EJBs, JavaServer pages (JSPs), servlets, and so on.

- The Web Services perspective combines tools to define, discover, and test web services.

- The Web Dynpro perspective provides a comprehensive environment for the model-driven design of user interfaces (UIs).

- The Java Dictionary perspective supports developers in defining data types and data structures as well as in creating and maintaining tables in the database.

- The Debugging perspective helps developers control debugging processes and thus analyze bugs in running applications.

With SAP NetWeaver Developer Studio, developers can immediately tap into the software life cycle management features of the SAP NetWeaver Development Infrastructure (NWDI), as shown in Figure 16-1. With a comprehensive offering in source code management, build automation, and software distribution, SAP's NWDI is designed for organizing the work of large teams of Java developers.

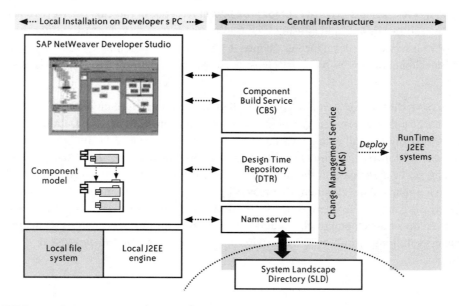

FIGURE 16-1. SAP NetWeaver Development Infrastructure

How do you create a service provider in Java?

In Chapter 15, we described how to service enable a Remote Function Call (RFC), creating a service from the inside out using ABAP. The process for service enabling a method in a Java class or EJB is quite similar, but it is worth taking a detailed look from the Java side. Similar to the example in Chapter 15, we will be providing employee address data through the web service we create in this section.

Since we are enabling existing functionality, we will assume that the EJB to be exposed already exists and that it has been imported into SAP NetWeaver Developer Studio or created in that development environment. We will also assume that an existing Enterprise Archive (EAR) project is associated with this EJB. In this example, we will work with a stateful session bean.

We start the Web Service Creation Wizard by right-clicking on the bean we want to service enable and selecting New → Web Service, as shown in Figure 16-2.

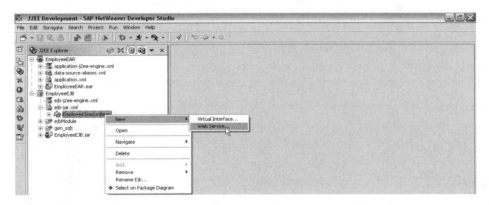

FIGURE 16-2. Service enabling an EJB

The Web Service Creation Wizard starts, as shown in Figure 16-3.

If you read Chapter 15, you may notice that the Java version of this wizard looks a bit different from the ABAP version. The Source Folder and Endpoint fields default to values appropriate for this service. We supply a Web Service Name—in this case, EmployeeHomeAddressWS. This is where we configure the web service as well.

Web services configuration allows you to define (through a pull-down menu) the technical characteristics of this service very easily. For example, you can specify whether it is stateful or stateless and what type of transport it uses (on this screen, SOAP over HTTP; another option would be SOAP over HTTPS to provide transport-level encryption). It also defines what authentication measures will be used for the service; choices include none, username and password (referred to as basic authentication), and authentication using digital certificates. You can change all of these settings later if desired, but this pull-down menu provides you with an easy way to configure many technical details right in the wizard.

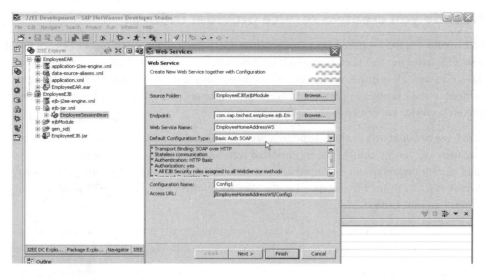

FIGURE 16-3. The Web Service Creation Wizard

We click Next to display the screen shown in Figure 16-4. On this screen, we select the methods we want to service enable. You could choose multiple methods or all of them. In this case, we selected one method that takes two strings and a java.util.date as input.

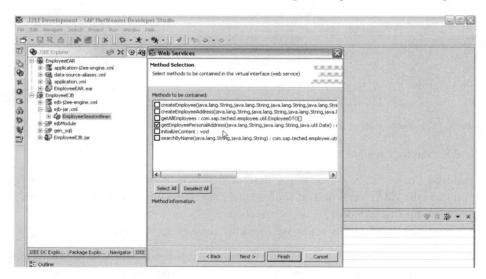

FIGURE 16-4. Selecting the method or methods to service enable

We click Next to display the screen shown in Figure 16-5. On this screen, Endpoint defaults to the session bean we pointed at when we started the wizard. The virtual interface defaults to the same name as the web service, with VI appended; similarly, the Web Service Definition has the same name with Wsd appended. The EAR project defaults to the EAR project associated with this EJB.

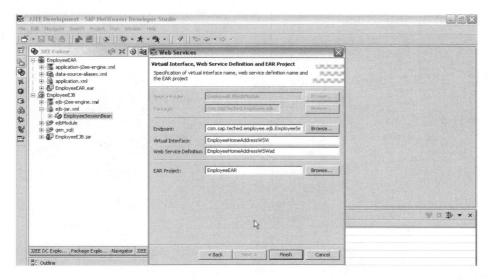

FIGURE 16-5. Specifying the virtual interface, web services definition, and EAR project

The virtual interface allows you to hide or rename parameters, simplifying or customizing an interface. (We will demonstrate this later in this example.)

All changes that we make will be propagated to the EAR project specified here.

We click Finish to display the screen shown in Figure 16-6. This screen summarizes the characteristics of the web service we created, including its configuration details (session handling, authentication level, authorization, and transport guarantee).

At this point, we tweak the virtual interface a bit. This is an optional step; it allows you to hide or rename parameters. In the J2EE Explorer (shown in Figure 16-7 in the left pane), we select the virtual interface for this web service.

In Figure 16-7, you can see that we changed the method name from getEmployeePersonalAddress to getEmployeeHomeAddress. We also assigned addressType a fixed value (HM for home), so this will not appear as an input in the web service.

The next step is to deploy the EAR file. We then click on the Web Services perspective to display the Web Services Navigator, shown in Figure 16-8.

The SAP Web Service Homepage is displayed in the upper-right pane. We click Test to display the screen shown in Figure 16-9.

This screen shows the operations for the web service; in this example, there is only one operation, and it is based on the method we selected. You can see that the method name change we made in the virtual interface (getEmployeePersonalAddress to getEmployeeHomeAddress) is reflected on this screen.

We click Test again to display the screen shown in Figure 16-10.

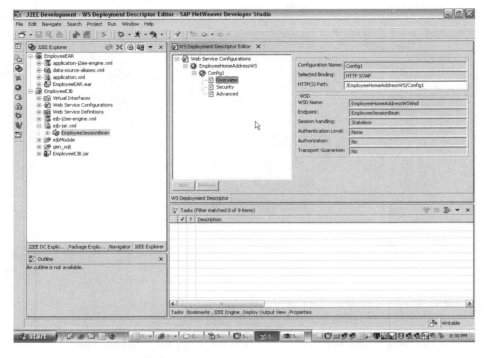

FIGURE 16-6. The newly created web service

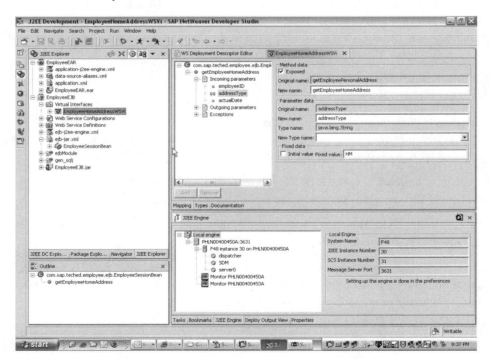

FIGURE 16-7. Modifying the virtual interface

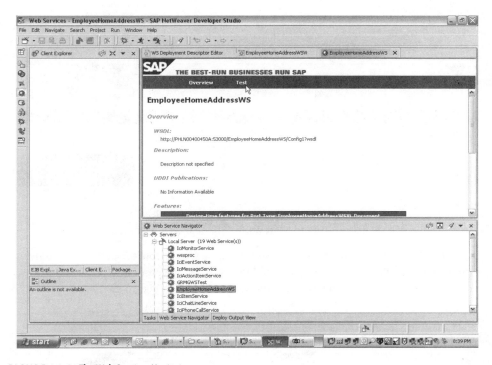

FIGURE 16-8. The Web Services Navigator

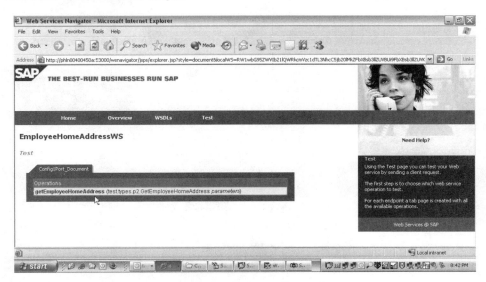

FIGURE 16-9. The SAP Web Service Homepage, which lists operations for the web service

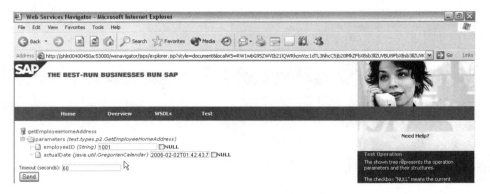

FIGURE 16-10. Testing the web service

Note that since we set addressType to HM, it doesn't appear as a parameter.

Note also that no Java coding was required to web service enable this EJB; everything, including the descriptor files, was generated for us. Now, we enter an employeeID (in this example, **1001**) and click Send to display the screen shown in Figure 16-11.

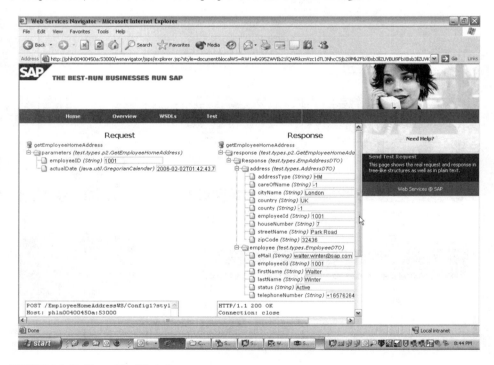

FIGURE 16-11. The results of the test

On this screen, you can see the request and the response for the web service. Near the bottom of the screen, you can see the very top of the SOAP request and response messages. You can wrap and unwrap the SOAP message to view the details of what is sent over the wire. Looking at these details can be helpful when troubleshooting a web service, especially for SOAP fault messages.

Figure 16-12 shows the beginning of a list of the Web Services Description Language (WSDL) files available for this service.

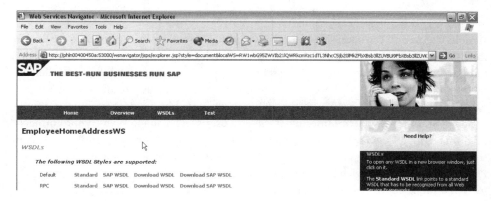

FIGURE 16-12. The styles of WSDL files from which to choose

Document style is typically the best choice, but a variety of WSDL styles are available.

You can see that it is easy to turn Java functionality into a web service. You don't have to write more Java and you don't even have to write any XML. While you can tweak everything by hand or through the SAP NetWeaver Developer Studio, the wizard gives you the power to create a web service, hide and rename parameters and methods, and configure the service quite easily.

How do you create a service consumer using Web Dynpro for Java?

Many enterprise services, including those provided by SAP in the Enterprise Services Inventory described in Chapter 8, will be implemented in ABAP. Since web services—and therefore enterprise services—are loosely coupled, the consumer of the service can be written in ABAP or Java. This section explores using Java to consume the ABAP web service created in Chapter 15.

Service consumers can be created in a variety of ways and visualized using Web Dynpro, JSPs, or ASPs, for example. In this section, we'll create a UI using Web Dynpro for Java. As mentioned earlier, Web Dynpro for Java is integrated into SAP NetWeaver Developer Studio as an Eclipse perspective.

Web Dynpro for Java uses the model-view-controller (MVC) paradigm, which clearly separates business logic and presentation logic. Its capabilities far exceed what we can discuss in this brief section; we will use many defaults in our example, and we will not show every screen in this process for the sake of brevity. Nonetheless, this example gives a basic feel for creating a service consumer in Web Dynpro.

To set the stage for this example, we open the SAP NetWeaver Developer Studio, choose the Web Dynpro perspective, and start a new Development Component Project (by choosing File → New → Development Component Project). In the Development Component Project, expand the Web Dynpro node for this new project in the Web Dynpro Explorer, right-click on Application, select Create → New, and fill in the fields required by the wizard.

Double-clicking on the component we created brings up a diagram view where we can see the MVC framework visually. This diagram view divides the screen in thirds, with a portion for the model at the bottom of the screen, a view (at the top), and the controller (in the middle). The model is where the business logic will reside; as a result, no default model is placed on the screen. The controller interacts with the model, reading and writing data, and the view determines what the end user sees. A single Web Dynpro project might have many models. A single model might have many controllers, and a single controller might have many views (for example, for different versions of an application for PDAs, cell phones, and web browsers). In our simple example, we will have a single model, a single controller, and a single view.

Creating the new Web Dynpro application generated a controller and a view, but now we need to import a model instead of creating one. To do so, we right-click in the model portion near the bottom of the screen and select Create Model. A dialog appears that asks us to specify the type of model. Although Web Dynpro is an SAP application development tool, you can use it to develop many types of client applications. SAP-related choices include adaptive RFC models and enterprise services models. Note that there are also options for non–SAP specific models such as web services models (which we will use here) and JavaBean models. For this example, we choose Import Web Service Model and click Next to display the screen shown (filled in) in Figure 16-13.

On this screen, we specify a model name and a package and select a WSDL source to answer the question every web services consumer must answer: where we will get the WSDL file? The WSDL might be located on the local server or on the local filesystem, or discovered using a Universal Description, Discovery, and Integration (UDDI) server (a UDDI server is included with SAP NetWeaver).

In this case, we select Local File System or URL and click Next to display the screen shown in Figure 16-14.

On the screen shown in Figure 16-14, we entered the URL for the WSDL file, cutting and pasting it from the tools in the ABAP environment. We can examine the WSDL file to review what inputs and outputs this service expects and what security options have been selected.

We click Next and then Finish. An informational message appears about reloading the project so that the changes we've made will be incorporated. We click OK. The newly created EmpAddrModel appears, as shown in Figure 16-15.

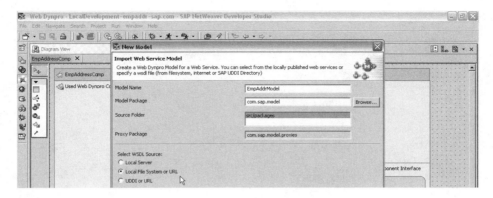

FIGURE 16-13. Importing a web services model in Web Dynpro for Java

FIGURE 16-14. Entering the URL for the WSDL file

At this point, we rebuild the project so that the changes are incorporated. To do so, we right-click on the development component project in the Web Dynpro Explorer, then choose Development Component → Build. After the project is rebuilt, we click OK.

The next step is to set up the controller to interact with the model. The controller will read and write data to the model.

We apply a template by right-clicking on the controller. We choose Service Controller and click Next to display the screen shown in Figure 16-16. It lists the models for this project (in this case, a single model).

We select the model and click Next to display the screen shown in Figure 16-17. This screen shows all the data supplied by the model; in this case, we chose to use everything, but we could filter what data we want to read and write.

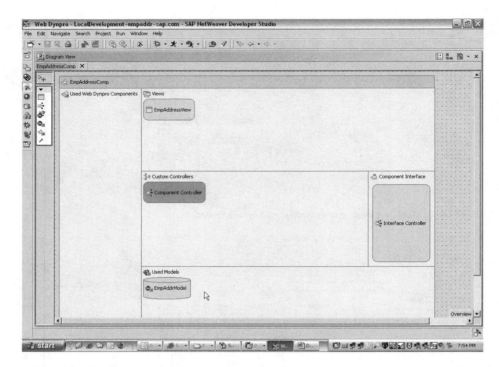

FIGURE 16-15. The newly created model

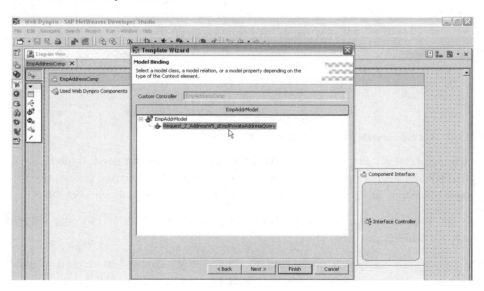

FIGURE 16-16. Binding the controller to the model

We click Next to display the screen shown in Figure 16-18. On the last screen, we selected the data we want to use; on this screen, we will generate the method call for the controller to invoke the web service.

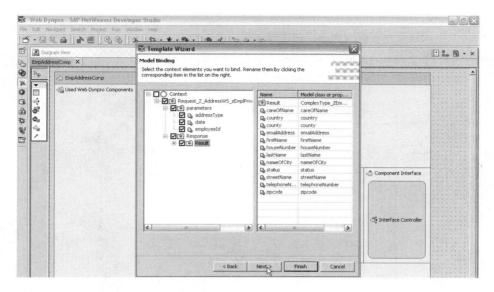

FIGURE 16-17. Choosing the data elements for the controller

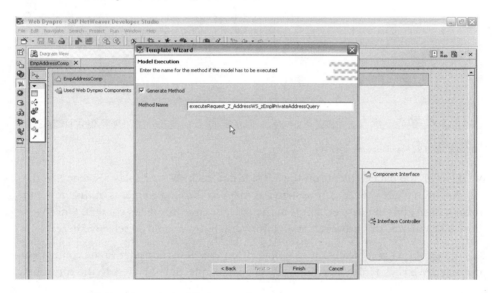

FIGURE 16-18. Generating the method call for the controller

We click Finish to generate the method. A line now appears, binding the controller to the model.

The next step is to make an association between the view and the controller. To do so, we use a line tool to draw a line from the view to the controller. Completing this line causes the Edit Context Mapping screen to appear. The data on the righthand side of this screen is the component controller; the data on the left side is the view controller. Initially, the left side is blank, and the right side shows the data that was made available through the connection between the model and the controller.

We select the data on the right and drag it to the left side to populate the view. After doing so, the screen should look like Figure 16-19.

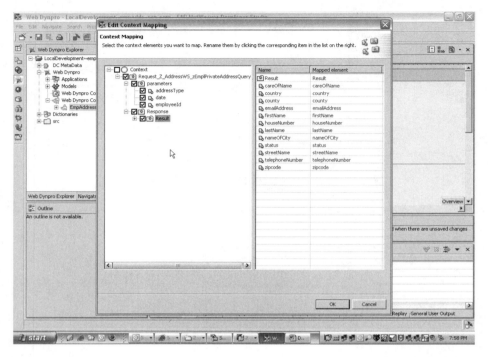

FIGURE 16-19. *Populating the view*

We select all the data elements on the left side and click OK to display a screen like the one shown in Figure 16-20. The system has mapped the data elements in the view controller's context to the data elements in the component controller's context. Since we chose all elements, this process is straightforward, but we could be selective here.

This screen shows graphically the mappings from the view controller to the component controller. We click Finish and a line will appear, connecting the view to the controller.

You could go to the view designer to create the interface; it offers the ability to create a complex GUI simply by dragging and dropping UI elements. To simplify the example, we simply right-click on the view and choose Apply Template. Since the web service requires input, we create a form by selecting Form and clicking Next. The Form View appears, as in Figure 16-21, where you can select elements. For this example, we select them all.

The elements appear in alphabetical order. You can rearrange them by selecting an option and using the up and down arrows on the right to move them up or down through the list. For example, it makes sense to move the input elements to the top of the list and to

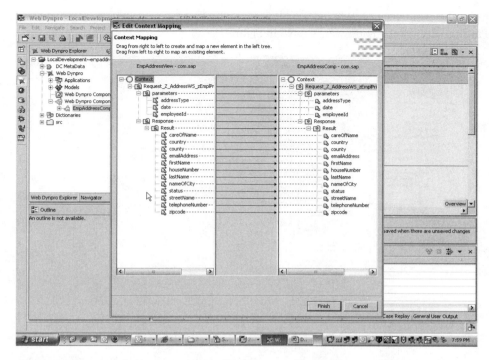

FIGURE 16-20. Mapping data between view controller and component controller

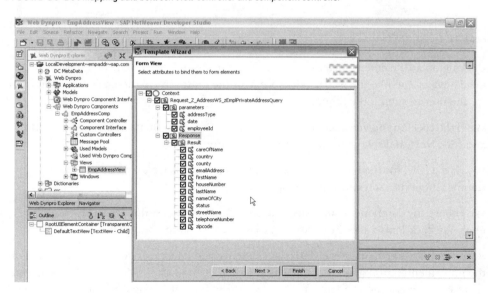

FIGURE 16-21. Selecting elements for the form

move the elements into the expected order for addresses. After they are arranged, we click Finish to display the Form view shown in Figure 16-22.

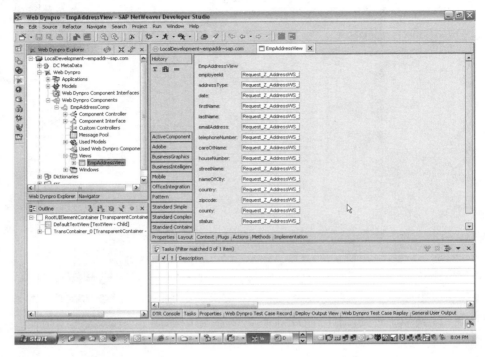

FIGURE 16-22. The Form view

Clicking on a UI element such as an input field lists its properties and values. Now you need a way to invoke the web service. It makes the most sense to add a command button for the user to submit the request.

We right-click on the view again and select Apply Template, then choose Action Button and click Next to display the screen shown in Figure 16-23.

We type a label for the button (in this case, Search) and click Next to display the Event Handler Properties screen shown in Figure 16-24.

We choose the component controller and specify a method (in this case, there is only one). We click Finish and the button appears. We rebuild the project.

At this point, you could rearrange the UI elements, add images, or do some Java coding on the implementation if desired; the IDE is based on Eclipse, as mentioned earlier. You can write your own action elements. In this case, no additional coding is needed; we simply deploy the project. We choose the application under Application in the Web Dynpro Explorer, right-click on it, and select "Deploy New Archive and Run."

The task view at the bottom of the screen shows messages about the progress of the deployment. After the deployment is complete, the client application displays in a browser

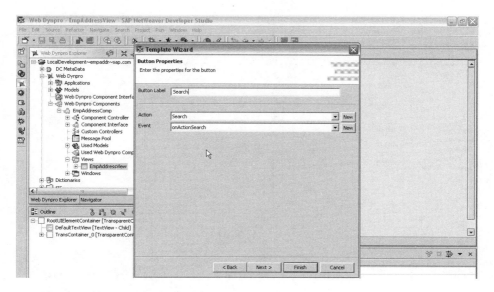

FIGURE 16-23. Adding a button to the form

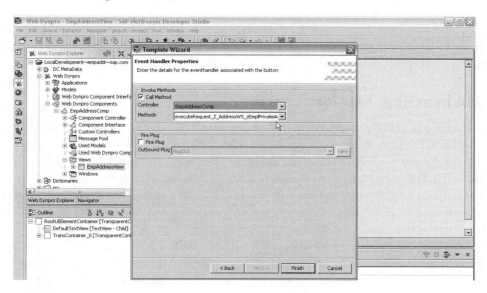

FIGURE 16-24. Specifying an event handler

window. The inputs are the first three fields; Figure 16-25 shows this form after pressing Search to retrieve the results of the query.

In this chapter, we examined how to create and consume services in Java using SAP NetWeaver Developer Studio and its many development facilities both for UI development and for coding projects. At various points in this process, you can glimpse the principles of ESA at work: we've seen abstraction that hides the complexity of XML from the developer, reuse of data types, and modeling as a development methodology. In presenting

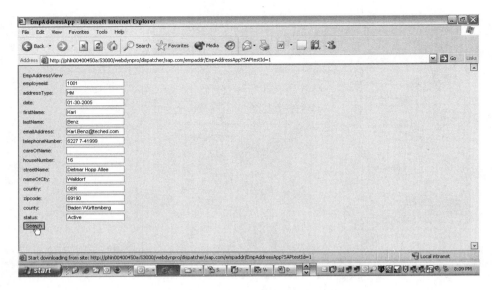

FIGURE 16-25. The Web Dynpro client application for consuming the ABAP web service

these examples, we have not even scratched the surface of the capabilities these tools offer Java developers. We refer you to the SAP Developer Network (SDN; *http://sdn.sap.com*) for documentation, articles, webinars, and courses as well as the opportunity to join a virtual community of Java developers using SAP tools and technologies.

ESA in action: Arcelor

One company actively using Java in its ESA implementation is Arcelor, and specifically its subsidiary, Profilarbed. Arcelor is one of the world's leading manufacturers of steel products for the automotive, construction, household appliance, and packaging industries. Formed in February 2002 by the merger of three steelmaking companies, Aceralia, Arbed, and Usinor, today Arcelor has annual revenues of 30 billion euros, with 95,000 employees in more than 60 countries producing 47 million tons of steel each year. Profilarbed is a subsidiary within Arcelor's portfolio of companies focused on the manufacture of steel sections and sheet piles for the construction industry. Profilarbed's IT department has created its own roadmap for the adoption of ESA with the goal being the rapid deployment of new services and composite applications in the pursuit of more flexible and efficient operations.

Profilarbed built its current IT landscape using SAP R/3 as the Enterprise Resources Planning (ERP) foundation, and it chose SAP NetWeaver as the platform for creating and recombining services. Profilarbed has already realized 20 years' worth of cost and efficiency advantages from its SAP applications and sees ESA as the gradual, natural extension of its investment. The company has already begun identifying and building the necessary services for the composite applications it envisions building in the next few years. The short-term goal is to abstract and write services in ABAP, call them using RFCs, and combine them into composite applications using Java. Additional services will be acquired from SAP. From this central pool of shared enterprise services overseen by IT, business analysts working in various departments will be given the provenance to compose applications as needed in order to streamline and consolidate existing systems and lower total cost of ownership (TCO).

For now, Profilarbed manually codes these composites in Java, which runs on SAP NetWeaver Application Server (SAP NetWeaver AS). Arcelor is waiting for next-generation modeling tools like the SAP Composite Application Framework (SAP CAF) to appear in SAP NetWeaver, which it expects will generate composite applications more easily and rapidly than its current hand-coded efforts. In the meantime, Profilarbed has begun grappling with the challenge of retraining its IT staff and prospective business analysts to think of applications as modular, object-oriented collections of services, which was one reason why Profilarbed chose Java as its development language. Not coincidentally, the company expects to reduce the time spent retraining staff further down the adoption path.

One of Profilarbed's first enterprise-services-based projects was the creation of a B2B purchase order entry application connecting several of its largest clients' systems to Profilarbed's own SAP R/3. Figure 16-26 shows Profilarbed's B2B project.

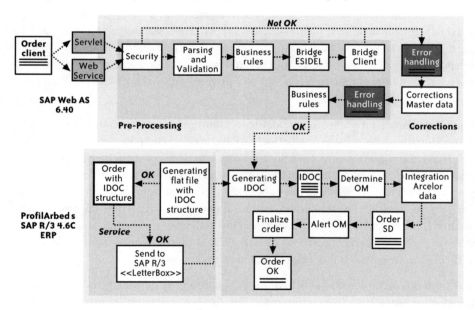

FIGURE 16-26. Profilarbed's B2B project

The order arrives via an XML message containing data written in ESIDEL, the European Steel Industry Data Exchange Language created by Eurofer, the European Confederation of Iron and Steel Industries. A procession of services orchestrated on SAP NetWeaver AS, validates, maps, and transforms the XML message into an IDOC used by SAP R/3. For

Master Data Management (MDM) purposes, a second IDOC is created to reconcile the order with Profilarbed's central system before the order is finally placed.

The five services orchestrating preprocessing in Figure 16-26 are examples of the services Profilarbed is already building and of which it intends to build many more.

ESA in action: TRW

Another example of a company using Java in its ESA implementation is TRW Automotive. TRW ranks among the world's leading automotive suppliers.

As a $12-billion-a-year business employing approximately 63,000 people in 25 countries, TRW is constantly looking for ways to improve product and process efficiency. To this end, TRW uses the Six Sigma Initiative to improve customer satisfaction, the quality of its business processes and products, and its methods of launching new products. TRW also employs the Six Sigma Initiative to create a culture capable of continuous process improvement.

TRW's Airbag Systems Group sought to simplify and automate its factory floor inventory and resupply procedures at its plants in Aschau and Laage, Germany, with the application of information logistics. They launched a Six Sigma "Black Belt" project that sought to identify redundancies and otherwise inefficient efforts in their supply chain. The project aimed to reconcile data from planning, ERP, Supply Chain Management (SCM), and factory floor applications into a single, integrated solution. Through this effort, TRW hoped to give floor personnel a real-time view of inventory and an automated resupply process. This would not only eliminate errors, but also drive down inventory costs by increasing consumption efficiency.

When it came time for implementation, the solution was to create a composite application automating this process using a variety of SAP NetWeaver components, including SAP Web Dynpro and homegrown enterprise services. The services allow the composite application to collect real-time data from the Unix-based production line host on the factory floor. That data is then passed to floor operators who monitor inventory levels, consumption patterns, and the time remaining until resupply is necessary. These operators know at a glance whether and when their production line will need to resupply, and they can order through the interface with two mouse clicks (if they choose to control the process on their own; usually, the process is completely automated).

TRW built this process with the help of the IT solution provider, znt-Richter, a German specialist for SAP NetWeaver technologies. The composite application maps the business process flow between the underlying systems, which include SAP R/3 and Unix-based inventory and production line systems. Each of these is linked via SAP NetWeaver Exchange Infrastructure (XI) to an SAP NetWeaver AS, which uses EJBs to wrap the business logic. SAP NetWeaver Portal provides the interface.

The project was TRW's first encounter with enterprise services, and company executives expect the results to be impressive, taking into account everything from productivity gains to reduced overtime. One of the lessons learned was the clear need for scalable and open technology platforms that will allow future efforts to develop at their own pace without architectural constraints. The company is confident that its enterprise services–enabled solution is flexible and scalable enough to link and add new plants to its solution and to adapt it to product development and external logistics processes. The combination of Six Sigma methodology and enterprise services–enabled solutions appears to be a key to real effectiveness gains.

PART SIX

Controlling Services

CHAPTER SEVENTEEN

ESA and IT Governance

IN ORDER TO ASSERT BETTER CONTROL OVER IT, ALIGN IT WITH BUSINESS OBJECTIVES, AND KEEP ITS potential benefits and risks in balance, corporations in recent years have paid considerable attention to the issue of IT governance. Also spurring this renewed attention are financial regulations, such as Sarbanes-Oxley, which call for improved documentation of IT systems and tighter controls over who uses them and to what end. The result is that enterprises have sought to bring to IT the kind of streamlined and rigorously defined business processes and reporting structures that IT has helped to make possible just about everywhere else in the enterprise.

If a formal definition of IT governance is required, it's hard to top the one provided by Jeanne W. Ross and Peter Weil in their book, *IT Governance* (Harvard Business School Press): "specifying the decision rights and accountability framework to encourage desirable behavior in the use of IT."

IT governance, they elaborate, provides a framework in which the decisions made about IT issues are aligned with the overall business strategy and culture of the enterprise. Governance is concerned, therefore, with setting directions, establishing standards and principles, and prioritizing investments.

Throughout this book, we have talked about how ESA ushers in fundamental changes in every area. It changes the relationship between business and IT, a relationship that is at the heart of most governance issues. In this chapter, we will see that ESA greatly simplifies governance. How so? ESA changes how the enterprise perceives, organizes, and manages many aspects of IT, divvying up financial and managerial responsibilities in radically new ways.

In the past, when business asked IT for changes to an application or system, that system was monolithic, and consequently the implications of the changes required a great deal of study and consideration. Enterprise services are granular. Corporations will have many, many enterprise services running. But because the function of each is discrete and the relationships among them are well understood, the process of approving a new service is far easier than that of approving a change to an new application. Needless to say, the budgetary requirements of such changes are far less as well.

ESA doesn't change the questions that IT governance attempts to answer, but it does change the answers—in important ways. The questions that are asked are fairly straightforward, even if different companies have answered them in different ways—through tight central control and mandates, perhaps, or in a decentralized approach that gives business units a good deal of autonomy. Among these questions: what standards is the enterprise adopting and enforcing in IT? Who in the organization is responsible for defining and building which pieces of IT? Who pays for this or that application or service? When are specific functions to be centralized or decentralized? What is the relationship of any one part of the company to the other parts? What does each department owe the other?

What are typical models for IT governance?

Traditionally, there have been two approaches to IT governance: *centralized* and *decentralized*. As its name implies, the centralized model calls for a central authority—the IT department, that is—to retain control over development budgets and the adoption of technical standards. To get new apps built, have old apps extended or modified, and procure new equipment and software, other business units within the organization must go to this central authority for approval and help.

The decentralized approach, which many corporations adopted as mainframe-based data processing gave way to client/server computing in the 1980s and 1990s, has shifted a certain amount of power over budgets and technical matters to business units and even to individual departments within those units. With less central oversight, these disparate groups of users can easily end up creating systems that over the long term do not work together particularly well. Semantic problems, such as differing definitions of "customer," for instance, can make it difficult for independently run systems to communicate and share information. In response to this, a small industry of application integration techniques, products, and companies has arisen.

What are the challenges and problems with existing models?

ESA simplifies the relationship between IT and business, yet standards remain as important as ever, if not even more important, to a successful deployment of ESA within any particular user organization. ESA calls for strict adherence to certain technical standards when creating enterprise services. Without standardized networking interfaces and semantic definitions, for instance, any enterprise services that an organization builds for itself will be unlikely to integrate properly with any other enterprise services, whether homegrown or acquired from SAP or its partners. Fluid integration, of course, is the primary goal of ESA. So, without the right policies and incentives in place to make sure that ESA-related standards are employed, ESA's essential value will be lost.

Standards policies are hardly a new, ESA-specific issue for IT. Enterprises have been grappling for years with how best to select, support, and enforce IT standards within their own ranks and across boundaries when dealing with suppliers, customers, and other business partners. When a corporation is powerful enough in its own industry, it can pretty much dictate the use of certain standards to any other firms with which it does business. Just look at the clout that Wal-Mart wields in retailing, as seen most recently in its mandate that suppliers must start adding a certain type of radio frequency identification (RFID) tag to the pallets they send its way. At the other end of the spectrum is Yahoo!, the web portal, which has forfeited the benefits of blanket IT standardization and permitted its disparate business units to develop and operate their IT systems pretty much as they see fit. In fact, Yahoo! may have little choice in the matter. Evidently, it has decided that this approach is the best one, financially and technically, in the kinds of volatile, high-growth, technology-driven markets where it does business. What's more, the web giant has acquired many of its business units as independent, self-sustaining startup companies which, by the time they join the Yahoo! fold, are well along in developing their own systems.

Wal-Mart and Yahoo! have chosen the approaches that are most appropriate to their respective marketplace and strategy. A key element of Wal-Mart's business strategy is to squeeze cost and inefficiency out of every possible business process, and that calls for a high degree of standardization in those business processes and in the IT systems that support them. Standardization of IT tends to hinder flexibility, but mass retailing is not subject to dramatic change. Success, therefore, is mainly a matter of progressively improving business processes and cost structures. To help keep IT costs down, Wal-Mart strives to standardize as much IT activity as possible, making it easier to replicate existing systems and teams wherever required and to keep training and operations costs to a minimum.

Yahoo!, in contrast, must continually scramble just to keep up with the fast-expanding, highly entrepreneurial web marketplace. There, new opportunities emerge and are jumped on virtually every day, it seems. Yahoo! can't afford to hinder its internal developers or newly acquired businesses by imposing on them more than a minimal slate of IT standards. It does, of course, pay for granting this freedom: it has to foot the bill for an exceptionally talented IT team whose ministrations are necessary to keeping Yahoo!'s plethora of systems running and integrating them at the relatively basic level of user interface (UI) and customer billing, for instance.

Most companies do not fit either one of these extreme molds: the highly centralized Wal-Mart mold or the highly improvisational Yahoo! mold. Instead, they will find themselves somewhere in between. Their challenge, therefore, is to work out a form of IT governance that's most appropriate to their circumstances. But they would do well to understand these extremes and glean from this picture a fundamental fact—namely, that in the IT organization, governance typically comes down to control. Who, it must be decided, has how much control over IT decisions, and therefore, control over expenditures of money?

How does ESA decrease the need for IT governance?

ESA reduces the need for IT governance dramatically. The reason for this is quite simple. Governance is about getting approval for changes, about power, about who wields that decision-making power—and how long such decisions take, given the speed of business change.

One way ESA significantly helps is by greatly reducing the incidence of decision making. Here is why existing enterprise services—and as much as 80 percent of the enterprise services you will ever need will come from SAP in the Enterprise Services Inventory—are already standardized. These services are therefore freely available to business analysts not only to consume, but also to use in composing new applications. The number of building blocks in the box, so to speak, is enormous. The only time that decisions must be made is when you need a building block that you don't currently have. Over time, as more services are created (and approved), the number of blocks in the chest increases, and it becomes more likely that the service you need is already in that chest. In this way, the granularity of enterprise services reduces the amount of time you spend on such decision making by reducing the number—and scope—of the decisions to be made. Such decision making is incremental rather than sweeping, reducing hassles for all concerned. Meanwhile, because enterprise services are available for composing new applications and modifying existing applications without the help of IT, business gains an unprecedented level of flexibility to change business processes at a high level.

How does ESA improve the relationship between business and IT?

In the past, the relationship between business and IT has at times been tense. Business wants agility to implement new strategies quickly. Requirements are handed off to IT and not only does it seem to take a long time to implement the required functionality, but often much is lost in the translation from requirements document to executable system. ESA promises to repaint this picture by, in a way, decoupling the IT side from the business side and giving each what it has always sought. For the first time, enterprises can reap the benefits of a uniform IT architecture while also enjoying a new level of flexibility in IT that's sufficient to truly meet business needs.

A fundamental principle of ESA is the separation of business logic from application logic. Business analysts gain the ability to define, change, and adapt business processes, supported by enterprise services. IT's responsibility is equally clear: it must manage the stack from the application logic down to the physical infrastructure. IT is in charge of the underlying platform for ESA: the Enterprise Services Repository. IT must also deal with operational issues, run server farms, secure the infrastructure, ensure that the network is running properly, and much more. ESA in essence improves the relationship between business and IT by making it clear who owns what and giving business a degree of independence to do what it needs to do without having an impact on IT.

This does not mean that IT and business never negotiate again, but by empowering business with agility to work with critical business processes and to compose applications from existing enterprise services, the need for an interface becomes narrower and the questions become smaller. Instead of approaching IT with a major change to a monolithic application, business gains the ability to make strategic changes without endangering the application ecosystem; again, giving each side what it has always wanted.

Where standardization becomes important—and where it is in the best interest of business itself—is in the development of new enterprise services. Enterprise services creation should be subject to a governance process to ensure that the new service "plays well" with existing services, that dependencies are well understood, that data types are standardized, and that reuse is maximized. Still, the question of whether to create an enterprise service is far smaller than the question of whether to customize the Customer Relationship Management (CRM) system, and the ability to reach a decision will be easier as well. But this begs provocative questions: who makes that decision? Who owns the enterprise services? Who has the authority to make decisions about them?

Who owns enterprise services? Who makes a decision about creating new services?

So far in this chapter, we have discussed only two models of governance: centralized and decentralized. A decentralized model ultimately works against standardization, and since enterprise services are built on standards to ensure interoperability, a decentralized model cannot be recommended. A centralized governance model is in some cases a good choice. In this scenario, all services are centrally owned, ensuring standardization. Everyone in the enterprise (with the proper roles and authorizations) can compose with those services freely, creating composite applications based on existing services. A decision-making process is needed only for the creation of new services. After all, a proposed new service might be more strategically created as an adaptation of an existing service, maximizing reuse instead of creating redundancy. No one will argue that new services must be subject to a decision-making process.

But there is another and perhaps better choice—a federal governance model that enables IT to do what it wants most and business units to do what they want most. A central authority exercises control of the underlying technology platform while business units create flexible, composite applications that take advantage of that platform. Dividing ownership of enterprise services by business unit is an alternative to centralized governance.

In fact, it now becomes possible to reorganize the business landscape as a set of domains,* or self-contained entities, within which lie most of the composite apps that will be built. The organization can be carved into domains in almost any way that makes sense: ownership of business processes by line of business is one possible method. Figure 17-1 shows the way one company organized its domains.†

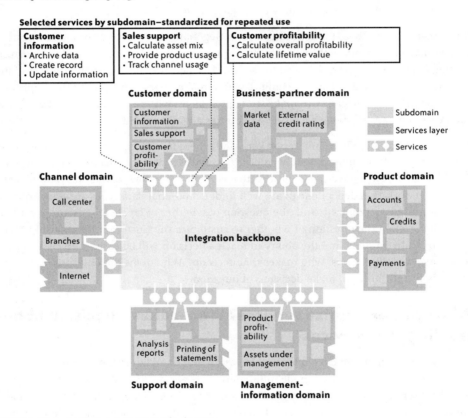

FIGURE 17-1. Restructuring governance by domains

* The authors would like to credit McKinsey & Company, Inc. with originating the concept of dividing business responsibilities by domain.

† This figure is reprinted by permission from Jürgen Laartz, Eric Monnoyer, and Alexander Scherdin, "Designing IT for Business: When Business and Computer People Put Their Heads Together, They Can Transform a Company's IT Architecture," *The McKinsey Quarterly*, number 3, 2003, pp. 76–86.

However, in a federal governance model, this brings up some interesting questions and issues: if domains own the services relevant to their business area, business units will find themselves negotiating about what services other domains can reuse for creating composite applications. This will open up new lines of communication among divisions as well as free business units from monolithic rules.

For example, instead of a one-size-fits-all policy for the entire enterprise, sales and marketing might have ownership of strategic enterprise services that empower that unit to try out new strategies to respond to changing market opportunities. Because the sales and marketing domain owns the services in question, it can create new composite applications using those services freely, without the need to consult other domains. Domains own services relevant to their needs. While some utility services might be centrally owned and available to all (a retrieval of customer data comes to mind), the door is open for a variety of approaches to divvying up enterprise services ownership. And instead of having IT own all of the services, the decisions about dividing services can be made in a way that makes the most sense from a business perspective. In this framework, business gains the agility it needs to move quickly, to compose broadly, and to innovate.

In this way, business units gain unparalleled flexibility. However, tradeoffs remain. The more authority the domains have, the more complex the relationships among domains may become. New sorts of negotiations will be necessary. Over time, however, the interface between domains and centralized governance will become clearer. Some enterprise services at first owned by a given domain may need to be centrally owned, and vice versa—these decisions are inevitable. Given time, businesses will strike the right balance between flexibility and complexity, allowing for maximum effectiveness in using ESA in support of strategic business processes.

What processes make sense for approving new enterprise services?

Discovering the right decision-making models and processes for approving enterprise services is a field still in its infancy. Clearly, dependencies must be considered, and redundancy is an important concern in building new enterprise services. However, companies are not alone in dealing with such decision-making processes. One model that all companies deploying enterprise services should consider is the Enterprise Services Community. This community, facilitated by SAP, is an important resource for all companies adopting ESA. Joining this community and participating in the process is a way to build new synergies. Local governance committees stand to benefit from participation in this community. For details on the Enterprise Services Community, see Chapter 6.

Governance is all about decision making, about who has the power to make those decisions, and about how quickly decisions will be made. We should clarify that ESA will not completely do away with the traditional tradeoff that has been made between uniformity and freedom. However, it will make that tradeoff much less painful and difficult for companies. The pendulum, as it were, won't swing as drastically as it has in the past between such disparate extremes. The granularity of services makes the decisions smaller. The separation of business logic from application logic gives businesses, for perhaps the first time, a clear way to divide governance issues along lines that make sense and offer all parties the flexibility they need to innovate while maintaining standards that keep costs low and efficiency high.

ESA in action: Whirlpool Corporation

Whirlpool Corporation practices a more decentralized form of governance. Whirlpool is the world's leading manufacturer and marketer of major home appliances with annual revenues of more than $13 billion, 68,000 employees, and nearly 50 manufacturing and technology research centers around the globe. The company markets its ovens, freezers, dishwashers, washing machines, and thousands of other products under the brand names Whirlpool, KitchenAid, Brastemp, Bauknecht, Consul, and others in more than 170 countries. The company's relentless focus on both customer service and continuous product innovation has already led its IT organization to embrace ESA as a means of enabling business process innovation that will help differentiate products and services and free up resources for reinvestment, instead of simply providing application support.

Instead of mapping out a strategic blueprint for ESA adoption from within a central architecture-planning unit (which was actually disbanded several years ago), Whirlpool Corporation has chosen a more tactical, incremental approach. Instead of implementing new enterprise services–based solutions and then consolidating the systems they replaced, Whirlpool Corporation is applying ESA principles when and where it can—converting SAP R/3 EDI messages into XML-based services, for example—while resolving to decompose these ad hoc services to more fundamental components when the chance presents itself. Figure 17-2 illustrates Whirlpool's business application vision. Instead of consciously designing an Enterprise Services Repository, for example, Whirlpool Corporation engineers intend to use the imminent replacement of their order management system as an opportunity to decompose the current system to the Remote Function Calls (RFCs) and the transactions that were called by them. Then they plan to recompose these into the first services that someday will fill an Enterprise Services Repository.

Whirlpool Corporation's overarching goal is flexible standardization. The company has already standardized around SAP R/3 as the foundation layer of its application hierarchy. This and other transactional systems are connected to the company's primary data center in Michigan and run on the same, consolidated SAP NetWeaver infrastructure. Whirlpool Corporation's governance model is more decentralized, with the core IT group defining 80 percent of a new composite application's functionality in terms of reusable services, then releasing the composite to regional units closer to the business need for implementation of the final interface and need-specific tweaking. That model—which manages to accommodate both reusable, standardized components *and* frontline initiatives—was expressly designed to drive product innovation. Whirlpool intends for its next step to be the standardization of entire manufacturing processes using services once modeling and messaging tools mature.

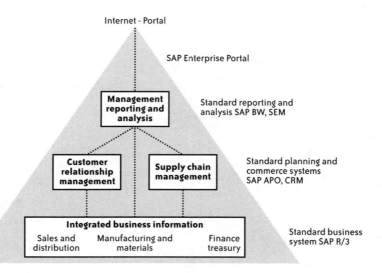

FIGURE 17-2. Whirlpool's business application vision

Until then, the company will continue using enterprise services to consolidate its menagerie of legacy systems. With SAP NetWeaver acting as the platform, legacy applications and data are migrated via the SAP NetWeaver Exchange Infrastructure (XI) and SAP NetWeaver Master Data Management (SAP NetWeaver MDM) to the core SAP R/3 systems, a process that has proven useful in sunsetting custom systems and those from other third-party vendors.

CHAPTER EIGHTEEN

ESA Life Cycle Management and Operations

AT THIS STAGE IN THE **ESA** EVOLUTION, IT'S UNDERSTANDABLE THAT WE SPENT THE BULK OF THIS BOOK focused on the construction and deployment of enterprise services rather than on life in a mature ESA environment still a decade away. But the challenges are known, and the answers are already being formulated.

It's important to understand that both life cycle management and operations are already experiencing a wrenching evolution independent of ESA's appearance on the scene. The overwhelming majority of the tools and practices developed for monitoring operations—i.e., whether the application is running normally, how busy it is, whether it's load balanced, etc. —were designed for an IT environment filled with homogenous, standalone entities…the world of SAP R/3 and its fellow monolithic applications. In that environment, the tools for installing, configuring, maintaining, and monitoring applications were built with the assumption that the only applications and systems that would be affected by further config-uration, applying patches, or full-fledged upgrades were the ones receiving the changes. Not much thought was given to interdependencies because there weren't many.

But that began to change in recent years, as first application-to-application integration and then the arrival of integration platforms such as SAP NetWeaver, as well as the wild proliferation of hardware stemming from mergers and acquisitions, best-of-breed investments, and systems orphaned by industry consolidation combined to spread application functionality and data across increasingly heterogeneous IT landscapes. Processes began to run across multiple systems, leading to the complex environment we know today, which is filled with unintended interdependencies and is serviced with operations and management tools ill equipped for understanding and working around them. Often the only option under the circumstances is the quick-and-dirty one: flood the zone with engineers to test as many systems in the environment as possible during downtimes and then keep those downtimes to an absolute minimum—a state of affairs that can be expensive and doesn't encourage consolidation aimed toward lowering total cost of ownership (TCO).

Now this state of affairs is about to become further complicated by the unprecedented flexibility of enterprise services, which promise to simultaneously decouple applications from systems, decouple the business logic from application functionality, and then granularize it into services and business objects, each one of which may have multiple instantiations supporting composite applications built on top of them. The landscape is poised to explode in potential complexity with these developments as newly independent layers of functionality and business logic are added to the platform, each of which may evolve at a faster rate than the underlying functionality called by the services. Another twist is the boundary-crossing nature of ESA, which will link automated processes within the company to partners, suppliers, and customers, without creating an entirely new set of interdependencies that will require an entirely new approach to monitoring and maintaining them.

Which operations and management problems will ESA actually solve?

Two operations and management problems that ESA will solve immediately come to mind. The first is strategic and the second is near and dear to CFOs' hearts: continuous availability of processes during software maintenance and lower TCO. Although we will discuss continuous availability and lower TCO in detail later in this chapter, let's consider both quickly them.

Continuous availability is the number one operational concern of SAP's customers: how can they upgrade or replace components without having an impact on running business processes? ESA offers a potential solution by decoupling business process and business logic—strategic differentiators that must always be available—from core functionality. The decoupling of business and process logic at the heart of ESA will enable business analysts to upgrade processes effectively using modeling tools without affecting the services below and the applications beneath the services. Conversely, it will become simultaneously possible to upgrade or even retire those underlying systems—first with new versions and later with services and other components which perform the same tasks—while never disturbing the business processes above, provided that a temporary rerouting of functionality has been planned for.

That planning is the key. While the number of moving parts may increase by several orders of magnitude, a standards-based management interface for each service will make it possible to monitor and orchestrate the nonfunctional, operational aspect of thousands of services from a central control center—the next-generation SAP NetWeaver Lifecycle Management discussed later in this chapter—with minimal effort. These developments are the first steps toward a new requirements-based management model in which the granular details of installations and upgrades are implemented automatically across the entire landscape based on a few high-level instructions, drastically reducing the number of tools and teams of testers necessary and thus lowering TCO. (We'll dub these new approaches and tools "ESA Lifecycle Management" to differentiate from the current situation.)

These are the goals, at least. As you'll discover in this chapter, much conceptualizing still needs to be done, new tools need to be created, and new skills must be acquired to make this vision a reality.

Figure 18-1 illustrates these phases.

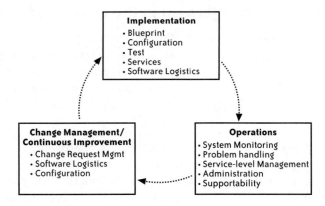

FIGURE 18-1. Phases of life cycle management

What is life cycle management?

Life cycle management refers to the tools and practices meant to support software customers throughout the entire life cycle of applications. It's composed of three phases:

Implementation
> The design, testing, and setup of business processes, landscapes, and systems. Implementation is especially concerned with the concept of *software logistics*, which might also be thought of as a software supply chain: what is the most effective and efficient way to sync Independent Software Vendors' (ISVs') application development with their customers' needs and then deliver new features without disrupting key processes?

Operations
> Running applications within the landscape once they've been installed and keeping them running smoothly. Tasks and responsibilities that might be filed under operations include ensuring that an application or enterprise service is running, checking to see

how busy it is, ensuring that it's load balanced, checking to see where it's currently deployed within the landscape, and checking whether any components are reporting errors. In this phase, the complexity of IT landscapes has so far outstripped the application-focused tools used for maintenance. New tools and management processes are needed to knit all of these functions into a single interface for maximum efficiency and lower TCO.

Continuous improvement and change management

Reconfiguring, patching, upgrading, and even replacing and/or consolidating applications and services within the landscape. This is perhaps the most critical of these three phases because many of any given company's most mission-critical applications have already been in use for years, just as the bulk of SAP's customers already own SAP R/3. The concept of software logistics is especially relevant in this phase as well: how often and how rapidly can IT improve and upgrade systems without incurring significant downtime?

What is life cycle management in the context of ESA?

ESA life cycle management adds two new duties to existing management of applications and management of landscapes, and those are *management of services* and *management of composite applications*. But the links between these layers are loosely coupled, unlike before. This makes it possible, as we'll discuss shortly, to administer and maintain applications, services, and the like independently of each other—the characteristic which guarantees continuous availability.

Decoupling of business logic from underlying functionality also means that for the first time, it will become possible to monitor the operations of the business process—i.e., is the operation of the process running smoothly—separately from the purely technical operation of the application or service—i.e., is it busy, is it load balanced, and so on. One of the goals of ESA life cycle management is to introduce business process awareness to life cycle management tools and procedures.

What are the challenges for life cycle management in the context of ESA?

The obvious challenges are the transition from implementing, operating, and upgrading potentially dozens of applications to managing literally thousands of enterprise services and business objects, and then managing the succeeding transition of functionality from retired applications to a galaxy of independent business objects.

These services and objects will be used to produce landscapes running business processes across multiple systems (which must be added or retired with no visible impact to the landscape) that must be able to change at will according to the commands of business analysts. And there needs to be a set of standards inherent in the business process platform that allows ISVs and customers alike to design and implement new services which will automatically possess the characteristics for doing this. These same standards must also empower IT to automatically manage a larger landscape and enable hardware providers such as Cisco, Sun, and Hewlett-Packard to create systems that can assume at least the partial burden of such tasks as load balancing and reliable message delivery.

The final challenge is to close the gap between managing the purely technical performance of a service and managing it in light of its greater significance to business processes. With the number of services operating within the landscape poised to explode—don't forget that services may have multiple instantiations—it becomes absolutely critical to be able to relate the technical importance of maintaining a service to its business importance. In other words, how do you make sure that your most valuable business processes are given operational priority ahead of less valuable ones? And how do you make sure *before* you install or upgrade a service that it won't take down or unintentionally alter a business process?

How will services be monitored in an ESA landscape? Where will the necessary metadata come from?

Just as enterprise services will use standardized interfaces to access the functional core of services, SAP envisions that three additional operations layers will be added to enterprise services for the purposes of administration, performance monitoring, and security. (For a discussion of security issues, see Chapter 19.)

ESA life cycle management tools will call upon these layers for installation, configuration, upgrades, load balancing, and prioritization of services within larger business processes. The tools for doing so will eventually be integrated into SAP NetWeaver to create a single, automated interface able to monitor or administer the entire landscape at a glance. SAP is currently focused on developing and driving the adoption of the standards and interfaces needed to make this vision a reality.

How does ESA affect implementation issues?

Even beyond configuration, the most important issue to be addressed in an ESA landscape is the possibility of conflicts, redundancies, and business process disruptions. As the granular complexity of the landscape increases with each service added, so does the possibility of something going wrong, and the ability of IT to debug or spot potential conflicts with the naked eye decreases proportionally. Furthermore, laboriously plotting the impact of a potential implementation by hand—i.e., configuring, testing, and debugging every single component that would be affected—isn't an optimal use of IT's time or resources.

SAP NetWeaver Lifecycle Management already does an excellent job of transforming high-level configuration instructions into granular application settings. But dealing with the flexibility inherent in an ESA landscape will require a still higher level of abstraction that would first include preconfigured and automatic initial setup of complete business scenarios. These would ideally shrink a six- to nine-month configuration process to an out-of-the-box installation preintegrated with SAP NetWeaver, with the latter being briefed by the installer on which components have been installed, which key performance indicators to monitor during operations, and so on.

A second aspect of this approach is a concept called *business scoping*. Scoping takes preconfiguration further, essentially installing a complete landscape of functionally that is dormant until initial configuration, at which time the administrator is presented not with extensive technical documentation on the scenarios contained within, but with a catalog of business processes and scenarios available within the landscape and described entirely in business terminology rather than technical specifications. The landscape then implicitly configures itself—activating business content, connecting services and business objects as needed, and the like. Instead of forcing customers to keep pace with the rapidly proliferating number of entities, the landscape hides its innermost technical workings during configuration and reconfiguration. All customers will need to know is what they would like done, not how it's done.

This is yet another example of the eventual evolution within ESA away from a specification model (where in this case, the implementation must be explicitly specified) and toward a requirement model, where the only administrator input necessary is the desired result. The responsibility for recognizing the relationship between technical functionality and business processes will be incorporated into the installation process itself.

How are operations affected by ESA?

On the software side, the creation of a standardized set of interfaces for administrating and monitoring enterprise services will go a long way toward consolidating and eliminating the often redundant and expensive toolset in use today. By grounding these standards in ESA, it will become possible to fold all of the necessary tools for load balancing, ensuring uptime, scheduling, running diagnostics, and so on, into SAP NetWeaver for automatic administration. That is exactly what SAP is doing.

Standardization will enable SAP to meet the landscape challenge by collapsing formerly individual and isolated tools into the central SAP NetWeaver Administrator—the central operations console of SAP NetWeaver. This systematic consolidation, which is already underway, will lower TCO while creating the link between the business process logic and the operational metadata, which will cause the latter to become contextually self-aware.

In practice, that means having administration tools that will do the following:

- Automatically recognize operational dependencies between services or composite applications
- Allocate system resources to services using their importance to business processes as a method for assigning priority
- Alert IT when service messages are not being received
- Ensure those messages are not lost and can be rerouted and make contingency plans for surges in system activity

Consolidating the tool in a single, remotely accessible user interface (UI) will only make the tasks of outsourcing system administration to data centers and receiving support from ISVs that much easier.

What is capacity planning in the world of ESA?

In general terms, *capacity planning* is the process of determining the required hardware resources for running enterprise solutions such as mySAP ERP or composite applications, for example. This includes initial estimates on required CPU server capacity, memory requirements, projected disk size and future growth, as well as frontend network-bandwidth requirements. It's possible to distinguish between different kinds of sizing: the initial size of your first hardware plans, adding load delta size after you go live, and upgrading your size when new solutions are added to an existing landscape. Sizing is achieved by translating business requirements into hardware requirements, as customers identify their bread-and-butter business processes and services, and SAP provides tools and guidelines to turn this information into hardware requirement predictions. What is the principle of sizing?

The theory is that each business process creates a load on the hardware that can be measured using standard performance monitors. This load is expressed in terms of CPU second for CPU usage, memory in megabytes, disk space in megabytes, and frontend network load in kilobytes transferred per user interaction step.

Abstraction of business logic from IT is enabled through operations, notifications, and synchronous and asynchronous messages to local or remote systems. When you look at the architecture from a business perspective, it is clear that different business objects have different complexities. For example, a sales order will be more powerful than a pay statement. Different operations may also have more impact on performance than others, and messages passed through the Adapter Framework create additional strain.

To prepare for these challenges, SAP will measure standard enterprise services along the criteria of CPU usage and memory and disk consumption and will turn the findings into a questionnaire where customers can fill in expected business application and volume requirements.

How do you size composite applications?

Composites aim at enabling efficient development of new applications that customers can adopt easily and that allow flexibility in backend connectivity. They are applications that use data and functions provided as services by backend systems and other underlying applications, and combine these into user-centric processes and pages, supported by their own business logic and specific UIs.

The scope of the composite application concept is broad and may be applied in various business cases. For example, small (lightweight) composites implement process logic only, and large composite applications such as SAP xApp Analytics add value at the persistence, object, and service layers.

Provided your software scales linearly, sizing is additive for composite applications. Their size is equal to the sum of their parts. What you can do in this context is begin from the standard sizing of the underlying services and add the requirements for your custom service. For example, you may want to integrate a third-party application with an SAP application via a unified UI, such as guided procedures, for example. You need to size the third-party application, the SAP application, and the load created by the new UI.

How does performance monitoring work in an ESA environment?

SAP NetWeaver contains a number of performance monitors that help you understand exactly which processes create which load in which component. Some monitors collect statistics on CPU utilization of different hardware servers, and others look at the runtimes of individual processes, on local servers as well as collecting performance KPIs from remote servers. There are tools for a quick bottleneck analysis, such as the XI Monitor; there are dedicated SQL traces for tuning access to the persistence layer; there are application traces for runtime analyses across packages and components; and there are familiar tools for measuring server-to-server communication, frontend network load, and rendering times on the browser. Figure 18-2 shows where the optimization potential is.

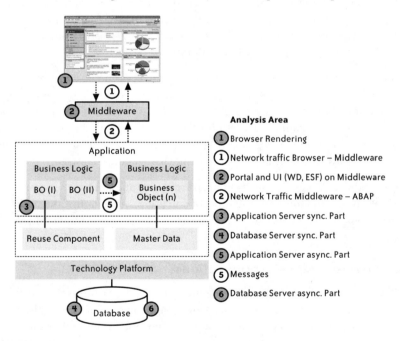

FIGURE 18-2. An overview of performance analysis

How does virtualization affect capacity planning?

Virtualization options (see the upcoming section, "What is adaptive computing and how does it relate to ESA?") can help with hardware landscape management by more flexibly deploying hardware, thus lowering TCO with less idle machine time. Although it's easy to virtualize disk storage and CPUs, memory presents more of a challenge. From a sizing perspective, peak requirements must be satisfied, and at some point, all resources must be tuned to meet these peak requirements. With sensible virtualization efforts, the individual peaks can be evened out, again lowering TCO.

If you look at Figure 18-3, you can see a typical load distribution at a customer site. CPU peak usage occurs at around 3:00 p.m. At that point, all services must be available to satisfy the CPU requirements. At other times, the virtualized CPU power may be taken to satisfy other needs—for example, serving web pages.

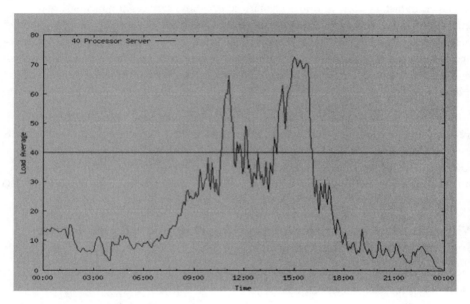

FIGURE 18-3. Load distribution at a customer site

How will ESA affect change management and software logistics?

The decoupling of business process logic from application functionality will lead to a profound evolution in change management, especially now that system downtime, that classic disincentive to software maintenance and upgrades, can be minimized if not eliminated outright.

In the current generation of software, potentially differentiating features that appear in each new version of a given release are inextricably tied to the bedrock functionality below. Any company considering an upgrade or a patch has had to weigh the financial and intangible costs (IT resources, the opportunity cost of downtime, etc.) against the potential advantages, and the more costly, critical, and complex the application, the less likely the company is to decide it's worth it. SAP's customers have stressed repeatedly that stability and continuous availability are key.

Decoupling the business layer from the application and business process platform layers frees each to evolve at its own pace. While the platform itself will not change rapidly—allowing companies to keep their mature systems in place, while ISVs such as SAP will continue to roll out new versions every 18 months as they have always done—the delivery and construction of new services and composite applications will likely become near-constant.

With the ability to ship products for the business layer rapidly and frequently, differentiating processes can be implemented and upgraded without having an impact on the application layer. In fact, as ESA continues its maturation, those services and business objects will drift downward to replace enterprise applications when they eventually reach the end of their lifespan. And because these services will contain the standard administration interfaces, IT will use SAP NetWeaver to automatically configure updates, analyze and pretest their potential impact on currently running systems, resolve conflicts and dependencies, and so on.

Software logistics will be transformed, as the rate of delivery and implementation will accelerate as the combination of service interfaces, SAP NetWeaver's centralized administration capabilities, and the adoption of specification model-style implementation and upgrade procedures reduce a formerly complicated and time-consuming procedure to a much simpler one, with little or no impact on the existing systems, greatly reducing TCO in the process.

What is the SAP NetWeaver Administrator? How will it adapt to the demands of an ESA environment?

The SAP NetWeaver Administrator (NWA) is a Web Dynpro-based tool for administration and monitoring, offering a central entry point to the whole SAP NetWeaver system landscape and enabling SAP NetWeaver administrators to perform all day-to-day operational tasks from within one console. The NWA unifies the most important administration and monitoring tools for Java and ABAP systems.

Based on a UI created in Web Dynpro, the NWA is fully accessible via a browser, and it consolidates previously separate tools for administration, troubleshooting, and problem analysis of the system landscape into a single environment. Using this tool, it's possible to start and stop instances, check configuration settings and logs, and monitor error-free functioning of components across the landscape for both Java and ABAP systems.

For Java, the NWA represents the crossover from various expert tools to an integrated, simple, and clear solution. It also completes the integration of the data sources for monitoring. For ABAP, the NWA represents the transition from many different expert transactions—some of which are difficult to use—to integrated, centrally available information.

The NWA comes with an Operations Handbook containing a large collection of guided procedures for various operational tasks. An authoring environment for guided procedures makes it possible to extend the predelivered SAP guided procedures or to develop new ones. Its open framework permits continual integration of ISV solutions.

What is adaptive computing and how does it relate to ESA?

While ESA represents an evolution in flexibility for applications, the concept of adaptive computing represents a similar increase in flexibility on the infrastructure level so that the demands of ESA applications can be met effectively. Using SAP NetWeaver, an adaptive computing virtualization layer is created to decouple applications and enterprise services from their underlying infrastructure. The goal is to run applications or services on many different servers without ever changing configurations.

What's behind adaptive computing?

Key to the adaptive computing concept is the separation of the IT infrastructure into four standardized building blocks: Computing, Network, Storage, and Control. These represent the primary components of today's data centers.

In this context, Computing not only stands for physical servers, but also for virtual computing nodes such as logical or virtual partitions (e.g., VMWare instances). Network, meanwhile, is used as a transport medium for the virtualization layer. Also important is Storage, which refers to the centralized storage that is home to application-specific components—an arrangement which eliminates the need to move data from one server to another. This is a key to the flexibility inherent in adaptive computing; moving an enterprise service from one physical server to another can literally take only minutes. The fourth building block, Control, is provided by SAP in the form of the Adaptive Computing Controller (ACC), which easily handles the management and assignment of enterprise services running on ever-changing hardware resources.

The advantage of virtualization is the flexible distribution of enterprise services and data across an IT landscape, regardless of their system of origin. Applications can be distributed according to the current business and system requirements. As soon as a server reaches its maximum capacity, the ACC is able to reallocate the load to available servers within the landscape flexibly, quickly, and smoothly.

Doing so first requires virtualizing applications. A new abstraction layer—the Adaptive Computing Virtualization Layer—will be implemented to remove the fixed coupling between application services and physical servers. Virtual IP addresses and logical host-names will ensure this.

The Adaptive Computing Controller

The Adaptive Computing Controller (ACC) enables SAP customers to manage available hardware resources dynamically and to assign enterprise services and other forms of functionality to them. The ACC allows IT departments to operate, observe, and manage an adaptive computing environment much as the next generation of the SAP NetWeaver Solution Manager is envisioned as the single point of control for software in ESA environments.

The Adaptive Computing Controller is composed of the following functions:

Configuration of logical and physical system landscapes
The individual components of a landscape can be grouped together at either a logical (i.e., functionality described) or a physical level. This makes it possible to reorganize the landscape into a hierarchy, which is a particularly effective management scheme for large landscapes. At a physical level, both individual servers and virtual units can be managed, which produces a high degree of flexibility. Mixed landscapes can be run with different hardware variants and operating systems.

Starting, stopping, and moving components
The ACC allows the administrator to assign parts of an SAP landscape such as databases or applications to the available servers easily and flexibly and to move software between servers in the shortest space of time.

Monitoring and recording service use in an adaptive computing landscape
The ACC makes it possible to monitor which enterprise services were assigned to which servers and when. This information can then be used for internal reporting and cost settlement, for example.

Planning and scheduling service use
The task planner in the ACC makes it possible to schedule the starting, stopping, and moving of components in an SAP landscape, enabling optimized planning for the deployment of the available resources.

Mass operations
The functions for mass operations enable the administrator to start several actions in parallel, in order to shut down a complete SAP solution on one IT landscape and start it up again on another. This simplifies and accelerates hardware updates or migrations when leasing contracts have expired, for example.

How do conventional infrastructure approaches compare to adaptive computing?

Compared to existing infrastructures, adaptive computing infrastructures eschew the traditional box-centric approach. Typically, an application is installed on its own dedicated server. In an adaptive computing environment, the application is decoupled from the server by virtualizing it. This means installations are not server based. Instead, they are available over the network. In using adaptive computing and its standardized building blocks, existing landscapes can be extended easily using the same operational concept. Backup and recovery can be handled on a logical landscape basis. Adaptive computing's resource model can help increase utilization of the existing IT infrastructure because sizing can be done for the entire landscape, which helps significantly in balancing the entire load.

What will adaptive computing mean for SAP's partners?

SAP works closely with its technology partners to ensure that the operating systems and storage components within the SAP environment meet the requirements of adaptive computing. To this end, the SAP Adaptive Computing Council was formed in October 2003 as a forum for ongoing information exchange and collaboration. One outcome of the forum is the Adaptive Computing Compliance Test, which customers can use to find out which partners offer a solution that meets the requirements of adaptive computing. This test consists of several steps, including a successful demonstration of the "start," "stop," and "relocate" functions. A large number of further compliance tests have been carried out since the first one in May 2004. Registered users can access the current version on the SAP Service Marketplace.

What does the introduction of ESA and its impact on life cycle management mean for IT departments?

The multilayered, multilifecycle environment created by ESA will require IT to master different skill sets and responsibilities corresponding to each layer, which will in turn likely divide IT departments into multiple teams.

One team will work to support business analysts and their modeling tools in creating and orchestrating new processes and a second team will traffic in software logistics, continually adding new services and business objects they have either created themselves or taken possession of from ISVs. A third team will tend to SAP NetWeaver, retiring and consolidating outmoded systems underneath, and a fourth will oversee all aspects of the physical infrastructure, applying adaptive computing techniques and distributing the impact of operations on the landscape. All the while, each team will be responsible for deploying, testing, monitoring, and maintaining the services and applications relevant to their layer.

Only one of these theoretical teams, the platform support team, will retain the bulk of its former skills and job descriptions. The rest of IT will assume new roles that require new skills and new training geared more heavily toward supporting the unprecedented rapidity of business process design. Most tools they will need in order to do so—and the tools that will bring business analysts directly into this equation—have yet to be designed. IT will need to master them, as well as the new standards, models, and metadata required to make all of this a reality.

Will life cycle management capabilities be available to ISVs?

As part of its efforts to drive standards for the operational layers of services, SAP intends to create standard interfaces for each service, others for a specification model, preconfigured installation interfaces, and still others built around the capabilities of SAP NetWeaver. This will guarantee that any service built on top of the platform by SAP or its customers or ISVs will contain the necessary attributes for automated ESA life cycle management.

SAP is also working with hardware partners such as Cisco Systems, Intel, EMC, Hewlett-Packard, and many others to create adaptive infrastructure components that are ESA and business process aware. Together, they will create another set of standards for embedded software that will assume operations and monitoring responsibilities. For instance, they could create a Cisco router containing a software layer that is capable of raising its own alerts when messages sent to a given service fail to be delivered or is capable of distributing the loads on a set of services not by technical criteria, but by their relative importance to the business processes they comprise. In other words, SAP and its partners are working together to create not just software, but essentially, hardware standards that for the first time will be business process aware. And these standards will be available to every ISV offering enterprise services. Finally, all services and composite applications, regardless of who built them, will enjoy the same capabilities for ESA life cycle management.

What additional capabilities does ESA offer in terms of allowing business analysts to determine which revenue-generating services should receive additional resources?

The ultimate challenge for companies is to focus not only on the technical implementation and operation of enterprise services but also on the business semantics of their implementation. Successful technical deployment is one thing—did the service install correctly, is it properly load balanced, etc.—but it's up to the business analyst to ensure that there are no gaps in functionality at the semantic level (e.g., is a process component missing), and she will need the tools to determine this.

To support the business analysts who will be driving the lifespan of business processes and composite applications in the top layer of the ESA life cycle, SAP intends to add functionality to its operations and modeling tools that will reflect and prioritize service performance relative to its performance in business processes. Faced with a dilemma in which two processes are competing for system resources, business analysts and their supporting IT really want to know which process is most critical from a business perspective as opposed to a purely technical one. (In the starkest terms, which one is making the most money?) SAP will build the standards enabling that linkage of business semantics and technical information directly into SAP NetWeaver.

CHAPTER NINETEEN

ESA Security

ONE OF THE MORE DAUNTING CHALLENGES FACING ENTERPRISE ARCHITECTS IS REINVENTING THE security model for business processes and the composite applications that support them. Traditionally, securing monolithic applications has simply been a matter of securing who had access to them, which meant that the user interface (UI) was the gateway and the natural point at which to guarantee the user's identity and permissions. Security inside the application itself was left to the vendor.

But in the world of ESA, service becomes the platform's problem, and defining access to services and the structure built on top of them is a more delicate, complex matter. Authentication at the UI is merely the first step; after that, the user's identity and role within the landscape must flow through composite applications, passed from service to service and checked by each, and the overall security of the process from one end to the other must be ensured. Further complicating matters is the fact that these services might comprise business processes which touch any number of external systems, including, perhaps, the host company's customers and/or partners, which raises another raft of issues.

An entirely new set of concerns, meanwhile, revolves around the sudden exposure of critical business processes to assault by malicious parties residing on the Web. Corporate firewalls may have eliminated most of the potential avenues for attack by hackers, corporate espionage, or what-have-you, but the new architecture often means that the overwhelming majority of SOAP messages now move through the still-open HTTP port, vastly diminishing firewalls' ability to screen traffic. In the age of enterprise services, corporations cannot afford to bury applications deep in their systems, which limits their effectiveness; nor can they afford not to see what's hiding inside every packet arriving at services, which requires new strategies and new security capabilities.

What security challenges face enterprise architects?

In the big-picture view, there are essentially two challenges: securing each service component with safeguards to protect against misuse, and securing the final composition—a process, or composite application—against attacks. The former task focuses on issues such as identity management, which includes the creation of user roles and authentication, access management, and the encryption of service messages. The latter has to do with securing the overall design of the application itself—has care been taken to ensure that there are no weak spots in the composition of the overall process where someone might attack? Providing the former is largely the responsibility of SAP and other Independent Software Vendors (ISVs) driving security standards and providing services; the latter is the result of competent designs that followed on security-friendly patterns of development. We'll address each of these in turn.

What are identity management and authentication?

Identity management is one of the essential parts of application security: defining which users exist and what roles they have (which access to what degree of functionality). It comprises creating and defining the list of users with access to the application (and now services) and assigning access rights in the form of roles. To accomplish this, SAP NetWeaver provides a set of tools and functionalities to allow customers to perform these tasks efficiently. Additionally, it is possible to integrate SAP NetWeaver with other identity management solutions through standard interfaces including the Lightweight Directory Access Protocol (LDAP) and the Service Provisioning Markup Language (SPML).

Authentication is the process by which a computer, computer program, or another user attempts to confirm that the computer, computer program, or user from whom the second party has received some communication is or is not the claimed first party. Creating a single-sign-on to composite applications depends on being able to pass authentication metadata from service to service.

How does identity management change within ESA?

It's no longer sufficient to secure the first service encountered by users in a business process (i.e., the interface); in fact, it never has been. Identity management–based security must extend across every system touched by the process about to be initiated because what's ultimately being exposed is not just a single service, but the entire business process.

What the user orders at the onset of the process must be verified and delivered at the end with the guarantees that: a) that is indeed what she ordered, and b) she is indeed entitled to request it. If the request were to pass through any unsecured service along its route, neither premise could be proven to have remained true.

From a service infrastructure standpoint, this responsibility will likely fall to the security operations layer in each. But it will also become necessary to integrate identity management processes and user profiles into a single repository. This repository will distribute that information to all the systems, providing them with the information required to assess the validity of a requirement, or it may be accessible from anywhere within the landscape, called by the system hit by the user's request, and provide the information in real time—essentially becoming an enterprise service itself. In the early stages of a company's ESA adoption, this might take the form of an LDAP integration effort. But as the environment continues to grow and evolve, the next step is federation—multiple identity repositories which contain different instantiations of the same user profile, and in which these various instantiations are linked. In practice, this would allow the external participants in cross-company processes to decide for themselves how much access and what role that user will have in its systems and which is resolved automatically when the user logs into her native environment.

What is access management?

Access management is the actual definition of roles—what should a salesperson have access to, or the CEO?—down to the level of which systems each role can access, or which processes they can initiate, or which documents they can open. The roles defined here will be used within identity management to permit users what they need to be permitted on the business level (the salesperson) as well as on a more technical level (the administrator). Access management defines the roles and enforces authorization—that the users have, in fact, the roles they have been assigned—and their corresponding permissions. Access management needs a valid identification of the user by the authentication subsystem, and the information concerning which users are assigned to which groups.

How does access management change within ESA?

Again, in an ESA environment in which each service must be secure and in which business processes flow across multiple systems in potentially multiple companies, there's a need for centralized access management. Additionally a federated model will be required for business processes that run across multiple companies in B2B scenarios.

Standards development for federated identity efforts is being driven by initiatives such as the Liberty Alliance Project, a global consortium of more than 150 companies, nonprofits, and government organizations that has been laying the groundwork on this issue since 2001. OASIS, which created the WS-Security and SAML standards, has also proposed WS-Trust and WS-Security-Policy for identity and access management purposes. (SAP is a founding member of the Liberty Alliance Project and is actively involved with OASIS.)

How are messages that are sent from enterprise services secured? What standards have been developed?

It does little good to create identity and access management repositories if the messages passed by the enterprise services themselves are unsecured and are open to attack or misuse. The messages carrying authentication and authorization metadata and confidential business data must be encrypted against prying eyes.

The most common standard for doing so is OASIS's WS-Security: SOAP Message Security (WSS-SMS) standard, which builds upon the XML Signature and XML Encryption standards. The consortium is continuing development of new specifications such as the Web Services Interoperability (WS-I) Basic Security Profile.

SAP NetWeaver supports WS-Security and the WS-I Basic Security Profile and will continue to support upcoming standards to ensure interoperability.

How do you develop secure composite applications without weaknesses?

The first step will be to develop security-friendly patterns of development, a set of frameworks for creating composite applications with inherently secure components. SAP will do its part by linking future versions of modeling tools such as SAP NetWeaver Visual Composer to the security operations layer of enterprise services, enabling enterprise architects to combine services in various combinations without explicitly focusing on security issues.

But developers will need additional frameworks and special security training to guide them in designing applications which will deflect common attacks such as cross-site scripting, in which malicious JavaScript code is entered into a web form, and while the code won't harm the host machine, it will load and infect the next unwitting customer who attempts to access your form. Learning to thwart these attacks isn't so much of an ESA issue as it is a development-of-best-practices issue, but these issues will become much more tangible when critical processes begin to poke their heads out beyond the corporate firewall.

SAP NetWeaver already includes frameworks to support secure programming. In addition, the SAP NetWeaver Developer's Guide includes a multiple-page security checklist for developers finishing their applications. The checklist leads off with questions such as:

- Is no security-relevant data stored on the client?
- Is the application free of back doors?
- Do all security implementations consist of a consistent and documented concept (and not "security by obscurity")?
- Does the system pass into a safe state in case of errors?

- Is the data stored in a secure way beyond the application session?

- Are no static keys used when encrypting data?

- Are encrypted data and keys always stored separately from each other, and can an attacker not implicate them?

Additional resources include the Secure Programming section on the SAP Developer Network (SDN; *http://sdn.sap.com*).

How will security between companies function and evolve in an ESA environment?

It's absolutely critical that intercorporate security function well, at all levels—from trust functions down to message-level encryption. Otherwise, companies will run the risk of disaster. It's especially important to understand that security cannot be implemented at the service level alone. Potential gaps or blind spots in business process logic make it imperative to create checks that monitor the entire process. For instance, say an office supply buyer at an airline is allowed to buy pencils from an online supplier and is channeled to that supplier's web services, which also link to Boeing's order system. If services in this case only check to see that someone from an airline is doing the ordering, that buyer might inadvertently have permission to buy a 747 in addition to pencils. Once a composite application is accessed—either by a human user or by a service call—it may find itself in the midst of process orchestration distributed across a variety of other composites, or perhaps in an environment in which one service will be executed in an entirely different security environment (another company, for example). A lot is at stake in ensuring that entire processes are protected, not just enterprise services.

It's also important to note that when it comes to processes that cross company borders or security domains, issues of trust cannot be resolved by software alone. The willingness of one company to receive an order or fulfillment request from another ultimately boils down to whether that company trusts that the request is legitimate. Before building a federated identity and access management model, it's necessary to sit down with partners to define what is and is not acceptable for granting authorized access to each other's users— and there may be surprisingly large gaps. One side might have employees register using their passport and then never check IDs after having done so, and the other, which works with a far-flung network of distributors, merely asks for an email address. And email is particularly vulnerable to interception.

Before one can build a secure, cross-company process, both sides must first agree on an answer to a critical question: what does it mean to be secure?

CHAPTER TWENTY

Standards and ESA

THE GLOBAL **I**NTERNET HAS EMERGED AS THE UBIQUITOUS COMMUNICATION MEDIUM FOR INDIVIDUALS and businesses alike. In order for this pervasive network to reach its full potential, interoperability between all connected computer systems is required. This pervasive network has increased the value of setting and adopting standards for everyone. And with a few exceptions here and there, the large technology companies that have the power to promote and enforce standards are coming to agreement on many key standards to a degree that has never been seen before.

In fact, out of frustration, the major players have changed the way standards are created. The old way—committees at standards bodies slogging through a lengthy and highly politicized design process—has given way to one in which technical committees composed of interested and motivated parties work fast and then make formal proposals to standards organizations. Without this mechanism, in fact, the Internet might never have escaped its original setting as a network available only to computer researchers and other scientists.

Large players such as IBM, Sun, Microsoft, and SAP have donated technology to the public domain to encourage standards setting, or have agreed to combine their disparate approaches. They have even created open community processes to gain active participation and buy-in from customers and partners.

This chapter is about how standards affect all layers of the ESA stack and, more importantly, how ESA can bring IT standards to life in a way that provides enormous business value to customers.

How do standards relate to ESA?

ESA is an approach to building complex IT systems by, in essence, selecting and assembling a set of building blocks known as services. As with any building blocks—fired-clay bricks, steel beams, or children's plastic blocks—there is much to gain from having all of them relate to, interact with, and connect to each other according to a set of precise and stable rules. Rooting the design and operation of these blocks in agreed-upon standards ensures a speedier design process, faster implementation of designs, and reduced need for maintenance: in short, lower total cost of ownership (TCO).

For physical blocks, these rules define shapes, angles, and sizes, the position of screw holes, and the patterns for dovetailed joints. In software, these rules, or interface standards, define the formats, content, and sequences of messages that building blocks, or services, are to exchange with each other under different circumstances. By standardizing these rules, or interface standards, across the enterprise, across IT systems, and ultimately across networks and ecosystems of business partners, the flow of information and the coordination of activities can be made much more efficient and effective. Moreover, the pervasive use of standards brings into being a new culture, or environment, in which to conceive, plan, and deploy IT.

Indeed, standards also help to remove longstanding barriers and facilitate the continuing alignment of business and technology strategies. Because it relies on standards-based interfaces up and down the technology stack, ESA makes it easier to compose new applications quickly. Existing enterprise services can be linked together, and if some new enterprise service is required, standards again facilitate its creation and assembly. The bottom line is that ESA brings enormous flexibility and the ability to match IT structures to business strategy. Likewise, since each enterprise service will be defined with equal input from business and IT managers, it will naturally embody the enterprise's thinking and approach to certain problems.

Isn't standardization between disparate brands of systems and between independent companies easier said than done?

In a literal sense, yes, standardization is much easier said than done. ESA is not magic. But it is, in fact, something quite new in the history of IT, a way of understanding, planning, and deploying sophisticated systems that finally unleashes the power of IT standards in ways that can help enterprises to reinvent the way their business operates and achieve business and technology goals that until now have appeared quite unreachable.

In a way, ESA is all about standards. It is designed from the ground up to fully exploit the power of IT standards to leverage existing technology investments, to improve developer productivity, and in turn, to lower the cost of developing, operating, and evolving the largest, most vital systems within an enterprise. This is a power that to date remains largely untapped.

ESA's deep reliance on standards frees the enterprise to think about, select, and refine the information that it needs to share in the execution of its business—information that it will share both within its own organizational boundaries and outside those boundaries, with its suppliers, business partners, and customers. Without standards, a great deal of energy must be spent on such basic tasks as making sure data is delivered in the right formats and figuring out how to get messages from point A to point B quickly, reliably, and securely.

IT standards come in many flavors. ESA brings them together and unlocks their inherent and collective value. A useful analogy can be made to rigging up a stereo system. Without standardized plugs and standardized signal levels in connecting wires, every home hi-fi system would have to be custom designed, perhaps requiring a full-fledged audio engineer to choose mutually compatible CD players, amplifiers, speakers, and so forth. The cost would likely be so high that only a few people would bother. Instead, audio products adhere to a stable set of technical standards that enable just about anyone to assemble components to achieve a particular set of goals (quality, amplification, economy), regardless of brand or internal design. Anyone can create a system that produces good if not superb sound. Indeed, because these standards were so well thought out in the first place, it's even possible to add entirely new kinds of components—wireless boxes streaming MP3 tracks from a distant PC, for instance—to stereo setups that were first put together during the era of turntables and vinyl LPs.

Now, the history of the software industry has largely been one of defining successive sets of standards, each one attempting to tame complexity by carving systems into manageable building blocks: macros in Assembly language, subroutines in FORTRAN, code libraries in C++, Enterprise JavaBeans (EJBs), and so forth. With each new genre of building block, software engineers sought to hide complexity and mind-numbing details to make it easier for programmers to construct larger and more functional systems.

ESA continues this tradition but elevates the approach to a much higher level of abstraction. By relying on (and hiding from view) a greater number of moving parts, as it were, ESA's building blocks are more powerful than those that have been available before. The difference is that ESA operates at the business rather than the technology level. ESA breaks down most previous barriers encountered in enterprise software, making it possible to create and stitch together blocks of functions, or services, which may execute on different computers operated by entirely different enterprises at vastly distant points on the globe.

None of this would be possible, though, without ESA embodying and enforcing the use of industry-defined standards to the degree that it does more than any previous software architecture. Equally important, ESA sets the stage for profitable exploitation of new IT standards as they emerge over time.

What kinds of standards does ESA rely on?

ESA encompasses and builds on three distinct categories of standards: technology, semantics, and portability. Figure 20-1 illustrates these categories. Let's examine each one briefly.

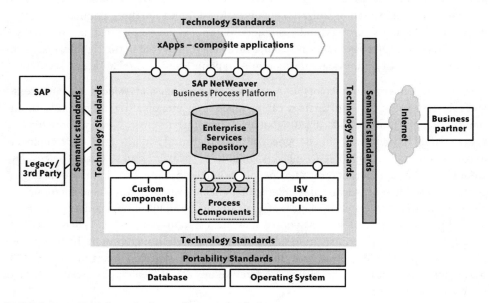

FIGURE 20-1. Portability, technology, and semantic standards

In order to create new enterprise services, developers must rely on certain programming methods, tools, languages, and interfaces. Together, these elements create a development environment that can ensure interoperability and reuse at many levels. Meanwhile, the basic interaction between any two enterprise services brought into play under ESA will be an exchange of data—a sequence of messages, that is, passed from one service or IT system to another. To make this possible, the two services need to share a standard way of talking, which is set forth in a variety of standards around the concept of web services. Along with ESA's programming and development tools, these standards provide the foundation of ESA's *technology standards*. You can find more about web services in Chapter 14.

Simply moving data from here to there is not enough, of course. The interactions between sender and receiver must take place in the proper order, according to a well-defined sequence upon which each party agrees. The message itself must be interpreted correctly, as it moves from one system to another. On top of that, a complex message may contain several types of data, and the systems need a way to extract one needle of data from a haystack of information. This is where so-called *semantic standards* come into play—precise rules that define what data, markup language, or "words" each message should contain and at which point during an exchange to send those messages.

Finally, it's of great value to customers if they can choose to create and deploy their applications—and enterprise services—on the IT platform that they deem best for the job. They can make this choice based on any criteria that are important to them: cost, compatibility with some piece of software already installed, or performance, among others. *Portability standards* address this issue and provide customers with greater freedom of choice in procuring hardware and software, now and in the future.

What is SAP's general approach to standards?

For 30 years now, the SAP name has been virtually synonymous with IT standards. The company prides itself on vigorously supporting and participating in all aspects of the standards-setting process and, equally important, on incorporating industry standards in all of its many software products. Indeed, SAP currently employs its own SAP NetWeaver composition platform, which embodies a wide range of IT standards, to create all of its service-oriented products and solutions.

Industry standards ensure that SAP NetWeaver integrates smoothly with other vendors' solutions and that the platform can align people, information, and business processes. Standards help to ensure accurate sharing of information, to improve the reuse of technology, to improve developer productivity, and to lower the cost of developing, operating, integrating, and maintaining IT systems.

Consider this. Without standards in place, it is difficult for different IT systems and organizations to exchange business documents, whether those documents are invoices, the definitions of web services, or digital certificates providing cryptographic protection of data. Without standards that define what information should look like and what it means, correctly understanding and processing that information becomes extremely difficult.

Likewise, when standards exist, the business logic and software required to process shared information needs to be developed just once. After that, the software can be used repeatedly. The same is true of skills: the use of standards means the technical skills that developers acquire will remain valuable for a longer period than would be the case otherwise even in those instances when developing new software is unavoidable.

SAP has long been an active supporter and contributor to the IT standards-setting process, using its decades of experience in building business applications to lead and influence many standards groups. SAP takes leadership positions in organizations such as the W3C, OASIS, OMG, Java Community Process (JCP), Eclipse, and the Web Services Interoperability Organization (WS-I) and actively participates in many of these organizations' working groups. To help make sure that solutions incorporating the standards defined by these groups are able to interoperate, SAP also leads the WS-I Sample Applications activity and conducts interoperability tests with competing platform vendors such as Microsoft and IBM. SAP has taken a particularly strong interest in defining semantic standards, identifying them as critical to integrating business applications—that is part of why semantic standards are the foundation of ESA.

Does ESA provide support for every major IT standard?

No, ESA does not provide support for every major IT standard. In fact, SAP has deliberately chosen not to implement every standard available. It has chosen to leave certain standards out of ESA because, based on its long experience in IT, the company recognizes that not all standards provide the right kind of value. Therefore, SAP focuses on choosing standards that will help businesses build the solutions they need, that guarantee interoperability with major platform partners.

Some of these standards may not be as widely accepted as others are. By throwing its support behind certain standards, SAP expects that it will be able to help them along and make them more widely accepted over time. One example of this is the Core Components standards put forward by a United Nations e-business standards group. Core Components, as we will describe further along in this chapter, bring significant value to customers and, yes, to SAP's internal development teams, too.

What are semantic standards, and how do they help build IT solutions?

Semantic standards—sometimes referred to as business standards—are an attempt to preserve meaning and lower the risk of misinterpretation as data is moved from one IT system to another. Without semantic standards to govern the structuring and tagging (with XML, for example) of individual chunks of data, what System A may perceive as valuable and vital information, System B may reject as gibberish.

Thus, semantic standards are absolutely key to today's IT activities, in which users are trying to weave together enterprise services, enable IT systems to collaborate, and link to their business partners and customers as closely as possible. While it's possible for a set of business partners to work out their own, closed set of semantic standards, it's much more practical and economical to employ the growing number of standards that industry associations are hammering out. The vast majority of the cost of building connections between systems derives from the work involved in understanding the semantics and business logic involved. Clearly, if the semantics are standardized, integration costs can be reduced significantly.

Are semantic standards simply sets of XML tags?

Semantic standards encompass more than the vocabularies of XML tags that many vertical industry groups have hammered out for their own purposes. Those vocabularies—the high-tech industry's RosettaNet is a typical example—focus on the format or content of electronic documents that two business partners are to exchange. And there is no question that those formats are critical to the successful use of enterprise services.

But document formats alone are not sufficient to define what's needed in a complex, cross-industry interaction. Of equal importance is the sequence—also called choreography—in which documents or data are to be exchanged. Because each industry's formats and choreographies are different, ESA has introduced a common understanding of those variances. Over time, ESA will encompass the standard enterprise services that businesses will need in order to interact at this level. As things stand today, there is too much variation in how each industry and company defines the way it does business. Some of this is necessary; for example, the aerospace industry and the steel industry have different business requirements, which can also vary by locale. The value-added tax, for example, is relevant in Europe but not in the U.S. Much of what businesses do is the same, however; sending and paying invoices is pretty much universal across industries, companies, and locales.

What is needed is a series of service interfaces, standard service definitions, or enterprise services that are defined in a way that can help partners operating in quite different industries to conduct their basic business processes efficiently, yet allow for controlled variation where needed. Ideally, this standardization would cover all aspects of enterprise services, from their naming—"order management"—to the network addresses where those services are accessible—*integration.companyX.com*—to the precise sequence of steps that a service automates.

SAP is helping to improve all of these types of semantic standards. The company is working closely with the UN/CEFACT, for instance, which has developed and continues to maintain the definitive international EDI standard, called UN/EDIFACT. SAP also chairs UN/CEFACT's Technologies and Methodologies Group (TMG), which is developing next-generation business information and collaborative process standards.

Semantic standards being supported by ESA include the following:

Data definitions
Define the format, structure, and semantics of the data exchanged between businesses (for example, on orders and invoices) as well as information exchanged between and stored by applications.

Collaborative process definitions
Sometimes called choreography standards or process orchestration, these standards define how two or more businesses collaborate by defining the sequence in which documents are exchanged. For example, an order sent to a supplier usually results in the return of an order response.

Core Components Technical Specification (CCTS)
Provides precise semantic definitions for business documents and processes.

Naming and Design Rules (NDR)
Specify how the core components developed by CCTS (such as address, full name, and line item) can be mapped to XML in a consistent way.

What are core components and how do they relate to SAP's concept of semantic standards?

Core components are reusable semantic building blocks that can be combined in various ways to create shared libraries of well-defined and widely interoperable business documents and processes. Many vertical industry groups have expressed strong interest in building business documents based on core components. Defining the guidelines for the development of core components is the task of SAP's Technique and Methodologies Group. Core components also serve as the basis of the enterprise services that SAP is creating. This ensures that business apps built on SAP NetWeaver will be able to map easily to the semantic standards that industry groups are developing.

Core components are chunks of data that are frequently used in most or perhaps all industries and that therefore lend themselves to being assigned standardized definitions and formats that don't vary from industry to industry. This frees standards-setting bodies in each industry from having to come up with their own definitions, encourages reuse of the components within higher-level and more complex documents, and reduces risk for all involved.

Examples? Typical core components are items such as amount, line item, and address. Every industry deals in such information, so there's no practical reason for each industry to define those entities uniquely. Indeed, adopting these core components reduces the cost of mapping between different formats and XML vocabularies used in different industries.

The need for core components is strongest in industries, such as chemicals, where producers do most of their business with customers operating in entirely different industries. Chemical makers, for instance, sell to the automotive, pharmaceutical, retail, aerospace, and even high-tech industries. Were the standards groups in each industry to adopt their own, unique definitions of "order" and "price," a chemical maker would face a dilemma when trying to integrate IT systems for the sake of closer collaboration and e-commerce. Should it insist that the other industries do things its way, or should it try to adopt each of the other's standards?

In contrast to electronic data interchange (EDI) standards, the core components approach does not attempt to define every possible type of data and every possible field that a data record might contain to serve every possible industry. Instead, it aims for the much more reasonable and practical goal of defining a minimum, or core, set of data items. Thus, each industry is free to build on this basic set and create the precise electronic documents it needs.

Which technology standards does SAP support, and how do they help build IT solutions?

Technology standards encourage interoperability at various levels of the stack. SAP supports technology standards associated with the Java programming language, web services, and the XML Schema Definition (XSD) language, to name just a few. This enables customers to design, develop, and deploy highly flexible composite applications that sacrifice nothing in terms of execution speed, functions, or security.

Consider, for example, the SAP NetWeaver Application Server (AS), a central component of SAP NetWeaver. It is fully compliant with the Java 2 Enterprise Edition (J2EE) standard. This platform also supports all of the major Java technologies, including:

- EJB

- The Portlet Specification (JSR 168)

- The Java Management Extensions (JMX) Specification

- JAX-RPC 1.0 for Web Services communication

SAP has been a member of the Java Community Process since 2001, and since 2002 it has been a member of the J2EE/J2SE Executive Committee, which guides the entire Java development process. It works with other leaders in the industry, such as IBM and BEA, on advancement of new Java standards such as Service Data Objects (SDO) and Service Composition Architecture (SCA). These specifications will define the future standards on how to build composite applications based on services.

Further bolstering SAP NetWeaver's support of standard technologies is the fact that it is built on Eclipse, the open source software development environment. By using Eclipse's integrated set of programming tools, SAP customers benefit from the sizeable Eclipse ecosystem. Indeed, SAP's development community is the second largest Eclipse-based community in the world. SAP is a member of the board that governs the Eclipse Foundation and it takes an active role in guiding the evolution and development of Eclipse as a whole.

What's an example of a critical technology standard?

Reliable messaging is one good example of a critical technology standard. Reliability in messaging comprises several factors. The first is simply that when a message is sent from a source to a destination, it doesn't get lost, even if it is sent over an inherently unreliable medium such as the Internet. It arrives at its intended destination within a certain time limit. In various business scenarios, it is additionally important that only one copy of a message is processed by the destination, in the expected sequence of messages, even if the source retries sending the message over and over again. For example, a purchase order must not be processed more than once; otherwise, more than the intended amount of goods and services will be ordered.

The mechanisms for ensuring this reliability have traditionally been designed into the applications operating at each end of such an electronic transaction. But now, with the rise of a standard called Web Services Reliable Messaging, or WS-RM, applications are no longer burdened with such details. Instead, as implemented in ESA, a facility within SAP NetWeaver takes care of it according to the rules of WS-RM. The advantage is that developers have one less task to bother with; they can simply trust SAP NetWeaver to ensure the reliability of messages whether exchanged between SAP applications or with applications from other vendors.

Which technology standards does SAP NetWeaver support?

SAP NetWeaver incorporates a comprehensive stack of technology standards that SAP intends to extend as additional standards become stable enough for production use.

The platform, with a declarative, model-driven environment that both programmers and business analysts can use to develop business solutions, builds upon existing service-oriented architecture (SOA) and web services standards. These standards fall into the following categories:

Basic web services
SOAP, Web Services Description Language (WSDL), Universal Description, Discovery, and Integration (UDDI), WS-Addressing, WS-Policy

Interoperability profiles
WS-I Basic Profile and Basic Security Profile

Security
XML Digital Signature, XML Encryption, SAML, and WS-Security

Reliable messaging
WS-Reliable Messaging

Web Services Policy Frameworks
WS-Policy

Web Services Addressing Core
WS-Addressing

Process definition
WS-BPEL

XML
XML Schema, XSLT

Service management
Distributed Management Task Force (DMTF) Common Information Model (CIM)

SAP actively participates in many of the organizations that are responsible for developing these and other standards, including:

W3C
Develops XML, XML Schema, XSLT, WSDL, and more. SAP is a gold-level sponsor of the Web Accessibility Initiative (WAI) and a member of the W3C Advisory Board that provides strategy-level guidance to the W3C management team.

OASIS
Develops standards such as UDDI, WS-Reliable Messaging, WS-Security, and WS-BPEL. SAP is a member of the OASIS Board of Directors that directs OASIS activities.

WS-I
Develops profiles of how web services standards should be used together. SAP is a member of the WS-I Board and leads the WS-I Sample Applications working group.

Java Community Process

Controls the development of the Java programming language. SAP is a member of several Java Specification Requests and leads JSR 165.

The Eclipse Foundation

Manages the development of the Eclipse development environment. SAP is a strategic member and has a seat on the Eclipse Board of Directors.

The Object Management Group (OMG)

Develops UML, XMI, and the Model Driven Architecture (MDA).

Liberty Alliance

Develops standards for managing identity on the Web.

DMTF

Develops management standards for integration technology and Internet environments.

How do portability standards help customers to build IT solutions?

Portability standards assure that customers have a range of choices when it comes to implementing each layer of the technology stack. These standards protect investments in applications software—software that is usually developed in-house at considerable expense. The standards accomplish this by essentially decoupling customers' apps from particular brands of database management systems and operating systems. This decoupling enables customers to port their apps between any of a variety of different IT environments with relative ease.

From its earliest days, SAP has made the inclusion and support of portability standards a key element of its value proposition. For example, SAP R/3—now mySAP ERP—has always been able to run on multiple computing platforms. Now, this portability has been carried to SAP NetWeaver, which is certified to run on multiple platforms, including:

- 32- and 64-bit versions of the Microsoft Windows operating system
- Linux
- IBM's AIX, OS/400, and z/OS
- HP's UX and Tru64
- Sun Microsystems's Solaris operating systems

SAP NetWeaver can also be used to build applications that will work with databases such as IBM's DB2 and Informix, Microsoft's SQL Server, and MaxDB.

What is SAP's relationship to industry-specific standards groups?

SAP develops solutions for specific industries and participates in many industry-specific standards groups. Some of these groups are listed in Table 20-1. Since these groups define business processes, data formats, and choreographies between businesses connected over the Internet, these organizations are of extreme importance for SAP. ESA has support for industry best practices built in and is interoperable with the most common industry practices as defined by these groups. Many of SAP's customers are members of these groups and SAP is engaged in critical dialog to contribute to the next generation of interindustry business processes, which are required to master the challenges of the global economy of the 21st century. Global supply chains, interoperability, and the quest for new efficiency within cross-industry business processes are the driving forces behind these groups.

TABLE 20-1. Industry- or application-specific standards groups

Industry or application type	Group
Aerospace	Spec2000
Agriculture	RAPID
Automotive	AIAG, Star Standard, and Odette
Chemical	CIDX
Consumer products and retail	GS1
High technology	RosettaNet
Manufacturing	S95, OPC, and MIMOSA
Oil and gas	PIDX
Mill products/paper	PapiNet
Financial reports	XBRL
Human resources applications	HR-XML

SAP is using what it learns from its ongoing work with these groups to ensure that technology standards initiatives in the W3C, OASIS, and WS-I—as well as the functionality of the SAP NetWeaver platform itself—reflect the specific needs of each vertical industry. SAP also makes its practical development experience available as a resource to vertical industry standards groups that are looking to adopt core components for semantic standards, web services, and XML for technology standards.

SAP is a member of the RosettaNet Executive Board and drives standards development at all levels. SAP is also a part of the RosettaNet Architecture team.

EPCglobal is concerned with the worldwide development of the radio frequency identification (RFID) standard. SAP is contributing heavily to the development of the EPCIS specification, which describes how to access RFID event data from trading partners. This specification defines integration in the supply chain.

GS1 GDSN™ (Global Data Synchronisation Network) is an automated, standards-based global environment that enables secure and continuous data synchronization, allowing all partners to have consistent item data in their systems at the same time. The SAP NetWeaver Master Data Management (SAP NetWeaver MDM) solution supports the 1SYNC specification.

SAP Research is also a strong contributor to the Athena project, which develops new tools and methodology for interoperability in the European Community. It is funded by the

European Commission. SAP is also actively supporting the foundation of the European Interoperability Center (EIC).

Are standards tested to ensure they provide interoperability?

Once standards are developed, each one must be tested to make sure that it achieves the interoperability between different vendors' systems that it was originally intended to foster. To ensure that ESA-based business solutions interoperate with solutions from other vendors, SAP runs tests with major platform vendors such as Microsoft and IBM. SAP also is a board member of WS-I, which includes companies such as IBM, Microsoft, Sun Microsystems, BEA, Oracle, and others. WS-I members collaborate on developing profiles that describe how web services specifications should be used together. SAP is also chair of the WS-I Sample Applications Working Group, which builds applications solely for the purpose of testing and proving that different suppliers' solutions can interoperate. These partners in turn support all ESA-related standards.

Which additional standards will ESA support in the future?

SAP intends, over time, to expand aggressively the range of standards supported by ESA, its goal being to make it as easy as possible for customers and software partners to adopt ESA as their primary development platform. SAP foresees a steady flow of new potential candidates in all three main areas of standards: technology, portability, and semantics. As it has in the past, SAP will work closely with customers and partners in deciding which standards to choose for inclusion in the ESA definition.

Two good examples of the kinds of new standards that are becoming available for ESA support are Service Component Architecture (SCA) and Service Data Objects (SDO).

Devised by a consortium of software makers including SAP, IBM, BEA Systems, and Oracle, these two specifications jointly address problems arising from the fact that it is increasingly difficult to construct standalone information systems. Today, most systems are connected to a collection of other systems running in different processes, different servers, and sometimes, different companies. Different elements of business logic often need to be accessed via different middleware technologies, each dependent on a context-specific association with certain software elements. Likewise, sources of data tend to produce result sets that vary in their organization and format, coupling business logic with data access.

SCA and SDO are designed to keep developers insulated from the complexities of this situation and thereby enable them to build new composite apps with relative ease. SCA specifies a programming model that assures a much-welcomed independence of business logic from middleware such as EJB, JMS, JAX-RPC, and JCA. This means that with SCA, an element of business logic may participate in different assemblies (systems) that each use different middleware technologies. SDO, meanwhile, provides a data manipulation model that is decoupled from physical data sources. This enables components to exchange composite data sets assembled from disparate data sources, which may be relational, XML, or API based, for instance.

SCA was designed following the principles of SOA and provides the means to compose autonomous assets that have been implemented using a variety of technologies and that expose a service contract. SCA enables location and activation transparency: the business logic or system encapsulated within service components and behind its contract can be reused and composed very efficiently into new solutions and systems, thereby facilitating the construction of connected systems.

Version 0.9 of the SCA specification was published in November 2005. It will take about one year before a final 1.0 version is published. Version 2.0 of the SDO specification was published in the same timeframe and the consortium is working toward a 3.0 version for the end of 2006.

INDEX

Dan Woods is CTO, editor, and founder of the Evolved Media Network, a firm that offers content creation, editorial, and publishing services to information technology, financial, electronic gaming, and biotechnology companies. In early 2006, Dan and Peter Thoeny started StructuredWikis.com, a firm created to help companies use Wikis in a corporate setting. As an author, Dan has written several books for developers and IT managers about Java technology, RFID, Enterprise Services Architecture, and open source. As a CTO, Dan has built technology for companies such as Time Inc. New Media and TheStreet.com.

Thomas Mattern is Solution Marketing Manager for Enterprise Services Architecture at SAP. Thomas has over 10 years experience in product marketing and management with a focus on distributed software architectures and enterprise application development. Prior to his current position, Thomas served as Product Marketing Manager in SAP's Global Marketing for mySAP Technology with a focus on SAP Web Application Server. Before joining SAP, Thomas was responsible for product marketing at In-Q-My Technologies, a Java application server company that was acquired by SAP. Earlier in his career, Thomas held consulting and technical account management positions at debis, Compuware, and Forté Software. Thomas is a frequent speaker and has written numerous articles about development tools, application servers, integration technology, web services, and service-oriented architecture. Thomas, who holds an engineering degree from University of Cologne, lives in Hoffenheim with his wife Suse and his two sons Elvis and Merlin.

COLOPHON

The cover image is original artwork. The cover fonts are Akzidenz Grotesk and Orator. The text font is Adobe's Meridien; the heading font is ITC Bailey.